Workplace Skills for Success with AutoCAD® 2011

BASICS

A Layered Learning Approach

Gary Koser, P.E.

Indian River State College

Dean Zirwas

Indian River State College

Prentice Hall

Boston   Columbus   Indianapolis   New York   San Francisco   Upper Saddle River
Amsterdam   Cape Town   Dubai   London   Madrid   Milan   Munich   Paris   Montreal   Toronto
Delhi   Mexico City   Sao Paulo   Sydney   Hong Kong   Seoul   Singapore   Taipei   Tokyo

Editorial Director: Vernon R. Anthony
Acquisitions Editor: Sara Eilert
Editorial Assistant: Doug Greive
Director of Marketing: David Gesell
Marketing Manager: Kara Clark
Senior Marketing Coordinator: Alicia Wozniak
Marketing Assistant: Les Roberts
Senior Managing Editor: JoEllen Gohr
Associate Managing Editor: Alexandrina Benedicto Wolf
Project Manager: Louise Sette
AV Project Manager: Janet Portisch

Senior Operations Supervisor: Patricia Tonneman
Operations Specialist: Deidra Skahill
Senior Art Director: Diane Ernsberger
Cover Designer: Jason Moore
Cover Art: SuperStock
Full-Service Project Management: Karen Fortgang, bookworks
Composition: Aptara®, Inc.
Printer/Binder: Edwards Brothers, Inc.
Cover Printer: Lehigh-Phoenix Color/Hagerstown
Text Font: Times New Roman

Certain images and materials contained in this publication were reproduced with the permission of Autodesk, Inc. © 2010. All rights reserved. Autodesk, AutoCAD, DWG, and the DWG logo are registered trademarks of Autodesk, Inc., in the U.S.A. and certain other countries.

Disclaimer:
The publication is designed to provide tutorial information about AutoCAD® and/or other Autodesk computer programs. Every effort has been made to make this publication complete and as accurate as possible. The reader is expressly cautioned to use any and all precautions necessary, and to take appropriate steps to avoid hazards, when engaging in the activities described herein.

Neither the author nor the publisher makes any representations or warranties of any kind, with respect to the materials set forth in this publication, express or implied, including without limitation any warranties of fitness for a particular purpose or merchantability. Nor shall the author or the publisher be liable for any special, consequential or exemplary damages resulting, in whole or in part, directly or indirectly, from the reader's use of, or reliance upon, this material or subsequent revisions of this material.

Credits and acknowledgments borrowed from other sources and reproduced, with permission, in this textbook appear on appropriate page within text.

Library of Congress Control Number: 2010926482

10 9 8 7 6 5 4 3 2 1

Prentice Hall
is an imprint of

www.pearsonhighered.com

ISBN-13: 978-0-13-215080-4
ISBN-10:   0-13-215080-8

The New Autodesk Education Press Series

Pearson/Prentice Hall has formed an alliance with Autodesk® to develop textbooks and other course materials that address the skills, methodology, and learning pedagogy for the industries that are supported by the Autodesk® Education software offerings that assist educators in teaching design.

Features of the New Autodesk Education Press Series

Job Skills. Coverage of computer-aided drafting job skills, compiled through research of industry associations, job websites, college course descriptions, and the Occupational Information Network database, has been integrated throughout the AEP books.

Professional and Industry Association Involvement. These books are written in consultation with and reviewed by professional associations to ensure they meet the needs of industry employers.

Autodesk Student Engineering and Design Community. The Autodesk Student Engineering and Design Community provides free Autodesk design software for download and learning resources to help you get started in your academic career. Join today; go to **www.autodesk.com/edcommunity**.

Features of *Workplace Skills for Success with AutoCAD® 2011: Basics*

This text presents a layered learning approach to using AutoCAD. That is, it is designed around a concept of layering the simple fundamental information used to create basic drawings, and then revisiting topics through project-based learning while increasing the difficulty of the drawings being created. Rather than discussing all commands in a sequence, this book uses a "draw-modify-dimension-print" cycle.

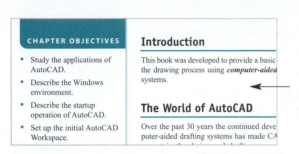

Chapter Objectives with a bulleted list of learning objectives for each chapter provide users with a roadmap of important concepts and practices that will be introduced in the chapter.

Key Terms are bold and italic within the running text, briefly defined in the margin, and defined in more detail in the comprehensive glossary.

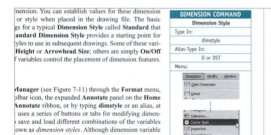

Command Grids appear in the margin, alongside the discussion of the command. These grids provide a visual of the action options using the toolbar, pull-down menu, command line, command alias, or tool icon, ensuring that the student is in the right place at the right time and correctly following the authors' direction.

Discipline Icons, placed in the margin alongside Chapter Tutorials and Chapter Practice Exercises, identify the discipline to which the exercise applies: **M** (Mechanical), **P** (Plumbing/HVAC), **G** (General), **A** (Architechtural), **E** (Electrical), or **C** (Civil). These icons allow instructors to quickly identify homework assignments that will appeal to the varying interests of their students and give students the opportunity to work on projects that have the most interest and relevance to their course of study.

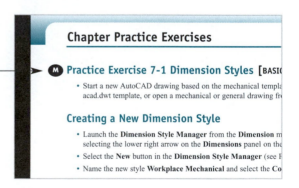

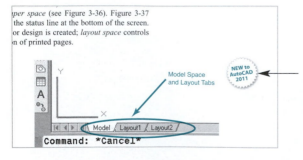

New to AutoCAD 2011 icons flag features that are new to the 2011 version of the AutoCAD software, creating a quick "study guide" for instructors who need to familiarize themselves with the newest features of the software to prepare for teaching the course. For those who do not update their software yearly, we have retained the New to AutoCAD 2010 icons for reference.

Job Skills boxes appear near material that relates specific unit content to the job skill necessary for success in the workplace.

ears various forms of the interface have
d and used based on commands such
RENCES, OPTIONS, and currently
CE. The Windows environment also stores
interface, set up as Profiles. You can use
ands to customize the interface for your
yle and application. These commands are
Chapter 12 of this book.
ou enter AutoCAD 2011 for the first time,
will appear with a ribbon located at the

NOTE:
The default color of the Model
Space background has been
changed in 2011 to dark gray.
This can be modified to any
color through the **Display** tab
on the **Options** by selecting
the **Colors**.

Note boxes present hints, tips, and tricks to enhance productivity. **For More Details** boxes provide a higher level of information to use as background, reference, or research.

EXERCISE 7-2 **CREATE ANGLE, RADIUS, AND ARC DIMENSIONS**

■ Start a new drawing in AutoCAD.

■ Draw one circle, one rectangle with fillets, and one rectangle with chamfers.

■ On the circle place a diameter dimension on the inside and another on the outside of the circle.

■ On each arc of the fillets place a radius dimension on the inside and outside in the drawing area. Also place an arc length dimension on the inside and outside of each fillet.

■ On each chamfer place an angular dimension at each end, alternating the acute and obtuse angles.

Exercise items are quick tutorials to show a command or present a concept.

Ⓖ **Tutorial 6-3: Inquiry—Civil**

1. Open the **Lots and Roads** drawing (see Figure 6-37) file from the student data files.

2. Use the **DISTance** command to verify the lot line dimensions shown.

3. Use the **LIST** command to determine the length of the roadway centerlines.

4. Check various lot areas using the **AREA** command. Which lot is the biggest? Which is the smallest?

5. Determine the units used in this drawing with the **STATUS** command. Change units and repeat Steps 3 and 4.

6. Close the drawing and **do not save** any changes.

To access student data files, go to **www.pearsondesigncentral.com.**

URLs in the margin direct students to the online student data files.

Chapter Tutorials present full instructions, either generic or discipline-specific. Disciplines include mechanical engineering, architectural, and civil engineering.

Ⓜ **Tutorial 6-2: Inquiry—Mechanical**

1. Open the **Welding Fixture Model** drawing file (see Figure 6-36) in the **Samples** folder of your AutoCAD program or access it from the student data files.

Chapter Test Questions

Multiple Choice

Circle the correct answer.

1. Which of the following commands will bring all objects in the drawing file into the display screen no matter where they are in space?

    c **Modify**
    d **Input**

4. The **CLEANSCREEN** command wi

Chapter Test Questions include Multiple Choice, Matching, and True or False Questions.

Chapter Projects are contextual projects and may involve research. They may also be assigned by the instructor for different learning styles or for extra credit.

Chapter Projects

Project 6-1 [INTERMEDIATE]

Using the **Inquiry** commands, find the "oldest" drawing in the AutoCAD **Samples** folder. Find the one with the least/most editing time. Which one has the smallest/largest file size? What are some of the block names in these drawings?

Chapter Practice Exercises

Ⓖ **Practice Exercise 6-1: PAN and ZOOM** [BASIC]

1. Start AutoCAD.

2. Pick the **File** menu and choose **OPEN**.

3. Using the drop-down area at the top of the **Select File** dialog box, go to the AutoCAD **Samples** folder or access the student data files.

4. Scroll through the list of drawing files (**.dwg**) and choose one to open by picking the **OPEN** button in the lower right of the dialog box:

   a. **Architectural Drawings**—8th Floor, Hotel, Hummer, Stadium, Taisei, or Wilhome

   b. **Building Services**—8th Floor

To access student data files, go to www.pearsondesignc

Chapter Practice Exercises are learner-oriented with minimal instructions. Some are discipline-specific, as noted earlier.

Instructor Resources

The **Online Instructor's Manual** provides answers to chapter exercises and tests and solutions to end-of-chapter problems; drawing files to get learners started; and lecture-supporting PowerPoint® slides.

To access supplementary materials online, instructors need to request an instructor access code. Go to **www.pearsonhighered.com/irc**, where you can register for an instructor access code. Within 48 hours after registering, you will receive a confirming e-mail, including an instructor access code. Once you have received your code, go to the site and log on for full instructions on downloading the materials you wish to use.

Student Resources

Pearson Design Central—Pearson has created an online community where students can share examples of their drawings and obtain resources for their drawing projects. Student data files needed for certain projects in this book can be obtained at **www.pearsondesigncentral.com.** URLs in the margin direct students to the online student data files.

Preface

Helping learners to become productive quickly within a 2D drawing environment is the primary goal of *Workplace Skills for Success with AutoCAD® 2011: Basics.* We use a layering approach in this text, first orienting the learner to the commands needed to complete fundamental drawings successfully and then gradually increasing the difficulty of the drawings being created through project-based learning. Instead of presenting all commands in a sequence, this text is designed around the "draw-modify-dimension-print" cycle.

This text is designed for a typical semester of instructor presentation and drawing lab time. By limiting the drawing lab time, instructors can complete each chapter in one week. Expanding the coverage with contextual projects can fill a traditional semester term. Each chapter consists of command content and presentation materials, as well as drawing activities and projects. Discipline-oriented practice activities are placed in each appropriate chapter, emphasizing the chapter content. These practice tasks and activities are from the three major computer-aided drafting disciplines: architectural, mechanical, and civil. This gives the instructor and students a variety of project-based exercises to demonstrate application of the chapter content.

Various methods are used to reinforce the concepts and skills. In some cases, an immediate tutorial or exercise is used. For more complicated concepts, a higher-level tutorial is presented. In many chapters, practice exercises offer learners an additional chance to practice their skills.

Through this layered-learning approach, learners build a foundation of skills based on a logical sequence and repetition, driven toward the end results of developing workplace skills and creating industry-style drawings in a timely fashion.

Features of This Text

- Words shown in ***bold italic*** are key terms the learner should know.
- **Note** boxes present hints, tips, and tricks to enhance productivity.
- **For More Details** boxes provide a higher level of information to use as background, reference, or research.
- **Job Skills** boxes appear near material that relates specific chapter content to the job skill necessary for success in the workplace.
- **Exercise** items are quick tutorials to show a command or present a concept.
- **Chapter Tutorials** are either generic or discipline-specific. Disciplines include mechanical engineering, architectural, and civil engineering.
- **Chapter Test Questions** include Multiple Choice, Matching, and True or False questions.
- **Chapter Projects** are contextual and may involve research. They may also be assigned by the instructor for different learning styles or for extra credit.
- **Chapter Practice Exercises** are learner-oriented with minimal instructions. Some are discipline-specific as noted above.

Features New to This Edition

- All new graphics covering the 2011 interface of AutoCAD 2011.
- Additional projects covering a variety of disciplines.
- Labeled icons identifying the new features of AutoCAD 2011.
- Two new chapters.

- An expanded glossary.
- 3D Workspace ribbons included in the appendices.
- Coverage of new **Hatch** and **Hatch Edit** ribbons.

Recommended Learning Path

We recommend that learners use the following method:

- Read the introduction to each chapter and give particular attention to **Chapter Objectives.**
- Listen to the instructor's presentation about the topics in the chapter.
- Participate in class discussions.
- Work through the **Exercises** carefully.
- Complete the **Chapter Practice Exercises** and **Chapter Tutorials** with an awareness of ways to increase productivity.
- Answer the **Chapter Test Questions** and verify the answers using AutoCAD.
- Read and use your text materials to apply the **Chapter Projects** and other references provided by your instructor.
- Present to your class additional examples of the concepts learned.

Acknowledgments

We want to thank the individuals whose contributions helped shape this textbook.

Chris Chamberlain
Delaware Technical and Community College, DE

James Freygang
Ivy Tech Community College, IN

Howard M. Fulmer
Villanova University

Dorothy Gerring
Pennsylvania College of Technology, PA

Jerry M. Gray
West Georgia Technical College, GA

DeDe Griffith
Lee College, TX

JoBeth Halpin
Triton College, IL

Carol Hoffman
The University of Alabama, AL

John Irwin
Michigan Technological University

Paul Lekang
North Dakota State College of Science, ND

Philip A. Leverault
Milwaukee Area Technical College, WI

Randal Reid
Chattahoochee Technical College

Luis Rios
Dona Ana Community College

Seymour Rosenfeld
Westchester Community College, NY

James Kevin Standiford
Arkansas State University, AR

Mel L. Whiteside
Butler Community College, KS

Style Conventions in *Workplace Skills for Success with AutoCAD® 2011: Basics*

Text Element	Example
Key Terms—Boldface and italic on first mention (first letter lowercase, as it appears in the body of the text). Brief definition in margin alongside first mention. Full definition in Glossary at back of book.	Views are created by placing *viewport* objects in the paper space layout.
AutoCAD commands—Bold and uppercase.	Start the **LINE** command.
Ribbon and panel names, palette names, toolbar names, menu items, and dialog box names—Bold and follow capitalization convention in AutoCAD toolbar or pull-down menu (generally first letter cap).	The **Layer Properties Manager** palette The **File** menu
Panel tools, toolbar buttons, and dialog box controls/buttons/input items—Bold and follow the name of the item or the name shown in the AutoCAD tooltip.	Choose the **Line** tool from the **Draw** panel. Choose **the Symbols and Arrows** tab in the **Modify Dimension Style** dialog box. Choose the **New Layer** button in the **Layer Properties Manager** palette. In the **Lines and Arrows** tab, set the **Arrow size:** to **.125**.
AutoCAD prompts—Dynamic input prompts are set in a different font to distinguish them from the text. Command window prompts are set to look like the text in the command window, including capitalization, brackets, and punctuation. Text following the colon of the prompts specifies user input in bold.	AutoCAD prompts you to *Specify first point*: Specify center point for circle or [3P/2P/Ttr (tan tan radius)]: **3.5**
Keyboard Input—Bold with special keys in brackets.	Type **3.5 <Enter>**

Contents

New to AutoCAD 2011

New to AutoCAD 2010

1

Introduction to AutoCAD

- Study the applications of AutoCAD.
- Describe the Windows environment.
- Describe the startup operation of AutoCAD.
- Set up the initial AutoCAD Workspace.

Introduction

This book was developed to provide a basic understanding of the drawing process using *computer-aided drafting (CAD)* systems.

The World of AutoCAD

Over the past 30 years the continued development of computer-aided drafting systems has made CAD a major component in the design and drafting process. According to Daratech, Inc., a research firm on computer trends and policies, currently more than 70 percent of all engineered drawings are produced by AutoCAD systems. Future CAD enhancements and integration are expected to increase the CAD influence in all aspects of designing, building, managing, and communicating. Every year CAD systems add more design capabilities, are reduced in cost, become more integrated with production, and increasingly use the Internet to communicate design.

Computer-aided drafting and design (CADD) systems are being used extensively in many fields, including architectural engineering (see Figure 1-1); mechanical engineering (see Figure 1-2); civil engineering and surveying, landscape architecture (see Figure 1-3), and the environment; structural engineering (see Figure 1-4); utility and infrastructure design; and manufacturing. Basically, any industry that uses a drawing is using CAD or CADD systems.

This book focuses on the initial drawing commands and the accurate placement of drawing entities. Since most of the CAD/CADD systems around the world are based on the product called AutoCAD® that was developed and is distributed by Autodesk®, Inc., this book will use AutoCAD as its base. Knowledge of AutoCAD drawing commands should be useful for other CAD systems that provide similar methods and techniques needed for precise work.

It is the authors' hope that students will gain a basic knowledge in using these accurate drawing methods and be able to apply this knowledge to other drawings in other disciplines.

computer-aided drafting (CAD): The process of producing engineering documentation through a computer.

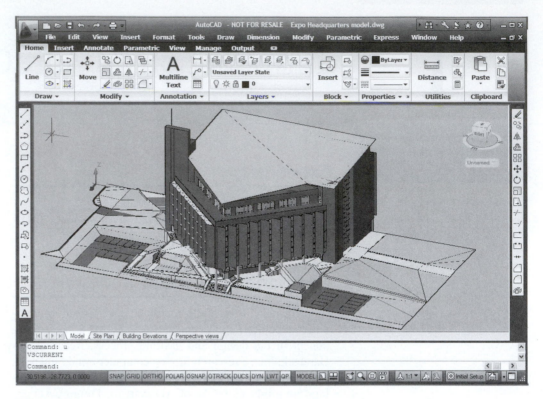

Figure 1-1
Office building

Figure 1-2
Welding fixture

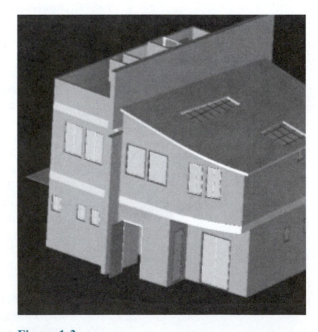

Figure 1-3
Two-story 3D house

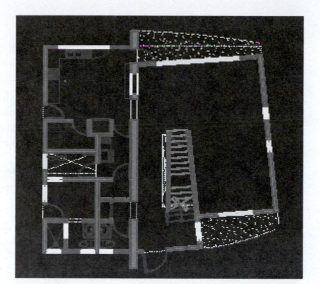

Figure 1-4
Two-story house floor plan

Industry Uses of AutoCAD

The following are typical scenarios of CAD projects and drawings for your information and as an introduction to the possible uses of computer-aided drafting and design.

Scenario 1—Architecture

You work for an architectural engineering consulting firm that is to draw a new office building in your area (see Figure 1-5). The architect has determined the basic dimensions of the building and located the stairs, elevators, and office space. You must draw this plan accurately and quickly. As you look at the building layout, the symmetry shows that drawing one wing and arraying it around the center of the building will speed production. Using CAD makes it possible to draw the building in a few hours and create a 3D model for rendering (see Figure 1-6).

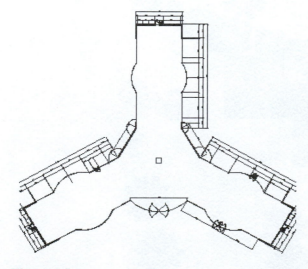

Figure 1-5
Office building floor plan

Figure 1-6
Office building rendering by Autodesk Max Design

Scenario 2—Civil Engineering

You work for the department of transportation. Your task is to draw a new road along the river. The survey crew has completed the topographic survey shown in Figure 1-7 using radial methods. Therefore, you have a file of angles and distances to each survey point. You must locate the points accurately for a proper design. Using the CAD system with units set for Surveyor's, you enter the bearings and distances to create the points. The Civil software, based on the points, develops a Triangular Irregular Net, which leads to the creation of the contours. The contours show points of equal elevation and aid in the placement of the road, intersections, and drainage (see Figure 1-8).

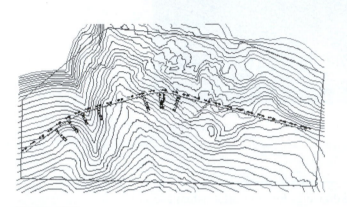

Figure 1-7

Civil engineering contours

Figure 1-8

Civil engineering street design

Scenario 3—Landscape Design

You work for a landscaping firm and are to design a playground in an existing park (see Figures 1-9 and 1-10). The park authority has given you information based on state plane coordinates

Figure 1-9

Landscape plan

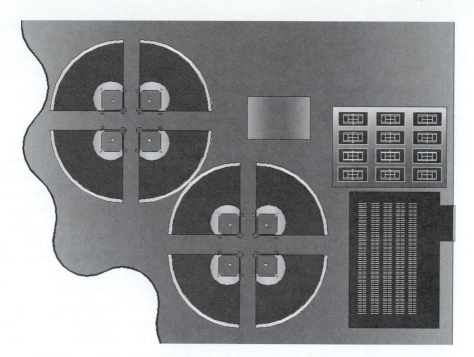

Figure 1-10

Landscape 3D view

(an absolute coordinate system that links to the Geographic Information System). Your work must result in a file that can be imported into the GIS and can be used by the construction company.

Scenario 4—Mechanical Engineering

You work for an industrial design development firm. Your client is applying for a patent on a toll road wireless transponder (see Figure 1-11). The client has given you an artist's sketch of the object and has requested a physical 3D model. Your office must develop the 3D model and extract the 2D production drawings for the patent application. Your model must be a compatible file to be printed with a 3D Rapid Prototyping printer.

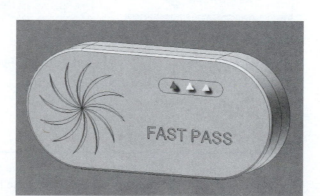

Figure 1-11

View of proposed case.

AutoCAD and the Windows Environment

As is most software today, AutoCAD *software* is based on Microsoft Windows. Windows has supported AutoCAD through several versions of its *operating system,* with the most current version of the Windows operating system being the common platform. Because of this, a solid working knowledge of a Windows program such as Microsoft Word, Excel, or PowerPoint is helpful. Though this is not required, you will increase your knowledge of your Windows operating system by running AutoCAD software. If you feel your knowledge of Windows is limited, consider taking an entry-level Windows operating class at a local community college or technical center. All file management actions such as **NEW, OPEN, SAVE, SAVE AS,** and **CLOSE** work as typical Windows-based commands. This is also true for edit action commands such as **CUT, COPY, PASTE, MATCHPROP,** and so on. This

software: Programs that control the operations of a computer and its peripherals.

operating system: The code that runs all commands for the computer system.

file management: The process of saving, copying, moving, and deleting the files produced by a computer system.

directory: A listing of files

means that any experience you have from current or previous versions of Windows will help in your *file management* procedures.

From launching the program to printing drawing files, you will find the experience of navigating the *directory* structure on your hard disk and managing files similar to other programs you have already used.

Starting AutoCAD

After successfully installing the AutoCAD software, you will have two basic options to launch the program and start a drawing session. The first method of starting the software is through the traditional **Programs** menu in the corner of the Windows environment. With the left mouse button pick the **Start** button (see Figure 1-12). Next you pick the **All Programs** (see Figure 1-13) selection and look for the **Autodesk/AutoCAD** listing. After picking the **Autodesk** group, you will have one more cascading menu from which you pick **AutoCAD 2011** (see Figure 1-14). The previous selections are made with a left mouse button click.

icon: A small picture used to launch a command.

desktop: The initial screen of a Windows operating system.

A second method to launch the program is to use the *icon* placed on the Windows *desktop* through the installation procedure. Locate the icon that looks similar to Figure 1-15. Double-click on the icon with the left mouse button, and this will launch the executable file to start the program. Both methods will take you to the same place—a new drawing session within the AutoCAD environment.

Figure 1-12

Start button

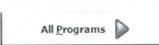

Figure 1-13

All Programs menu

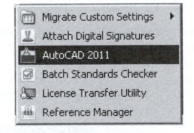

Figure 1-14

Autodesk submenu

Figure 1-15

AutoCAD desktop icon

Initial AutoCAD Setup

Upon beginning an AutoCAD session, you may find the screen interface a bit overwhelming. The appearance of the interface will depend on how the last user left the program. AutoCAD will open based on the settings of the last user's session or on an AutoCAD workspace.

AutoCAD Workspaces

NEW to AutoCAD 2011

Over the years various forms of the interface have been created and used based on commands such as **PREFERENCES, OPTIONS,** and currently **WORKSPACE.** The Windows environment also stores the current interface, set up as Profiles. You can use these commands to customize the interface for your particular style and application. These commands are presented in Chapter 12 of this book.

When you enter AutoCAD 2011 for the first time, the interface will appear with a ribbon located at the

NOTE:

The default color of the Model Space background has been changed in 2011 to dark gray. This can be modified to any color through the **Display** tab on the **Options** by selecting the **Colors.**

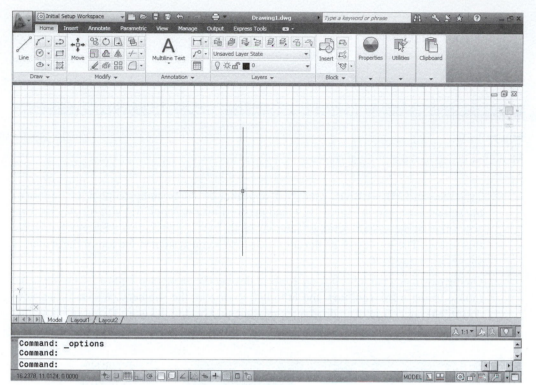

Figure 1-16

Initial AutoCAD screen

NEW to
AutoCAD
2011

top of the screen (see Figure 1-16). This is the AutoCAD initial setup workspace as defined in AutoCAD 2011 software. This basic look has been the same for many previous versions of AutoCAD, allowing you to understand and use any release of AutoCAD. To make this setup easier to use for drawings and for this text, make the following changes.

1. At the bottom of the screen on the left is the ***status bar*** which houses a series of drawing aid icons (see Figure 1-17). Right-click the mouse to show the pop-up menu. Left-click the mouse on **Use Icons** to remove the check mark. This will convert the icons to words as shown in Figure 1-18.

status bar: A series of on/off buttons for drawing aids related to the operations of the current drawing session.

Figure 1-17

Drawing aids or status line with icons

Figure 1-18

Drawing aids or status line with letters

Figure 1-19

Input to place the menu bar

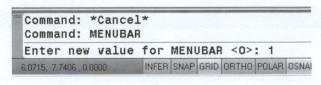

Figure 1-20

Menu bar added to the top of the screen

2. Type the word **MENUBAR,** which will appear at the command prompt at the bottom of the screen as shown in Figure 1-19, and press **<Enter>.** AutoCAD will display the current value of the system setting **Menubar** as 0. Type a **1** and press **<Enter>** to change this setting. The result will be the addition of the menu system at the top of the screen as shown in Figure 1-20.

3. On the new menu bar left-click on **Tools** to display the menu (see Figure 1-21). Move the mouse to the word **Toolbars** and left-click to display the submenu. Move to the word **AutoCAD** and left-click to display the next menu. Move to the word **Draw** and left-click to place the **Draw** toolbar on the screen. The result should be similar to Figure 1-22.

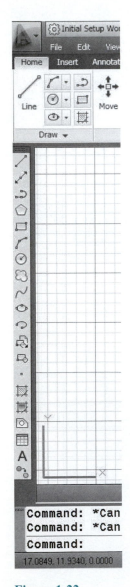

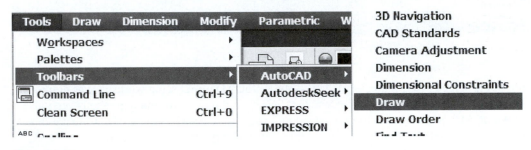

Figure 1-21

Draw toolbar access

4. On the new menu bar left-click on **Tools** to display the menu (see Figure 1-23). Move the mouse to the word **Toolbars** and left-click to display the submenu. Move to the word

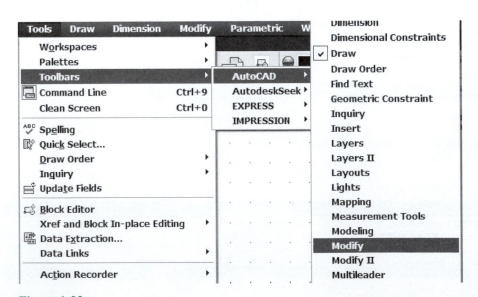

Figure 1-22

Draw toolbar in place

Figure 1-23

Modify toolbar access

AutoCAD and left-click to display the next menu. Move to the word **Modify** and left-click to place the **Modify** toolbar on the screen. The result should be similar to Figure 1-24.

5. The resulting screen as shown in Figure 1-25 will be the standard setup used in this text.

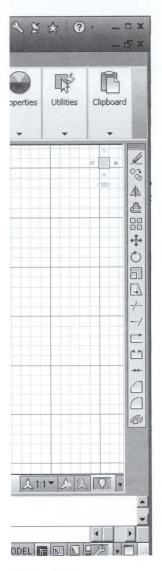

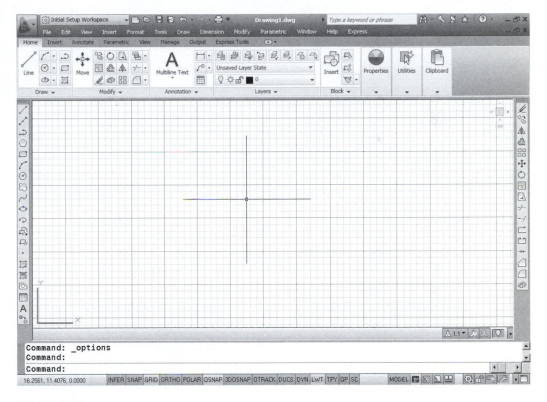

Figure 1-24

Modify toolbar in place

Figure 1-25

Standard AutoCAD screen for this text

Chapter Summary

In this chapter, we introduced you to the concept of CAD/CADD (computer-aided drafting and design), explained the operation of the AutoCAD software, and presented an overview of its applications and functions in the Microsoft Windows operating system environment. First, you were presented with typical examples of AutoCAD drawings generated for projects in the fields of architecture, civil engineering, landscape design, and mechanical engineering. Then you learned about AutoCAD functions in the Windows operating system environment: the Windows-based file management commands (**NEW, OPEN, SAVE, SAVE AS,** and **CLOSE**) and the edit action commands (**CUT, COPY, PASTE,** and **MATCHPROP).** Finally, you were introduced to the initial AutoCAD screen and some of the components that make up the AutoCAD interface.

2 Quick-Start Tutorials

CHAPTER OBJECTIVES

- Explain the operation of the basic DRAW and MODIFY commands: LINE and ERASE.

- Demonstrate the steps involved in the setup of a drawing.

- Create Quick-Start drawings.

- Discuss selecting objects to modify.

Introduction

To make the opening chapters of this text more meaningful, let's begin with two Quick-Start Tutorials to introduce you to one method of the drawing process. These quick-start exercises are meant to give you an overall experience in drawing setup and basic command execution. You will be guided through the tutorials with a step-by-step series of instructions. The following is a short introduction to the basic commands that you are about to use.

LINE Command

Lines are created by specifying the endpoints of each line segment. After you execute the **LINE** command the command prompt (see Figure 2-1) will ask you to *Specify first point*. After you input the first point by picking a location with the left mouse or entering coordinates, the command prompt (see Figure 2-2) will ask you to *Specify next point*. Upon the input of the second point a line will be created between the two selected points. After the completion of the first line, the command will stay active, continuing to prompt you to *Specify next point* until you choose to end the sequence by pressing either the space bar or the **<Enter>** key, the **<Esc>** key (to cancel the operation), or the right mouse button (see Figure 2-3) to select the **Enter/Cancel** command from the right mouse menu.

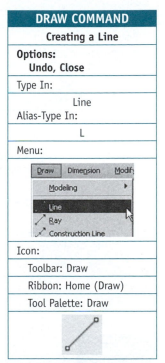

DRAW COMMAND
Creating a Line
Options: Undo, Close
Type In:
Line
Alias-Type In:
L
Menu:
Icon:
Toolbar: Draw
Ribbon: Home (Draw)
Tool Palette: Draw

```
Command: *Cancel*
Command: line

Specify first point:
```

Figure 2-1

Initial **LINE** command prompt

```
Specify next point or [Undo]:
Specify next point or [Undo]:

Specify next point or [Close/Undo]:
```

Figure 2-2

Succeeding prompts for the **LINE** command

Figure 2-3

Right-click menu for the **LINE** command

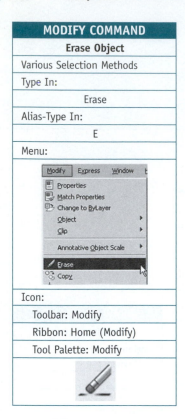

MODIFY COMMAND
Erase Object
Various Selection Methods
Type In:
Erase
Alias-Type In:
E
Menu:

Icon:

Toolbar: Modify

Ribbon: Home (Modify)

Tool Palette: Modify

The **LINE** command has two options: **Close** and **Undo.** Options to a command are displayed within the square brackets in the prompt line (see Figure 2-2). To execute a command's option you identify the capital letter from the word in the prompt line and type in that upper- or lowercase letter, followed by **<Enter>.** After two or more line segments are created you can execute the **Close** option to create one more line segment that will close the shape back to the first selected endpoint that started the sequence. This will end the command.

When the **Undo** option is executed from within the **LINE** command, the last point of input will be released and allow the user to respecify the endpoint of that line segment. Be aware that continuous execution of the **Undo** function will step back through all endpoints specified during this line activity.

ERASE Command

The **ERASE** command is used to delete entities from the drawing file. As with all **Modify** commands, after you select the command you will be prompted to *Select objects* (see Figure 2-4). After you have selected the entities and pressed **<Enter>,** the selected entities will be erased from the drawing file and screen. An alternative method to using the **ERASE** command is to select an entity when a command is not in progress and press the **<Del>** key, thus removing the entity from the drawing file. Remember, the program is in neutral when the prompt line reads *Command*. This is when you can use the alternative method mentioned.

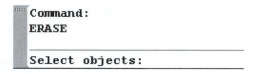

Figure 2-4

Initial **ERASE** command prompt

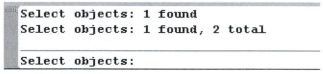

Figure 2-5

Select objects prompts in **ERASE** command

Selecting Objects

Figure 2-6

AutoCAD Desktop icon

When you enter any **Modify** command, the prompt *Select objects* will appear in the command line, and the screen cursor will be replaced by a small square known as a *pick box* (see Figure 2-5). This pick box is referred to as a *single-selection pick box* and is used to select the single entity that is below the box when a left mouse click is executed. By moving the pick box over any object on the screen and left-clicking, you select that entity and place it into the current selection set. Selected objects will appear in a dashed form to signify they are part of the currently selected set for modification. You may continue to select other objects that need to be placed into the selection set by simply moving the pick box over other entities and using a left mouse click. This process will continue until you complete your selections and finish the selection process by pressing **<Enter>** or the right mouse button for a menu to stop the selection or to cancel the selection.

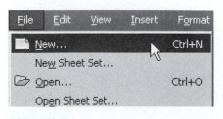

Figure 2-7

File menu options

Quick-Start Tutorial 1

1. Locate the **AutoCAD** icon on the desktop. Double-click the icon to start the program (see Figure 2-6).

2. From the **File** menu select **New** (see Figure 2-7).

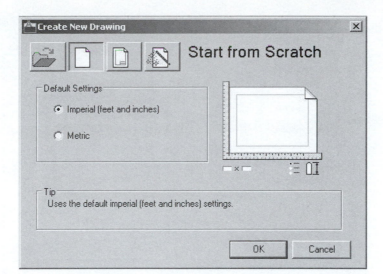

Figure 2-8

Start from Scratch dialog box

3. From the **Create New Drawing** dialog box, pick the second icon from the left to choose **Start from Scratch** as the method to start. Verify imperial units are chosen and pick **OK** with the left mouse button (see Figure 2-8). If the **Select template** dialog box appears (see Figure 2-9), pick **acad.dwt** as the template to use for this tutorial.

4. From the **Tools** menu select the **Drafting Settings** entry near the bottom of the menu (see Figure 2-10).

5. In the **Drafting Settings** dialog box select the **Snap and Grid** tab (see Figure 2-11).

6. In the **Snap** section, change the **Snap Y spacing** value to **.25.** This is done by double-clicking the current value, which will be highlighted with a blue box, and typing in the new value. Be sure the

NOTE:

• The system variable **STARTUP** will establish whether the Figure 2-8 or Figure 2-9 dialog box is used.

• The display of a grid has changed slightly in 2011 with the addition of vertical and horizontal grid lines. This change will better represent typical engineering graph paper.

• This can be changed to a series of dots in 2D model space by changing the **Grid style** in the **Drafting Settings** dialog box (see Figure 2-11).

NEW to AutoCAD 2011

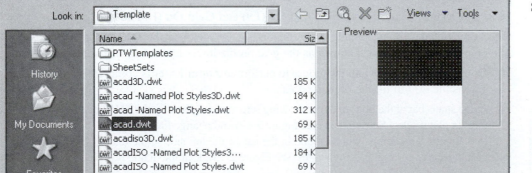

Figure 2-9

Select template dialog box

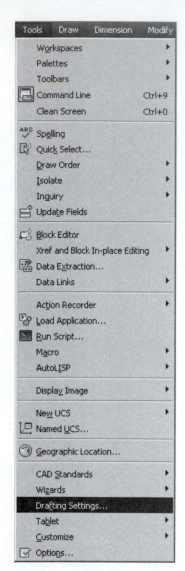

Figure 2-10

Tools menu for Drafting Settings

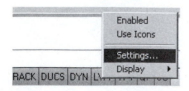

Figure 2-12

Accessing lineweight settings

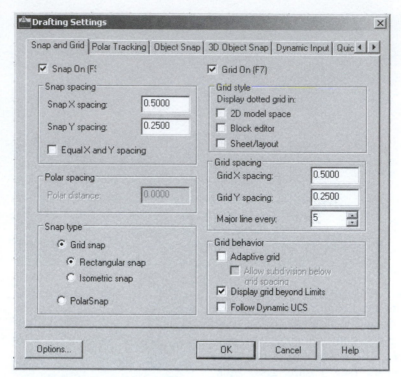

Figure 2-11

Drafting Settings dialog box

Equal X and Y spacing box does not have a check mark in it. The **Snap type** should be set to **Rectangular snap.**

FOR MORE DETAILS   More detailed information on the **LINE** and **ERASE** commands can be found in Chapter 5 of this book.

---

7. In the **Grid** section, change the **Grid Y spacing** value to **.25.** This is done by double-clicking the current value, which will be highlighted with a blue box, and typing in the new value.

8. Place a check mark in both the **Snap On (F9)** and **Grid On (F7)** boxes.

9. Accept all the changes made in the dialog box by selecting the **OK** button. You should now see a series of dots, known as the *grid,* in the lower left corner of the screen.

10. Double-click the wheel on the mouse to perform a **Zoom Extents** command, which repositions the grid to fill the drawing area.

11. In the status bar at the bottom of the drawing screen, right-click on the **LWT** button. From the pop-up menu select **Settings . . .** (see Figure 2-12) and change the lineweight for this drawing to 0.40 mm. This setting can be found in the list on the left side of the dialog box. Be sure to check the box to **Display Lineweight** (see Figure 2-13). Exit the dialog box by selecting **OK.**

12. In the **Draw** menu, select the **LINE** command (see Figure 2-14) or use the **LINE** command on the **Home** tab of the ribbon (see Figure 2-15). Create Drawing QS-1 shown in Figure 2-16, drawing each line as shown from grid point to grid point. The pointing device will snap to each grid point owing to the drafting settings. Every line may require you to restart the **LINE** command. This may require the occasional use of the **ERASE** command, which is found in the **Modify** menu shown in Figure 2-17 or on the **Modify** panel of the **Home** tab on the ribbon (see Figure 2-18).

13. When the drawing is complete save your work. Go to the **File** menu and select **SAVE** (see Figure 2-19). You should enter a unique name, such as QS-1, for the drawing file, and press <**Enter**> (see Figure 2-20).

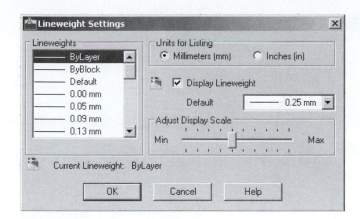

Figure 2-13

Lineweight Settings dialog box

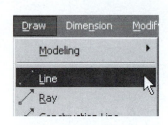

Figure 2-14

Draw Line menu

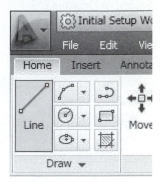

Figure 2-15

LINE command on the **Home** tab of the AutoCAD ribbon

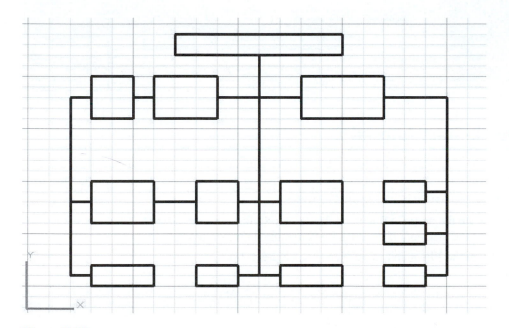

Figure 2-16

The QS-1 Drawing

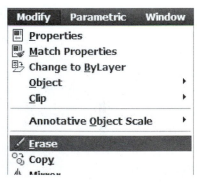

Figure 2-17

ERASE command on the **Modify** menu

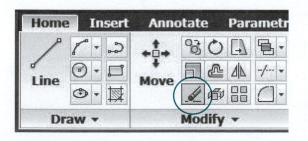

Figure 2-18

ERASE on the **Modify** panel of the **Home** tab of the ribbon

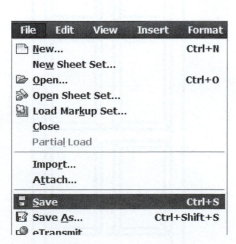

Figure 2-19

File Save menu

Figure 2-20

Saving of Drawing QS-1

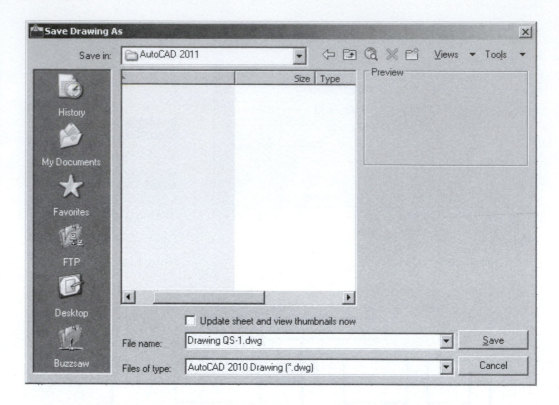

Quick-Start Tutorial 2

The following is a second quick-start tutorial with an architectural flair (see Figure 2-21). This will require you to change the unit type and adjust both X and Y values in the **Snap** and **Grid** areas. Complete the drawing as follows.

1. Locate the **AutoCAD** icon on the desktop (refer to Figure 2-6). Double-click the icon to start the program. If the program is running, move to step 2.

2. From the **File** menu select **New** (see Figure 2-22).

Figure 2-21

Drawing of six-panel door for Drawing QS-2

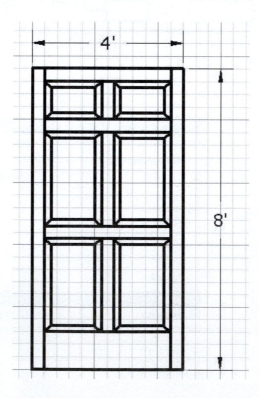

Figure 2-22

File New

3. From the **Create New Drawing** dialog box, pick the second icon from the left to choose **Start from Scratch.** Verify imperial units are chosen and pick **OK** with the left mouse button (see Figure 2-23). If the **Select template** dialog box appears (see Figure 2-24), pick the **acad.dwt** template for this tutorial.

> **NOTE:**
> The system variable **STARTUP** will establish whether the Figure 2-23 or Figure 2-24 dialog box is used.

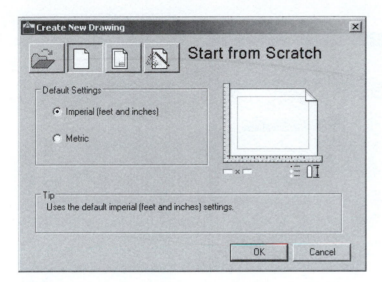

Figure 2-23

Start from Scratch dialog box

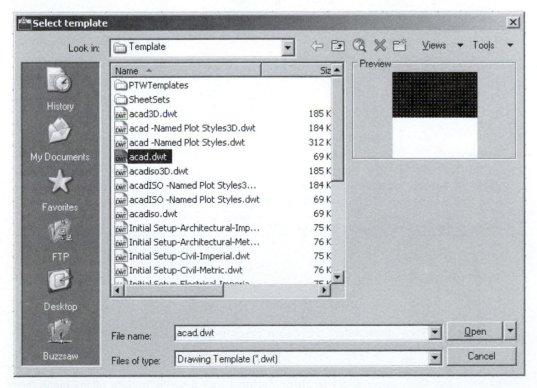

Figure 2-24

Select Template dialog box

4. In the **Format** menu (see Figure 2-25) select **Units . . .** near the bottom of the menu.

5. In the **Drawing Units** dialog box (see Figure 2-26), locate the drop box for the **Length Type** and change the units to **Architectural**.

6. From the **Format** menu select **Drawing Limits** (see Figure 2-27). Enter a value of **0,0** <**Enter**> for the lower left-hand corner and a value of **10′,15′** <**Enter**> (see Figure 2-28) for the upper right-hand corner.

Figure 2-25

Format menu for the **UNITS** command

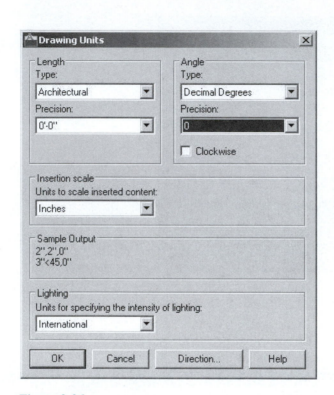

Figure 2-26

Drawing Units dialog box

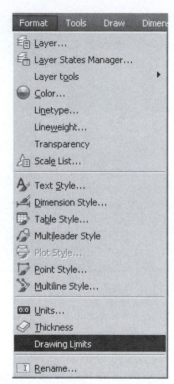

Figure 2-27

Format menu for the **DRAWING LIMITS** command

```
Command:
LIMITS
Reset Model space limits:
Specify lower left corner or [ON/OFF] <0'-0",0'-0">:

Specify upper right corner <1'-0",0'-9">: 10',15'
```

Figure 2-28

LIMITS command prompts

7. From the **View** menu select the **Zoom** cascading menu. From the **Zoom** cascading menu select **All** (see Figure 2-29). This will reset the drawing area to match the limits just established.

8. From the **Tools** menu select **Drafting Settings . . .** near the bottom of the menu (see Figure 2-30).

9. In the **Drafting Settings** dialog box select the **Snap and Grid** tab (see Figure 2-31).

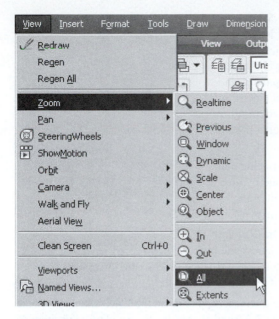

Figure 2-29

View Zoom All menu

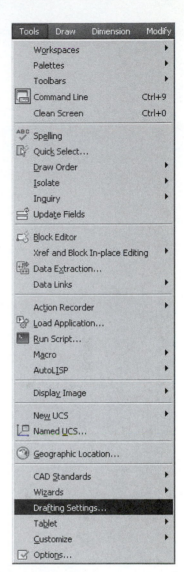

Figure 2-30

Tools menu

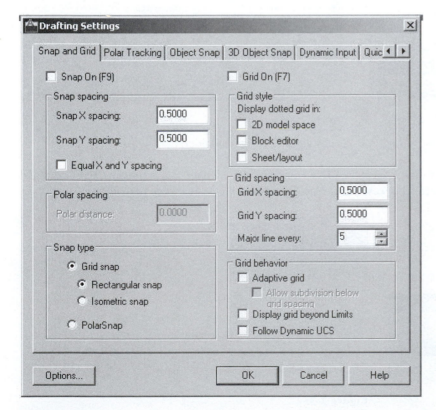

Figure 2-31

Drafting Settings dialog box for Drawing QS-2 before steps 10 and 11

10. In the **Snap** section, change the **Snap X spacing** and **Snap Y spacing** values to **2″**. This is done by double-clicking the current value, which will be highlighted with a blue box, and typing in the new value. Be sure the **Equal X and Y spacing** and **Adaptive grid** boxes do not have a check mark in them. The **Snap type** should be set to **Rectangular snap**. Also be sure the **Grid behavior** area has no check marks for this drawing.

11. In the **Grid** section, change the **Grid X spacing** and **Grid Y spacing** values to **4″**. This is done by double-clicking the current value, which will be highlighted with a blue box, and typing in the new value.

NOTE:

The display of a grid has changed slightly in 2011 with the addition of vertical and horizontal grid lines. This change will better represent typical engineering graph paper.

This can be changed to a series of dots in 2D model space by changing the **Grid style** in the **Drafting Settings** dialog box (see Figure 2-31).

12. Place a check mark in both the **Snap On (F9)** and **Grid On (F7)** boxes. Accept all the changes made in the dialog box by selecting the **OK** button. You should now see a series of dots, known as the grid, in the lower left corner of the screen.

13. In the status bar at the bottom of the drawing screen, right click on the **LWT** button. From the pop-up menu select **Settings . . .** (see Figure 2-32) and change the lineweight for this drawing to 0.40 mm. This setting can be found in the list on the left side of the dialog box. Be sure to check the box to **Display Lineweight** (see Figure 2-33). Exit the dialog box by selecting **OK.**

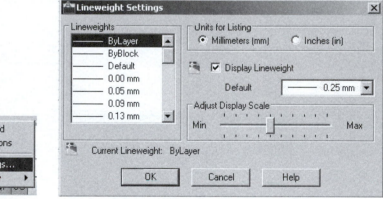

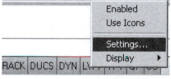

Figure 2-32

Accessing lineweight settings

Figure 2-33

Lineweight Settings dialog box

14. In the **Draw** menu, select the **LINE** command (see Figure 2-34) or use the **LINE** command on the **Home** tab **Draw** panel (see Figure 2-35) and create the drawing in Figure 2-21

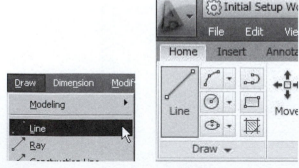

Figure 2-34

Draw Line menu

Figure 2-35

LINE command on the **Home** tab on the AutoCAD ribbon

with each line as shown. You may need to restart the command with every line. This may require the occasional use of the **ERASE** command, which is found in the **Modify** menu (see Figure 2-36) or on the **Home** tab **Modify** panel (see Figure 2-37).

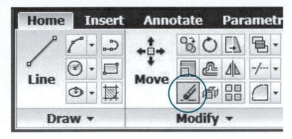

Figure 2-36

ERASE on the **Modify** menu

Figure 2-37

ERASE on the **Modify** panel of the **Home** tab

15. When the drawing is complete save your work. Go to the **File** menu and select **SAVE** (re-fer back to Figure 2-19). You may enter a name for the drawing file (refer to Figure 2-20), and press **<Enter>** to complete the **Save** operation.

Chapter Summary

In this chapter, you were introduced to two Quick-Start Tutorials, which gave you the opportunity to create simple drawings. At first you learned about the operation of the basic **LINE** and **ERASE** commands. Next, we discussed the concept of Selecting Objects for the purpose of modifying the selected objects. Finally, we explained the main concept of the chapter—step-by-step instructions for creating drawings.

3

AutoCAD Interface

- Identify the parts of the AutoCAD interface.
- Explain the operation of the ribbon, dialog boxes, and menu systems.
- Describe the special function keys, Help files, and command aliases.

Introduction

The AutoCAD interface is divided into several subareas or windows, such as menu bars and dialog boxes. In this chapter, we will take a closer look at each of these areas and their operations. Along with the AutoCAD interface, we will discuss the specialty keys, Help files, command aliases, and mouse operations that are unique to the system.

Identification of Interface Areas

The interface can be divided into several subareas or windows.

Title Bar

At the top of the screen is a Windows bar (typically black) known as the *title bar* indicating that you are in the AutoCAD program (see Figure 3-1). At the center of this top bar, the name of the current file is listed. The file location may precede the name. On the right side of this title bar are three icons typical of the Windows environment. These icons are used to **Minimize, Maximize,** and **Exit,** respectively, the AutoCAD software (see Figure 3-2). You can change the AutoCAD window to any size by pulling the edges of the current window. The first two buttons aid in sizing the window quickly, and the third exits the program. If drawings have been edited, AutoCAD will request confirmation to save changes before closing the software.

The Ribbon

ribbon: A strip of panels that contain command icons organized by specific tasks connected to the AutoCAD workspaces.

The *ribbon* is a special form of the tool palette found across the top of the drawing screen. The ribbon contains a set of control panels that are organized by commands (see Figure 3-3). The ribbon reduces screen clutter caused by displaying several toolbars and/or tool palettes. Commands are presented in a single location and command interface. The ribbon panels contain more information than a typical tool palette. Several panels have an expandable panel on which additional information becomes visible when you work within the active panel. Just click on the control panel's title bar arrow (see Figure 3-4) to expand the panel and show the

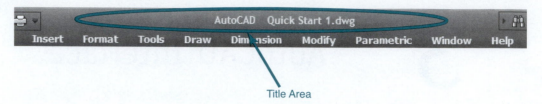

Title Area

Figure 3-1

Title bar with drawing name at center

Figure 3-2

Title bar, right side

Min., Max., and Exit
Drawing Session

Figure 3-3

Home ribbon

Figure 3-4

Arrows to expand ribbon
panels

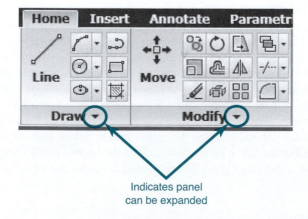

Indicates panel
can be expanded

slide-out portion of the panel containing the additional commands. Right clicking on any area of the ribbon will bring up a context-sensitive menu with **Tabs** and **Panels** options (see Figure 3-5) for selecting the commands you want in your ribbon. The ribbon can be displayed with three different looks: tabs, panel titles, and panel buttons. To change the look of the ribbon, simply select the down-arrow icon located to the right of the ribbon tabs. From that list choose the ribbon's display mode from the drop list (see Figure 3-6). When floating, the ribbon can be transparent and auto-hide, as do other palettes. Dragging a panel off the ribbon will display the panel as a "sticky panel" (see Figure 3-7). Sticky panels remain

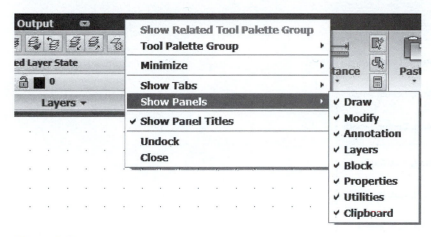

Figure 3-5

The right-click menu on the ribbon

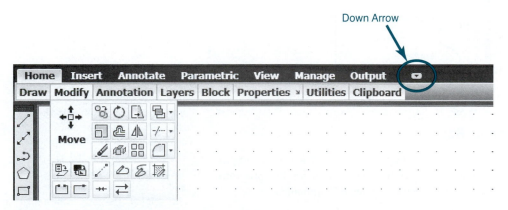

Figure 3-6

Condensed ribbon with the **Modify** panel expanded

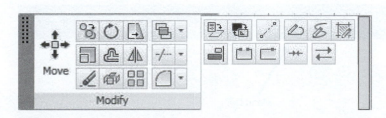

Figure 3-7

Ribbon panel as a detached sticky panel

displayed even when you are selecting commands from other panels (see Figure 3-8). Unlike tool palettes with commands, the ribbon has no options for changing entity properties as a preset condition. Therefore, the icons in the ribbon are the same as the icons used in a toolbar when displayed in detail.

NOTE:

See Appendix B to view the various ribbons available.

Figure 3-8

ARC command on the **Home** ribbon

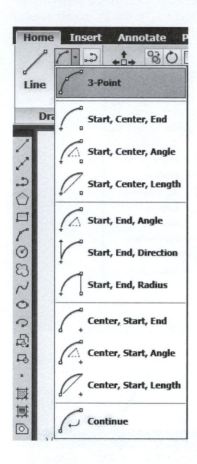

Menu Bar

The menu bar (see Figure 3-9) and browser (see Figure 3-16) contain the pull-down menus for the program. Each word represents a series of commands.

NOTE:

If you are not seeing the menu bar, type the word **MENUBAR** at the command prompt and press **<Enter>**. AutoCAD will display the current value of the system setting **Menubar** as 0. Type a **1** and press **<Enter>** to change this setting. The result will be the addition of the menu system at the top of the screen as shown in Figure 3-9.

Menu Bar

Figure 3-9

AutoCAD menu bar

When you make a selection from this menu list, a menu will drop down, exposing a series of related commands, submenus, and dialog boxes. The most-often-used commands and options can be found in the pull-down menus. Beginning users will need to get used to the organization of the commands within the pull-down menu areas. This familiarity will come with experience, but at this point in the learning curve, new users should merely become acquainted with a few graphical features in the pull-down menus.

First, notice how the placement of the toolbar icons in the menus shown helps you connect each icon to the corresponding command.

As you look at a pull-down menu such as the **Draw** menu in Figure 3-10, you will see several small black triangles. Each triangle indicates that there is a submenu known as a *cascading menu* (see Figure 3-11). You must make a selection from the menu that cascades out to the right (or left, depending on screen position) of the original selection. The actual commands are located on the last menu. Any text to the left (or right) of the last menu is considered organizational and not an actual command.

A second graphical feature is an *ellipsis,* a series of three periods following a word (see Figure 3-12). This symbol indicates a dialog box related to the command selected.

Dialog boxes appear as floating windows on the screen (see Figure 3-13). You need to address the information in the dialog box and either accept or cancel the dialog before you will have access to the main program interface again. Dialog boxes allow you to randomly input information related to the command chosen and, in some cases, preview what would be

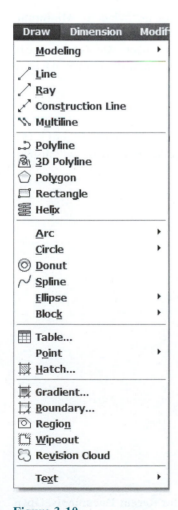

Figure 3-10

Full **Draw** menu

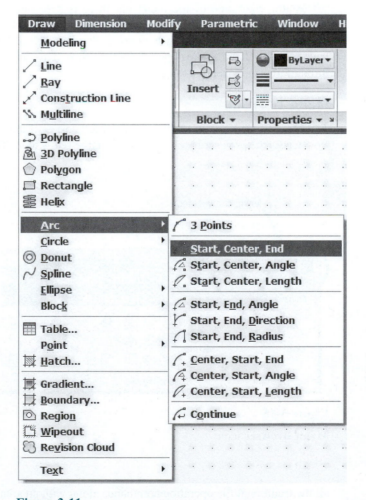

Figure 3-11

Draw menu with cascading submenu for arcs

Figure 3-12

Draw menu with ellipsis

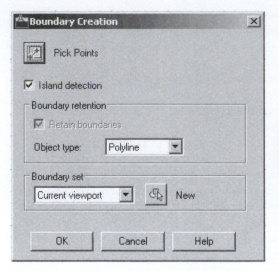

Figure 3-13

Boundary dialog box from the **Draw** menu

Figure 3-14

Drawing session upper right icons

the results of the input prior to accepting the change. We will present more information on the various fields within a dialog box later in this chapter.

At the right side of the menu bar there is a second set of the Windows **Minimum, Maximum,** and **Close** icons (see Figure 3-14). This set of buttons is for the individual drawing file you have open during the current drawing session. When using AutoCAD you can have multiple drawing files open at a single time. This set of buttons will help you navigate through multiple open drawing files.

Menu Browser

The **Menu Browser** is located in the upper left corner of the display screen (see Figure 3-15). You access the browser by clicking on the large red **A** icon. The **Menu Browser** will display

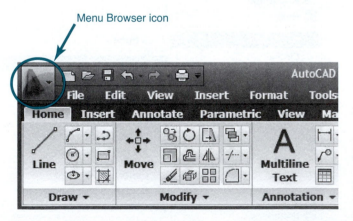

Figure 3-15

Menu Browser icon

all the traditional file operation commands along with an area for **Recent Documents, Open Documents,** and **Recent Action.** When you pass the mouse over any item in the left column, a corresponding list of actions will show up in the right column, allowing you to select the item to activate the command (see Figures 3-16a and 3-16b).

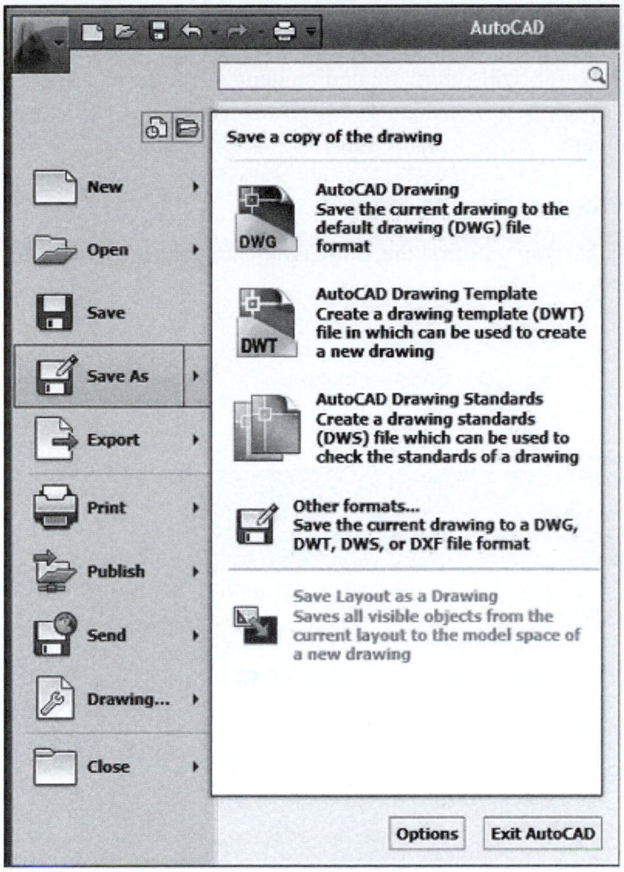

(a)

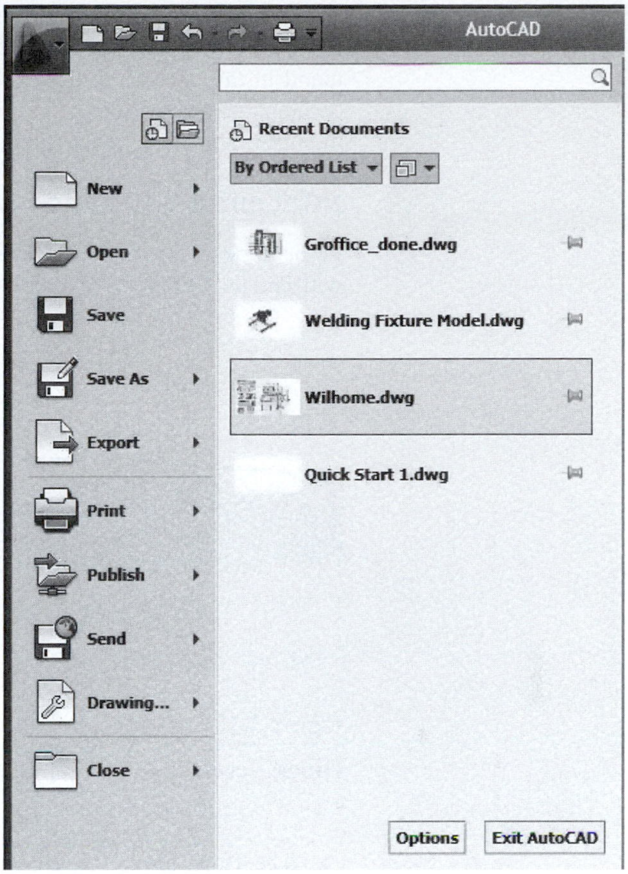

(b)

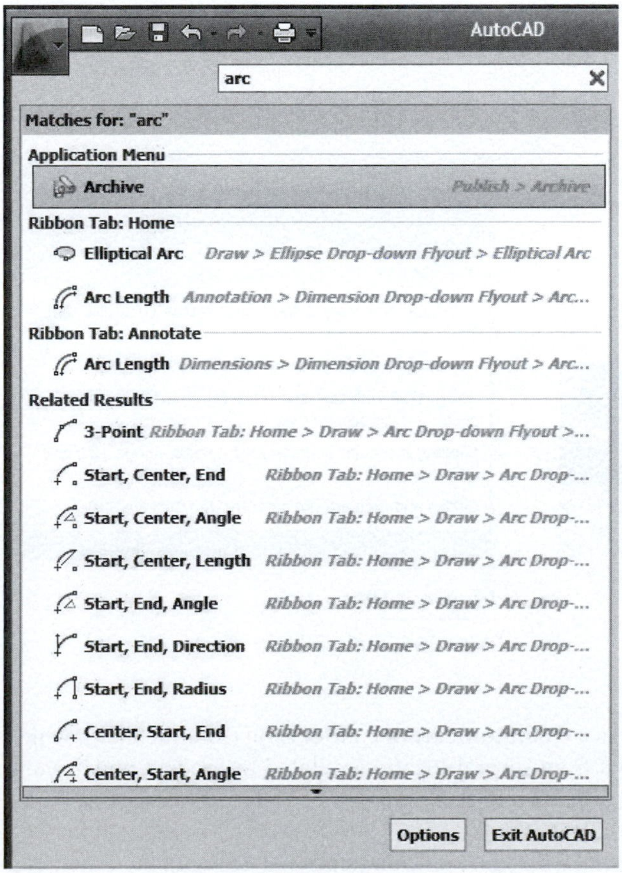

(c)

Figure 3-16

Menu Browser (a) results, (b) expanded for recent work, and (c) with search line

A second feature of the **Menu Browser** is the **Search Field** (see Figure 3-16c), which is located in the upper right portion of the **Menu Browser.** You can type in any phrase or command in this area, and the resulting search will return related content in the form of menu commands, basic tooltips, command prompt text strings, or tags from which you can access the information or execute the command.

InfoCenter and Quick Access

In the upper right corner of the menu bar you will find the **InfoCenter**, and at the top left you will find the **Quick Access** toolbar (Figure 3-17).

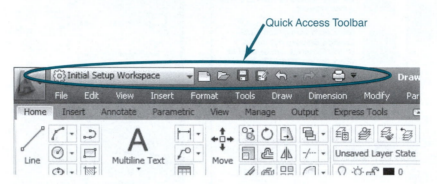

Figure 3-17

Quick Access toolbar at top of page

The **InfoCenter** (Figure 3-18) gives you several options to access help-related topics. You obtain help by selecting the **Search** icon and typing in your question. The program will then search multiple locations for your answer and display them as links for you to choose the type of help you are looking for (Figure 3-19). Answers may come from several locations such as the **Command Reference Guide,** the **Customization Guide,** the **User Reference Guide,** or other location.

Figure 3-18

InfoCenter at top for help

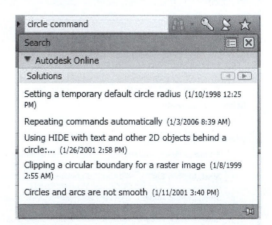

Figure 3-19

Autodesk Online Help display

The next item on the menu bar is a **Communication Center** icon (satellite dish), which will list a variety of announcements from several locations related to product updates and subscription programs along with articles and tips on productivity and knowledge-based command enhancements (Figure 3-20).

The final item on the **InfoCenter** menu bar is an icon (star) that accesses the **Favorites,** a location similar to the Favorites list of any Web browser. This is the area in which you save

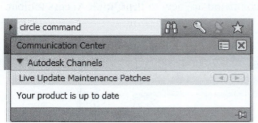

Figure 3-20

Help menu showing Autodesk Channels

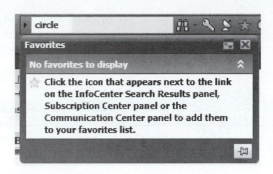

Figure 3-21

InfoCenter Favorites display

topics that you want to revisit. You can add links to the **Favorites** from the **Communication Center** by clicking on the star icon to the right of the help topic. This will place the link in the **Favorites** list under the appropriate area based on where it comes from (Figure 3-21).

2011 Version

The **Quick Access** toolbar can hold icons for frequently used commands. This toolbar is customizable and contains a predefined set of commands that are controlled by the current workspace. You can add, remove, and/or reposition commands within the **Quick Access** toolbar through a right-click menu option. Along with the right-click options, the **Quick Access** toolbar includes a new flyout option. You can access the flyout menu by selecting the down arrow on the right end of the **Quick Access** toolbar. The flyout contains a list of common tools from which you can select to include on the **Quick Access** toolbar (see Figure 3-22). There is limited room in the location for the **Quick Access** toolbar, so if you continue to add commands to this toolbar, it will roll into a flyout style to accommodate the extra commands. By default the **Workspace** flyout list will be at the far left side of the toolbar. This flyout will contain all of the defined workspaces in the drawing system. You will be able to change your current workspace by simply choosing one from the

NEW to
AutoCAD
2011

> **NOTE:**
>
> If there is no active drawing file open, the only commands that will appear in the toolbar will be **New, Open,** and **Sheet Manager.**

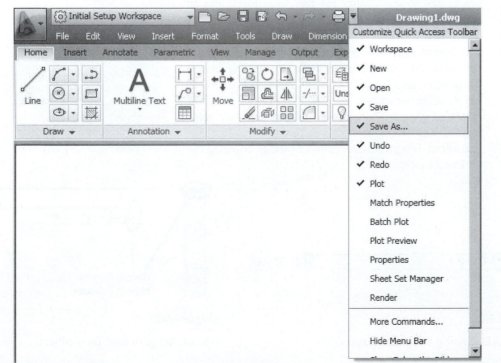

Figure 3-22

Quick Access customization options

NEW to
AutoCAD
2011

flyout list. In the **2D Drafting and Annotation** workspace, the following commands will be available in the default mode: **NEW, OPEN, SAVE, SAVEAS, PLOT, UNDO,** and **REDO.** The **Workspace** flyout and the **Save As** command are new to the **Quick Access** toolbar.

Figure 3-23

AutoCAD Classic workspace toolbars

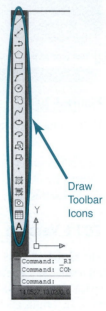

Draw Toolbar Icons

Figure 3-24

Draw toolbar

Toolbars

toolbar: A collection of icons representing various commands or operations.

Toolbars, located below the menu bar or in other locations, show a series of icons, representing AutoCAD commands or operations (see Figures 3-23, 3-24, and 3-25). You can select one of these icons with the left mouse button, and the program will execute the AutoCAD command related to that icon. AutoCAD 2011 has more than 30 predefined toolbars available. Four are located at the top of the screen in the **AutoCAD Classic** workspace, with one each on the left and the right side of the drawing area. Each of these toolbars is organized with similar commands common to the title of the toolbar. Unlike the pull-down menu, not all commands can be found on a toolbar, and you have the option of what toolbars you want displayed and at what location. Toolbars can be docked on any of the four sides of the screen, or they may be left undocked, or floating around the drawing area (see Figure 3-26). Each docked toolbar has a double bar located on the left edge known as a *grab bar* (see Figure 3-27). Selecting this grab bar while holding down the left mouse button and using a dragging motion allows you to move or undock a toolbar, changing the toolbar's location.

> **NOTE:**
>
> For the novice user, it may be beneficial to use the pull-down menus to execute commands initially. This will familiarize you with the organization of commands built into the software.

Modify Toolbar Icons

Figure 3-25

Modify toolbar

Figure 3-26

AutoCAD floating toolbar for layers

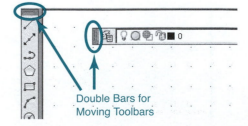

Double Bars for Moving Toolbars

Figure 3-27

AutoCAD grab bars for toolbars

Figure 3-28

AutoCAD toolbar as a single row

Figure 3-29

AutoCAD toolbar as a double row

When a toolbar is in a floating mode, its shape can be reconfigured, based on the number of icons on the toolbar (see Figures 3-28 and 3-29). To dock a floating toolbar, pick the grab bar with the left mouse button depressed and drag it to where you wish to dock it. When the toolbar gets to the docked location, the ghost image of the toolbar will change shape, at which time you let go of the mouse button and dock the toolbar in that location. Toolbars provide a faster way of executing frequently used commands. There is a learning curve required to identify which picture or icon will execute which commands, but once you are familiar with the program, you will become adept at executing commands using the toolbars. (See Appendix B for a complete list.)

JOB SKILLS

Identifying a command's icon will increase your daily productivity.

Drawing Area and Scroll Bars

The next area of the interface is the largest. This large window is known as the *drawing area*. This is where you will develop your drawings. The background color is gray as the default (see Figure 3-30), but this can easily be changed to any color you desire by accessing the **Screen Display** tab of the **OPTIONS** command.

> **NOTE:**
> The default color of the model space background has been changed in 2011 to dark gray. This can be modified to any color through the **Display** tab on the **Option** dialog box by selecting the **Colors** button.

drawing area: The large center area of the screen where the drawing is created.

FOR MORE DETAILS   The drawing area may at times contain tool palettes with blocks for inserting, commands for certain operations, hatch patterns, and entity properties for modifications. These palettes are discussed in Chapter 13.

The size of the drawing area is established in units and based on the template chosen. On the initial startup the size of the area is 12 units by 9 units. You can adjust this area to equal any size required to create your drawings in full-size units or at full size.

JOB SKILLS

All drawings created in a CAD world are full size. The traditional drafting scale is applied during the creation of layout space for printing purposes.

It is not uncommon to have a drawing area of $100' \times 150'$, $24'' \times 18''$, or $3 \text{ km} \times 2 \text{ km}$. These sizes might be used to represent a small single-family residential lot, a part in an airplane, or a subdivision. The physical size of the window itself does not change. You can adjust the drawing

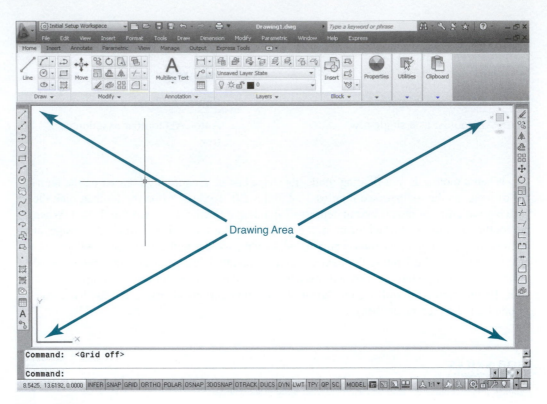

Figure 3-30

Autocad Drawing Area

limits to control the value, in specific units of measurement, to have the drawing area represent an area large enough to handle the design at a full scale. When working with larger values for your drawing limits, you will need to use a series of viewing commands such as **ZOOM** and **PAN** to manipulate the view within the drawing area window.

Along the right side and the bottom of the drawing window are two slider boxes known as *scroll bars* (see Figure 3-31). You can slide the screen left or right or up and down by clicking on the arrows within the scroll bar boxes.

The drawing area can also display two visual drawing aids. Using the **GRID** command, you can turn on a *grid*. In AutoCAD 2006 and earlier versions this was a series of regularly spaced dots. In AutoCAD 2007 it became grid lines (see Figure 3-32). Then, located in the

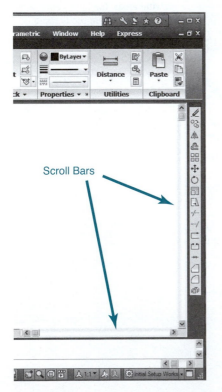

Figure 3-31

AutoCAD drawing area with scroll bars

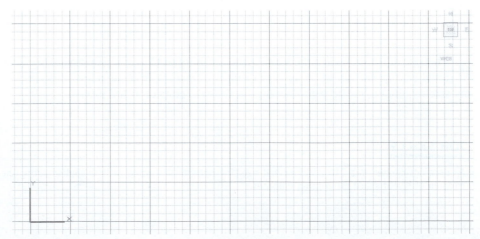

Figure 3-32

AutoCAD drawing area with grid lines

lower left corner of the drawing area is the *user coordinate system (UCS) icon* (see Figure 3-33). The **UCSICON** command gives information related to 3D space orientation and coordinate input. Both of these drawing aids are invisible to the plotting process, which means they do not print.

Navigation Bar

New to AutoCAD 2011 is the **Navigation** bar, along with a few changes to the **ViewCube,** which was introduced in the 2010 release. The **ViewCube** is a tool used predominately in 3D space. The tool is now available in the 2D wireframe visual style (see Figure 3-34). Although the **ViewCube** is primarily used with 3D models, the clockwise/counterclockwise part of the tool is quite useful when you want to rotate your point of view in the current XY plane. The addition of the **Navigation** bar to the **2D Annotation** workspace has been an additional tool for the control of a 2D drawing by providing access to the most frequently used viewing commands from a single interface. The bar contains the **Navigational Wheel, Pan, Zoom Extents, Orbit,** and **Show Motion** options (see Figure 3-35). By default the Navigation bar is docked on the right side of the screen but can be docked on any of the screen sides. The **Navigation** bar is completely customizable, allowing you to choose the viewing tools you use most often.

Model Space and Layout Space Tabs

Directly below the drawing area, to the lower left of the screen, there are three buttons used to switch between *model space* and *layout* or *paper space* (see Figure 3-36). Figure 3-37 shows the alternative **Model** and **Layout** icons in the status line at the bottom of the screen. *Model space* refers to the space where a drawing or design is created; *layout space* controls the views of a drawing or design for the production of printed pages.

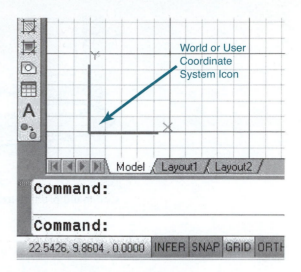

Figure 3-33

AutoCAD drawing area with coordinate system icon

user coordinate system (UCS) icon: Shows the positioning and direction of the XY axis in space.

Figure 3-34

ViewCube in 2D model space

Figure 3-35

Navigation toolbar

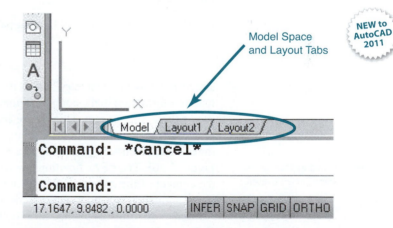

Figure 3-36

AutoCAD **Model** and **Layout** tabs

Command Line

The *command line* is typically located below the drawing area (see Figure 3-38). Its function is to communicate with the user through questions and statements based on the commands currently active, and it is much like a toolbar.

Its default location is below the drawing area, but like toolbars, it can be undocked to a floating style or repositioned somewhere else on the edges of the drawing area (see Figure 3-39).

One difference between toolbars and the command line area is that when the command line window is undocked and floating, the window can have a transparency value. This value

Figure 3-37

Alternative **Model** and **Layout** (paper space) icons

command line: The screen location that reflects input and command options.

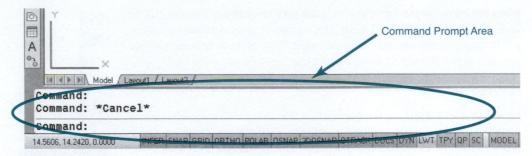

Figure 3-38

Command prompt area

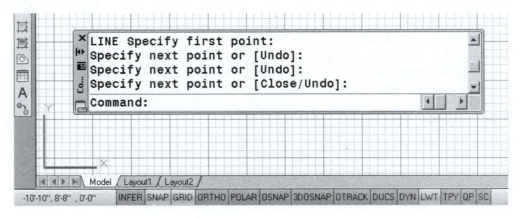

Figure 3-39

Floating command area on a floating palette

allows the drawing geometry behind the command line window to be seen. The most current line of information in the command line area is the bottom line. By default, the command line shows three lines of text. This can be adjusted to other values based on your preferences, but three lines are recommended for seeing AutoCAD responses, answer options, and error messages. All the lines are recorded in a text window, available by pressing the **<F2>** key (see Figure 3-40). The **<F2>** function key will turn a *text screen* window on and off, showing all the content of the command line since the beginning of the current drawing session.

text screen: A window that shows the history of the commands used.

Commands can be typed directly onto the command line and executed by hitting the **<Enter>** key from this point. Previous commands and operations may be "copied and pasted" at the command line and executed again. Any typing that occurs on the command line must be followed by pressing the **<Enter>** key to execute the command.

Status Bar

status bar: A series of readouts and on/off buttons, for drawing aids, located on the bottom of the screen.

The bottom area of the interface is the *status bar* located under the command line window. The status bar houses a series of on/off buttons or toggles referred to as *drawing aids*. On the left end of the status bar there is a coordinate or display readout (see Figure 3-41). When coordinate display is turned on, the current position of the cursor will read out as X, Y, and Z coordinates. Other variations of this information are available by cycling with left mouse picks in this area. To the right on this status bar is a series of drawing aid buttons, including **SNAP** and **GRID**. The button labeled **QP** was new for 2009 (see Figure 3-42). These buttons act as toggle switches to turn these drawing aids on or off. When a drawing aid is *on,* the button appears in a depressed or sunken mode. Figure 3-43 shows the alternative status line drawing aid icons. At the right end of the status bar there is a small downward-pointing arrow that will bring up a short menu (see

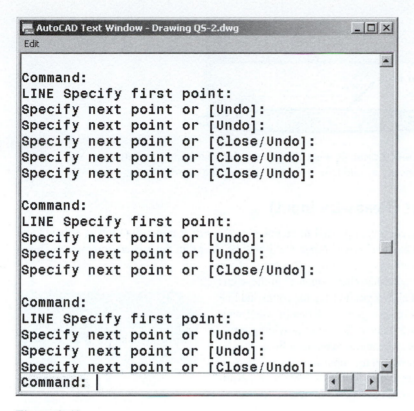

Figure 3-40

AutoCAD text window

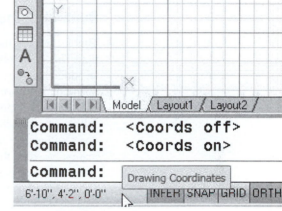

Figure 3-41

Drawing coordinate display area

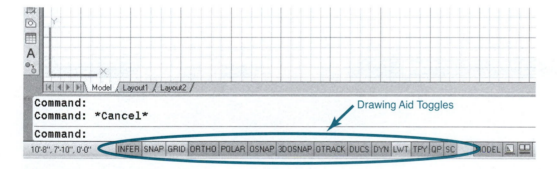

Figure 3-42

Drawing aid toggles on status line

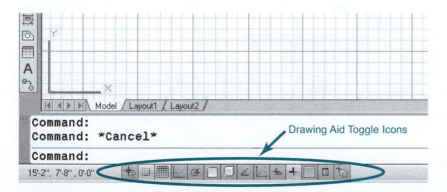

Figure 3-43

Drawing aid toggles on icons in the status line

Figure 3-44

Drawing control icons on the
right side of the status line

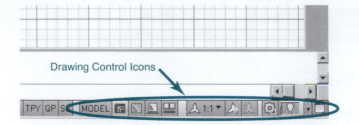

Drawing Control Icons

Figure 3-44). This menu controls what buttons will be visible on the status bar. You can customize which buttons are available by selecting them in the pop-up menu.

Dynamic Input (Heads-Up Input)

This feature lets the command prompt to be linked to the cursor rather than left in a fixed location. This feature is called *dynamic input,* and it will be shown in the related commands. This is an addition to the drafting tools settings. The status of your operation is shown with the other "toggles" in the status line. Dynamic input allows you to have the command line follow wherever the cursor goes. A series of small windows will appear at the cursor location, providing information based on the current command (see Figure 3-45). The <**Tab**> key will switch the input fields (see Figure 3-46), and the down arrow key will show any options available for the current command (see Figure 3-47).

> **NOTE:**
>
> Dynamic input can be switched on/off through the **DYN** button in the status bar.

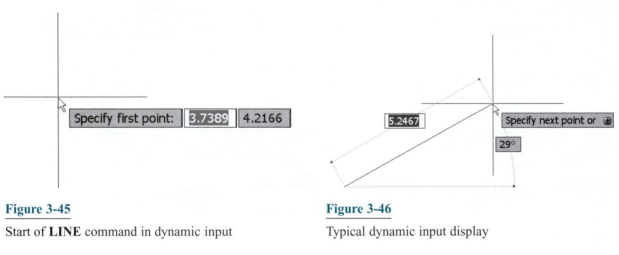

Figure 3-45

Start of **LINE** command in dynamic input

Figure 3-46

Typical dynamic input display

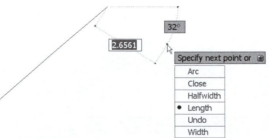

Figure 3-47

Options available in a **Dynamic Input** command

Drawing Status Bar

The drawing status bar is located on the right end of the status bar. This area has a series of icons used to control the drawing's **Scale Annotations, View, Workspace,** and other commands (see Figures 3-48 and 3-49).

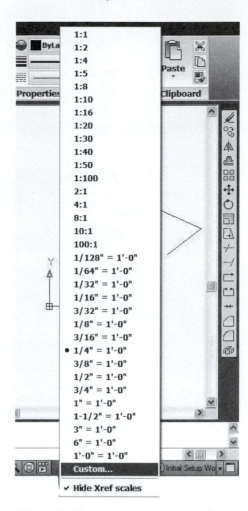

Figure 3-48

Status bar for **Annotation Scale**

Figure 3-49

Status bar **Annotation Scale** list

Annotations can be scaled automatically for various layout viewports as well as model space. When annotation objects are created, they are scaled to the active annotation scale. This will size all the entities to the proper relationship for that viewport. The icons in the drawing status bar will turn automatic scaling on or off. You will be able to set the annotation scale and the visibility of the annotation objects. Other icons in this area lock the positions of the toolbars and windows, control the **CLEANSCREEN** operation (which will hide/unhide all toolbars and windows), and allow you to select the elements you want displayed in the status bar area.

These tools are specific to model space and layout space. Different icons will appear depending on what space you are in.

Dialog Boxes, Function/Specialty Keys, and Help Files

Dialog boxes appear as windows during a drawing session. As mentioned earlier, some commands in the pull-down menus are followed by an ellipsis. When you select one of these commands, a dialog box will appear. You will then have an opportunity to set values and make selections related to the command. There are several styles or methods for inputting this information.

dialog box: A window that appears on top of the drawing screen for random input of a command.

radio buttons: Buttons used to select an option in a dialog box.

Numerical fields require you to single-click, or swipe across the current value, turning the field blue (see Figure 3-50). Then you can change the value through keyboard entry. You can also make choices from a *drop-down list*, which requires you to click on the black triangle (see Figure 3-51). You can select from a list of options called **radio buttons** (see Figure 3-52), or toggle check marks in boxes to activate or deactivate the option (see Figure 3-53).

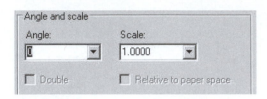

Figure 3-50

Dialog box with numerical field highlighted

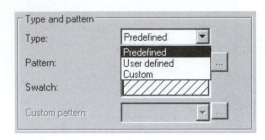

Figure 3-51

Dialog box with drop-down list

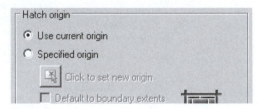

Figure 3-52

Dialog box with radio buttons

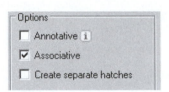

Figure 3-53

Dialog box with check boxes

These methods give you the ability to address any area of the dialog box at any time. Along with the previous methods, dialog boxes can contain a series of buttons or commands that will launch other dialog boxes. Remember, you must address the topmost dialog box and either accept or cancel this box before moving back through the remaining dialog boxes and back to the main interface. Some dialog boxes have an option to preview the results of the current values. By testing the values through the preview window, you can make changes to the values before actually placing the entities in the drawing file.

function keys: Typically, 12 programmable keys across the top of the keyboard.

Across the top of the keyboard is a row of *function keys*. This series of keys labeled <F1> through <F12> are programmable for functions within AutoCAD. Generally they are used as on/off toggles. Table 3-1 shows the function keys and their actions.

TABLE 3-1	Function keys
F1	Help
F2	Text Screen
F3	Object Snap
F4	3D Object Snap
F5	Isoplanes
F6	Dynamic UCS
F7	Grid Display
F8	Ortho Mode
F9	Snap Mode
F10	Polar Tracking
F11	Object Tracking
F12	Dynamic Commands

TABLE 3-2	Typical control key commands				
Key Code	**Command**	**Key Code**	**Command**	**Key Code**	**Command**
Ctrl+0	CleanScreen	**Ctrl+1**	Properties Palette	**Ctrl+2**	Design Center
Ctrl+3	Tool Palettes	**Ctrl+4**	Sheet Set Manager	**Ctrl+5**	
Ctrl+6	dbConnect	**Ctrl+7**	Markup Set Manager	**Ctrl+F4**	Closes Drawing
Ctrl+A	Selects All Objects	**Ctrl+B**	Snap Toggle	**Ctrl+C**	Copy to Clipboard
Ctrl+D	Dynamic UCS Toggle	**Ctrl+E**	Isoplane Toggle	**Ctrl+F**	Osnap Toggle
Ctrl+G	Grid Toggle	**Ctrl+L**	Ortho Toggle	**Ctrl+K**	Hyperlink
Ctrl+N	Starts New Drawing	**Ctrl+O**	Open Drawing	**Ctrl+P**	Plot/Print Dialog
Ctrl+Q	Exit/Quit AutoCAD	**Ctrl+R**	Cycles through Viewports	**Ctrl+S**	Save Drawing
Ctrl+T	Tablet Toggle	**Ctrl+V**	Paste from Clipboard	**Ctrl+U**	Polar Toggle
Ctrl+W	Selection Cycling	**Ctrl+X**	Cut to the Clipboard	**Ctrl+Z**	Undo

Specialty Keys

Along with the function keys, AutoCAD uses the functionality of the control keys. It has a series of **<Ctrl>** (control key) and character keystroke combinations that perform predefined commands. To execute a control keystroke function, both the **<Ctrl>** key and the character must be depressed at the same time. Several of these combinations are the same in all Windows-based programs; **<Ctrl>** + **<S>** for **SAVE** and **<Ctrl>** + **<C>** for **Copy to Clipboard** are examples. Others are unique to AutoCAD software. Table 3-2 lists the typical control keystroke combinations used within AutoCAD. Figure 3-54 shows the typical location of the **<Ctrl>** key for most keyboards.

Control Key

Figure 3-54

The control key

Escape, Delete, and Arrow Keys

Certain keys have specific commands attached to them. For example, the **<Esc>** (escape) key will end, stop, or cancel any currently active command. Some commands require you to press the **<Esc>** key twice to fully cancel the active command, but most commands will cancel after a single **<Esc>** keystroke. The **<Del>** (delete) key can act as an **ERASE** function. You can select an entity on the screen and hit the **<Del>** key to erase the entity from the file. Finally, the arrow keys typically located between the alpha keyboard and the numeric keypad can be used to nudge entities around the drawing environment. See Figure 3-55 for a typical location of these keys.

TABLE 3-3	Single-character command aliases
Single-Character Aliases (Typical)	
A	ARC
B	BLOCK
C	CIRCLE
D	DIMSTYLE
E	ERASE
F	FILLET
G	GROUP
H	HATCH
I	INSERT
J	JOIN
L	LINE
M	MOVE
O	OFFSET
P	PAN
R	REDRAW
S	STRETCH
T	MTEXT
U	UNDO
V	VIEW
W	WBLOCK
X	EXPLODE
Z	ZOOM

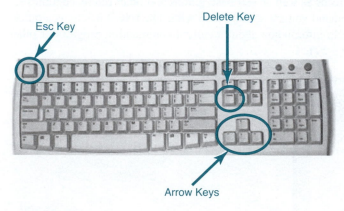

Esc Key

Delete Key

Arrow Keys

Figure 3-55

Useful keys

Command Aliases

Command aliases are an alternative method of launching a command. Most aliases are one to three keystrokes followed by the **<Enter>** key. For example, **L** initiates the **LINE** command, **E** begins the **ERASE** command, and so on (see Table 3-3). This shortcut method of invoking a command saves on the time it takes to track down a command in the traditional pull-down menu area or to find an icon. Not all commands have an alias alternative. A complete list of command aliases is stored in a text file named acad.pgp, which can also be modified to the operator's desires. This list can be found in Appendix C along with other character aliases available in AutoCAD.

Online Help Files

Help files can be found in the **Help** menu, by typing in the command **HELP,** or by pressing **<F1>.** From this menu a traditional help window, similar to all Windows-based programs, is where you can conduct content searches, review a program index, and post questions pertaining to all topics within the AutoCAD program. The right side of the window (see Figure 3-56)

Figure 3-56

Typical **Help** screen layout

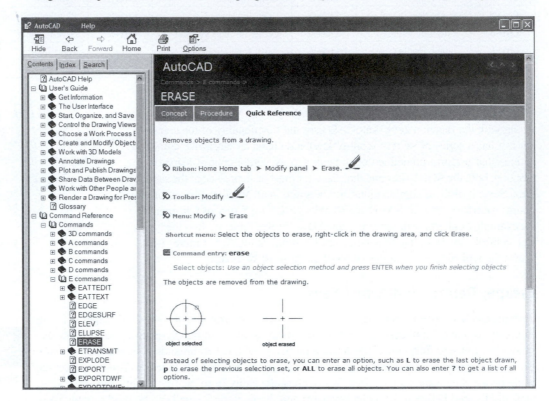

is the topic content side, with three tabs—**Concept, Procedure,** and **Quick Reference.** The content side shows graphics screens as well as text descriptions and other reference topics related to the active topic or command you are seeking help with. The **INFO** palette is a quick, interactive assistant showing help information about a current command in progress or other related information (see Figure 3-57).

Figure 3-57

INFO palette

Tooltips

Tooltips are an interactive form of help that describes, through pop-up information, commands related to toolbars, menu browsers, ribbon panels, and dialog boxes. The tooltip provides relevant information about links to items such as commands, object snaps, and drafting operations. You activate a tooltip by pausing the mouse over an item for a short time. In the **Options** dialog box, the **Display** tab defines the length of time allowed to display the tooltip. After this predefined length of time a small window appears with the tooltip displayed within (see Figure 3-58). If you continue to hover the mouse over the item, an expanded version of the tooltip will appear offering additional information about the command in question (see Figure 3-59).

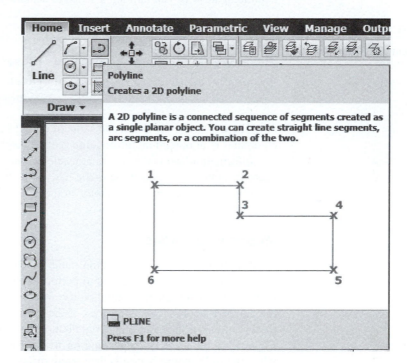

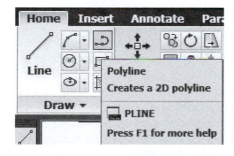

Figure 3-58

Polyline tooltip help

Figure 3-59

Polyline tooltip help expanded

Online Resource

The **Help** menu contains several live links to Autodesk websites that have information addressing product support, training, and customizing AutoCAD plus access to AutoCAD user groups (see Figure 3-60). If you have an active Internet connection, selecting one of these menu choices will launch an Internet session taking you to the link location. There are many Internet sites devoted to AutoCAD, and several links will start you in the right direction with additional help and links related to users' questions.

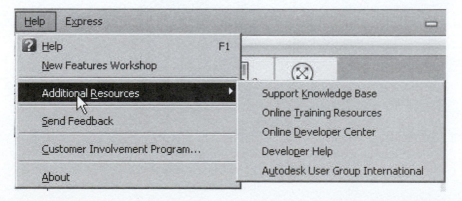

Figure 3-60

Additional Resources submenu

Command Line Details

As mentioned earlier, the command line is a window where operators can directly type in AutoCAD commands. This window will then display command prompts and messages regarding the active commands (see Figure 3-61). The most current line is located at the bottom of the window, allowing preceding lines of text to scroll upward and out of the command line display onto the text screen. When the word *Command* is shown in the active command line, this means the program is ready and waiting for an instruction. Any command or alias can be entered directly into the command line. To execute the typed command you must press the **<Enter>** key on the keyboard. Once a command is in operation the command line will communicate with you through a series of statements about the current command.

Figure 3-61

Typical command line in action

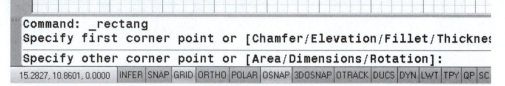

```
Command: _rectang
Specify first corner point or [Chamfer/Elevation/Fillet/Thicknes
Specify other corner point or [Area/Dimensions/Rotation]:
15.2827, 10.8601, 0.0000   INFER  SNAP  GRID  ORTHO  POLAR  OSNAP  3DOSNAP  OTRACK  DUCS  DYN  LWT  TPY  QP  SC
```

There are two visual clues to some of the information seen in the command line. Once a command is in operation, information will be displayed in square brackets and in parentheses. Information inside the square brackets will be options for the current commands. To execute an option, you must type in the letter(s) of the word that is capitalized. Information in parentheses is referred to as *default* information. To accept any default value, you simply press the **<Enter>** key on the keyboard.

Mouse Operations

Most input devices are three-button mouse devices. In some cases the middle button is replaced with a wheel programmed to perform certain viewing or display commands. The left button is the pick, select, or input button. When it is depressed, the command highlighted by the cursor executes. This is the case if the arrow is on a word in a menu or on an icon in a toolbar or on a ribbon panel. The right button is used for a context-sensitive pop-up menu (see Figures 3-62 and 3-63). Depending on whether a command is active or where the arrow is when the right mouse button is depressed, different menus will display.

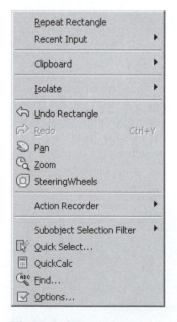

Figure 3-62

Typical right-click menu

Figure 3-63

Typical right-click menu when a command is active

If you hold the **<Ctrl>** key down and then depress the right mouse button, an **Object Snap** menu appears at the location of the cursor (see Figure 3-64).

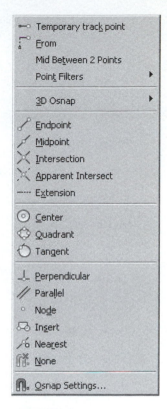

> **JOB SKILLS**
>
> Demonstrate an efficient use of previous commands by using **Recent Input.** This can be found on a right-click menu.

AutoCAD has preprogrammed the center button for viewing commands. By rolling the wheel you will perform a **ZOOM** command, which changes the magnification of the drawing. When you roll the wheel forward, you perform a **ZOOM IN** command. When you roll the wheel backward, you perform a **ZOOM OUT** command. When you are using the wheel, the current location of the cursor will be the center of the **ZOOM** operation. A third display command known as **PAN** (no change in magnification, just movement based on the cursor movement) is executed when you push down on the wheel and keep the wheel depressed as you move the mouse around.

Figure 3-64

Object Snap right-click menu

Chapter Summary

In this chapter, we introduced you to the basics of the AutoCAD interface and its features. We explained the title bar, ribbon and control panels, menu bar and drop-down menus, dialog boxes, menu browser, **InfoCenter,** toolbars, drawing area, and scroll bars. We also covered navigational tools, model space/layout space tabs, command line, status bar, dynamic input, and drawing status bar operations. We then showed you how to access AutoCAD commands and options through dialog boxes, check boxes, radio buttons, function/specialty keys (**<F1>** through **<F12>**, **<Ctrl>**, **<Esc>**, **<Del>**, and arrows). Finally, we discussed command aliases, mouse operations, as well as how to obtain help from the pull-down menu, tooltips, live Autodesk website links, and command line details.

Chapter Test Questions

Multiple Choice

Circle the correct answer.

1. An arrow to the right of an entry in the pull-down menu means
   a. Window to follow
   b. Cascading menu to follow
   c. Command execution
   d. Dialog box to follow

2. What does the ellipsis to the right of an entry in the pull-down menu mean?
   a. Window to follow
   b. Cascading menu to follow
   c. Command execution
   d. Dialog box to follow

3. The space bar in the AutoCAD program will act as another _____ key.
   a. Cancel
   b. Escape
   c. Delete
   d. Enter

4. To stop or cancel a command in AutoCAD, you would press the _____ key.
   a. Cancel
   b. Escape
   c. Delete
   d. Enter

5. The double grab bar on the side of a toolbar is used to _____ a toolbar.
   a. Float
   b. Close
   c. Dock
   d. Delete

Matching

Write the number of the correct answer on the line.

a. **Navigation** bar _____

b. Shortcut _____

c. Radio buttons _____

d. Alias _____

e. Status bar _____

1. Used to select an option in a dialog box

2. Special toolbar that contains viewing commands

3. Alternative method of launching a command

4. An icon on the desktop to start a program

5. Contains drawing aids

True or False

Circle the correct answer.

1. **True or False:** The middle wheel on a mouse can be used for viewing control.

2. **True or False:** All the commands in the pull-down menus can be found in a toolbar.

3. **True or False:** The look of the AutoCAD interface is set at the factory and cannot be changed.

4. **True or False:** The **ORTHO** drawing aid will produce objects perpendicular to each other.

5. **True or False:** A right click on the mouse will bring up a context-sensitive menu.

Chapter Projects

Project 3-1 [BASIC]

Which icon in the **Standard** toolbar will fly out to show more options?

Project 3-2 [BASIC]

What is shown at the bottom of the **File** menu immediately above **EXIT**?

Project 3-3 [INTERMEDIATE]

Check with technical firms in your area to learn which CAD software and which CAD standards they are using.

Project 3-4 [INTERMEDIATE]

Examine Microsoft Office software. Find the icons that are common to both the AutoCAD and the Office products and create a list. Are the actions the same in both programs?

Project 3-5 [BASIC]

Fill in the identifying names in Figure 3-65. See this figure in the student data files.

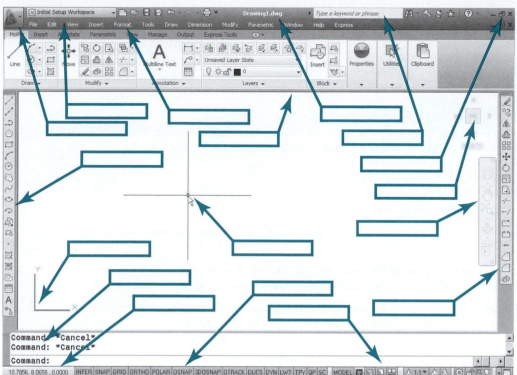

To access student datafiles, go to
www.pearsondesigncentral.com.

Figure 3-65

Basic setup quiz

Chapter Practice Exercises

Practice Exercise 3-1: *File Management* [BASIC]

1. Start AutoCAD using the Desktop icon or menus.

2. Examine each of the menus to learn the location of commands and when submenus or dialog boxes will appear.

3. Move the mouse slowly over various icons to see the command name (tooltip) for that icon.

4. Pick the **File** menu and choose **OPEN** (see Figure 3-66).

5. Using the drop-down area at the top of the **Select File** dialog box, find the student data files.

To access student datafiles, go to
www.pearsondesigncentral.com.

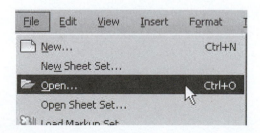

Figure 3-66

File Open menu

6. Scroll through the list of drawing files (.dwg) in the **Sample** folder and choose one to open by picking the **Open** button in the lower right of the dialog box:

   a. **Architectural Drawings**—8th Floor, Hotel, Hummer, Stadium, Taisei, Willhome, Campus, Kitchen, or Stadium North
   b. **Building Services**—8th Floor
   c. **Civil Drawings**—Hotel or SPCA Site Plan
   d. **Facilities Management**—Db__samp
   e. **Landscaping**—SPCA Site Plan
   f. **Mechanical**—Oil Module, Welding Fixture 1, Welding Fixture Model, Chevy, Truck Model, or Watch
   g. **Presentation**—Hotel, Hummer, Stadium, Welding Fixture Model, Campus, Chevy, Kitchen, Stadium North, or Truck Model
   h. **Process Piping**—Oil Module
   i. **Structural**—MKMPlan or Oil Module

7. Practice using the mouse wheel to **PAN** and **ZOOM** on these drawings.

8. Access various commands and watch the command line for instructions. Pressing **<Esc>** will cancel any operation.

9. To end your work session on a drawing, go to the **File** menu and pick **CLOSE**. Pick the answer **No** so that no modifications are saved at this time. If you want to open and examine another drawing, go back to Step 4.

10. To end your AutoCAD session, go to the **File** menu and pick **EXIT.** If a drawing is active, answer **No** to the prompt in the command line so that no modifications are saved at this time. The program then ends.

4

Creating and Working with AutoCAD Files

CHAPTER OBJECTIVES

- Understand the concepts of file management.
- Identify the file extensions used in AutoCAD.
- Use ANSI and ISO drawing templates.
- Create user-defined templates for various engineering disciplines.

Introduction

Now that you have completed a quick tutorial, we turn to the drawing file setup and the file management process. By creating templates you can begin each new design with the same approach to the process of completing a drawing. These templates will be the foundation of the drawing process in any engineering discipline.

File Management

File management is the saving, storage, archiving, and organization of the product created in a drawing session. AutoCAD drawings produce a file with a *.dwg* file extension. Security and organization are two main issues when saving or archiving drawing files.

Since most computers use Windows as the operating system, the file management commands within the AutoCAD program are the same ones found in any Windows-based program. Commands such as **NEW, OPEN, SAVE, SAVEAS,** and **CLOSE** are the basic operations related to file management. These commands can be found in the **File** pull-down menu (see Figure 4-1) and on the center section of the **Quick Access** toolbar (see Figure 4-2). Procedures for each of these commands are executed only on the single file that is currently active, even though AutoCAD has the ability to have multiple drawing files open at one time. These commands allow you to name files, save files, retrieve files, and manipulate the locations where files are stored. It is considered good practice to store drawing files in various folders referred to as *directories*. Drawing files should never be saved in folders containing any of the AutoCAD system files. Making a separate subdirectory or folder on your local hard drive and saving files into that folder will help secure your drawing files, as well as keep the program system files safe from modifications. Beginning users need to develop day-to-day habits regarding the management of their files.

.dwg: The file extension used for all valid AutoCAD drawing files.

> **NOTE:**
> Drawing files should never be saved in folders containing any of the AutoCAD system or program files.

Figure 4-1

File menu

Figure 4-2

Quick Access toolbar for file management functions

JOB SKILLS

CAD operators are responsible for the tracking of their daily work within the company file management system. This includes revision versions as well as archived files from past projects.

Beginning a New Drawing Session

template: A predefined series of variables saved in a file for the purpose of starting a new drawing file.

Use the **NEW** command to open the **Select template** dialog box (see Figure 4-3). You can then choose a basic, generic AutoCAD *template* or one of several preprogrammed templates established for various engineering disciplines. After accepting a style of template, you will exit the dialog box by clicking on the **OPEN** button, thus starting a new drawing session. All new drawing sessions are temporarily named DRAWING1.dwg, and any sequential new drawing sessions are named DRAWING2.dwg, DRAWING3.dwg, and so on. You should rename this drawing and store it in the correct folder or directory using the **SAVE** or **SAVE AS** command. If the system variable **STARTUP** is set to a value of 1, executing the **NEW** command will result in the **Create New Drawing** dialog box (see Figures 4-4, 4-5, and 4-6). This **Create New Drawing** dialog box has three choices available. You may **Start from Scratch** (see Figure 4-4), **Use a Template** (see Figure 4-5), or **Use a Wizard** (see Figure 4-6).

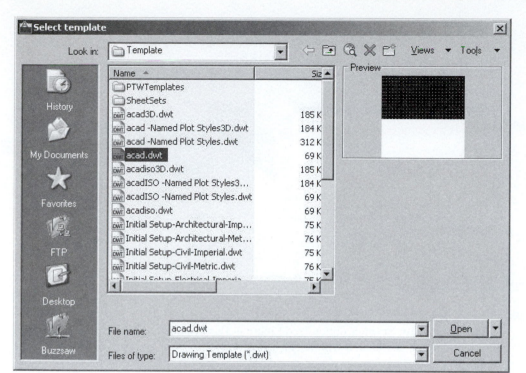

Figure 4-3

Select template dialog box

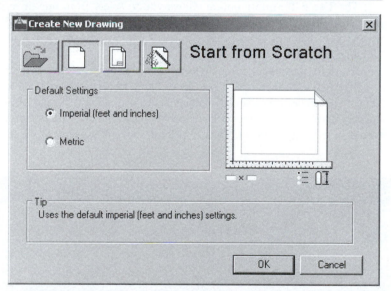

Figure 4-4

Create New Drawing
screen—**Start from Scratch**

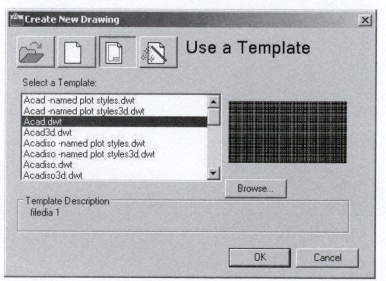

Figure 4-5

Creating a new drawing using
a template

Figure 4-6

Creating a new drawing using the Wizard

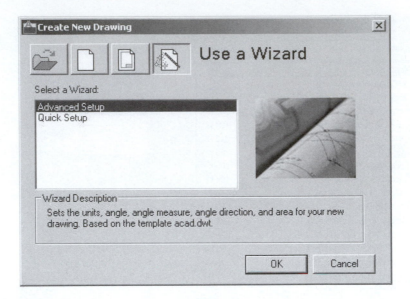

ANSI (American National Standards Institute): A government-controlled series of standards for engineering.

ISO (International Standards Organization): An internationally controlled series of standards for engineering, manufacturing, and other technical issues.

wizard: A tool that uses a step-by-step routine to complete a task.

The **Start from Scratch** option (see Figure 4-4) will allow you to select either imperial or metric units, and then it will launch a session based on the standard default acad.dwt template.

The **Use a Template** option allows you to select from one of over 60 predefined templates (see Figure 4-5). These templates are based on sheet sizes and drafting standards such as **ANSI** (American National Standards Institute) or **ISO** (International Standards Organization) practices.

In addition, standard templates are included from various other countries.

The **Use a Wizard** option (see Figure 4-6) has two choices: **Quick Setup** and **Advanced Setup**. The *wizard* uses a series of dialog boxes with options to establish settings used in controlling the drawing's input methods and overall environment. **Quick Setup** allows you to set the type of units used, along with the size or limits of the drawing area (see Figures 4-7 and 4-8). The

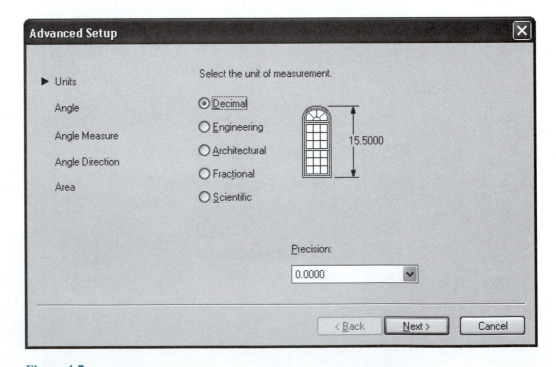

Figure 4-7

Wizard screen for **Units**

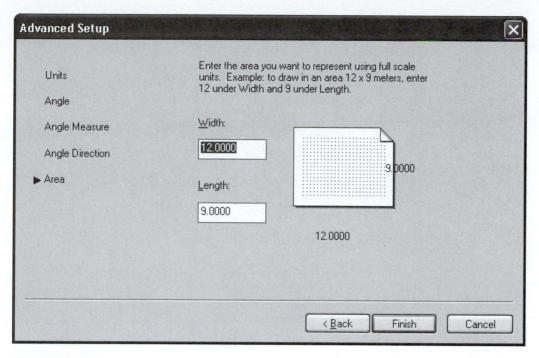

Figure 4-8
Wizard screen for **Area**

Advanced Setup asks the same two questions as the **Quick Setup**, along with additional questions related to type of angles, angle measurement, and angle direction (see Figures 4-9, 4-10, and Figure 4-11). Your selections are established along with the default acad.dwt template file for the new drawing.

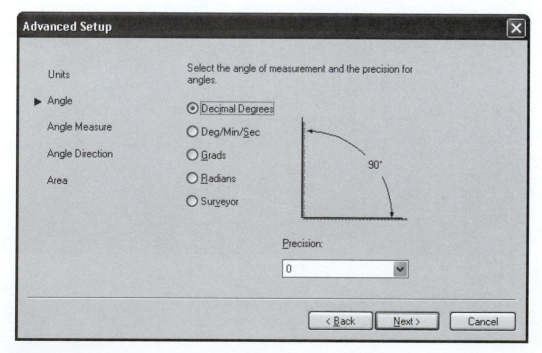

Figure 4-9
Wizard screen for **Angle**

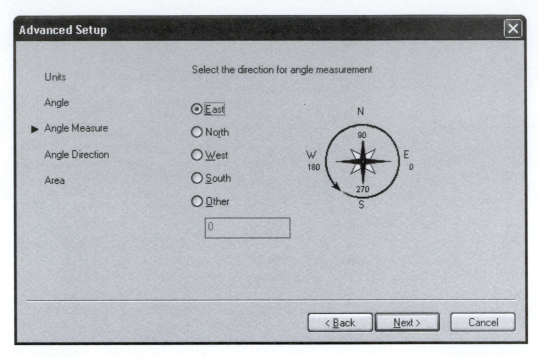

Figure 4-10

Wizard screen for **Angle Measure**

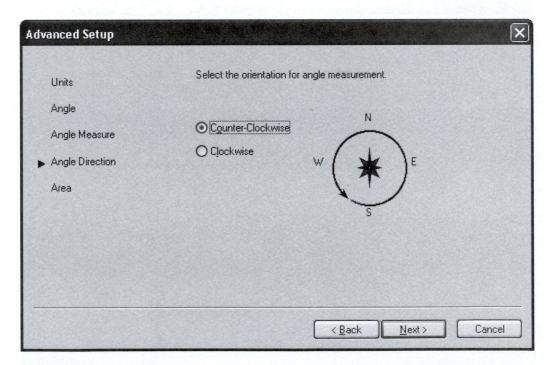

Figure 4-11

Wizard screen for **Angle Direction**

Saving Files

You have three options for saving your work: **SAVE**, **QSAVE**, and **SAVEAS**. The first time a **SAVE** command is executed, the **Save Drawing As** dialog box appears (see Figure 4-12). At this time you can navigate the system drives to go to a specific directory and rename the drawing file. Remember, AutoCAD will place a generic name such as Drawing1.dwg, Drawing2.dwg, and so forth, on all files that have not yet been saved. It is to your advantage to invoke a **SAVE** command as soon as possible. Once an initial **SAVE** command has been completed, any future execution of a **SAVE** command will result in the execution of a **QSAVE** command. This command will simply update the previously saved file to the current status of the file. If you would like to change the location the file is saved in or change the name of the saved file, you must invoke the

> **NOTE:**
> - The **SAVEAS** command can now be found on the **Quick Access** toolbar.
> - AutoCAD 2010 introduced a new file format. You will not be able to open a 2010 or 2011 file in previous versions of AutoCAD without executing a **SAVEAS** command and changing the file type to a previous file format.

SAVEAS command. **SAVEAS** will allow you to change the name of the file, the location it is being saved in, and the format in which it is saved (see Figure 4-13). On execution of the **SAVEAS** command, the existing file will become a copy (with an extension suffix of *.bak* as explained next). When a new name is entered, it will result in an automatic closure of the previous file you were working on.

.bak: A standard file name extension used by many programs to be the last saved version of a document, spreadsheet, or drawing before the most recently saved version.

Auto Saved and Backup Files

AutoCAD does have an automatic save function. This system variable, **SAVETIME**, is set by default to save the active drawing every 120 minutes. It can be changed in the **Options**

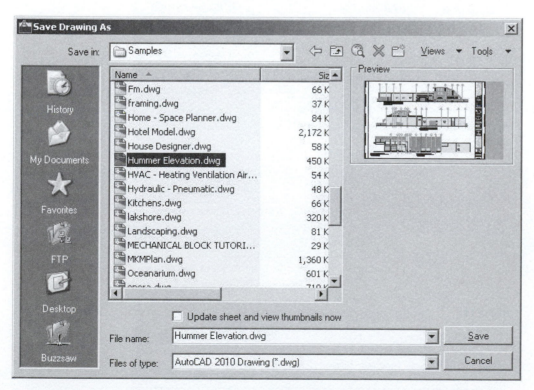

Figure 4-12

Save Drawing As dialog box

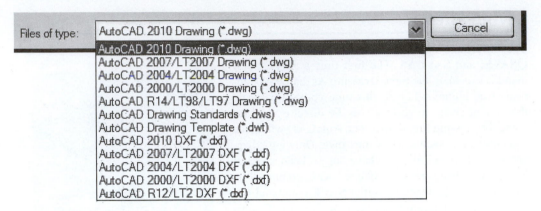

Figure 4-13

Save Drawing Options drop-down list

dialog box under the **Open and Save** tab (see Figure 4-14). There you will find a check box to activate the feature, along with a time field for **Minutes between saves**. It is a good practice to reduce the time field to approximately 10 to 15 minutes. You can do a great deal of work in 120 minutes that you may not want to do over in case of a system crash, power failure, or similar problem. Individual user habits or established office practices will vary when related to this issue. It is important to note that the **Auto Saved** file (typically with a default extension suffix of .sv$ or .ac$) is not saved in the same location as the drawing file saved with the **QSAVE** command. Check the file path location in the **Options** dialog box under the **Files** tab to find the location of automatically saved files (see Figure 4-15).

Figure 4-14

Options dialog box, **Open and Save** tab, for **Automatic save** time setting

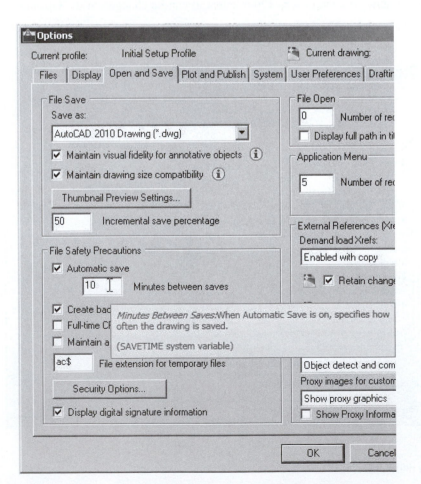

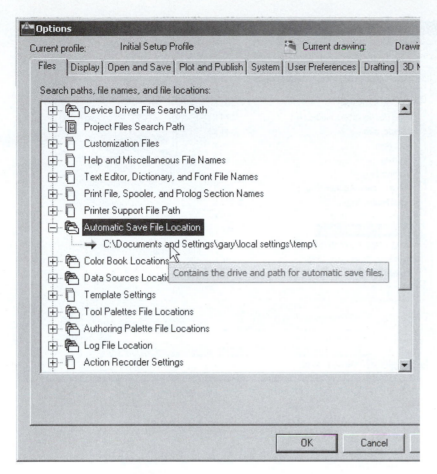

Figure 4-15

Options dialog box, **File** tab, for location of **Automatic Save** files

Along with automatically saving, each time an existing file is saved, AutoCAD creates a backup copy of the original file or updates it if the file already exists. This feature is also controlled in the **Options** dialog box. The file will be created in the same directory as the AutoCAD .dwg file. The only difference is that its file name will have a .bak extension. This file can be renamed through typical Windows procedures to have a .dwg extension, if needed, to recover the file as a valid AutoCAD drawing file.

Opening a Drawing

The **OPEN** command will allow you to retrieve an existing AutoCAD drawing file. After executing the command you will be presented with the **Select File** dialog box (see Figure 4-16). In this dialog box you will be able to navigate your system drives to locate directories and select a drawing file. Most valid AutoCAD drawing files will show a thumbnail preview in the upper right area of the dialog box. By default, this dialog box filters for drawing files with a .dwg file extension. At the bottom of the dialog box there is a field for file types, which can be changed to search for other types of files such as .dxf (data exchange files), .dwt (template files), or .dws (drawing standards files) (see Figure 4-17). Once the file is located and selected, you can select the **Open** button in the lower right area of the dialog box to retrieve the data from the file and begin the drawing session.

Figure 4-16

Open drawing dialog box

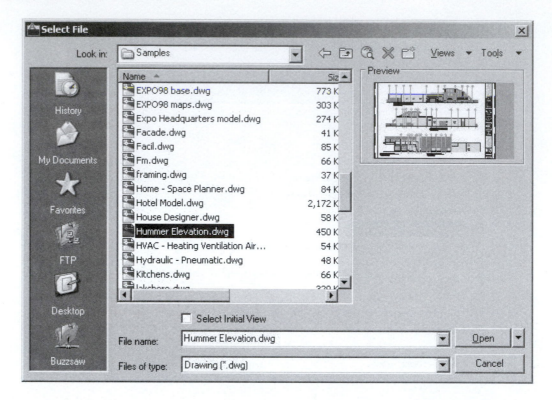

Figure 4-17

File type drop-down to filter for the type of drawing

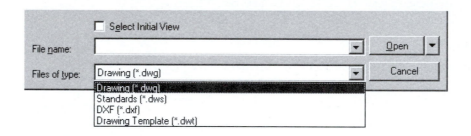

A second method of opening files is to select the file from the Windows Explorer program. Any valid AutoCAD drawing file (one with a .dwg extension) can be located through the Explorer or the My Computer function; then you can double-click with the left mouse button on the file to launch the AutoCAD software and open the contents of the drawing file selected (see Figure 4-18). A third method of accessing an AutoCAD drawing is to set up a desktop icon (see Figure 4-19) by either using the **AutoCAD** icon as a base with the drawing name specified or placing the drawing name on the desktop as an icon directly when the file is being saved (see Figure 4-20).

NOTE:

Be watchful for the AutoCAD Alert shown in Figure 4-21. It is telling you that the drawing you are about to open is already in use by someone else (or maybe it is currently open in your session). Generally, you do not want to work on a drawing that is currently in use. Ask the person using it to release it to you before doing any further editing.

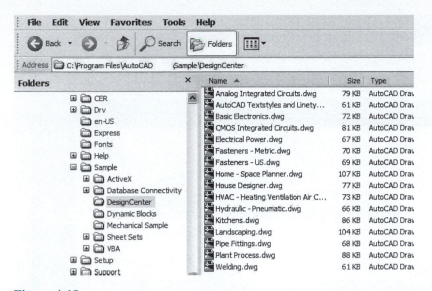

Figure 4-18

Explorer dialog showing AutoCAD files

Figure 4-19

AutoCAD desktop icon to open a drawing directly

Figure 4-20

Figure 4-21

Open file duplicate warning message

Working with Multiple Drawing Sessions

As mentioned earlier, AutoCAD is capable of having several drawings open in a single session. This is referred to as a *Multiple Design Environment* (MDE). Drawings can be viewed in several arrangements. A single floating window is the default mode (see Figure 4-22).

Drawings can also be *cascaded* (see Figure 4-23), exposing the title bar of each file, *tiled horizontally* or *tiled vertically* on the screen (see Figure 4-24). You can navigate through multiple active drawing files by selecting the name of the drawing from the **Window** menu (see Figure 4-25). If one of the other display modes is active, you may simply click on the title bar of the drawing you want to activate. Switching drawings when the multiple drawings are tiled requires you only to move the cursor into the file and click anywhere within that drawing's viewport. If the system variable **TASKBAR** is set to a value of 1, each open drawing will appear as an icon on the Windows taskbar. Simply selecting the icon from the bottom taskbar will activate that drawing.

There are several commands or actions that can take place between multiple drawings.

JOB SKILLS

Users will often share information between drawings through drag-and-drop techniques. This can be easily accomplished when drawings are tiled vertically or horizontally.

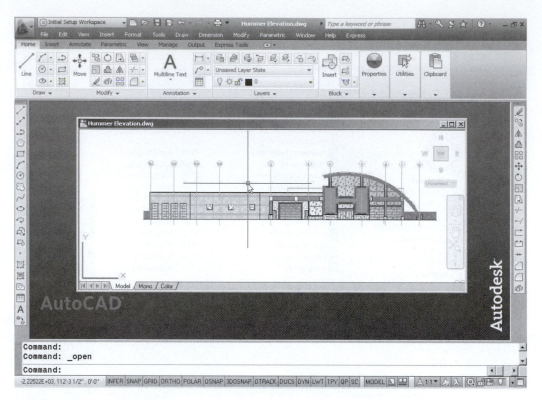

Figure 4-22

Single drawing in floating window

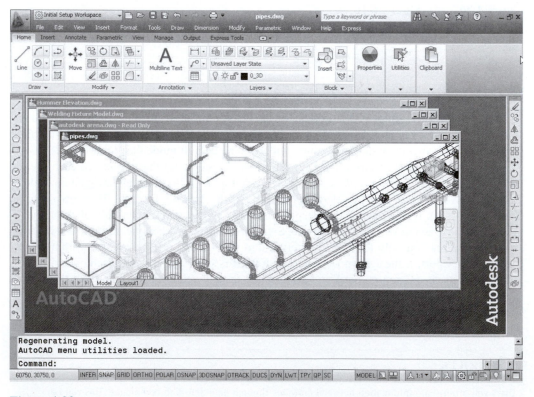

Figure 4-23

Multiple drawings in floating cascade windows

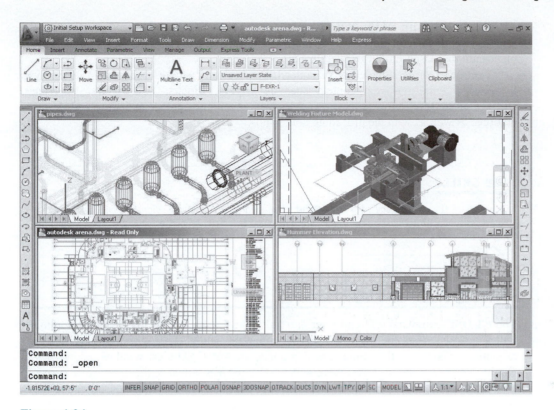

Figure 4-24

Multiple drawings in tiled viewports

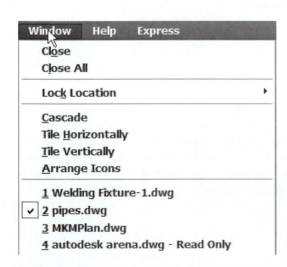

Figure 4-25

Window menu showing open drawings

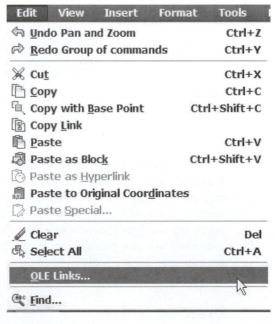

Figure 4-26

Edit menu

Figure 4-27

Cut, Copy, and **Paste** icons

Figure 4-28

Cut, Copy, and **Paste** icons from the **Clipboard** panel on the **Home** tab on the ribbon

The traditional Windows commands **CUT**, **COPY**, and **PASTE** are available from the **Edit** menu (see Figure 4-26), by the combination control keystrokes shown on the menu, and on the Standard toolbar (see Figure 4-27). These commands also are available from the **Clipboard** panel on the **Home** ribbon (see Figure 4-28).

The **COPY with BASE POINT** and the **PASTE SPECIAL** commands ensure that the transfer of objects maintains their accuracy as related to their specific drawings. These commands are discussed further in later chapters.

The use of the **DesignCenter** (Chapter 10) and the tool palettes (Chapter 14) allows you to transfer definition-based content such as **Layers, Blocks, Text Styles, Linetypes, Dimension Styles, Layouts,** and **Properties** from one file to another with drag-and-drop operations, as well as with the preceding commands.

JOB SKILLS

Demonstrate the use of **Copy with Base Point** when using the Windows versions of the **Cut**, **Copy**, **Paste** sequence. This will increase the accuracy of your placement no matter what the destination file format is.

Closing and Exiting

The **CLOSE** command will end your currently active drawing file session. This command will affect the current file while still leaving you in the AutoCAD program. In most cases the execution of a **CLOSE** command will produce an AutoCAD alert window asking if you would like to save the file (see Figure 4-29). Selecting **Yes** will save the drawing or specified file, and selecting **No** will close the session and discard all changes made during the drawing session.

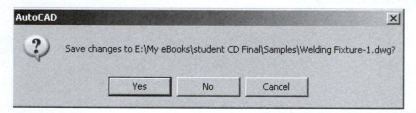

Figure 4-29

AutoCAD save message

The **CLOSE** command is found in three locations, the **File** menu (see Figure 4-1), the **Window** menu (see Figure 4-25), and the **Menu Browser** (see Figure 4-30). If there are multiple drawing files open, you may choose the **CLOSE ALL** selection under the **Window** menu to close all the files currently opened. To close the drawing session and exit the program, use the **EXIT** command in the **File** menu. As in the **CLOSE** command, the **EXIT** command will also produce the "Save changes" question if changes have been made to the drawing (see Figure 4-29).

Drawing Units

Next, we will create the environment of a typical drawing session. The following commands are all found in the **Format** menu (see Figure 4-31). Initially you should select units, establish drawing limits, and develop and execute a layering scheme. Addressing these commands when beginning a new file will help you to organize and control the creation of the drawing entities.

First and foremost, you need to select the type of units with which you will be working. The **UNITS** command on the **Format** menu will launch the **Drawing Units** dialog box (see Figure 4-32). Here you can address the type or style of input units you will use for both linear input (see Figure 4-33) as well as angular input (see Figure 4-34). By default, the linear

Figure 4-30

Menu Browser showing the **CLOSE** option

Figure 4-31

Format menu

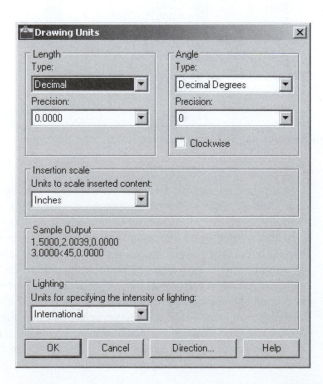

Figure 4-32

Drawing Units dialog box

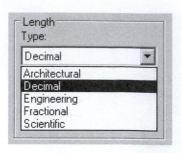

Figure 4-33

Length units drop-down list

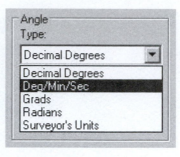

Figure 4-34

Angle units drop-down list

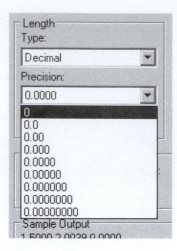

Figure 4-35

Decimal length units precision

units are set to **Decimal** input with four-place precision (see Figure 4-35). Other choices found in the **Length** drop-down list include **Architectural** (see Figure 4-36), **Engineering** (see Figure 4-37), **Fractional** (see Figure 4-38), and **Scientific** (see Figure 4-39).

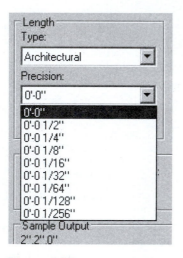

Figure 4-36

Architectural length units precision

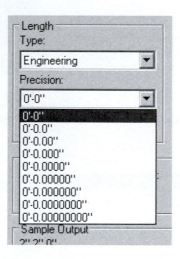

Figure 4-37

Engineering length units precision

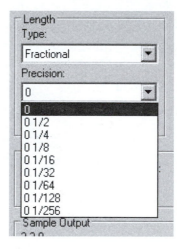

Figure 4-38

Fractional length units precision

Keep in mind that the **Decimal** style is used for imperial units (feet or inches) as well as metric units. All the styles have a precision value. This controls the accuracy of a number when displayed in various inquiry commands. It does not influence dimensions, as they are controlled by the dimension style. The default precision is four-place accuracy. Familiarize yourself with the precision options and format as they relate to each input style.

Angular inputs are addressed on the right side of the **Drawing Units** dialog box. Once again, the default is a **Decimal** input style with four-place accuracy (see Figure 4-40). Other angle input choices are **Degree/Minutes/Seconds** (see Figure 4-41), **Grads** (see Figure 4-42), **Radians** (see Figure 4-43), and **Surveyor's Units** (see Figure 4-44), and are found under the **Angle Type** drop-down arrow. Each of these styles has a precision field to control the accuracy of the display of input information. Refer to these figures as examples of the angular input styles and their related precision controls.

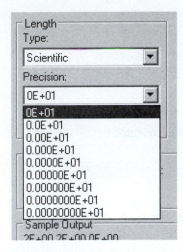

Figure 4-39

Scientific length units precision

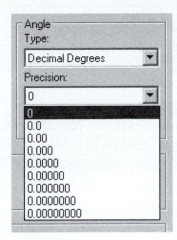

Figure 4-40

Decimal angle units precision

Figure 4-41

Deg/Min/Sec angle units precision

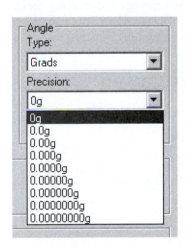

Figure 4-42

Grad angle units precision

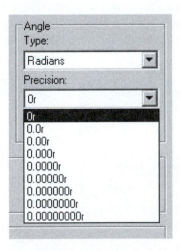

Figure 4-43

Radian angle units precision

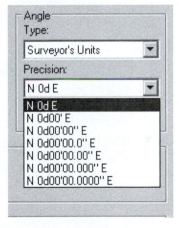

Figure 4-44

Surveyor's Units angle units precision

Drawing Limits

Now that you have selected your input units, you can start to develop the drawing area. The command **LIMITS** or **Drawing Limits** in the **Format** menu (see Figure 4-31) establishes an electronic drawing zone in which to produce the drawing. This zone is created by establishing the lower left corner and the upper right corner of the area. The points of the drawing limits are established with absolute coordinates (X, Y), where the first number is a horizontal distance and the second number is a vertical distance from the origin in a Cartesian coordinate system.

These values are entered in the current **Units** settings. This area should be large enough to accept all the entities required for the drawing in **full size**. Typical default drawing limits are 12 units by 9 units. This area could be used for small mechanical parts or electronic components. For most situations the lower left limit

> **NOTE:**
>
> Drawings should be made at full size or with actual dimensions. The drawing is scaled to fit the paper when the plotter device and paper size are chosen in the **PLOT** command.

full size: Drawing something in a 1 unit = 1 unit scale such as 1″ = 1″ or 1′ = 1′ or 1 m = 1 m.

Figure 4-45

LIMITS command prompt
line 1

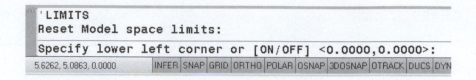

Figure 4-46

LIMITS command prompt
line 2

```
Reset Model space limits:
Specify lower left corner or [ON/OFF] <0.0000,0.0000>:
Specify upper right corner <12.0000,9.0000>:
```
```
5.6262, 5.0863, 0.0000    INFER SNAP GRID ORTHO POLAR OSNAP 3DOSNAP OTRACK DUCS DYN
```

should be **0,0** (see Figure 4-45) so that you are always in positive X and Y coordinates. If you are going to do a typical residential floor plan, more appropriate upper right input might be 100′-00″, 75′-00″ (see Figure 4-46), whereas a civil application required for a subdivision could be upward of 10,000′-00″, 10,000′-00″.

For architectural and engineering unit formats, a single quotation mark or foot mark (′) is used; otherwise AutoCAD will assume the input unit is in inches. For the scientific format, the **E** must be inputted to complete the precision.

Controlling the drawing limits will help with certain **VIEW** commands, displaying a grid, and plotting files. Figures 4-47 and 4-48 show the location of the **ZOOM ALL** command, which will reset the drawing area to the established limits if no other entities are present.

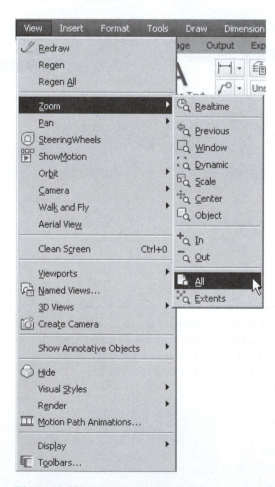

Figure 4-47

View Zoom All menu for resetting the drawing area

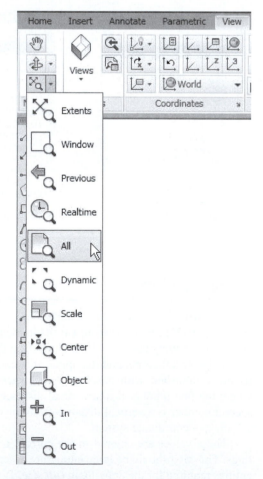

Figure 4-48

ZOOM commands on the **Navigate** extension on the **Views** panel on the ribbon

Layer Concepts and Settings

The layering of a drawing file is a concept relating to the organization and control of drawing entities. *Layers* are like clear overlay sheets to which entities or drawing elements can be attached. These overlays can control certain properties of an entity attached to the layer as well as the visual display of the layer's content.

layer: A property attached to an entity for an organizational and control purpose.

FOR MORE DETAILS   Various organizations including many government agencies require the use of the U.S. National CAD Standards for drawings (www.nationalcadstandard.org). This standard includes Layering Guidelines and Sheet Naming Conventions as developed by the American Institute of Architects (www.aia.org) and the Construction Specifications Institute (www.csinet.org).

The general concept of layers is to assemble similar entities on individual layers. For instance, you may have an individual layer for object lines, hidden lines, centerlines, dimensions, or text. Although there are layering standards in place throughout the various industries, the development and implementation of a layering scheme is up to the user. Layering practices are not automated in standard AutoCAD. You must continuously be aware of the concepts involved with layering, as well as the commands, to maintain the organizational advantages of a properly layered drawing file.

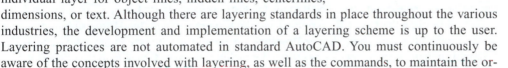

Figure 4-49

Layer toolbar

There are no limitations to the number of layers in a drawing file. The initial default layer is named **0** (see Figures 4-49 and 4-50). Each layer must have a unique name. When you first create a layer, the generic default name Layer1 is assigned to it. Any sequential layers are named Layer2, Layer3, and so on. You can rename layers immediately following their creation, or at a later time. To do that, slowly double-click on the layer name in the **Layer Properties Manager** palette (see Figures 4-51 and 4-52) initiating a rename procedure. Layers address the properties **Color, Linetype, Lineweight, Transparency, Plot Style,** and visibility. They control the visibility of the content display in several modes: **On/Off, Freeze/Thaw, Lock/Unlock.** In addition to properties and displays, layers can control the ability to plot (print) information from user-designated layers using the **PLOT** command.

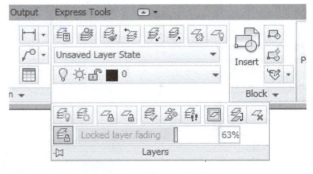

Figure 4-50

Layers panel on the **Home** ribbon

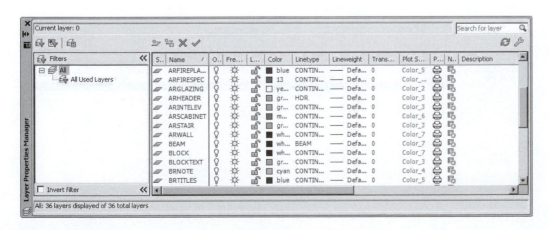

Figure 4-51

The **Layer Properties Manager** palette for model space

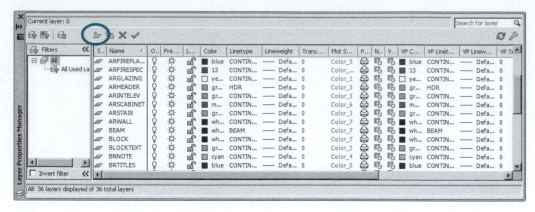

Figure 4-52

Layer Properties Manager palette in layout space

Layer Setup

Layers can be created and controlled through the **Format** menu under **Layer . . .** (see Figure 4-30) as well as through the **LAYER** command and the **Layers** panel on the **Home** ribbon. Use one of these methods to launch the **Layer Properties Manager** palette (see Figures 4-51 and 4-52). From this palette, new layers can be created by picking the **New Layer** icon (see Figure 4-53). This will add a layer named **Layer1** to the **Manager** window (see Figure 4-54). A layer's color can be changed by picking the **Color** box (see Figure 4-55). This will bring up the color selection window. The **Linetype** field allows you to assign a specific linetype to all entities attached to the layer (see Figure 4-56). Keep in mind that you may have to load the linetype first to have the style available for assignment. The next property is lineweight (see Figure 4-57). As with the other properties, a lineweight can be assigned to all entities attached to a layer. *Lineweight* is the ability to make an object look thicker or bolder than other objects.

lineweight: A width value that can be assigned to all graphical objects except TrueType® fonts and raster images.

Figure 4-53

New Layer icon

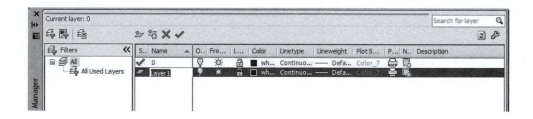

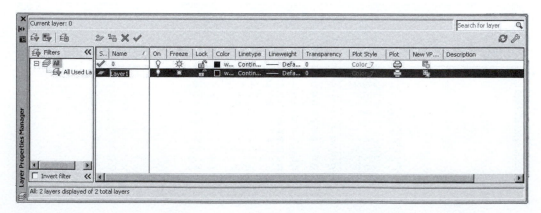

Figure 4-54

New Layer naming area in model space

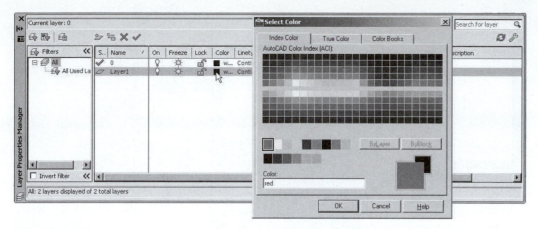

Figure 4-55

Color selection for layers

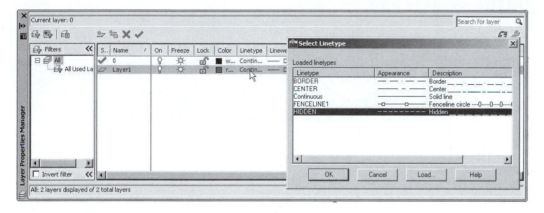

Figure 4-56

Linetype selection for layers

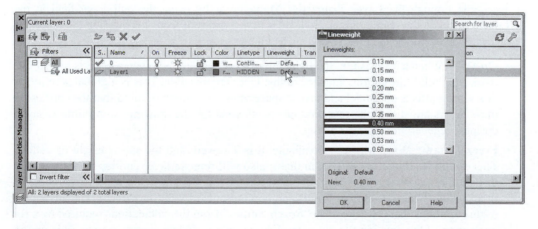

Figure 4-57

Lineweight selection for layers

Typically a lineweight would be about .030 mm (.0120″), but certain drafting standards may have different lineweights for various linetypes. Depending on your template selection, the plot style property may be available for selection (see Figure 4-58). As mentioned earlier, the second advantage of a properly layered drawing file is the ability to control the display of a layer's content (see Figure 4-59). **On/Off, Freeze/Thaw, Lock/Unlock, Transparency,** and

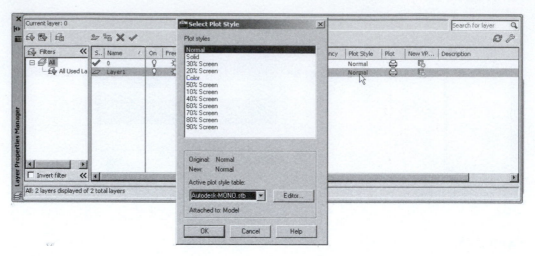

Figure 4-58

Plot Style selection for layers

Figure 4-59

Completed layer specifications for model space view

Plot Style are the options for controlling the visibility of a layer's content. These controls are accessible through the **Layer Properties Manager** or by using the pull-down field in the **Layers** panel on the **Home** ribbon. Both areas have a series of icons for toggling these options on or off. The options and their results are as follows:

- **On/Off**   When a layer is **On**, the lightbulb is bright or yellow. When a layer is turned **Off** (dark lightbulb), the entities attached to that layer are invisible. This is a global activity, as this setting affects all model and layout space viewports. Keep in mind that the entities on these layers are still in the regeneration calculations for the drawing, so no time is saved during a regeneration of the drawing.

- **Freeze/Thaw**   When a layer is available, it is **Thawed**, and the sun is bright or yellow. This option is similar to **On/Off,** in that it also will remove layer entities from the visual display. This is also a global layer operation on the left side, meaning it will freeze objects in all views. **Freeze** is similar to **Off** and is represented by the snowflake. The advantage of this option is that it will remove "frozen entities" from the calculations required by a regeneration of the drawing file, thus speeding up redraw and regeneration time. This option has a higher level of protection than the **On/Off** option for the layer entities.

- **Lock/Unlock**   When a layer is **Locked,** all the entities on that layer remain visible, but the entities are not accessible and cannot be modified. Entities can be placed only on **Unlocked** layers. You will be able to object snap to various entities on a locked layer, but you will not be able to alter that entity in any way. This is a global action and affects all viewports.

- **Transparency**   Transparency will control the visibility of a layer's content through a percentage value. A value of 100 percent equals full visibility, whereas anything less than that would reduce the visibility of the layer's content (see Figure 4-60).

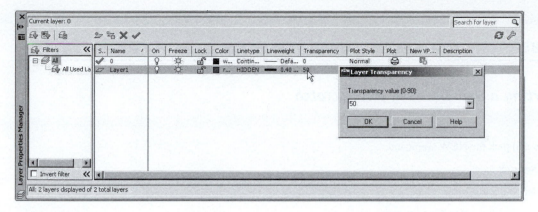

Figure 4-60

Transparency input for layers

- **Plot/NoPlot**   This option gives you control over which layers will be used for calculations in the plotting process. Any layer can be assigned a **NoPlot** status, preventing the layer's content from being printed. This option is best used for layers containing construction geometry, internal notes, sketches, scrap entities, and other record information. These layers are utilized during the building of a drawing and do not need to be a part of the final drawing.

   Other columns on the right side of the display (see Figure 4-61) may be present if the current viewport is in layout space. They represent a **Freeze/Thaw** toggle for the layer in the **Current Layout View** and in future **New Layout** viewports as well as other control specifications for layer based entities. (Layouts are discussed in Chapter 8.)

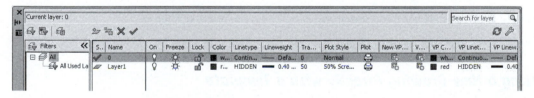

Figure 4-61

Layer Properties Manager for layouts

Chapter Summary

In this unit we introduced you to the creation, saving, storage, archiving, and organization of drawing files in AutoCAD. You learned how to start a new drawing either from scratch, by using templates, or by using the wizards and were introduced to the ANSI and ISO drafting standards on which the templates are based. You then learned how to manage drawing files with the **NEW, OPEN, SAVE, QSAVE, SAVEAS,** and **CLOSE** commands and the proper use of file directories and extensions. The process of working with several drawings open in a single session, or a Multiple Design Environment (MDE), was explained, as well as the selection of units and the establishment of drawing limits to create the environment of a drawing session. Finally, we investigated the creation and use of layers, which are properties that are attached to entities in a drawing and that resemble clear overlay sheets. In general, the concept of layering in AutoCAD is the organization and control of drawing entities by assembling similar entities on individual layers.

Chapter Tutorials

Ⓖ Tutorial 4-1: *Starting a New Drawing from Scratch*

1. Start AutoCAD.

2. Access the **File** menu and pick the **NEW** command.

3. Pick the **Start from Scratch** icon.

4. AutoCAD will complete the initial setup.

5. Access the **File** menu and pick the **SAVE** command.

6. Using the system drive drop-down at the top of the dialog box, navigate to your **Workskills** folder.

7. Enter the name **T4-1** in the location and save the drawing.

Ⓖ Tutorial 4-2: *Starting a New Drawing with Advanced Setup*

1. Start AutoCAD.

2. Access the **File** menu and pick the **NEW** command.

3. Pick the **Use a Wizard** icon.

4. Pick the **Advanced Setup** option.

5. On the screens pick the following options:
   a. **Decimal** units
   b. **Surveyor's** angles
   c. **East** as angle measurement
   d. **Counterclockwise** as angle direction
   e. Area with **15** for length and **12** for width
   f. Pick **Finish** and AutoCAD will complete the setup.

6. Access the **File** menu and pick the **SAVE** command.

7. Using the system drive drop-down list at the top of the dialog box, navigate to your **Workskills** folder.

8. Enter the name **T4-2** in the location and save the drawing.

Ⓖ Tutorial 4-3: *Starting a New Drawing Directly with a Template*

1. Start AutoCAD.

2. Access the **File** menu and pick the **NEW** command.

3. Pick the **Use a Template** icon.

4. Pick the **Architectural**, **English units**, **named plot style.dwt** template from the list displayed.

5. Pick **OK** and AutoCAD will complete the setup.

6. Access the **File** menu and pick the **SAVE** command.

7. Using the system drive drop-down list at the top of the dialog box, navigate to your **Workskills** folder.

8. Enter the name **Arch_Drawing** in the location and save the drawing.

Tutorial 4-4: *Opening a Drawing and Adding Layers*

1. Start AutoCAD.

2. Access the **File** menu and pick the **OPEN** command.

3. Using the system drive drop-down list at the top of the dialog box, navigate to your **Workskills** folder.

4. Find the **Arch_Drawing** file from Tutorial 4-3 and pick the **OPEN** command.

5. Access the **Format** menu and pick the **LAYER** command.

6. Add layers as listed below:
   a. **WALLS** with color **Red** and linetype **Continuous**
   b. **DOORS** with color **Blue** and linetype **Continuous**
   c. **WINDOWS** with color **Green** and linetype **Continuous**
   d. **FOUNDATION** with color **Red** and linetype **Dashed**
   e. **TEXT** with color **Red** and linetype **Continuous**
   f. **DIMENSIONS** with color **Cyan** and linetype **Continuous**
   g. **BORDER** with color **Magenta** and linetype **Continuous**

7. Access the **File** menu and pick the **SAVE** command to place the updated drawing in the directory.

Chapter Test Questions

Multiple Choice

Circle the correct answer.

1. To save a drawing under a new name, what command would you use?
   a. **SAVE**
   b. **RENAME**
   c. **QUICK SAVE**
   d. **SAVEAS**

2. A layering scheme will aid in a drawing's
   a. Organization
   b. Content
   c. Accuracy
   d. File size

3. Which of the following is **not** a display function within layers?
   a. **On/Off**
   b. **Freeze/Thaw**
   c. **Plot/NoPlot**
   d. **Lock/Unlock**
   e. **Transparency**

4. To save a drawing file in a different format, what command would you use?
   a. **SAVE**
   b. **RENAME**
   c. **QUICK SAVE**
   d. **SAVEAS**

5. Which of the following is **not** a valid drawing unit to use?
   a. Scientific
   b. Fractional
   c. Object-based
   d. Architectural

Matching

Write the number of the correct answer on the line.

a. .dwg _____

b. .bak _____

c. .dwt _____

d. .sv$ _____

e. .dws _____

1. AutoCAD drawing template

2. AutoCAD backup file

3. AutoCAD auto saved file

4. AutoCAD drawing file

5. AutoCAD drawing standards

True or False

Circle the correct answer.

1. **True or False:** Users can start a new drawing file from a drawing wizard.

2. **True or False:** Drawing area is the same as drawing limits.

3. **True or False:** Only one drawing file can be open at a time.

4. **True or False:** Layers can have properties attached to them.

5. **True or False:** All file management commands are similar to the ones used in other Windows-based programs.

Chapter Projects

Project 4-1 [BASIC]

Describe the differences between manual drafting and CAD.

Project 4-2 [INTERMEDIATE]

Research the various standards used by AutoCAD (AIA, U.S. National CAD, British, DIN, and JIS) and others. Which is most appropriate for your drawings and why?

Project 4-3 [INTERMEDIATE]

Examine the **Select File** dialog box. How could you search for and find a file? Research and explain the differences in the left column icons for **History, My Documents, Favorites,** and **Desktop**. What is the fastest way to find a drawing?

Chapter Practice Exercises

Ⓜ Practice Exercise 4-1: *Creating a Basic Template* [BASIC]

1. Start a new drawing in AutoCAD using the acad.dwt template.

2. For **UNITS** set the following:

Distance	**Decimal**
Distance Precision	**0.000**
Angle	**Decimal Degrees**
Angle Precision	**0.000**
Lighting	**International**

3. For **LIMITS** set the following:

Lower Left	**0,0**
Upper Right	**15,12**

4. For **LINETYPES** add the following:

   BORDER
   CENTER
   DASHED
   PHANTOM

5. For **LAYERS** add the following:

   PART with color **Red** and linetype **Continuous**
   ASSEMBLY with color **Blue** and linetype **Continuous**
   LINES with color **Green** and linetype **Continuous**
   CENTERLINES with color **Cyan** and linetype **Centerlines**
   HIDDEN with color **Magenta** and linetype **Dashed**
   PHANTOM with color **Blue** and linetype **Phantom**
   TEXT with color **Red** and linetype **Continuous**
   DIMENSIONS with color **Cyan** and linetype **Continuous**
   BORDER with color **Magenta** and linetype **Border**

6. Save as a **Template** file type using the **SAVEAS** command with the name **ACAD_Template** in your **Workskills** folder.

Ⓜ Practice Exercise 4-2: *Creating a Mechanical Template* [BASIC]

1. Start a new drawing in AutoCAD using the ANSI-A.dwt template.

2. For **UNITS** set the following:

Type	**Decimal**
Distance	**Decimal**
Distance Precision	**0.00**
Angle	**Decimal**
Angle Precision	**0.00**
Lighting	**International**

3. For **LIMITS** set the following:

Lower Left	**0,0**
Upper Right	**11.00,8.50**

4. For **LINETYPE** load the following linetypes:

BORDER, CENTER, PHANTOM, HIDDEN

5. For **LAYERS** create the following layers:

OBJECT LINE	**GREEN**	**CONTINUOUS**
CENTERLINE	**YELLOW**	**CENTER**
HIDDEN LINE	**RED**	**HIDDEN**
HATCH	**CYAN**	**CONTINUOUS**
CONSTRUCTION JUNK	**MAGENTA**	**CONTINUOUS**
TEXT	**BLACK**	**CONTINUOUS**
DIMENSIONS	**BLUE**	**CONTINUOUS**

6. Save your work as a **.dwt** (template) file type using the **SAVEAS** command with the name **Mech_Template** in your **Workskills** folder.

Ⓐ Practice Exercise 4-3: *Creating a Basic Architectural Template* [BASIC]

1. Start a new drawing in AutoCAD using the **Architectural**, **English units**, **color plot style.dwt** template.

2. For **UNITS** set the following:

Distance	**Architectural**
Distance Precision	**1/8″**
Angle	**Deg, Min, Sec**
Angle Precision	**0d00′00″**
Lighting	**International**

3. For **LIMITS** set the following:

Lower Left	**0′-0″,0′-0″**
Upper Right	**100′,80′**

4. Execute the **ZOOM ALL** command from the **View** menu to reset the drawing area display to reflect the new drawing limits.

5. For **LINETYPES** add the following:

BORDER
CENTER
DASHED

6. For **LAYERS** add the following:

WALLS with color **Cyan** and linetype **Continuous**
DOORS with color **Green** and linetype **Continuous**
WINDOWS with color **Green** and linetype **Continuous**
FOUNDATION with color **Red** and linetype **Dashed**
TEXT with color **Red** and linetype **Continuous**
DIMENSIONS with color **Red** and linetype **Continuous**
BORDER with color **Magenta** and linetype **Border**

7. Save as a **Template** file type using the **SAVEAS** command with the name **ACAD_Building** in your **Workskills** folder.

C **Practice Exercise 4-4:** *Creating a Basic Roadway Design Template* [BASIC]

1. Start a new drawing in AutoCAD using the acad.dwt template.

2. For **UNITS** set the following:

Distance	**Decimal**
Distance Precision	**0.000**
Angle	**Decimal Degrees**
Angle Precision	**0.000**
Lighting	**International**

3. For **LIMITS** set the following:

Lower Left	**−100,−100**
Upper Right	**5000,5000**

4. Execute the **ZOOM ALL** command from the **View** menu to reset the drawing area display to reflect the new drawing limits.

5. For **LINETYPES** add the following:

   BORDER, CENTER, DASHED, PHANTOM

6. For **LAYERS** add the following:

   ROADWAY with color **Red** and linetype **Continuous**
   DRAINAGE with color **Blue** and linetype **Continuous**
   SIDEWALKS with color **Green** and linetype **Continuous**
   CENTERLINES with color **Cyan** and linetype **Centerlines**
   PIPES with color **Magenta** and linetype **Dashed**
   WATERLINES with color **Blue** and linetype **Phantom**
   TEXT with color **Red** and linetype **Continuous**
   DIMENSIONS with color **Cyan** and linetype **Continuous**
   BORDER with color **Magenta** and linetype **Border**

7. Save as a **Template** file type using the **SAVEAS** command with the name **ACAD_Civil** in your **Workskills** folder.

C **Practice Exercise 4-5:** *Creating a Subdivision Design Template* [BASIC]

1. Start a new drawing in AutoCAD using the acad.dwt template.

2. For **UNITS** set the following:

Type	**Engineering**
Distance	**Decimal**
Distance Precision	**0.000**
Angle	**Surveyor**
Angle Precision	**N0d00'00"E**
Lighting	**International**

3. For **LIMITS** set the following:

Lower Left	**0,0**
Upper Right	**1000'.000,1000'.00**

4. Execute the **ZOOM ALL** command from the **View** menu to reset the drawing area display to reflect the new drawing limits.

5. For **LINETYPE** load the following linetypes:

   BORDER, CENTER, PHANTOM, DASHED

6. For **LAYERS** create the following layers:

LOT LINE	**GREEN**	**PHANTOM**
ROADS	**RED**	**CONTINUOUS**
R.O.W.	**YELLOW**	**CONTINUOUS**
CENTERLINE	**RED**	**CENTER**
SIDEWALKS	**CYAN**	**CONTINUOUS**
BOUNDARY	**MAGENTA**	**BORDER**
EASEMENTS	**BLUE**	**DASHED**

7. Save your work as a **.dwt** (template) file type using the **SAVEAS** command with the name **Subdivision_ Template** in your **Workskills** folder.

5 Fundamental Drawing and Modifying Commands

CHAPTER OBJECTIVES

- Use the Cartesian coordinate system.
- Define the world coordinate system in AutoCAD.
- Explain input methods.
- Demonstrate object snap functions.
- Use drawing aids.
- Use the basic selection methods.
- Create and modify basic entities.

Introduction

Now that we have established a few variables within our template file, it's time to create and modify a few basic entities. All CAD systems have the ability to create lines, circles, arcs, text, and so on. The differences among CAD systems lie in the methods and options for creating and modifying entities. The draw-modify-dimension-print cycle is a standard approach to the completion of a drawing in a basic AutoCAD system.

Accuracy within the AutoCAD system relies on understanding the *Cartesian coordinate system*. AutoCAD has several input methods that help you create the accurate entities. Understanding the various input methods will ensure accuracy when creating and modifying drawing entities.

Cursor control, drawing aids, and the use of input methods as they relate to the Cartesian coordinate system are the foundation of the accuracy required for creating these entities. We will first take a look at how each of the basic entities is created, and then we will explore the various input methods available to accurately control the creation of these entities. All the following commands can be found on the **Draw** menu (see Figure 5-1), the **Draw** toolbar (see Figure 5-2), or the **Draw** panel on the **Home** ribbon (see Figure 5-3).

Cartesian coordinate system: A three-dimensional system where the X direction is horizontal, the Y direction is vertical, and the Z direction is coming out of the paper toward the reader.

Figure 5-1

Draw menu

Elementary Entities

Line

Lines are created by specifying the endpoints of each line segment. After executing the **LINE** command, the command prompt will ask you to *Specify first point*. After the input of the first point, the command prompt will ask you to *Specify next point*. The input of the second point will create a line between the two selected points. After the completion of the first line, the command will stay active, continuing to prompt you to *Specify next point* until you choose to end the sequence by either pressing the <Enter> key, the right mouse button to select a command from the pop-up menu, or the <Esc> key to cancel.

NOTE:

A review of geometric definitions related to Cartesian coordinates, geometric shapes, and the right-hand rule will help you understand the terms used in the creation of entities in CAD systems.

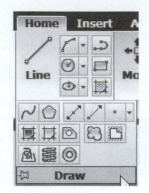

Figure 5-2

Draw toolbar

Figure 5-3

Draw panel on the **Home** ribbon

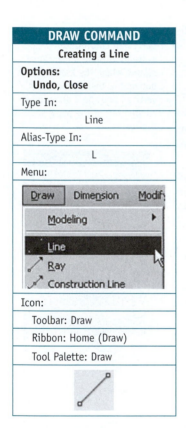

DRAW COMMAND
Creating a Line
Options: **Undo, Close**
Type In:
Line
Alias-Type In:
L
Menu:
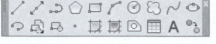
Icon:
Toolbar: Draw
Ribbon: Home (Draw)
Tool Palette: Draw

The **LINE** command has two options. Remember that options to a command are displayed within the square brackets in the prompt line. To execute a command's option, you identify the capital letters from the word in the prompt line and type in the letters, followed by pressing **<Enter>**. After two or more line segments are created, you can execute the **Close** option to create one more line segment that will close the shape back to the first selected point or beginning point for the command. The second option is the **UNDO** command. When the **Undo** option is executed from within the **LINE** command, the last point of input will be released, allowing you to respecify the endpoint of the line. Be aware that continuous execution of the **Undo** function will step back through all endpoints specified during the active line sequence.

EXERCISE 5-1 **CREATE A LINE**

■ Start AutoCAD and begin a new drawing.

■ Select the **LINE** command from the **Draw** menu, **Draw** toolbar, or the **Draw** panel on the **Home** ribbon.

■ Select a location on the screen with the left mouse button to establish the first endpoint of the line.

■ Move the cursor to a new location and establish the other endpoint of the line with the left mouse button (see Figure 5-4).

■ Continue moving around the screen drawing lines by clicking on the left mouse button (see Figure 5-5).

■ To finish the command simply type **C** and hit **<Enter>** (see Figure 5-6).

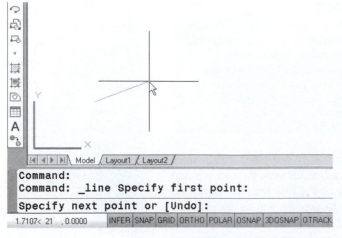

Figure 5-4

LINE command start

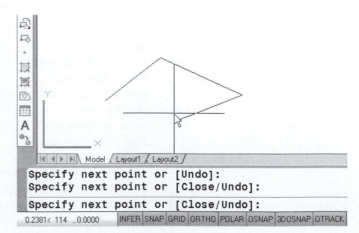

Figure 5-5

LINE command continued

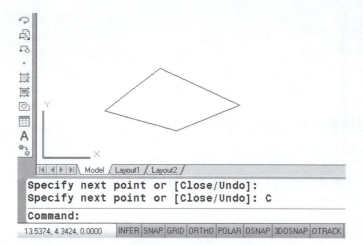

Figure 5-6

LINE command completed with **Close** option

Circle

There are six different ways to create a circle. The two basic methods require an input for the **Center Point** of the circle and a second input for either a **Radius** or **Diameter** value. By default a rubber-band line will appear after the selection of the center point. You can establish the value of the second input by dragging the rubber-band line out to the desired length or by typing in a numeric value.

- **Center, Radius** The first point establishes the center point for the circle; the second input is used as the radius for the circle.
- **Center, Diameter** The first point establishes the center point for the circle; the second input is used as the diameter for the circle.

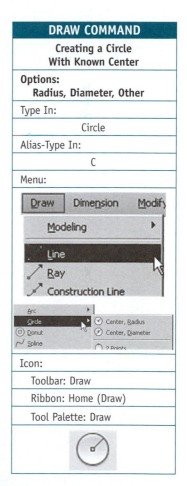

FOR MORE DETAILS Additional options for creating a circle will be presented in Chapter 9.

EXERCISE 5-2 **CREATE A CIRCLE**

- Start AutoCAD and start a new drawing or continue with the drawing from the previous exercise.
- Select the **CIRCLE** command from the **Draw** menu and **Center, Radius** on the cascading menu or from the **Draw** panel on the **Home** ribbon.
- Select a location on the screen with the left mouse button to establish the center point of the circle.
- Drag the cursor to a new location to establish the radius of the circle and select that point with the left mouse button (see Figure 5-7).
- Select the **CIRCLE** command from the **Draw** menu and **Center, Radius** on the cascading menu.
- Select a location on the screen with the left mouse button to establish the center point of the circle (see Figure 5-8).
- Key in a value of **3**, then press **<Enter>** for the value of the circle radius (see Figure 5-9).

Arc

Although there are 11 ways to create an arc, most of the methods are based on prompting the user for start points, end points, and center points in various orders. The simplest and quickest way to create an arc is with the **3 Points** method. By selecting three points on the screen,

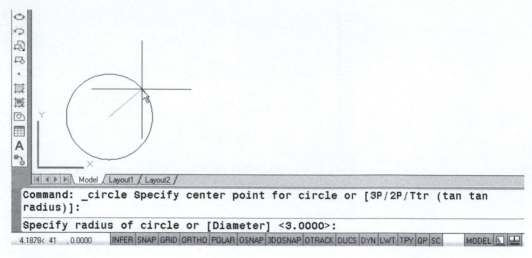

Figure 5-7

CIRCLE command start

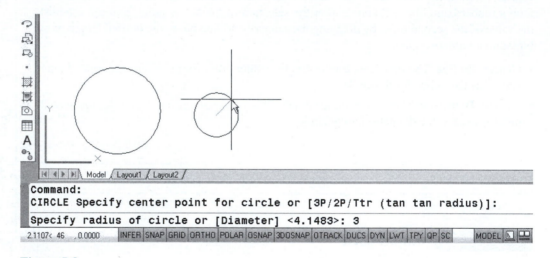

Figure 5-8

CIRCLE command continued

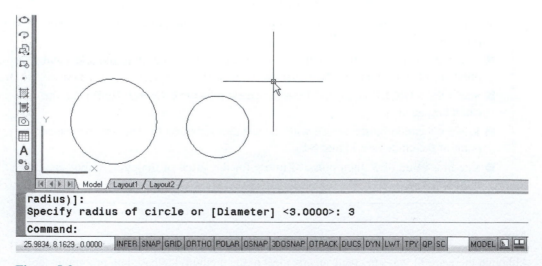

Figure 5-9

CIRCLE command completed at specific radius

you will be creating an arc that passes through all three selected points with the two points farthest apart as the start point and the endpoint.

FOR MORE DETAILS   Additional options for creating an arc will be presented in Chapter 9.

> **EXERCISE 5-3**   **CREATE AN ARC**
>
> ■ Start AutoCAD and start a new drawing or continue with the drawing from the previous exercise.
>
> ■ Select the **ARC** command from the **Draw** menu and **3 Points** on the cascading menu, **Draw** toolbar, or the **Draw** panel on the **Home** ribbon.
>
> ■ Select a location on the screen with the left mouse button to establish the first endpoint of the arc (see Figure 5-10).
>
> ■ Drag the cursor to a new location to establish the second point of the arc and select that point with the left mouse button (see Figure 5-11).
>
> ■ Move the cursor to a third location to establish the remaining endpoint of the arc. Select that point with the left mouse button (see Figure 5-12).

DRAW COMMAND
Creating an Arc With 3 Points
Options: **Pick Points, Other Options**
Type In:
Arc
Alias-Type In:
A
Menu:
Icon:
Toolbar: Draw
Ribbon: Home (Draw)
Tool Palette: Draw

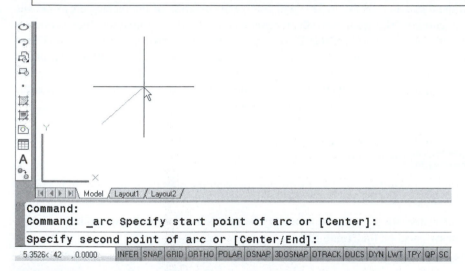

Command:
Command: _arc Specify start point of arc or [Center]:
Specify second point of arc or [Center/End]:

5.3526< 42 , 0.0000   INFER SNAP GRID ORTHO POLAR OSNAP 3DOSNAP OTRACK DUCS DYN LWT TPY QP SC

Figure 5-10

ARC command start

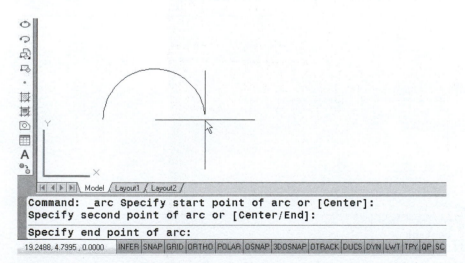

Command: _arc Specify start point of arc or [Center]:
Specify second point of arc or [Center/End]:

Specify end point of arc:

19.2488, 4.7995 , 0.0000   INFER SNAP GRID ORTHO POLAR OSNAP 3DOSNAP OTRACK DUCS DYN LWT TPY QP SC

Figure 5-11

ARC command continued

Figure 5-12

ARC command completed

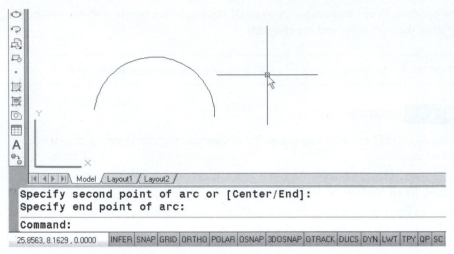

DRAW COMMAND
Creating a Rectangle With 2 Diagonal Points
Options: Chamfer, Elevation, Fillet, Thickness, Width, Dimension Area, Rotation
Type In:
RECTANG
Alias-Type In:
REC
Menu:

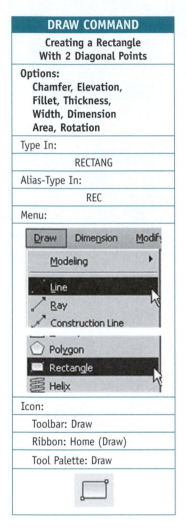

Icon:
Toolbar: Draw
Ribbon: Home (Draw)
Tool Palette: Draw

Rectangle

The **RECTANGLE (RECTANG)** command will prompt you to specify the *First Corner Point* and the *Other Corner Point*. This will control the creation of the rectangle by opposite or diagonal corners. All four lines of the rectangle created will be joined together as one entity. Options for the **RECTANGLE** command include **Chamfer, Elevation, Fillet, Thickness,** and **Width**. Options can be executed to establish beveled (**Chamfer**) or rounded (**Fillet**) corners. The **Elevation** and **Thickness** options are related to the creation of a three-dimensional rectangle, and the **Width** option creates the lines that give the rectangle a wider line value. We will learn more about these options in Chapter 9.

EXERCISE 5-4 **CREATE A RECTANGLE**

■ Start AutoCAD and start a new drawing or continue with the drawing from the previous exercise.

■ Select the **RECTANG** command from the **Draw** menu, **Draw** toolbar, or the **Draw** panel on the **Home** ribbon.

■ Select a location on the screen with the left mouse button to establish the first corner of the rectangle (see Figure 5-13).

■ Drag the cursor to a new location to establish the diagonal corner of the rectangle. Select that point with the left mouse button (see Figure 5-14).

Figure 5-13

RECTANG command start

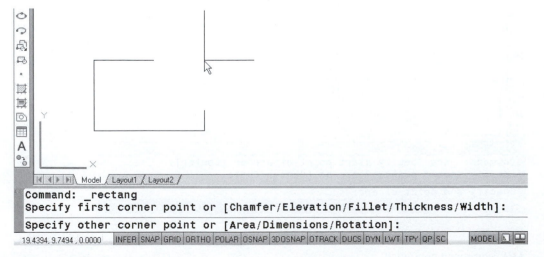

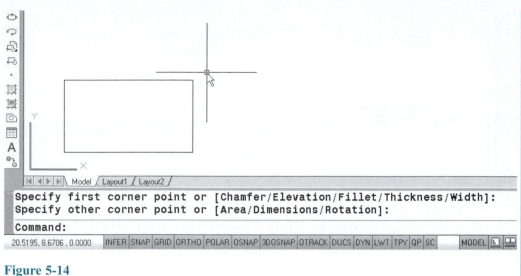

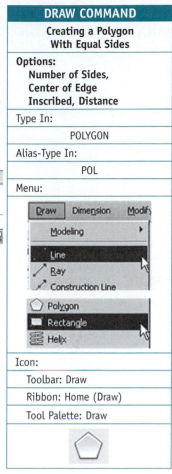

DRAW COMMAND
Creating a Polygon With Equal Sides
Options: Number of Sides, Center of Edge Inscribed, Distance
Type In: POLYGON
Alias-Type In: POL
Menu:
Icon:
Toolbar: Draw
Ribbon: Home (Draw)
Tool Palette: Draw

Figure 5-14

RECTANG command completed

Polygon

The **POLYGON** command produces a multisided ***regular polygon*** in the drawing. This command uses a series of prompts that you will be required to answer. Polygons are based on a center point and a radius or edge. They will then be constructed either ***inscribed*** within the circle or ***circumscribed*** about the outside of the circle.

The radius value can be considered across the flats (circumscribed) or across the corners (inscribed). The following is the sequence of command prompts issued during the construction of the polygon.

> Enter number of sides:
> Specify center of polygon or [Edge]:
> Enter an option [Inscribed in circle/Circumscribed about circle] <I>:
> Specify radius of circle:

Be aware that if you make an input error during the sequence, you will have to cancel the command (<**Esc**> key) and start it again. There is no method to back up through the sequence to change any previous inputs.

regular polygon: A multisided closed figure with all sides equal and interior angles equal.

inscribe: To construct an entity inside a circle.

circumscribe: To construct an entity on the outside of a circle.

EXERCISE 5-5   **CREATE A POLYGON**

■ Start AutoCAD and start a new drawing or continue with the drawing from the previous exercise.

■ Select the **POLYGON** command from the **Draw** menu, **Draw** toolbar, or the **Draw** panel on the **Home** ribbon.

■ Enter the number of sides you want in your polygon (see Figure 5-15).

■ Specify a location on the screen for the center point of the polygon with the left mouse button.

■ Type in an **I**, then press <**Enter**> to inscribe the polygon inside the circle (see Figure 5-16).

■ Drag the cursor out to specify the polygon radius, and select that location with a left mouse click (see Figure 5-17).

Figure 5-15

POLYGON command start

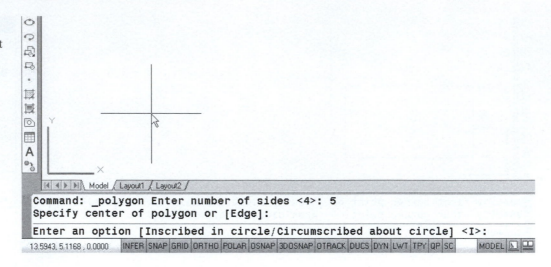

Figure 5-16

POLYGON command
continued

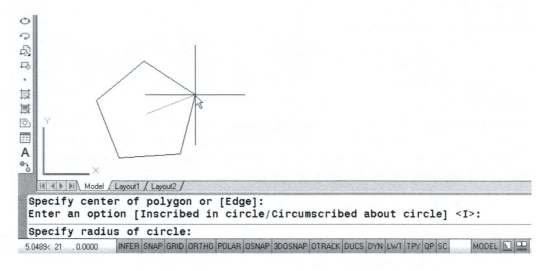

Figure 5-17

POLYGON command
completed

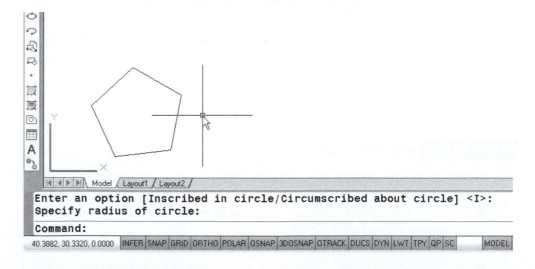

polyline: A sequence of line segments created as a single object. The segments can be straight-line segments, arc segments, or a combination of the two that are connected through a vertex point.

Polyline

A *polyline* is a series of two-dimensional line segments or arcs connected into a single object. Polylines can be made up of straight segments or arc segments connected through a point known as a *vertex*. Polylines are created by selecting the vertex point that represents the endpoints of the lines or arcs. It is possible to combine line segments with arc segments to form one polyline. Polylines may form a closed figure, which allows for the calculation of area, perimeter, and other properties. When you create an arc segment, the default option for the arc is tangent to the previous line segment. You can specify other methods to define the arc through options such as the angle, center point, direction, second point, or the radius of the arc you want to create (see Figures 5-18 and 5-19).

```
Command: _pline
Specify start point:
Current line-width is 0.0000
Specify next point or [Arc/Halfwidth/Length/Undo/Width]:
Specify next point or [Arc/Close/Halfwidth/Length/Undo/Width]:
```

Figure 5-18

Polyline prompts for line segments

```
Current line-width is 0.0000
Specify next point or [Arc/Halfwidth/Length/Undo/Width]:
Specify next point or [Arc/Close/Halfwidth/Length/Undo/Width]: a
Specify endpoint of arc or
[Angle/CEnter/CLose/Direction/Halfwidth/Line/Radius/Second pt/Undo/Width]:
```

Figure 5-19

Polyline prompts for arc segments

The following options apply to the creation of a polyline. You can exercise these options at any time when creating a polyline simply by typing in the letter that is capitalized in the option name.

- **Arc** In the line segment drawing mode, this option switches the operation to the creation of tangential arc segments. The arc segment will be tangent to the last endpoint created unless some other option is chosen to create the arc.
- **Close** Closes the polyline back to the first point of the initial segment as long as there are two or more segments defined in the polyline.
- **Halfwidth** Specifies the width from the center of a wide polyline line segment to one of its edges. Two values are required: one for the beginning of the segment and one for the end of the segment.
- **Length** Creates a line segment at a specific length. The new segment created will be at the same angle as the previous segment. If the last segment was an arc, the new line segment will be tangent to the endpoint of the previous arc.
- **Line** In the arc drawing mode, this option switches the operation to the addition of line segments to the polyline.
- **Undo** Removes the last segment created in the sequence allowing you to reenter a new point.
- **Width** Prompts you for a starting width of the segment and an ending width of the segment. The ending width defaults to the value stated for the starting width. You can taper the width of the polyline simply by entering a different value for the ending width.

DRAW COMMAND
Creating a Polyline
Options: Arc, Close, Line, Halfwidth, Length, Width, Undo
Type In: Polyline
Alias-Type In: PL or PLINE
Menu:

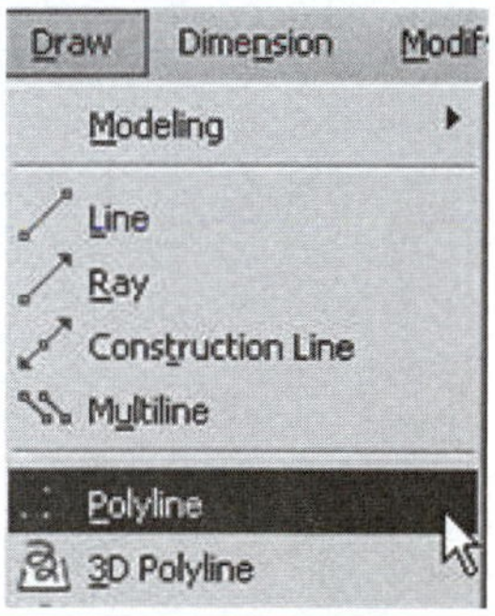

Icon:
Toolbar: Draw
Ribbon: Home (Draw)
Tool Palette: Draw

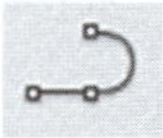

EXERCISE 5-6   **CREATE A POLYLINE**

- ■ Start a new AutoCAD drawing.
- ■ Select the **POLYLINE** command from the **Draw** menu, the **Draw** toolbar, or the **Draw** panel on the **Home** ribbon.
- ■ Enter **4,4** for the first vertex and press **<Enter>**.
- ■ Enter **8,8** for the next vertex and press **<Enter>**.
- ■ Enter an **A** to enter the **Arc** mode and press **<Enter>**.
- ■ Enter **12,6** and **8,2** as the next two vertices.
- ■ Enter an **L** to enter the **Line** mode, and press **<Enter>**.
- ■ Enter **4,2** for the next vertex and press **<Enter>**.
- ■ Enter a **C** to close the polyline back to the initial point.
- ■ The result should be as shown in Figure 5-20.

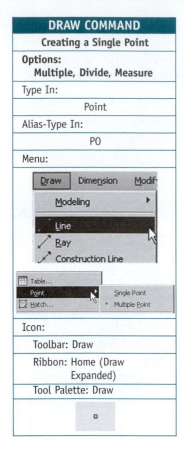

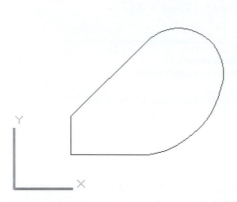

Figure 5-20

Result of **POLYLINE** exercise

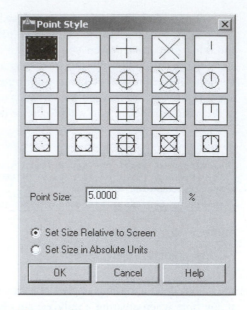

Figure 5-21

Point Style dialog box

Point

A *point* is a location in space. Points have no physical characteristics such as length, width, or height. When you select the **POINT** command, the X, Y, and Z coordinates are recorded for that position. Because points have no physical characteristics, they can be displayed as a variety of graphic outputs. By default the point will show up as a dot on the screen. The system variable **PDMODE** controls the graphic display of a point.

Figure 5-21 shows available point styles. Only one point graphic output can be used in a drawing file. All points in the drawing will have the same graphic output.

Creating Grid and Snap Controls

grid: A symmetrically spaced pattern.

A *grid* is a series of dots spaced in a rectangular pattern on the screen. The rectangular pattern of dots will extend over the area you specify as the drawing limits (typical default area is from 0,0 to 12,9 in English units). Using the grid is similar to placing a sheet of graph paper under a drawing. The grid helps you align objects and visualize the distances between them. The visual display of the grid can be turned on or off in the status line and is transparent to the print process, meaning it will not plot.

snap: The ability to exactly choose a known location.

Snap is a user-defined value that restricts the movement of the cursor based on the value to be found. The **On/Off** status of **SNAP** can also be controlled through the status line. When **SNAP** is turned on, the cursor seems to adhere or "snap" to an invisible rectangular grid.

The combination of these two commands can produce a visual display of dots along with a controlled motion of the cursor, which can be useful for specifying precise input with the arrow keys or the pointing device. Although the **SNAP** and **GRID** settings can be equal, causing the cursor movement to snap to each grid dot, the settings can be set up in such a way that they have a proportional relationship to each other. You can change the grid and snap values in the **Tools** menu under **Drafting Settings** (see Figure 5-22). You can also right-click on the word **SNAP** or **GRID** in the status line and select **Settings** from the pop-up menu (see Figure 5-23). If you zoom in or out of your drawing, you may need to adjust grid and snap spacing to be more appropriate for the new magnification.

Snap spacing does not have to match grid spacing. For example, you might set a wide grid spacing to be used as a reference but maintain a closer snap spacing for accuracy in specifying points. The **SNAP** and **GRID** spacings are based on *x* and *y* values. If the "Equal X and

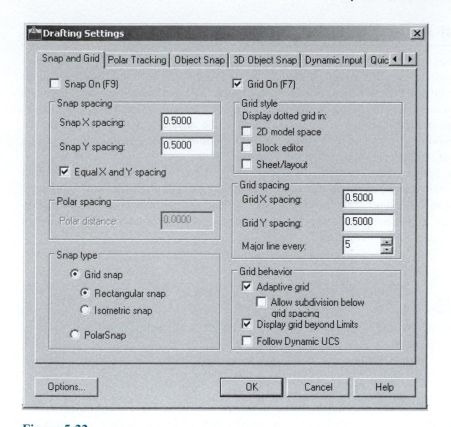

Figure 5-22

The **Drafting Settings** dialog box for **SNAP** and **GRID**

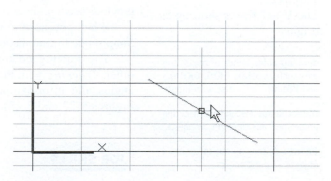

Figure 5-23

Right-click menu for **GRID** toggle

Y spacing" box is checked, you can change the *x* value and the *y* value will change to match it. If you need a rectangular look, remove the check mark and you may enter a new value for the *y* field in the dialog box, resulting in a rectangular grid and/or snap.

This dialog box also has a setting in (see Figure 5-22) called **Snap type**. The choices are **Rectangular snap, Isometric snap,** and **PolarSnap**. The selection of an isometric style will result in the rotation of the grid and snap values to an isometric axis receding in both directions (approximately 35°). Refer to Figures 5-24 and 5-25 to see the difference in the styles available.

The options in the **Grid Behavior and Grid Style** area are self-explanatory regarding the basic layout for placement of lines.

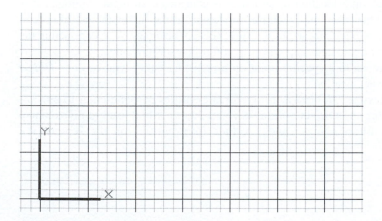

Figure 5-24

A rectangular grid line display

Figure 5-25

Isometric grid line display

direct distance entry: Input method that works on a mouse direction and an input of the distance value.

absolute coordinate system: Input method based on an *x, y,* and *z* value related to a fixed origin.

relative coordinate system: Input method based on an *x, y,* and *z* value related to a floating or moving origin.

relative polar coordinate system: Input method based on an angle and a distance related to a floating or moving origin.

Precision Input Methods

Several different input methods are available to you to precisely locate an object. Based on information you are working with, one method may be more beneficial than another, but all are available for use at any time and in any combination. The goal regarding input methods is to maintain the level of accuracy while doing a minimal amount of mathematical calculation. Data can be input through *direct distance entry*, the *absolute coordinate system*, the *relative coordinate system*, and the *relative polar coordinate system*. These methods offer a wide choice of philosophies and are the most common styles.

Some of these methods work in a formula style, meaning there is a specific syntax that needs to be followed, i.e., **X,Y** or **@X,Y** or **@distance<angle**. The @ (at) symbol implies the method of input is floating origin based. The < (less than) symbol indicates the information is a polar angle. Other input methods benefit from the use of drawing aids or object snaps to increase the accuracy of the input.

> ## JOB SKILLS
>
> Mastery of the Cartesian coordinate system and its relationship to data entry is essential to a drawing's accuracy.

world coordinate system: Base location of the fixed origin position—typically 0,0,0—and the relationship of the XY plane.

user coordinate system: An alternative position of the Cartesian coordinate system based on user input.

origin: The fixed position of a Cartesian coordinate system. The origin has an *x, y* value of 0,0.

Cartesian Coordinates

AutoCAD draws only on an XY plane that is initially defined by the *world coordinate system (WCS)* and is represented by the X-Y icon in the lower left corner of the drawing screen. In this configuration, the positive *X*-axis is horizontal, the positive *Y*-axis is vertical, and the positive *Z*-axis is coming out of the screen toward the operator (see Figure 5-26).

The XY plane's orientation can be redefined in a *user coordinate system (UCS)*. This method repositions the drawing's origin at some other location or orientation to a drawing's entities. The point at which the *X* and *Y* axes intersect is called the *origin* and is assigned a coordinate value of **0** for X and **0** for Y, expressed as **0,0**. Values are assigned from the origin with the appropriate sign (+ or −) based on the direction from the origin. Movement to the right and upward is positive, and movement to the left and downward is negative if the orientation is similar to that in Figure 5-26.

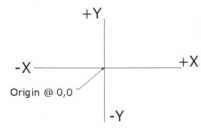

Figure 5-26

The *X* and *Y* axes showing the origin

drawing aids: Series of on/off toggles such as **SNAP**, **GRID**, **ORTHO**, and **POLAR** that assist with input.

Object Snap: Method for selecting predefined positions on an object.

ORTHO: A drawing aid to create objects at right angles.

tracking: A way to locate points relative to other points on the drawing.

Cursor Control

Cursor control refers to the movement of the screen pointer or crosshairs. The cursor movement is generated by mouse movement or in some cases use of the arrow keys on a keyboard. A left click on a location or an entity is considered an input. Although it is rather hard to control the exact input with free movement of the cursor, the use of several different *drawing aids* in combination can ensure a great deal of accuracy. As mentioned in the previous section, the use of a grid and snap will help control cursor movement.

When you need to attach to a specific point on an existing entity, you can use *Object Snap* mode to find that exact location.

The drawing aid known as *ORTHO* is used to create entities perpendicular to one another. *Tracking* with **Polar** and **Object** options is yet another method used to invoke snap angles and information filters using *x* and *y* values from entities on the screen (see Figures 5-27 and 5-28).

> ## JOB SKILLS
>
> Mastery of the various drawing aids found on the status line will increase efficiency, accuracy, and productivity.

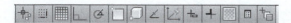

Figure 5-27

Cursor control toggles at the base of the screen, also known as the status line

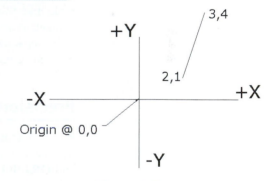

Figure 5-28

Status line toggle icons for cursor control

Direct Distance

Direct distance entry uses a mouse direction and a typed input distance to specify the location. With direct distance input, you can quickly specify a point relative to the last point you entered. At any AutoCAD prompt asking for a point location, you can point the mouse's rubberband line in the direction needed and enter a numeric value through the keyboard, followed by pressing **<Enter>**. This will create a line or entity in the direction of the mouse with the length equal to the value typed in. The **ORTHO** and **Polar Snap** drawing aids can be used in conjunction with direct distance entry to increase accuracy in mouse direction.

Absolute Coordinate System

> **NOTE:**
> You could also include the third dimension (Z) as the height of the entity, making the entry X,Y,Z for a true 3D drawing.

Absolute coordinate values are based on a fixed position location from the base known as the origin (**0,0**). The origin is where the X and Y axes intersect in the Cartesian coordinate system. Use an absolute coordinate when you know the precise x and y values of the point coordinate. For example, the coordinate **3,4** specifies a point **3** units along the X-axis and **4** units along the Y-axis from the origin. To use absolute coordinate values to specify a point location, enter an x value and a y value separated by a comma. The syntax looks like this: **X,Y** followed by **<Enter>** (see Figure 5-29).

The x value is the positive or negative distance, in units, along the horizontal axis. The y value is the positive or negative distance, in units, along the vertical axis. All absolute coordinate input is related to the current position of the origin. To calculate X and Y movement, it will be necessary to know the x,y values of the previous inputted point. Remember to add values when moving to the right and upward, and subtract values when moving to the left and downward.

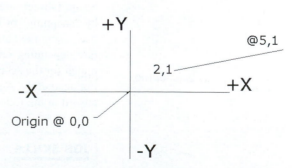

Figure 5-29

Using absolute coordinates

Relative Coordinate System

Relative coordinate input is related to a floating origin. Relative coordinate values are based on the last point entered as if it were a temporary origin value of **0,0**. Movement can then be calculated from the temporary origin located at the last point of input (see Figure 5-30). As in the absolute coordinate system, X movement is horizontal, and Y movement is vertical. Use a relative coordinate when you know the position of a point in relation to the previous point. To specify a relative coordinate, precede the coordinate with an **@** sign. For example, the coordinate **@3,4** specifies a point **3** units along the X-axis and **4** units along the Y-axis from the last point specified.

You must keep in mind the syntax required for relative input and the positive and negative values of the input, since this will control the direction of the movement from the origin. This input method should eliminate the need to add and subtract values from the previous point of input.

Figure 5-30

Using relative coordinates for placement of line

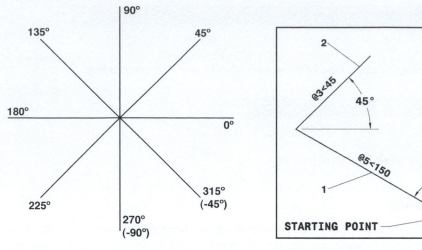

Figure 5-31

Angles in AutoCAD

Figure 5-32

Relative polar coordinate entries

Polar Coordinate System

Polar coordinate input is based on an angle and a distance. By default, the direction east equals **0** degrees, and angles increase in the counterclockwise direction (a positive angle value) and decrease in the clockwise direction (a negative angle value) (see Figure 5-31). For example, entering **@1<315** is the same as entering **@1<−45**. The angle conventions for the current drawing are set under the **UNITS** command. Polar coordinates can be entered as either absolute (measured from the origin) or relative to the previously entered point. To specify a relative coordinate, precede the distance with an @ sign. The correct syntax looks like this: **distance<angle** or **@distance<angle** (see Figure 5-32). The first number is taken as a distance and the second number is taken as the angle. These two values need to be separated by the less than (<) sign, which in turn treats the numeric input as polar coordinate values.

Precision Drafting Controls

Precision drafting controls are referred to as *drawing aids*. We have already covered the two drawing aids known as **GRID** and **SNAP. Object Snap, Object Tracking, Polar Tracking**, and **ORTHO** are the remaining drawing aids available when the program is asking for an input. Like **GRID** and **SNAP** all these aids are easily toggled on or off from the status line below the drawing area (see Figure 5-27 or 5-28), and a right click on the button will access a setting command to adjust the values of the option. The most used of these aids is **Object Snap. Object Snap** is the best way to attach new elements to existing entities in the drawing by "snapping" or linking to a specified location on an existing object already in the drawing file. Using the cursor control input method without **Object Snap** will generally not be accurate depending on the level of zoom applied. Even with maximum zoom, one's eye is no match for the accuracy of a CAD system. Therefore, snapping is an important tool for drawing accurately. AutoCAD offers a wide range of snap options for use in a drawing, as discussed in the following sections.

JOB SKILLS

A drawing's integrity is based on accurate placement of geometry. In today's CAD/CAM world there is no room for run-ons (overshoots) or gaps (undershoots) between entities. Operators must use **Object Snap** to ensure accuracy in their work.

Object Snap

Object Snap (OSNAP) constrains a point specification to exact locations, such as a midpoint or an intersection, on existing objects. Using object snap is a quick way to locate an exact position on an object without having to know the coordinate or draw construction geometry. For example, you can use object snap to draw a line from the center of a circle to the midpoint of an existing line segment. You can specify an object snap whenever AutoCAD prompts for a point. Let's take a look at the most common **Object Snap** functions (see Figures 5-33 and 5-34).

* **ENDpoint** Snaps to the endpoint of either a line or an arc or to any vertex on a polyline.
* **MIDpoint** Snaps to the midpoint of either a line or an arc or to the midpoint of any segment on a polyline.
* **CENter** Snaps to the center point of a circle, an arc, or an ellipse.
* **QUAdrant** Snaps to the 0, 90, 180, or 270 degree point on a circle, an arc, or an ellipse.
* **INTersection** Connects to the exact location where two existing entities cross in a geometric plane or in space (apparent intersection).
* **PERpendicular** Snaps to a point at a right angle to the entity selected.
* **TANgent** Calculates the exact point where a line, circle, or arc connects with a second line, circle, or arc. Recall that the definition of tangency is that two entities touch at one point and only one point.
* **NODe** Snaps to a point entity.
* **NEArest** Connects an entity to another entity at the closest location selected. This function is a little less accurate than other methods, but it will ensure that the two entities do connect in space without leaving a gap or overshooting the object.

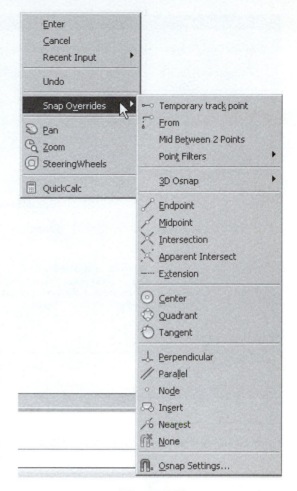

Figure 5-33

Right-click menu for **Object Snap**

FOR MORE DETAILS   This is not a complete discussion of the **Object Snap** functions. We will visit the more advanced methods in future chapters.

Figure 5-34

Object Snap toolbar

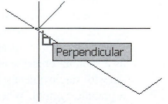

Figure 5-35

Tooltip and symbol for **Object Snap**

When an **Object Snap** function is active, AutoCAD displays a marker and a tooltip whenever you move the cursor over or near an active snap point (see Figure 5-35). This feature provides a visual clue that indicates which object snaps are in effect. Each object snap has a unique symbol identifying the function, as shown in Figures 5-36 and 5-37.

There are a variety of ways to turn on object snaps. If you choose an individual object snap from the toolbar shown in Figure 5-34 or enter the object snap name on the command line, the object snap stays in effect only for the next point you specify. You also can set a *running object snap*, with one or more object snaps that remain in effect as you work. You do this by accessing the **Drafting Settings** dialog box (see Figure 5-36) or by right-clicking on

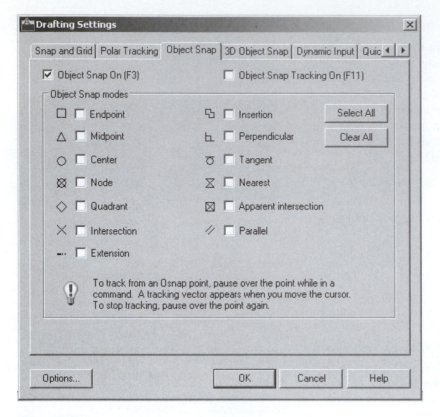

Figure 5-36

Tools Drafting Settings for continuous **Object Snaps**

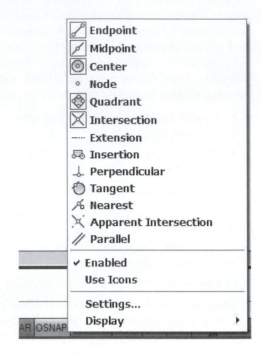

Figure 5-37

Status line **Object Snap** settings

the **OSNAP** button on the status line (see Figure 5-27 or 5-28) and selecting **Settings** to access the same **Drafting Settings** dialog box and select the **Object Snap** tab. A choice of **NONE** in the right-click menu or toolbar will turn off both single and running object snaps for the next input.

When you specify an object snap, the cursor changes to an object snap target box. When you select an object, AutoCAD snaps to the eligible object snap point closest to the center of the target box. If you need to use the same object snap repeatedly, you can set it as a running object snap, which means it stays on until you turn it off. For example, you might set **Center** as a running object snap if you need to connect the centers of a series of circles with a line. As with single object snaps, the aperture, or target box, identifies the object snap position with a graphic symbol. When you turn on multiple running object snaps, AutoCAD uses the object snap most appropriate to the object you select and the cursor location. If two potential snap points fall within the selection area, AutoCAD snaps to the eligible point closest to the center of the target box.

Object Tracking

Object Tracking allows you to hover over an existing object snap position and track from that position at a specified angle. Object tracking is used in combination with object snaps. By default, object tracking will track in a horizontal or vertical direction from the object snap position. This feature can also be set to track in increments of the **Polar Angle Settings** (see Figures 5-38 and 5-39). This aid filters out the x or y value of the position and makes that value available to input the next position. You will notice the dotted "tracking" line when the cursor passes over a valid object snap position. You can then move down the tracking line to select a position along the line for the next input.

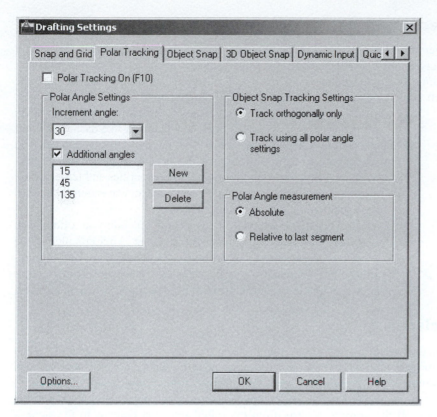

Figure 5-38

Polar Tracking settings tab in the **Drafting Settings** dialog box

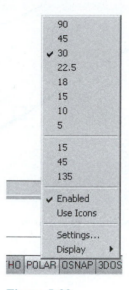

Figure 5-39

Polar Tracking right-click menu from status line

Polar Tracking

Polar Tracking is sometimes referred to as *angle snap*. This drawing aid allows you to specify an angle as an incremental value (again, see Figures 5-38 and 5-39). When active, the cursor will snap to the angle's value in an incremental fashion as the cursor is moved around the drawing screen.

If the **Polar Angle Settings Increment angle** value is set for 45, the function will snap to 45, 90, 135, 180, 225, and so on, around the drawing screen. When the cursor is in the range of the angle value (or a multiple of the value) a dotted "tracking" line appears along with a display of the current distance and angle.

Ortho

ORTHO is a drawing aid that creates entities that are perpendicular to previous entities regardless of the screen cursor's position. This function will track only cursor movement that is parallel to the world or a user-defined coordinate system *X*- or *Y*-axis. When active, **ORTHO** generates all inputs perpendicular to the previously inputted position. This function cannot be used in conjunction with the **Polar Tracking** drawing aid.

Object Selection Methods

Now that we have discussed the creation of a few basic entities, we need to focus on modifying entities that are on the screen. AutoCAD in general is a command-driven program. This means you pick a command (verb) first and then the entities (noun) for the operation. When working with the series of commands found in the **Modify** menu, you will always be prompted to *Select objects* as part of the command sequence.

There are several different ways of selecting entities within AutoCAD. Let's take a look at some of the basic selection methods.

Single Selection

When you enter any **Modify** command, the prompt *Select objects* will appear in the prompt line, and the screen cursor will be replaced by a small square known as a *pick box*. This is referred to as a *single-selection* pick box and is used to select the single entity that is below the box when a left click is executed (see Figure 5-40). By moving the pick box over any object on the screen and left-clicking, you select that entity and place it in the current selection set. Selected objects will appear in a dashed or highlighted form to signify they are part of the current selection set. You may continue to select other objects that need to be placed in the selection set by simply moving the box over other entities and left-clicking. This process will continue until you complete your selections and finish the selection process by pressing <**Enter**>.

This selection method will select only one entity at a time even if there are multiple entities under the pick box. After completing the selection process, you will be prompted for additional information regarding the command originally executed. When the **Modify** command is completed, all the entities in the selection set will be affected.

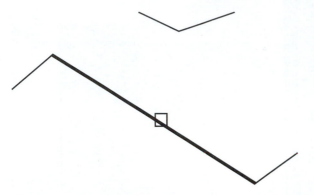

Figure 5-40

Pick box single selection

window selection: A selection method in which only the entities completely inside the selection window are selected.

crossing window: A rectangular area drawn to select objects that are within and that cross the window's borders.

Window Selections

Other selection methods allow you to select multiple entities in one selection operation. When you are being prompted to *Select objects* and there is no entity under the pick box, you can select that position and start a selection method known as *implied windowing*. Implied windowing allows you to create a box on the screen to encompass all entities you wish to select (see Figure 5-41). If the movement away from the initial selection point is to the right, a *window selection* is in effect. If the movement is to the left, a *crossing window* is executed.

The window selection box will appear as a solid box with a light blue background, indicating the window method is active. The window selection method requires that the complete entity must be within the window to be selected. Only entities that are completely inside the window are placed in the selection set. After completing the window you will remain in the select object mode to make other selections. As previously mentioned you must complete the selection process by pressing <**Enter**>. This window method will select all entities, even those that lie directly on top of others.

Crossing Window Selection

As in the previous method, an implied window is invoked when a left click is made and there is not an entity under the pick box. When you make a move to the left of the initial point, a crossing window will appear. The crossing window is displayed as a dashed box with a green background (see Figure 5-42). Any entity that is touched by the crossing style window or is completely inside the crossing style window will be placed in the selection set. As mentioned before, after completing the crossing window you will remain in the select object mode to make

Figure 5-41

Implied window selection when going from left to right (solid line boundary)

Figure 5-42

Implied crossing window selection when going from right to left (dashed line boundary)

other selections. Again you must complete the selection process by pressing <**Enter**>. This crossing window method will select all entities, even those entities that lie directly atop others.

FOR MORE DETAILS   Although there are many other selection methods, these three selection methods are sufficient for basic operations. We will be looking at the other methods in Chapter 9.

Elementary Modifying of Entities

One of the biggest advantages of a CAD system is the ability to modify existing geometry for other uses. Even though the erasing of objects and the undoing of previously executed commands are part of the **Modify** menu, most modifying commands are used to either alter existing geometry or create more geometry from existing entities currently in the drawing file. As a general rule of thumb, you will spend more time in the **Modify** menu than in the **Draw** menu. This may not be the case for all users, but an efficient production session will more likely adhere to this concept. If entities already exist, use those entities rather than create a new set of entities from scratch. All the following **MODIFY** commands can be found in the **Modify** menu, the **Modify** toolbar, or the **Modify** panel on the **Home** tab on the ribbon (see Figures 5-43, 5-44, and 5-45).

JOB SKILLS

CAD operators should always look for an opportunity to use and modify geometry already created. This will increase speed and consistency during the drawing session.

MODIFY COMMAND
Erase Objects
Various Selection Methods
Type In:
Erase
Alias-Type In:
E
Menu:

Icon:
Toolbar: Modify
Ribbon: Home (Modify)
Tool Palette: Modify

Figure 5-43

Modify menu

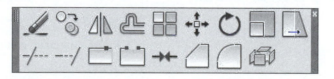

Figure 5-44

Modify toolbar

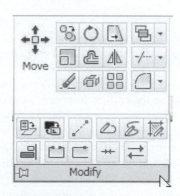

Figure 5-45

Modify panel expanded on the **Home** ribbon

Erase

The **ERASE** command is used to delete entities from the drawing file. As with all **Modify** commands, after you select the command you will be prompted to *Select objects*. After you have completed selecting entities and pressed **<Enter>**, the selected entities are erased from the drawing file. An alternative method to using the **ERASE** command is to select an entity when a command is not in progress and hit the **<Del>** key on the keyboard, thus removing the entity from the drawing file. Remember, the program is in "neutral" when the prompt line reads Command. This is when you can use the alternative method.

EXERCISE 5-7   **PRACTICE THE ERASE COMMAND**

- Start a new drawing.
- From the **Draw** menu pick the **LINE** command and create a rectangle with diagonal absolute coordinates of **1,1** and **4,4**.
- From the **Modify** menu access the **ERASE** command (see Figure 5-46).
- Select two lines (see Figure 5-47) with the pick box and press **<Enter>** to remove the objects (see Figure 5-48).

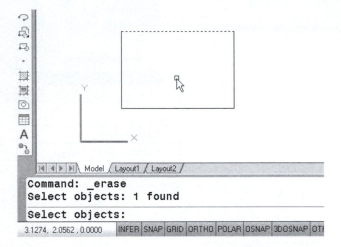

Figure 5-46

ERASE command start

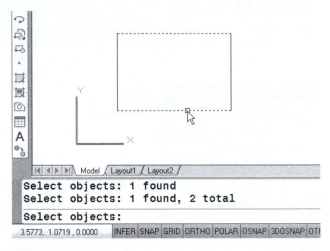

Figure 5-47

ERASE command continued

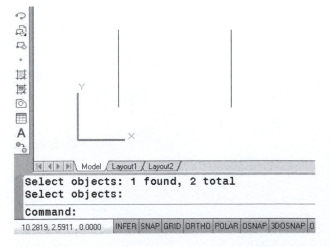

Figure 5-48

ERASE command completed

Move

The **MOVE** command allows you to select entities and physically move the entities from one location to another. This command will prompt you to select objects. After you have finished selecting objects, you will be prompted for a base point that will be used as a control point and a second point or displacement value for the new location for all the selected entities. Remember that a second point can be established through any of the input methods described earlier. The use of a precise input method will greatly increase the accuracy of the move.

EXERCISE 5-8   **PRACTICE THE MOVE COMMAND**

- Start a new drawing.
- From the **Draw** menu pick the **LINE** command and create a rectangle with diagonal absolute coordinates of **1,1** and **4,4**.
- From the **Modify** menu access the **MOVE** command.
- Select two lines with the pick box (see Figure 5-49) and press **<Enter>** to complete the selection process.
- Pick a base point for the start of the move (see Figure 5-50).
- Pick the position for the objects to be located after the move (see Figure 5-51).
- Notice that the objects are in the new location only (see Figure 5-52).

Copy

The **COPY** command is similar to the **MOVE** command. This command also prompts you to *Select objects*. After you have finished selecting objects, you will be prompted for a base point to be used as a control point and a second point or displacement value for the new location for

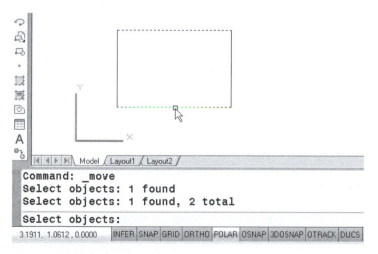

Figure 5-49

MOVE command start

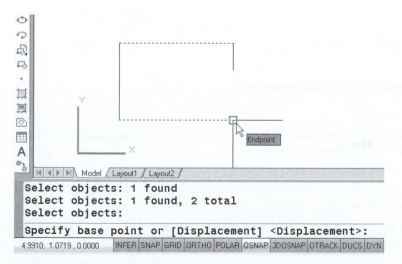

Figure 5-50

MOVE command continued

MODIFY COMMAND
Move Objects
Various Selection Methods
Type In:
Move
Alias-Type In:
M
Menu:
Icon:
Toolbar: Modify
Ribbon: Home (Modify)
Tool Palette: Modify

MODIFY COMMAND
Copy Objects
Various Selection Methods
Type In:
Copy
Alias-Type In:
CO or CP
Menu:
Icon:
Toolbar: Modify
Ribbon: Home (Modify)
Tool Palette: Modify

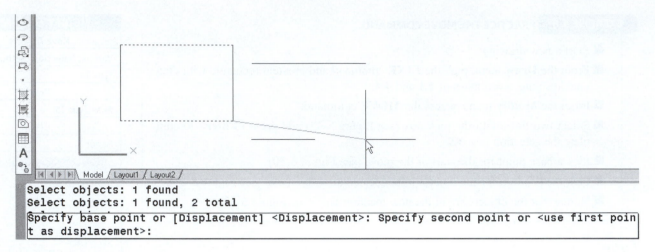

```
Select objects: 1 found
Select objects: 1 found, 2 total
Specify base point or [Displacement] <Displacement>: Specify second point or <use first poin
t as displacement>:
```

Figure 5-51

MOVE command continued

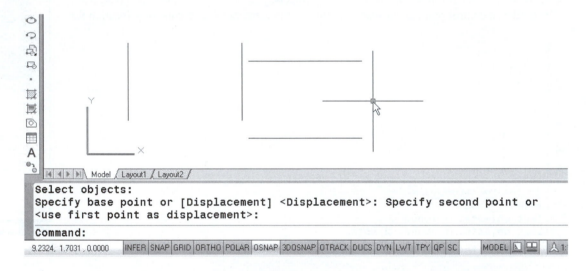

```
Select objects:
Specify base point or [Displacement] <Displacement>: Specify second point or
<use first point as displacement>:

Command:
```

```
9.2324, 1.7031 , 0.0000    INFER SNAP GRID ORTHO POLAR OSNAP 3DOSNAP OTRACK DUCS DYN LWT TPY QP SC    MODEL 🔲 🖵    人 1:
```

Figure 5-52

MOVE command completed

all the selected entities. The difference between the two commands is that the original selected entities will remain in their original location and a second copy of the selected entities will go to the new location specified. Once a second point is specified, you will be able to place multiple copies of the selection set in as many locations as needed by simply left-clicking in a new location. Recall that a base point and a related second point can be accurately positioned with the use of an **Object Snap** drawing aid or any other input method described earlier.

EXERCISE 5-9   **PRACTICE THE COPY COMMAND**

- Start a new drawing.
- From the **Draw** menu pick the **LINE** command and create a rectangle with diagonal absolute coordinates of **1,1** and **4,4**.
- From the **Modify** menu access the **COPY** command.
- Select two lines with the pick box (see Figure 5-53) and press **<Enter>** to complete the selection process.
- Pick a base point for the start of the copy (see Figure 5-54).
- Pick the position for the objects to be located after the move (see Figure 5-55).
- Notice that the objects are in the new location as well as the original positions (see Figure 5-56).

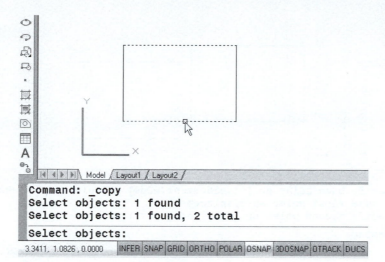

Figure 5-53
COPY command start

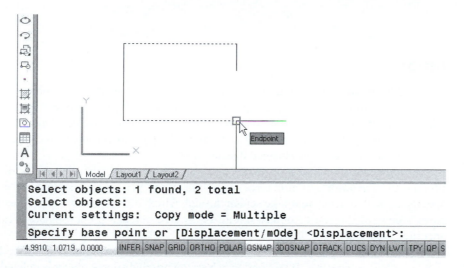

Figure 5-54

COPY command continued

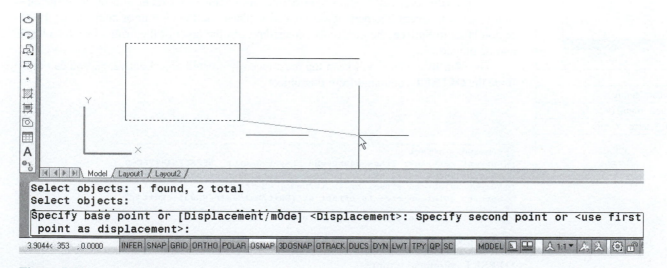

Figure 5-55

COPY command continued

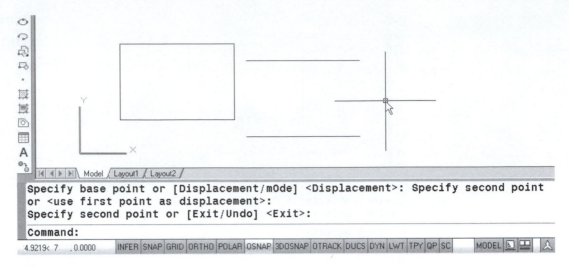

```
Specify base point or [Displacement/mOde] <Displacement>: Specify second point
or <use first point as displacement>:
Specify second point or [Exit/Undo] <Exit>:

Command:
```

Figure 5-56

COPY command completed

MODIFY COMMAND
Offset an Object
Options:
Distance, Through, Side to Offset, Erase, Layer, Multiple, Undo
Type In:
Offset
Alias-Type In:
0
Menu:
Icon:
Toolbar: Modify
Ribbon: Home (Modify)
Tool Palette: Modify

Offset

The **OFFSET** command produces a copy of the object selected (source object) a specified distance away or through a selected point. First you are prompted to *Specify offset distance*, where you can key in a specified distance. Next, you *Select a source object*. Last, you are asked to *Specify point on side to offset* to determine both the direction in which the offset copy will be produced and the established distance away.

If you enter a null response (by pressing <**Enter**>) to the *Specify offset distance* prompt, the **Through** option is invoked. In this option you select a source object and then specify a point somewhere on the screen through which the offset copy is produced. In both cases a copy of the source object and all the source object's properties are created at the specified location.

There are two options within the **OFFSET** command (see Figure 5-57). The **Erase** option has a **Yes** or **No** value. If this option is **Yes**, the original source object is deleted when the second point or side of object is selected. The second option addresses the **Layer** function. As mentioned earlier, in default mode, **OFFSET** makes a copy of the selected source object with all the same properties. The **Layer** option has a value of **Current** or **Source**. If this option is set to **Current**, the new object created is placed on the current or active layer. If the option is set to **Source**, the new object created retains the layer of the original source object and its properties.

The **Multiple** option will keep the most recently created object active, so you can continue the **OFFSET** command from that object.

```
Command: _offset
Current settings: Erase source=No  Layer=Source  OFFSETGAPTYPE=0
Specify offset distance or [Through/Erase/Layer] <Through>: 1.5
Select object to offset or [Exit/Undo] <Exit>:
Specify point on side to offset or [Exit/Multiple/Undo] <Exit>:

Select object to offset or [Exit/Undo] <Exit>:
```

Figure 5-57

OFFSET command prompts

EXERCISE 5-10 CREATE OFFSET OBJECTS

- Start a new drawing.
- From the **Draw** menu place a line and a circle in the drawing.
- From the **Modify** menu pick the **OFFSET** command.
- Enter **0.5** for the offset distance and press **<Enter>** (see Figure 5-58).
- Pick the line as the offset object.
- Pick a location above the line for placement of the offset object (see Figure 5-59). *Note:* Distance is already set, so this step is only for direction. The command continues to be available.
- Pick the circle as the offset object.
- Pick a location outside the circle for placement of the offset object (see Figure 5-60).
- Press **<Enter>** to stop the command (see Figure 5-61).

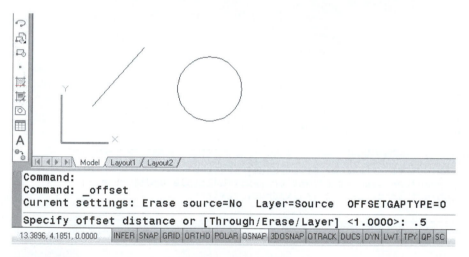

Figure 5-58

OFFSET command start

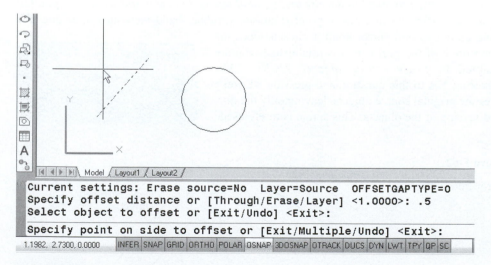

Figure 5-59

OFFSET command continued

Figure 5-60

OFFSET command continued

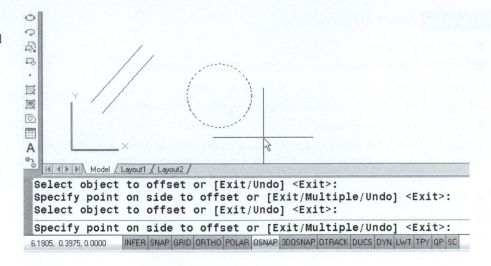

Figure 5-61

OFFSET command completed

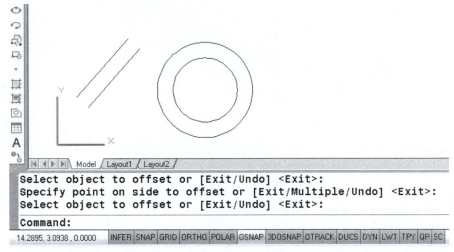

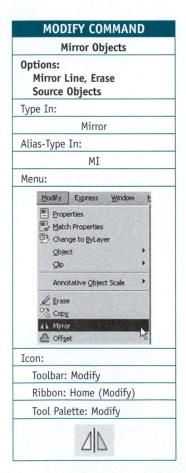

MODIFY COMMAND
Mirror Objects

Options:
    Mirror Line, Erase
    Source Objects

Type In: Mirror
Alias-Type In: MI
Menu:
Icon:
Toolbar: Modify
Ribbon: Home (Modify)
Tool Palette: Modify

Mirror

The **MIRROR** command flips a series of selected objects in a symmetrical fashion over a defined mirror line (see Figure 5-62). After selecting the objects to work with and pressing **<Enter>**, you are prompted to *Specify first point of mirror line*: and *Specify second point of mirror line*:. After the first mirror point is chosen, a rubber-band view moves, as does the cursor, until a second mirror point is chosen. Once the second point of the mirror line is established, you are prompted to *Erase source object? Yes/No <N>*. Answering **Yes** to this question and pressing **<Enter>** erases the original source objects, leaving only the mirrored version of the objects. This action is rarely used.

> **NOTE:**
>
> Use the **ORTHO** drawing aid to ensure a mirror image over the *X*- or *Y*-axis.

Figure 5-62

Mirror line and result

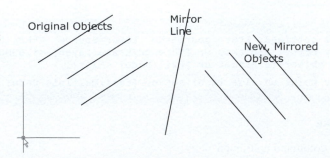

EXERCISE 5-11 CREATE A MIRROR OBJECT

- Start a new drawing.
- From the **Draw** menu place three lines similar to the lines on the left in Figure 5-62 in the drawing.
- From the **Modify** menu pick the **MIRROR** command.
- Select two of the lines as the objects to be mirrored and press <**Enter**> to end the selection process.
- For the "First point" use an **ENDpoint Object Snap** to select one end of the line not chosen above.
- Move the mouse to the other end of this line and watch the rubber-banding of the mirrored object.
- For the "Second point" use an **ENDpoint Object Snap** on the other end of the line not chosen.
- Answer **No** to the question regarding the erasing of objects.

Arrays

The **ARRAY** command creates a copy of the selected objects in a patterned format. There are two types of arrays, **Rectangular** and **Polar**. A **Rectangular Array** produces copies based on a rectangle or orthogonal pattern. A **Polar Array** produces copies based on a center point and a circular pattern. The controls for both are found in the **Array** dialog box (see Figure 5-63) under the **Modify** menu, on the **Modify** toolbar, or on the expanded **Modify** panel on the **Home** ribbon. When you select the radio button near the top of the dialog box corresponding to the type of array you want to produce, the dialog box screen reflects the information needed for that particular option.

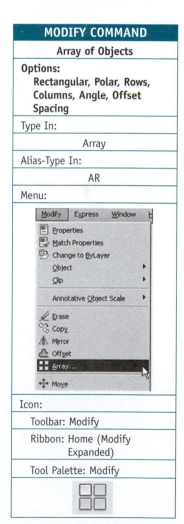

MODIFY COMMAND
Array of Objects
Options: Rectangular, Polar, Rows, Columns, Angle, Offset Spacing
Type In:
Array
Alias-Type In:
AR
Menu:
Icon:
Toolbar: Modify
Ribbon: Home (Modify Expanded)
Tool Palette: Modify

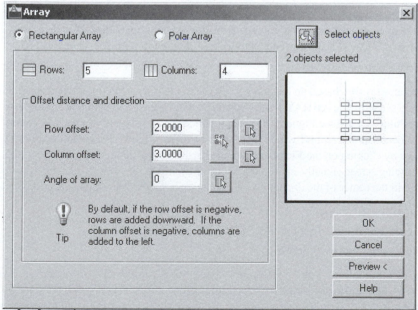

Figure 5-63

ARRAY command dialog box for rectangular layouts

Rectangular Array. Rectangular arrays (see Figure 5-64) form a pattern based on two dimensions. The **Rows** dimension is parallel to the *X*-axis, and the **Columns** dimension is parallel to the *Y*-axis. You need to select the objects you want to pattern and establish the number of **Rows** and **Columns** needed for the array. Then, you enter the distance between **Rows** and the distance between **Columns**. Keep in mind that the distance between rows or columns is from the lower left corner of one object to the lower left corner of the next object or from one center to the next center. This distance is made up of the distance across the object as well as the distance between the objects. The direction in which the pattern will form is based on the positive or negative values of the **Rows** and **Columns** distances. For example, two positive values produce an array in the first quadrant (positive X and Y), whereas two negative values produce an array in the third quadrant (negative X and Y). The remaining field in the dialog box is for the angle of the array. The **Angle** value rotates the array around the lower left point of the pattern. After you have entered the required information in the dialog box, you can execute the **Preview** button to see the results of the values inputted. If you like the preview results, you can **Accept** the input or return back to the **Array** dialog box through the **Modify** button.

After Array

Before Array

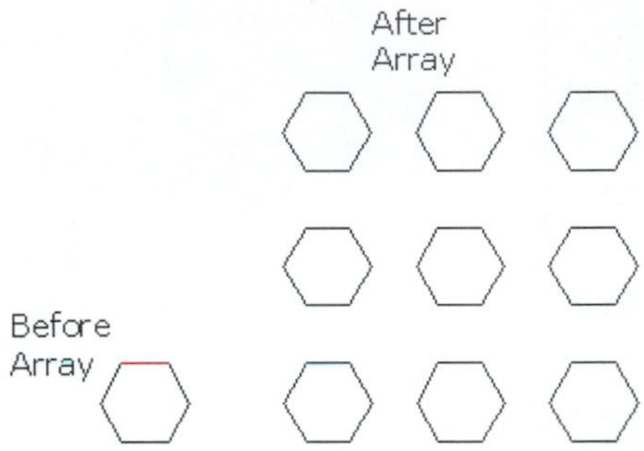

Figure 5-64

Rectangular array results

EXERCISE 5-12 **CREATE A RECTANGULAR ARRAY**

- Start a new drawing.
- From the **Draw** menu pick the **RECTANGLE** command and create a rectangle with diagonal absolute coordinates of **0,0** and **2,1**.
- From the **Modify** menu access the **ARRAY** command.
- Verify that the top button is set to the **Rectangular Array** option.
- Set the following parameters in the dialog box as shown in Figure 5-63:
  - **Rows: 5**
  - **Columns: 4**
  - **Row offset: 2**
  - **Column offset: 3**
- In the upper right area of the dialog box, pick the **Select objects** icon and choose the rectangle in the drawing.
- With the left mouse button, pick the **Preview** option from the lower right command area.
- If the array looks correct, pick **Accept** from the options provided. If it does not look correct, make the appropriate changes and preview it again.

Polar Array. Polar arrays are based on the number of copies needed, a center point, and an angle to fill. You begin by selecting the **ARRAY** command and switching the radio button near the top of the dialog box to **Polar Array** (see Figure 5-65). Next, you select the objects you want to pattern and establish the center point around which the pattern will be produced. You can do this by coordinate entry or by clicking on the **Pick center** button in the **Array** dialog box and selecting a point from the drawing screen. Finally, choose the **Method** by which the array is calculated from the drop-down list in the center of the dialog box. There are three methods available, as follows:

- **Total number of items** (including the original) and **Angle to fill**
- **Total number of items** (including the original) and **Angle between items**
- **Angle to fill** and **Angle between items**

Depending on which method you choose, you need to complete the information by establishing the **Total number of items** and the angle information. When you have entered all the information in the dialog box, you can execute the **Preview** button to see the results (see Figure 5-66). If you like the results of the preview, you can **Accept** the input or return to the dialog box through the **Modify** button.

Items that are arrayed may be rotated as they are copied or held with the same orientation as the original based on the check box in the lower left corner of the **Polar Array** dialog box.

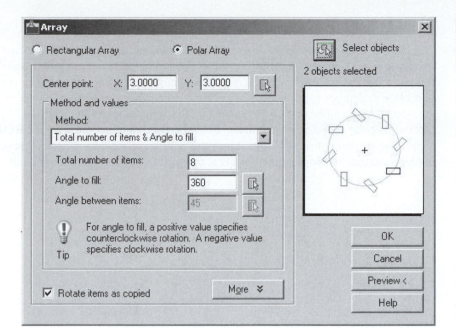

Figure 5-65

Polar Array dialog box for polar (circular) layout

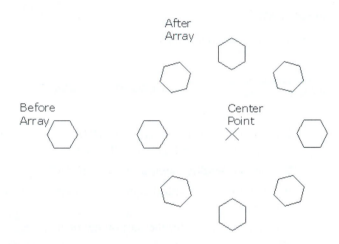

Figure 5-66

Polar array results with rotation

EXERCISE 5-13 **CREATE A POLAR ARRAY**

■ Start a new drawing.

■ From the **Draw** menu pick the **CIRCLE** command and create a circle with center coordinates of **0,0** and a radius of **0.4**.

■ From the **Modify** menu access the **ARRAY** command.

■ Verify that the top button is set to the **Polar Array** option.

■ Set the following parameters in the dialog box:
  • **Center point: 3,3**
  • **Method: Total number of items & Angle to fill**
  • **Total number of items: 8**
  • **Angle to fill: 360**

■ In the upper right area of the dialog box, pick the **Select objects** icon and choose the circle in the drawing.

■ With the left mouse button, pick the **Preview** option from the lower right command area.

■ If the array looks correct, pick **Accept** from the options provided. If it does not look correct, make the appropriate changes and preview it again.

<table>
<tr><td colspan="2">MODIFY COMMAND</td></tr>
<tr><td colspan="2">Rotate Objects</td></tr>
<tr><td colspan="2">Options:
  Various Selection
  Methods, Copy, Undo</td></tr>
<tr><td colspan="2">Type In:</td></tr>
<tr><td colspan="2">Rotate</td></tr>
<tr><td colspan="2">Alias-Type In:</td></tr>
<tr><td colspan="2">RO</td></tr>
<tr><td colspan="2">Menu:</td></tr>
</table>

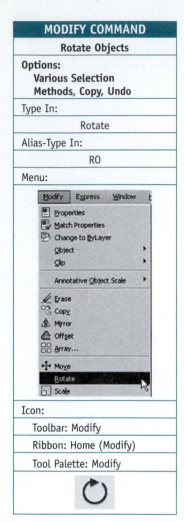

Icon:

Toolbar: Modify

Ribbon: Home (Modify)

Tool Palette: Modify

Rotate

The **ROTATE** command spins or rotates the selected entities around a specified base point. After you finish selecting the entities, you will be prompted for a base point, which is the control point the entities rotate around. After selecting a base point you can then specify a rotation value in degrees (see Figure 5-67) or use a **Reference** option to reference two points on the screen, which move that line to a specific rotated position. Remember that 0° points to the east on the polar coordinate system, and 0° is also the default location for the **ROTATE** command. The second option is **Copy.** This option will leave the original selection set of objects in place and create a copy of the objects at the specified rotation and base point.

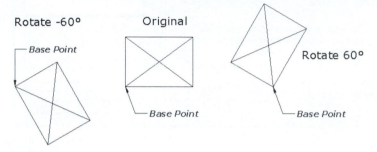

Figure 5-67

ROTATE command operations

EXERCISE 5-14 **PRACTICE THE ROTATE COMMAND**

- Start a new drawing.
- From the **Draw** menu pick the **LINE** command and create a rectangle with diagonal absolute coordinates of **1,1** and **4,4**.
- From the **Modify** menu access the **ROTATE** command.
- Select two lines with the pick box and press **<Enter>** to complete the selection process.
- Pick a base point for the start of the rotation.
- Pick the location for the objects to be located after the rotation by moving the mouse. A left mouse click will set the new location.
- Notice that the objects are in the new location only.

Scale

The **SCALE** command allows you to increase or decrease the size of the selected objects proportionally in all three directions. This scale operation will be in reference to a user-defined base point. As with all the previous commands, you need to select the objects to work with. After finishing the selection process, you will be prompted for a base point. This is the point the object will grow toward or grow away from. After defining the base point, you will enter a scale factor, or you can also move the mouse to dynamically view the scaled size.

The current size of the selected objects is considered a factor of 1.0 (see Figure 5-68). Any number larger than 1.0 will increase the size of the objects proportionally; for example, entering **2** will scale to twice the current size, or entering **4** will scale to four times the current size. Any number under 1.0 will reduce the size of the selected objects by the percentage entered; for instance, inputting **0.5** will reduce the selected set to half the current size, or inputting **0.25** will reduce it to one-fourth the current size. For the most accuracy, a rational number should be entered at the **Scale Factor** prompt.

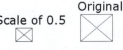

Figure 5-68

SCALE command examples

The **SCALE** command has two options. The **Reference** option allows you to dynamically select two points on the current entity with the mouse and then enter a value for the new **Reference Length**, which will set the scale factor for the selected set. The second option is the **Copy** option. This will leave the original selection set of objects in place and create a copy of the objects at the specified scale factor and the base point.

EXERCISE 5-15 PRACTICE THE SCALE COMMAND

- Start a new drawing.
- From the **Draw** menu pick the **LINE** command and create a rectangle with diagonal absolute coordinates of **1,1** and **4,4**. Also draw the diagonals using the **LINE** command.
- From the **Modify** menu access the **SCALE** command.
- Select the lines that make up the rectangle and press **<Enter>** to complete the selection process.
- Select the lower left corner of the rectangle for the base point.
- Enter a value of **3.0** for the **Scale Factor** and press **<Enter>**. This will triple the size of the original rectangle.
- Repeat the **SCALE** command and this time enter a scale factor value of **0.5**. This should reduce the size of the rectangle by half.

Polyline Edit (PEDIT)

Polyline segments have a series of editing options that are not available to a single line segment. To edit a polyline, you use the **PEDIT** command found in the **Modify** menu under **Objects**. The options here include **Fit** or **Spline** for creating curved lines and a **Join** option for adding other objects to an existing polyline. You can also **Decurve** any polyline that has had the **Fit** or **Spline** option applied to it. The following list further describes the options available under the **PEDIT** command (see Figure 5-69):

- **Open** Opens the polyline by removing the last segment as long as there are two or more segments defined in the polyline.
- **Join** Adds lines, arcs, or other polylines to the end of an existing open polyline. This option will remove any fitted or splined curve information contained in the polyline definition.
- **Fit** Creates a smooth curve out of arcs that pass through the defined vertices of a polyline. The arcs will be based on tangent information specified by predefined formulas.
- **Spline** Creates a spline-based curve similar to a B-spline that passes through the first and last vertices as long as the polyline is open. Again, the arcs will be based on tangent information specified by a formula different from that of the **Fit** option.
- **Decurve** Removes any additionally inserted vertices that were inserted during the application of a **Fit** or **Spline** edit option. The results will be a straight-line segmented polyline.
- **Width** Prompts you for a starting width and an ending width of the segment. The ending width will default to the value stated for the starting width. You can taper the width of the polyline simply by entering a different value for the ending width.

```
Command: pedit
Select polyline or [Multiple]:
Enter an option [Open/Join/Width/Edit vertex/Fit/Spline/Decurve/Ltype
gen/Undo]: e
Enter a vertex editing option

[Next/Previous/Break/Insert/Move/Regen/Straighten/Tangent/Width/eXit] <N>:
```

Figure 5-69

Polyline edit prompts

MODIFY COMMAND
Scale Objects
Options: Copy, Reference, Various Selection Methods
Type In: Scale
Alias-Type In: SC
Menu:
Icon:
Toolbar: Modify
Ribbon: Home (Modify)
Tool Palette: Modify

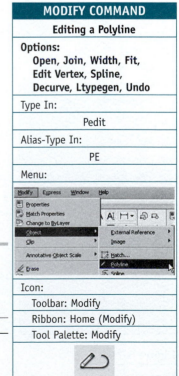

MODIFY COMMAND
Editing a Polyline
Options: Open, Join, Width, Fit, Edit Vertex, Spline, Decurve, Ltypegen, Undo
Type In: Pedit
Alias-Type In: PE
Menu:
Icon:
Toolbar: Modify
Ribbon: Home (Modify)
Tool Palette: Modify

Figure 5-70

The **Undo** and **Redo** arrows on the **Quick Access** toolbar

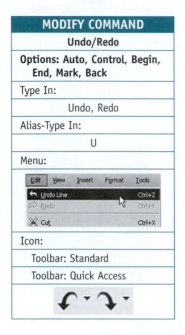

MODIFY COMMAND
Undo/Redo
Options: Auto, Control, Begin, End, Mark, Back
Type In:
Undo, Redo
Alias-Type In:
U
Menu:

Figure 5-71

Format menu

Undo/Redo

The **UNDO** command reverses the action of the last command executed. This is considered a basic modifying command even though it is not found in the **Modify** menu.

You will find this command in the **Edit** menu, in the **Standard** toolbar, or in the **Quick Access** toolbar (see Figure 5-70). The **UNDO** command may act like an **ERASE** command, but it is much more. When you invoke an **UNDO** command all the steps used during the execution of the command are also reversed. For example, if you turn on **ORTHO** during the execution of the command, **ORTHO** will be turned off when the **UNDO** command is executed. Multiple **UNDO** functions can be selected from the toolbar icon as you hold down the left mouse button and choose the command you want from the pop-up menu. To reverse an **UNDO** command, you can choose the **REDO** command. This will reverse the **UNDO** operation and restore the file to the status prior to the **UNDO** command. As with the multiple **UNDO** function, there is a multiple **REDO** function that is executed in the same manner.

Elementary Object Properties

All entities created in a drawing file have a series of properties attached to them. These properties can be classified into three areas: general, entity specific, and style based. The general properties that are attached to all objects are layer, color, linetype, scale, and lineweight. Entity-specific properties come in the form of geometry, such as the length of a line or the center point coordinates of a circle or arc. Style-based properties refer to a value that is part of a larger definition-based style. Examples include use of arrowheads in a dimension style, justification of a text string, or the rotation of a block insertion. Although most properties are assigned and controlled by the user, the general properties assigned to entities in a new drawing session all have a default version related to Layer **0**. For instance, an entity is white in color with a continuous linetype when attached to Layer **0**. As mentioned earlier, part of the drawing setup is to establish a layering scheme for organizational purposes. This is where you start to address object properties by assigning some of the general properties to a layer, all the while maintaining awareness of the layer that is active. At this time, let's take a look at the general properties of every entity when it is created. All these properties can be controlled through the **Format** menu (Figure 5-71), the **Properties** toolbar (Figure 5-72), or the **PROPERTIES** command found in the **Modify** menu or on the **Home** ribbon (Figure 5-73).

Figure 5-72

Properties toolbar

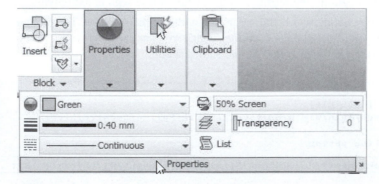

Figure 5-73

Properties panel expanded on the **Home** ribbon

Layer

Each entity is attached to a layer. Layers are identified by giving each one a unique name. An entity can be attached to only one layer at a time. Which layer an object is attached to is up to the user and depends on the current layering scheme. Remember that AutoCAD does not have an automatic layering feature, and the organization of layers is defined by the user or individual office practices. See Chapter 4 for the discussion of layer visibility options.

JOB SKILLS

An understanding of layering concepts and procedures is essential in a well-organized drawing file. Most offices will have established layering guidelines for operators to follow.

Color

You can assign a color to an object by selecting the color through the **Select Color** dialog box (see Figure 5-74). This dialog box contains the standard AutoCAD colors along with a tab that contains a color index, a tab for mixing True Color, and a tab for color books like the PANTONE® series of colors.

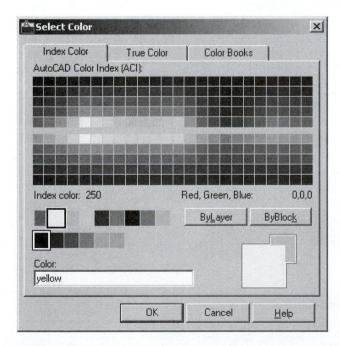

Figure 5-74

Select Color dialog box

JOB SKILLS

The use of a drawing template, as described in Chapter 4, can aid in establishing layers, colors, linetypes, and lineweights in a drawing.

Linetype

The linetype property controls the noncontinuous linetype patterns loaded into the drawing file. By default, linetype is set to continuous. If a noncontinuous pattern such as center or hidden is needed, you must first load the linetype definition from the **Linetype Manager** dialog box (see Figure 5-75) and then assign the linetype property to a specific pattern and to an entity or layer.

Lineweight

The lineweight property refers to the width of the line when the entity is printed and can be scaled for the current drawing display. Lineweights can be established in English or metric values as shown in the **Lineweight Settings** dialog box (see Figure 5-76). This property is also available through a layering scheme.

> **NOTE:**
>
> Linetype scale **(LTS)** is the system value that will control the space of a noncontinuous linetype. All noncontinuous linetype definitions have a spacing value that is based on a 1.0 value. Increasing the **LTS** will cause the pattern's spacing to stretch out, and decreasing the **LTS** will cause the pattern's spacing to shorten.

Figure 5-75

Linetype Manager dialog box

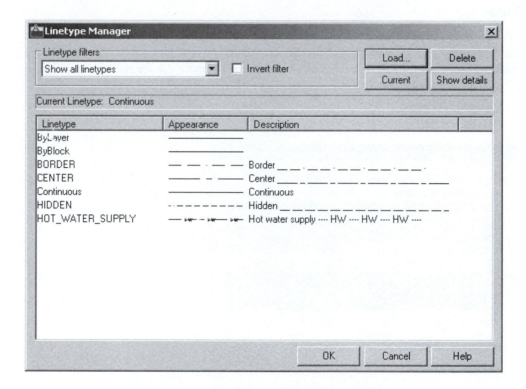

Figure 5-76

Lineweight Settings dialog box

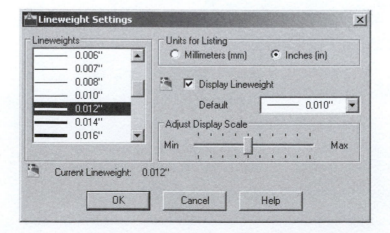

Chapter Summary

In this unit we practiced creating and modifying such basic entities as lines, circles, arcs, rectangles, polylines, and polygons in AutoCAD. You were introduced to the various commands (found on the **Draw** and **Modify** menus and toolbars) used to perform these and similar operations. We then explained the basics of the Cartesian coordinate system as well as the different input methods used to precisely locate an object including grid and snap for cursor control, direct distance entry, the absolute and relative coordinate systems, and the relative polar coordinate system. You then learned about various precision drafting controls including Object Snap (OSNAP) functions, **Object Tracking, Polar Tracking,** and **ORTHO.** Next, we discussed some of the different methods used to select objects for AutoCAD operations (single selection, window selection, and crossing window selection). You then proceeded to learn the modifying commands, focusing on those used to either alter existing geometry **(OFFSET, MIRROR, ARRAY, ROTATE,** and **SCALE)** or create more geometry from existing entities. Finally, you learned the entity properties that are attached to all objects in AutoCAD: layer, color, linetype, scale, and lineweight.

Chapter Tutorials

Ⓖ Tutorial 5-1: *Using Absolute Coordinates to Draw*

In this tutorial you will use AutoCAD to create the drawing in Figure 5-77 using the absolute coordinates shown to draw the lines.

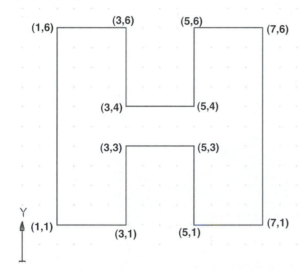

Figure 5-77

Drawing for Tutorial 5-1

1. From the **File** menu choose **NEW** to begin a new drawing.

2. From the **Format** menu choose **Drawing LIMITS** and enter **0,0** for the lower left corner and **11,8.5** for the upper right corner to complete the command.

3. From the **View** menu, pick **Zoom** and then pick **All** to resize the drawing area to your limits.

4. Access the **LINE** command from the icon, the **Draw** menu, or the **Draw** panel on the **Home** ribbon, or by typing **LINE**. Enter **1,1** as the first point (see Figure 5-78) and press **<Enter>**.

```
Command: line
Specify first point: 1,1

Specify next point or [Undo]:
```

Figure 5-78

Command line prompts

5. Continuing in the **LINE** command, enter the following coordinates to complete the drawing. After each set of coordinates press **<Enter>** to go to the next coordinate request entry:

   a. **1,6**
   b. **3,6**
   c. **3,4**
   d. **5,4**
   e. **5,6**
   f. **7,6**
   g. **7,1**
   h. **5,1**
   i. **5,3**
   j. **3,3**
   k. **3,1**
   l. **1,1** (This last entry could be a **C** for **Close**, as this returns the end of the line segment to the origin of the drawing line.)

6. Access the **File** menu and select the **SAVEAS** command. Maneuver to your **Workskills** folder as shown in Figure 5-79, enter the name **Tutorial 5-1**, and save this drawing.

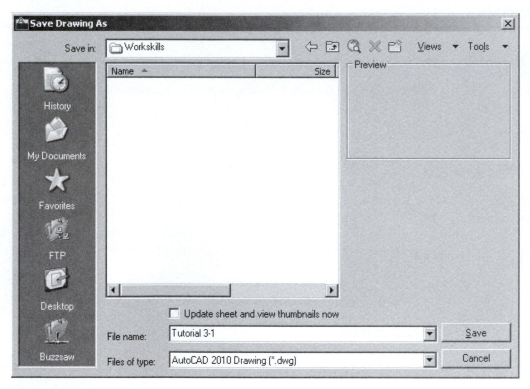

Figure 5-79

SAVEAS command dialog box for Tutorial 5-1

Tutorial 5-2: *Using Relative Coordinates to Draw*

In this tutorial you will use AutoCAD to create the drawing in Figure 5-80 using the relative coordinates shown to draw the lines.

1. From the **File** menu, choose **NEW** to begin a new drawing.

2. From the **Format** menu, choose **Drawing LIMITS** and enter **0,0** for the lower left corner and **11,8.5** for the upper right corner to complete the command.

3. From the **View** menu, pick **Zoom** and then pick **All** to resize the drawing area to your limits.

4. Access the **LINE** command from the icon, the **Draw** menu, the **Draw** panel on the **Home** ribbon, or by typing **LINE**. Enter **1,1** as the first point (see Figure 5-81) and press **<Enter>**.

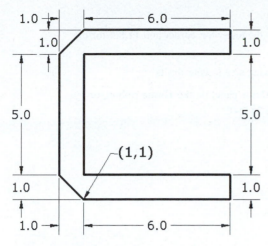

Figure 5-80

Drawing for Tutorial 5-2

```
Command: line
Specify first point: 1,1

Specify next point or [Undo]: @6,0
```

Figure 5-81

LINE command prompt for Tutorial 5-2

5. Continuing in the **LINE** command, enter the following information to complete the drawing. After each set of coordinates, press **<Enter>** to go to the next coordinate request entry:

 a. **@6,0**
 b. **@0,1**
 c. **@-6,0**
 d. **@0,5**
 e. **@6,0**
 f. **@0,1**
 g. **@-6,0**
 h. **@-1,-1**
 i. **@0,-5**
 j. **@1,-1** (This last entry could be a **C** for **Close** or a **1,1**, as this returns the end of the line segment to the origin of the drawing line.)

6. Access the **File** menu and select the **SAVEAS** command. Maneuver to your **Workskills** folder as shown in Figure 5-79, enter the name **Tutorial 5-2**, and save this drawing.

Ⓖ Tutorial 5-3: *Using Relative Polar Entries for Drawing*

In this tutorial you will use AutoCAD to create the drawing in Figure 5-82 using the relative coordinates shown to draw the lines.

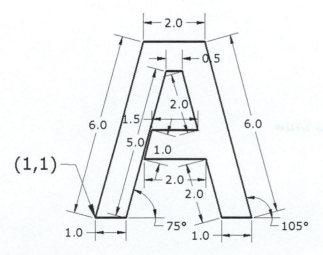

Figure 5-82

Drawing for Tutorial 5-3

1. From the **File** menu, choose **NEW** to begin a new drawing.

2. From the **Format** menu, choose **Drawing LIMITS** and enter **0,0** for the lower left corner and **11,8.5** for the upper right corner to complete the command.

3. From the **View** menu, pick **Zoom** and then pick **All** to resize the drawing area to your limits.

4. Access the **LINE** command from the icon, the **Draw** menu, or the **Draw** panel on the **Home** ribbon, or by typing **LINE**. Enter **1,1** as the first point (see Figure 5-83) and press **<Enter>**.

```
Command: line
Specify first point: 1,1

Specify next point or [Undo]: @6<75
```

Figure 5-83

LINE command prompt for Tutorial 5-3

5. Continuing in the **LINE** command, enter the following coordinates to complete the drawing. After each set of coordinates, press **<Enter>** to go to the next coordinate request entry:

   a. **@6<75**
   b. **@2<0**
   c. **@6<-75**
   d. **@1<180**
   e. **@2<105**
   f. **@2<180**
   g. **@1<75**
   h. **@1.5<0**
   i. **@2<105**
   j. **@.5<180**
   k. **@5<255**
   l. **@1<180** (This last entry could be a **C** for **Close** or a **1,1**, as this returns the end of the line segment to the origin of the drawing line.)

6. Access the **File** menu and select the **SAVEAS** command. Go to your **Workskills** folder as shown in Figure 5-79, enter the name **Tutorial 5-3**, and save this drawing.

Ⓖ Tutorial 5-4: *Using Absolute, Relative, and Polar Entries for Drawing*

In this tutorial you will use AutoCAD to create the drawing in Figure 5-84 using the various input methods shown to draw the lines.

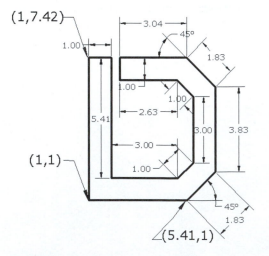

Figure 5-84

Drawing for Tutorial 5-4

1. From the **File** menu, choose **NEW** to begin a new drawing.

2. From the **Format** menu, choose **Drawing LIMITS** and enter **0,0** for the lower left corner and **11,8.5** for the upper right corner to complete the command.

3. From the **View** menu, pick **Zoom** and then pick **All** to resize the drawing area to your limits.

4. Access the **LINE** command from the icon, the **Draw** menu, or the **Draw** panel on the **Home** ribbon, or by typing **LINE**. Enter **1,1** as the first point (see Figure 5-85) and press **<Enter>**.

```
Command: line
Specify first point: 1,1

Specify next point or [Undo]: 1,7.42
```

Figure 5-85

LINE command prompt for Tutorial 5-4

5. Continuing in the **LINE** command, enter the following coordinates to complete the drawing. After each set of coordinates, press **<Enter>** to go to the next coordinate request entry:

   a. **1,7.42**
   b. **@1,0**
   c. **@0,-5.41**
   d. **@3,0**
   e. **@1<45**
   f. **@0,3**
   g. **@1<135**
   h. **@-2.63,0**
   i. **@0,1**
   j. **@3.04,0**
   k. **@1.83<-45**
   l. **@0,-3.83**
   m. **5.41,1**
   n. **1,1** (This last entry could be a **C** for **Close**, as this returns the end of the line segment to the origin of the drawing line.)

6. Access the **File** menu and select the **SAVEAS** command. Go to your **Workskills** folder as shown in Figure 5-79, enter the name **Tutorial 5-4**, and save this drawing.

Ⓐ Tutorial 5-5: *Using Direct Distance Entries for Drawing*

In this tutorial you will use AutoCAD to create the drawing in Figure 5-86 using the relative coordinates shown to draw the lines.

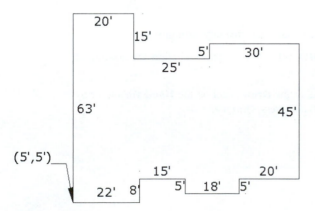

Figure 5-86

Drawing for Tutorial 5-5

1. From the **File** menu, choose **NEW** to begin a new drawing.

2. From the **Format** menu, choose **UNITS**. Set the **Length Type** to **Architectural** and the **Length Precision** to **0'-0'** and pick **OK** when completed, as shown in Figure 5-87.

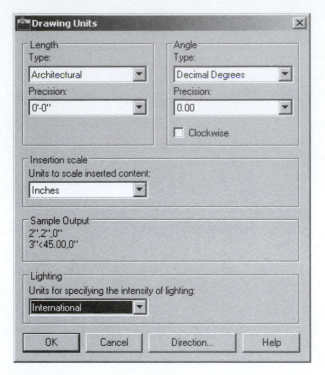

Figure 5-87

Units dialog box for Tutorial 5-5

3. From the **Format** menu, choose **Drawing LIMITS** and enter **0,0** for the lower left corner and **100′,80′** for the upper right corner to complete the command (see Figure 5-88). Remember that **UNITS** are set to **Architectural** and the foot mark (single quotation mark) is required input for most distances. Otherwise, AutoCAD will consider the distance input to be in inch units.

```
Command: limits
Reset Model space limits:
Specify lower left corner or [ON/OFF] <0'-0",0'-0">:

Specify upper right corner <1'-0",0'-9">: 100',80'
```

Figure 5-88

LIMITS command prompts

4. From the **View** menu, pick **Zoom** and then pick **All** to resize the drawing area to your limits.

5. From the status bar at the bottom of the screen, pick **ORTHO** and turn it on. This will allow the drawing of objects in only a horizontal or vertical orientation.

6. Access the **LINE** command from the icon, the **Draw** menu, or the **Draw** panel on the **Home** ribbon, or by typing **LINE**. Enter **5′,5′** as the first point (see Figure 5-89) and press **<Enter>**.

```
Command: line
Specify first point: 5',5'

Specify next point or [Undo]: 22'
```

Figure 5-89

LINE command for Tutorial 5-5

7. Continuing in the **LINE** command, enter the following distances while moving the mouse in the proper direction. After each distance entry, press **<Enter>** to go to the next request entry:

   a. Mouse moving **East**; enter **22′**
   b. Mouse moving **North**; enter **8′**
   c. Mouse moving **East**; enter **15′**

d. Mouse moving **South**; enter **5′**
e. Mouse moving **East**; enter **18′**
f. Mouse moving **North**; enter **5′**
g. Mouse moving **East**; enter **20′**
h. Mouse moving **North**; enter **45′**
i. Mouse moving **West**; enter **30′**
j. Mouse moving **South**; enter **5′**
k. Mouse moving **West**; enter **25′**
l. Mouse moving **North**; enter **15′**
m. Mouse moving **West**; enter **20′**
n. Mouse moving **South**; enter **63′** (This last entry could be a **C** for **Close** or a **5′,5′**, as this returns the end of the line segment to the origin of the drawing line.)

8. Access the **File** menu and select the **SAVEAS** command. Go to your **Workskills** folder as shown in Figure 5-79, enter the name **Tutorial 5-5**, and save this drawing.

Tutorial 5-6: Using Object Snaps for Drawing

In this tutorial you will use AutoCAD to create the additional lines shown in Figure 5-90 using the drawing from the previous tutorial (Figure 5-86) as the base drawing, or access this figure in the student data files.

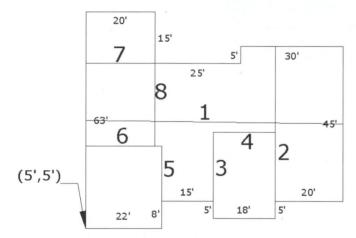

Figure 5-90

Drawing for Tutorial 5-6

1. From the **File** menu, choose **OPEN** to access the drawing **Tutorial 5-5** from your **Workskills** folder to begin the session.

2. From the **Tools** menu, choose **Drafting Settings.**

3. Select the **Object Snap** tab and place check marks in the boxes for **ENDpoint, MIDpoint,** and **INTersection** (see Figure 5-91).

4. Access the **LINE** command from the icon, the **Draw** menu, on the **Draw** panel on the **Home** ribbon, or by typing **LINE.** Add the lines to the drawing as follows:

a. **Line 1**—pick the **MIDpoint** of the 43′ wall and connect to the **MIDpoint** of the 63′ wall.
b. **Line 2**—pick the **ENDpoint** at the south end of the line, type **PER** (see Figure 5-92), and press **<Enter>** to connect to the 30′ wall at a right angle, or 90°, to complete the line.
c. **Line 3**—pick the **ENDpoint** at the south end of the line. Move the mouse due north (be sure **ORTHO** is on), enter **20′**, and press **<Enter>** for a direct distance input.
d. **Line 4**—continuing from **Line 3** move to **Line 2,** type **PER,** and press **<Enter>** to connect to the wall at a right angle, or 90°, to complete the line.
e. **Line 5**—pick the **ENDpoint** at the south end of the line. Move the mouse due north (be sure **ORTHO** is on), type **16′**, and press **<Enter>** for a direct distance input.
f. **Line 6**—continuing from **Line 5** move to the 63′ wall, type **PER,** and press **<Enter>** to connect to the wall at a right angle, or 90°, to complete the line.

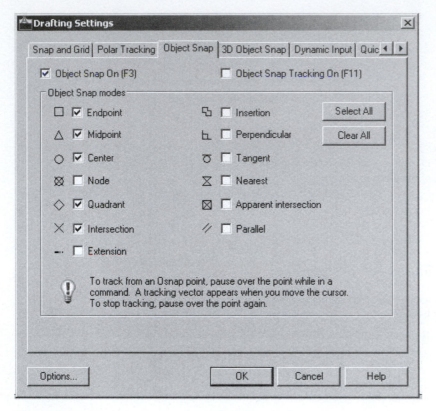

Figure 5-91

OSNAP Drafting Settings dialog box for Tutorial 5-6

```
Command: line
Specify first point: end
of

Specify next point or [Undo]: per
```

Figure 5-92

LINE command prompt for Tutorial 5-6

    g. **Line 7**—pick the **ENDpoint** at the east end of the wall, move to the 63′ wall, type **PER,** and press
        <Enter> to connect to the wall at a right angle, or 90°, to complete the line.

    h. **Line 8**—pick the **ENDpoint** at the north end of the wall, move to **Line 6,** type **PER,** and press **<Enter>**
        to connect to the wall at a right angle, or 90°, to complete the line.

  5. Access the **File** menu and select the **SAVEAS** command. Go to your **Workskills** folder as shown in Figure 5-79,
     enter the name **Tutorial 5-6,** and save this drawing.

Tutorial 5-7: *Using Surveyor's Units for Drawing*

In this tutorial you will use AutoCAD to create the drawing in Figure 5-93 using relative coordinates and surveyor's
units to draw the lines.

  1. From the **File** menu, choose **NEW** to begin a new drawing.

  2. From the **Format** menu, choose **UNITS**. Set the **Angle Type** to **Surveyor's Units**, set the **Angle Precision** to
     0d00′00″, and pick **OK** when finished, as shown in Figure 5-94.

  3. From the **Format** menu, choose **Drawing LIMITS** and enter **1000,1000** for the lower left coordinate and
     3000,3000 for the upper right coordinate to complete the command (see Figure 5-95).

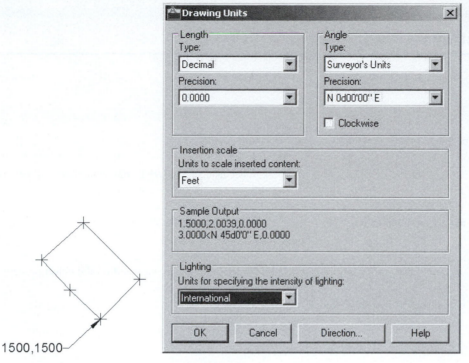

1500,1500

Figure 5-93

Drawing for Tutorial 5-7

Figure 5-94

Units dialog box for Tutorial 5-7

```
Reset Model space limits:
Specify lower left corner or [ON/OFF] <0.0000,0.0000>: 1000,1000
Specify upper right corner <12.0000,9.0000>: 3000,3000
```

Figure 5-95

LIMITS command prompt for Tutorial 5-7

4. From the **View** menu, pick **Zoom** and then pick **All** to resize the drawing area to your limits.

5. Access the **LINE** command from the icon or the **Draw** menu, or by typing **line** at the command prompt. Enter **1500,1500** as the first point and press **<Enter>**.

6. Continuing in the **LINE** command, enter the following distances and bearings. After each entry, press **<Enter>** (see Figure 5-96).

   a. **@180<n46d56'23"w**
   b. **@176<n43d34'57"w**
   c. **@240<n48d34'20"e**
   d. **@340<s44d45'11"e**
   e. **@236.33<s44d47'01"w**

7. Access the **File** menu and select the **SAVEAS** command. Go to your **Workskills** folder, as shown in Figure 5-79, enter the name **Tutorial 5-7**, and save this drawing.

```
Command:
Command: _line Specify first point: 1500,1500
Specify next point or [Undo]:
```

Figure 5-96

LINE command prompt for Tutorial 5-7

Chapter Test Questions

Multiple Choice

Circle the correct answer.

1. Grid and Snap settings can be found in the _____ dialog box.
   a. Options
   b. Drafting Standards
   c. Properties
   d. Object Snap

2. Which of the following is **not** a valid input method?
   a. Absolute
   b. Relative coordinates
   c. Direct distance
   d. Object-based

3. The origin of the absolute coordinate system has a value of
   a. 1,1
   b. 0,1

   c. 0,0
   d. 1,0

4. When using a **MODIFY** command, users will be prompted to:
   a. List objects
   b. Select objects
   c. Draw the objects
   d. Assign objects

5. Which of the following is **not** a valid object property?
   a. Linetype
   b. Layer
   c. Color
   d. Coordinate

Matching

Write the number of the correct answer on the line.

a. Absolute coordinates _____

b. Relative coordinates _____

c. Polar coordinates _____

d. Direct distance _____

e. Cursor control _____

1. Mouse movement

2. X,Y

3. @X,Y

4. Distance<angle

5. Mouse direction and a distance

True or False

Circle the correct answer.

1. **True or False:** Only one input method can be active at a time.

2. **True or False:** The pick box is used for the selection of multiple objects.

3. **True or False: ORTHO** mode will lock cursor movement to the *X*- or *Y*-axis.

4. **True or False:** Polar tracking is referred to as angle snap.

5. **True or False:** A crossing window requires the object to be completely inside the window.

Chapter Projects

Ⓐ Project 5-1 [INTERMEDIATE]

Your instructor will divide the class into groups. Each group will measure one of the classroom buildings on campus and determine the spacing of support columns, beams, roof beams, and other information. Make a drawing and show the location of stairs and elevators. Which method for input did you use?

Ⓐ Project 5-2 [INTERMEDIATE]

Measure the building where you live and do the same as in the preceding project.

Ⓐ Project 5-3 [INTERMEDIATE]

Take a field trip to an office construction site or visit an existing building and check the drawings for accuracy and compare them against the construction. How accurate do you need to be?

Chapter Practice Exercises

Figures 5-97 to 5-116 represent typical general, architectural, civil, and mechanical drawings that can be drawn using the techniques and commands explained in this chapter. Dimensions and text on the drawings are given for informational purposes only and should not be drawn at this time.

- To begin the drawing process for each drawing, access the **File** menu and pick **NEW.** (Use the acad.dwt template if this is requested.)

- If the drawing will use feet and inches, set **UNITS** for **Architectural**. This command is found in the **Format** menu.

- Next, set **LIMITS** for the drawing to resize the screen to hold the drawing. This command is in the **Format** menu. The lower left corner should be set to **0,0** with the upper right set to numbers just beyond the maximum *X,Y* of the figure.

- Then process the **ZOOM ALL** commands using the keyboard, **View** menu, or icon. This will resize the screen to view the complete drawing as described by the limits.

- Access the **LINE** command to begin drawing the figure. Various linetypes may be added to show hidden or centerlines.

- Remember to save your drawing every 10 to 15 minutes to avoid losing your work. Save the drawings in your **Workskills** folder with the figure number as the file name.

Ⓜ Practice Exercise 5-1: *Absolute Coordinate Input* **[BASIC]**

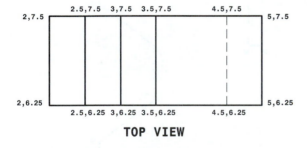

TOP VIEW

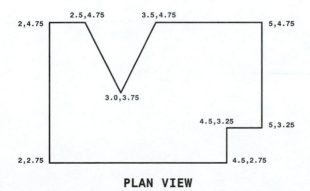

PLAN VIEW

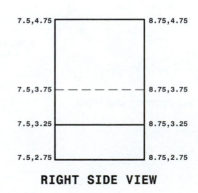

RIGHT SIDE VIEW

Figure 5-97

Practice Exercise 5-1 drawing and input

Ⓐ Practice Exercise 5-2: *Absolute Coordinate Input—Architectural* [BASIC]

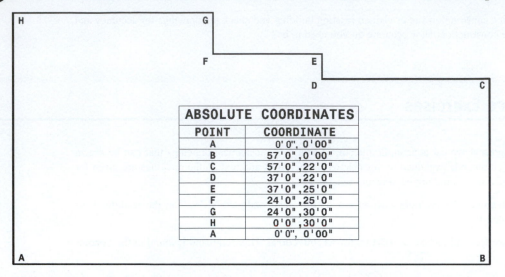

ABSOLUTE COORDINATES	
POINT	COORDINATE
A	0'0", 0'00"
B	57'0",0'00"
C	57'0",22'0"
D	37'0",22'0"
E	37'0",25'0"
F	24'0",25'0"
G	24'0",30'0"
H	0'0",30'0"
A	0'0", 0'00"

Figure 5-98

Practice Exercise 5-2 drawing and input with architectural units

Ⓜ Practice Exercise 5-3: *Relative Coordinate Input* [BASIC]

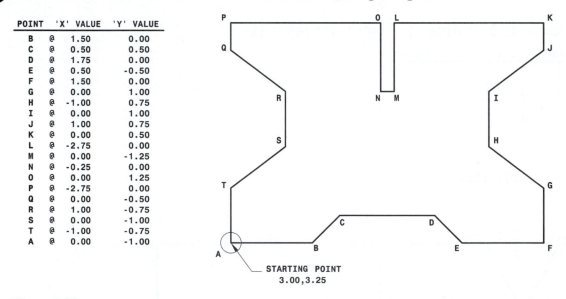

POINT	'X' VALUE	'Y' VALUE
B @	1.50	0.00
C @	0.50	0.50
D @	1.75	0.00
E @	0.50	-0.50
F @	1.50	0.00
G @	0.00	1.00
H @	-1.00	0.75
I @	0.00	1.00
J @	1.00	0.75
K @	0.00	0.50
L @	-2.75	0.00
M @	0.00	-1.25
N @	-0.25	0.00
O @	0.00	1.25
P @	-2.75	0.00
Q @	0.00	-0.50
R @	1.00	-0.75
S @	0.00	-1.00
T @	-1.00	-0.75
A @	0.00	-1.00

STARTING POINT
3.00,3.25

Figure 5-99

Practice Exercise 5-3 drawing and input

Ⓐ **Practice Exercise 5-4:** *Relative Coordinate Input—Architectural* [BASIC]

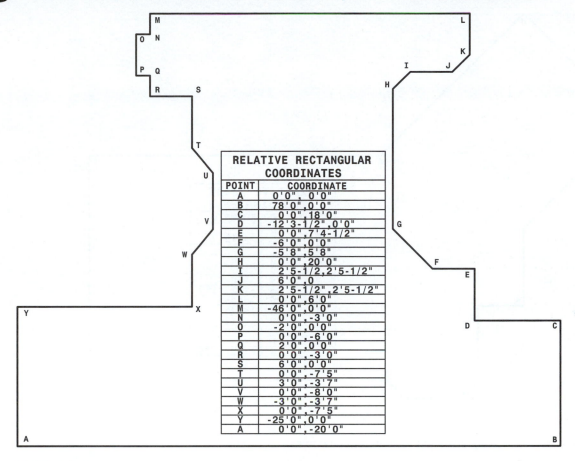

RELATIVE RECTANGULAR COORDINATES	
POINT	COORDINATE
A	0'0", 0'0"
B	78'0",0'0"
C	0'0",18'0"
D	-12'3-1/2",0'0"
E	0'0",7'4-1/2"
F	-6'0",0'0"
G	-5'8",5'8"
H	0'0",20'0"
I	2'5-1/2,2'5-1/2"
J	6'0",0
K	2'5-1/2",2'5-1/2"
L	0'0",6'0"
M	-46'0",0'0"
N	0'0",-3'0"
O	-2'0",0'0"
P	0'0",-6'0"
Q	2'0",0'0"
R	0'0",-3'0"
S	6'0",0'0"
T	0'0",-7'5"
U	3'0",-3'7"
V	0'0",-8'0"
W	-3'0",-3'7"
X	0'0",-7'5"
Y	-25'0",0'0"
A	0'0",-20'0"

Figure 5-100

Practice Exercise 5-4 drawing and input with architectural units

Ⓜ **Practice Exercise 5-5:** *Polar Coordinate Input* [BASIC]

LINE	DISTANCE	ANGLE
AB	2.00	0
BC	1.20	25
CD	1.20	65
DE	1.25	55
EF	1.25	145
FG	1.30	180
GJ	2.25	270
JK	2.00	180
KN	2.25	90
NO	1.30	180
OP	1.25	215
PQ	1.25	305
QR	1.20	295
RA	1.20	335 (OR CLOSE)
1-2	1.50	0
2-3	2.00	90
3-4	0.50	0
4-5	0.707	45
5-6	0.50	0
6-7	0.50	90
7-8	2.371	162
8-9	2.371	198
9-10	0.50	270
10-11	0.50	0
11-12	0.707	315
12-13	0.50	0
13-1	2.00	270 (OR CLOSE)

DRAW INTERIOR LINES USING OBJECT SNAP OPTIONS

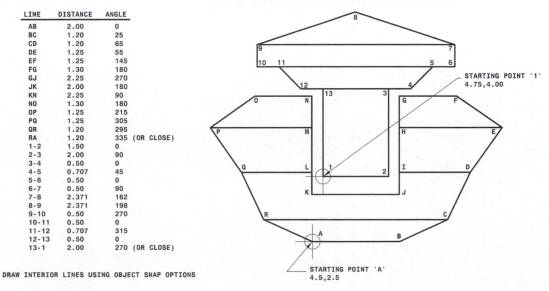

STARTING POINT '1'
4.75,4.00

STARTING POINT 'A'
4.5,2.5

Figure 5-101

Practice Exercise 5-5 drawing and input

A **Practice Exercise 5-6:** *Polar Coordinate Input—Architectural* [BASIC]

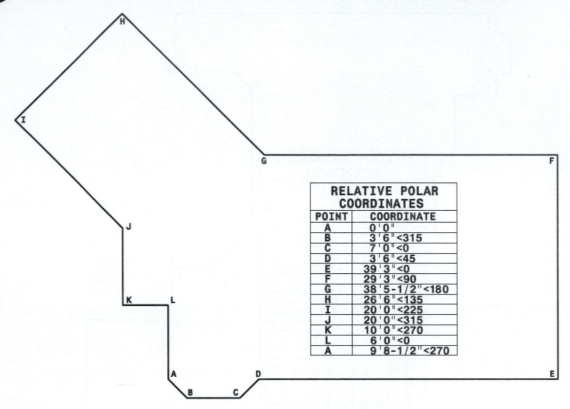

RELATIVE POLAR COORDINATES	
POINT	COORDINATE
A	0'0"
B	3'6"<315
C	7'0"<0
D	3'6"<45
E	39'3"<0
F	29'3"<90
G	38'5-1/2"<180
H	26'6"<135
I	20'0"<225
J	20'0"<315
K	10'0"<270
L	6'0"<0
A	9'8-1/2"<270

Figure 5-102

Practice Exercise 5-6 drawing and input with architectural units

G **Practice Exercise 5-7:** *Isometric Grid Work* [INTERMEDIATE]

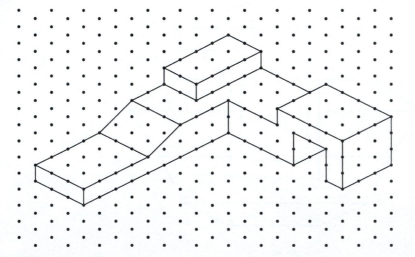

Figure 5-103

Practice Exercise 5-7 drawing and input using the Isometric
Snap and Grid at *Y* = .5

Ⓖ Practice Exercise 5-8: *Absolute Input Boxes* [BASIC]

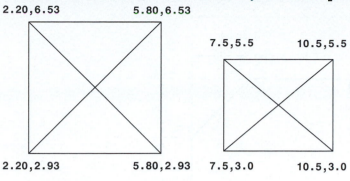

Figure 5-104

Practice Exercise 5-8 drawing and input

Ⓐ Practice Exercise 5-9: *Grid and Snap—Architectural* [BASIC]

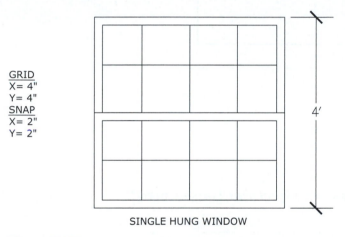

Figure 5-105

Practice Exercise 5-9 drawing and input

Ⓐ Practice Exercise 5-10: *Isometric Grid Work—Architectural* [INTERMEDIATE]

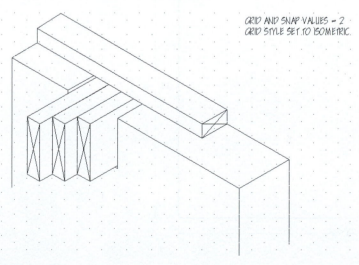

Figure 5-106

Practice Exercise 5-10 drawing and input

Ⓜ Practice Exercise 5-11: *Absolute Input—Mechanical* [INTERMEDIATE]

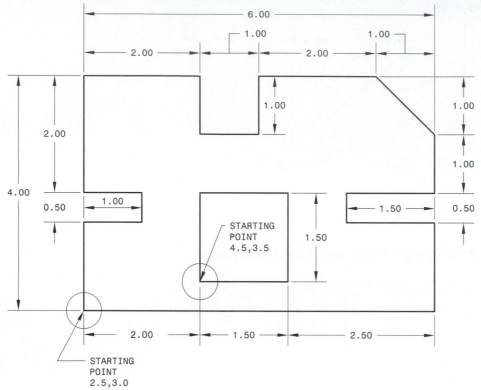

Figure 5-107

Practice Exercise 5-11 drawing and input

Ⓐ Practice Exercise 5-12: *Direct Distance—Architectural* [INTERMEDIATE]

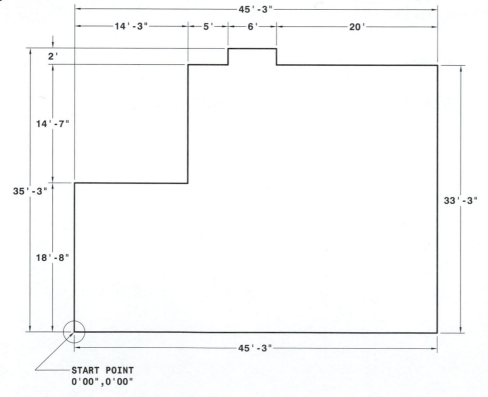

Figure 5-108

Practice Exercise 5-12 drawing and input

M **Practice Exercise 5-13:** *Relative Input Mechanical* [INTERMEDIATE]

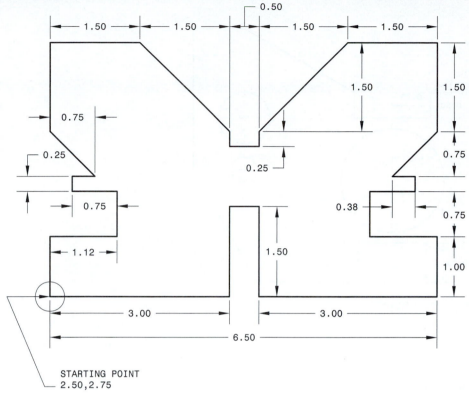

Figure 5-109

Practice Exercise 5-13 drawing and input

A **Practice Exercise 5-14:** *Relative Coordinate Input—Single Line Floor Plan* [INTERMEDIATE]

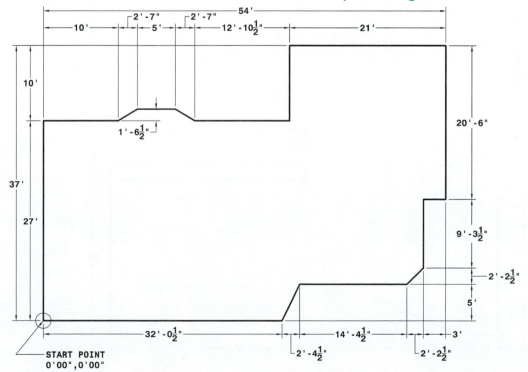

Figure 5-110

Practice Exercise 5-14 drawing and input

M **Practice Exercise 5-15:** *Gasket—Mirror* [INTERMEDIATE]

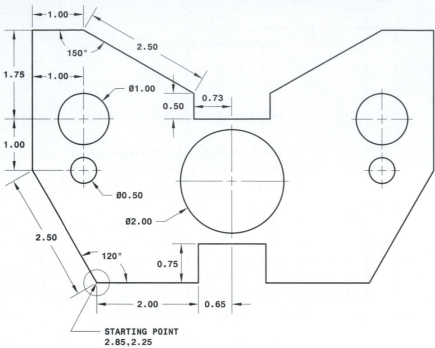

Figure 5-111

Practice Exercise 5-15 drawing and input

A **Practice Exercise 5-16:** *Polar Coordinate Input—Single Line Floor Plan* [INTERMEDIATE]

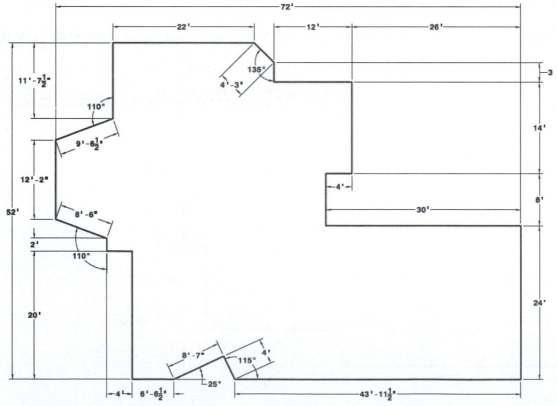

Figure 5-112

Practice Exercise 5-16 drawing and input

G **Practice Exercise 5-17:** *Geometric Construction—1* [BASIC]

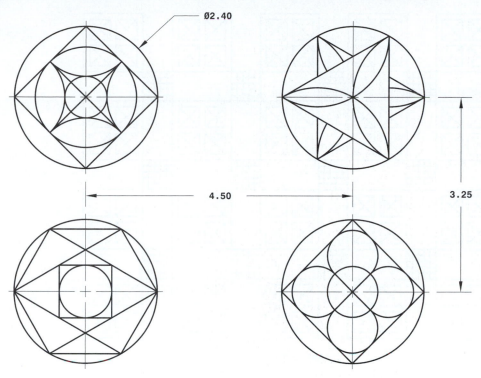

Figure 5-113

Practice Exercise 5-17 drawing and input

G **Practice Exercise 5-18:** *Geometric Construction—2* [INTERMEDIATE]

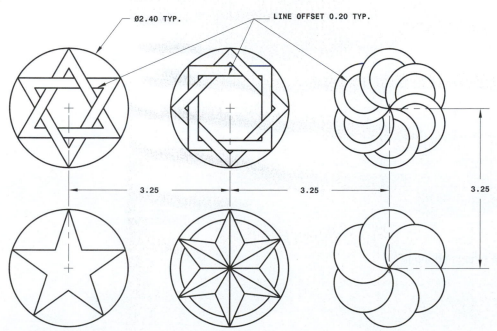

Figure 5-114

Practice Exercise 5-18 drawing and input

G **Practice Exercise 5-19:** *Rectangle Pattern* [INTERMEDIATE]

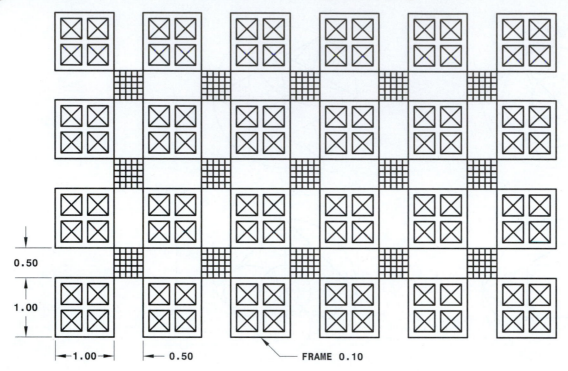

Figure 5-115

Practice Exercise 5-19 drawing and input

C **Practice Exercise 5-20:** *Polar Input—Civil* [INTERMEDIATE]

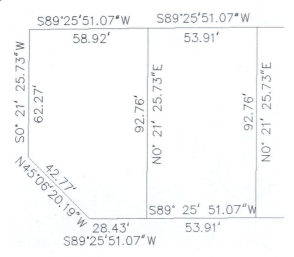

Figure 5-116

Practice Exercise 5-20 drawing and input

6 Fundamental Viewing and Inquiry Commands

CHAPTER OBJECTIVES

- Understand drawing regeneration.
- Use real-time mouse control.
- Understand view control commands.
- Retrieve information from entities.
- Perform inquiries related to the **DISTANCE** and **AREA** commands.
- Set individual system variables.

Introduction

AutoCAD has no limitations on the size of the environment in which a drawing is created. Whether you are working on a circuit board, a floor plan, or a bridge, all entities that make up a drawing should be drawn in real-world units at full size. No matter how big the drawing is, you have to be able to move around the entire file to look at various parts of the drawing. You need to view the whole drawing—the extents—as well as the smallest detail in it.

Viewing a Drawing

Your ability to control the display is found in the **View** menu (see Figure 6-1). Commands such as **ZOOM IN**, **ZOOM OUT,** and **PAN** give you complete control of the drawing area display. **ZOOM** refers to the computer's ability to magnify the screen similar to the way a camera lens can zoom in on a subject being photographed. **PAN** gives you the ability to move across the drawing at the current magnification to a part of the drawing that is presently off the screen to better see that area to add or revise entities. When a television camera shows the crowd at a football game, it is panning by moving along an invisible path and keeping the same magnification.

View commands can be performed at virtually any time and from several locations. The **View** menu (see Figure 6-1) houses many of the commands that pertain to the screen display. Other locations include the **Zoom** toolbar (see Figure 6-2), a section of the **Standard** toolbar (see Figure 6-3), the **View** toolbar (see Figure 6-4), the **View** ribbon (see Figure 6-5), the scroll bars, a mouse wheel, and the command line. Depending upon where you execute the viewing command from, it can be a *transparent command*.

A transparent command is one that can be executed during the activity of another command; it does not disrupt or cancel the original command. When the viewing command is completed, you are returned to the original command in progress with no interruptions to that sequence.

transparent command: A command that can be executed from within an active command; when completed the initial command resumes.

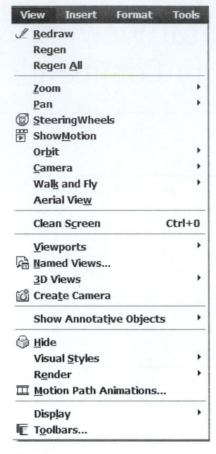

Figure 6-1

View menu

Figure 6-2

Zoom toolbar

Figure 6-3

View icons in the
Standard toolbar

Figure 6-4

The **View** toolbar

Figure 6-5

View ribbon

REDRAW Versus REGEN

regeneration: The process of calculating the screen image and displaying the results.

REDRAW: The process of displaying the screen image based on the last recorded memory.

Before we get into the actual viewing commands, you need to understand the differences between **REDRAW** and **REGEN** (regeneration) (see Figure 6-6). Both of these commands will in essence refresh the screen display. *Regeneration* is a more comprehensive version of the process. *REDRAW* removes the display from the screen and paints the display back on based on the last recorded memory of the display.

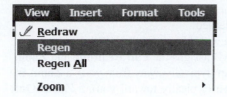

Figure 6-6

View menu for **REDRAW** and **REGEN**

REGEN removes the display from the screen and sends all information in the drawing database back to the central processing unit (CPU) to reprocess the file before it paints the display back on the screen. This is why **REGEN** is considered a more comprehensive version of the drawing database restoration. **REDRAW** is seen as a quicker screen refresh command. Both of these commands are found at the top of the **View** menu. If you are working in a multiple *viewport* configuration (see Figure 6-7), you may choose to invoke a **REGENALL** command to regenerate all viewports. This will cause regeneration to be processed in all viewports in the same command.

viewport: Display of a drawing in an AutoCAD session.

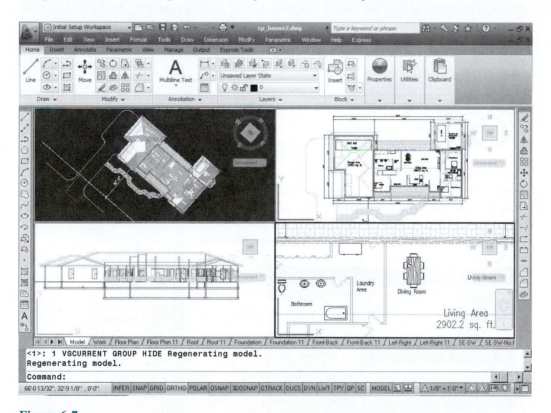

Figure 6-7

Four tiled viewports

Zoom and Pan Realtime

The quickest way to zoom and pan around a drawing is with the mouse wheel. If you do not have a wheel on the mouse, invoking the **Zoom Realtime** command (see Figure 6-8, right icon) gives your left mouse button the ability to change magnification of the drawing by moving vertically (up for **Zoom In,** down for **Zoom Out**). Without a mouse wheel the **Pan Realtime** command (see Figure 6-8, left icon) allows the left mouse button to move the drawing around the display area.

NOTE:

If you do not have a mouse with a wheel, we highly recommend this minimal investment as a productive tool that will quickly be a valuable aid in creating AutoCAD drawings.

Figure 6-8

Pan and **Zoom Realtime** icons in the **Standard** toolbar

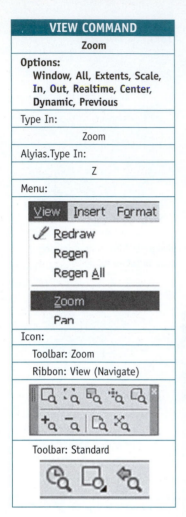

zoom: To reduce or increase magnification of the screen image.

When the **PAN** command is moving to the edge of the window, it will continue to move the drawing in that direction until the mouse button is released.

If your system is equipped with a mouse that has a wheel between the left and right mouse buttons or a rocker-type middle mouse button, AutoCAD assigns the **Pan Realtime** and **Zoom Realtime** features to this button. By rolling the wheel up (typically away from you), a **Zoom In** command will be executed. By rolling the wheel down (typically toward you), a **Zoom Out** command is invoked. The center of the **Zoom** operation is based on the location of the cursor or crosshairs as you spin the wheel. To use the **Pan Realtime** you must press and hold down the wheel, at which time the screen cursor will change to a "hand" icon, signifying the **PAN** command is in effect. As you move the mouse, the drawing will move in the same direction.

A major advantage of executing the viewing commands with the mouse is that these commands are performed as a transparent version of the command. Furthermore, by double-clicking the wheel, you execute a **Zoom Extents** command, modifying the magnification to show the extents of all entities currently in the drawing and available for viewing. **Zoom Extents** is not a transparent command and cannot be executed while you are in another command.

When you use the mouse for **ZOOM** and **PAN** operations, there are limitations to the level of magnification that can be viewed. The amount of magnification will go up only to the point of change that does not require a regeneration of the entire drawing database. A symbol may appear to indicate that you have reached this limit. If this limit is reached, simply **REGEN** the drawing file, and a new set of magnification boundaries will be generated.

Zoom

Under the **View** menu you will find the **Zoom** submenu. This entry leads to a cascading menu of various *zoom* options (see Figure 6-9) or in the **Navigate** panel flyout on the **View** ribbon (see Figure 6-10), all of which perform some type of screen magnification modification. Most of the versions found here are considered full versions of the command and can cause an automatic regeneration of the drawing database, which may be time-consuming. We will discuss some of these options now and reserve others for later chapter topics.

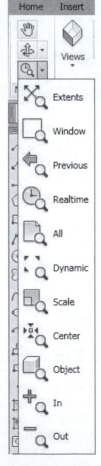

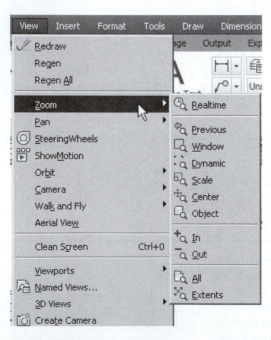

Figure 6-9

Zoom submenu from **View** menu

Figure 6-10

Zoom command flyout from the **Navigate** panel on the **View** ribbon

Zoom Window

Zoom Window (see Figure 6-11) prompts you to construct a window by establishing first one corner and then the opposite, diagonal corner. The area in which the window is created becomes the next magnification of the drawing screen. The actual magnification is calculated based on the longest side of the window while the proper aspect ratio of the X and Y screen dimensions is maintained.

Zoom All

The **Zoom All** (see Figure 6-12) option calculates the largest screen magnification possible as it relates to the current drawing limits. If drawing entities exist outside the drawing limits, the **Zoom All** command calculates the magnification based on the location of all the entities regardless of their location in the drawing. This is not a transparent command and may result in a regeneration of the drawing file.

Zoom Extents

The **Zoom Extents** (see Figure 6-13) option is similar to the **Zoom All** command in that it will calculate the largest magnification possible based on all the entities in the drawing file, regardless of the current drawing limits. If a **Zoom Extents** produces what appears to be a blank screen, you need to look carefully around the top or right edge of the screen for any entities. These entities are located far from the main drawing and need to be erased. You can then execute a second **Zoom Extents** command to produce a more accurate display. Remember that **Zoom Extents** brings all objects in the drawing file into the display no matter where they are in space. This is not a transparent command and may result in a regeneration of the drawing file.

> **NOTE:**
> The **Zoom Extents** command can also be executed by double-clicking the wheel on the mouse.

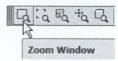

Figure 6-11

Zoom Window icon from the **Zoom** toolbar

Figure 6-12

Zoom All icon from the **Zoom** toolbar

Zoom Previous

The **Zoom Previous** (see Figure 6-14) option returns the screen display to the previous zoom magnification you were last working with. You can step back (up to 10 times) through a series of previous display screens by repeating the command.

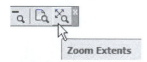

Figure 6-13

Zoom Extents icon from the **Zoom** toolbar

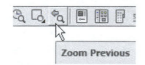

Figure 6-14

Zoom Previous icon from the **Standard** toolbar

Pan

Pan gives you the ability to slide the current screen display in all four directions to expose parts of the drawing file that may be just off the screen. In the **View** menu there is a cascading menu with the various **PAN** operations (see Figure 6-15). Except for **Pan Realtime,** these commands move a specific direction and distance. If you hold down the left mouse button and drag the hand icon around the screen when using the **Pan Realtime** command (see Figure 6-16), the display will move in accordance with the mouse movement, keeping the current zoom magnification. Even if the PAN symbol moves to the edge of the drawing screen, you can continue to pan the view by continuing to move the mouse and holding down the left mouse button.

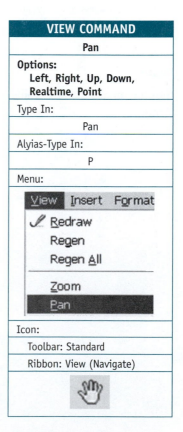

VIEW COMMAND
Pan
Options: Left, Right, Up, Down, Realtime, Point
Type In:
Pan
Alyias-Type In:
P
Menu:
View Insert Format / Redraw Regen Regen All Zoom Pan
Icon:
Toolbar: Standard
Ribbon: View (Navigate)

pan: The ability to slide the screen or shift the screen display around with no change in magnification.

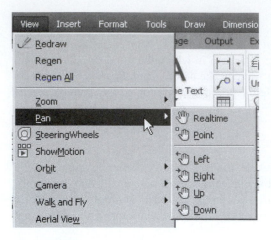

Figure 6-15

Pan submenu from the **View** menu

Figure 6-16

Pan Realtime icon from the **Standard** toolbar

JOB SKILLS

It is essential for you to be able to move around a large drawing file by using a variety of viewing commands and techniques. A complete understanding of creating views and saving named views along with various **ZOOM** commands and the realtime **PAN** and **ZOOM** is necessary. This will keep the regeneration time during a drawing session to a minimum.

Drawing Inquiry

Inquiry: The process of retrieving information from a drawing file.

You can access drawing file information through the *Inquiry* submenu found in the **Tools** menu (see Figure 6-17). This set of commands extracts information from the database pertaining to individual drawing entities as well as the complete drawing files. Commands such as **ID**

Figure 6-17

Inquiry submenu on the **Tools** menu

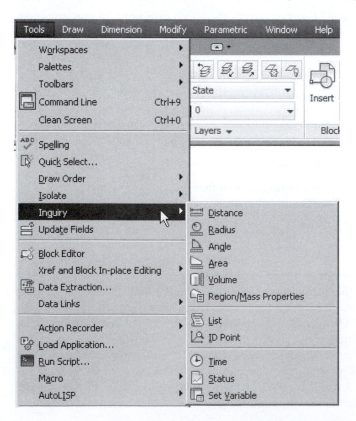

Point, **LIST, DISTance,** and **AREA** will give you information regarding the entities selected. The **TIME** and **STATUS** commands reveal summary information attached to the complete drawing file. **Set Variable** has to do with basic AutoCAD settings that are discussed later.

When you execute a drawing inquiry, the information requested shows up in the text window. Remember that the **<F2>** function key is used to toggle or flip between the text window and the AutoCAD graphics screen. Entity-based inquiries can also be made from the **Inquiry** toolbar (see Figure 6-18) or the **Utilities** icons on the **Home** ribbon (see Figure 6-19).

List

The **LIST** command will prompt you to *Select objects*. After the selection set is chosen, the text screen will display all information about the selected entities individually. The type of entity and its general properties as well as geometry-specific information such as the length, projected lengths, and coordinates of the start point and endpoint of lines, center coordinates and radius of circles, vertex coordinates, length, and area of polylines, and more will be read from the drawing database (see Figure 6-20). Geometry-based information will differ depending on the type of entity selected.

ID Point

The **ID Point** command (see Figure 6-21) will present in the text window the absolute coordinates (X, Y, and Z) of the location selected and is shown in the current drawing units (see Figure 6-22). You may select the location with a mouse pick or use any of the **Object Snap** options to ensure accuracy.

> **NOTE:**
> Executing a **CLEANSCREENON** command will remove all the toolbars and tool palettes from the screen display, leaving only the command line, the menu bar, and the drawing window expanded to the largest possible size. The **CLEANSCREENOFF** command will restore the previous, complete screen display. **CLEANSCREEN** is a system variable that can be turned on/off by a **<CTRL> + <0>** key combination or from the item in the **View** menu or from the **Tools** menu.

Figure 6-18

Inquiry toolbar expanded

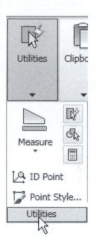

Figure 6-19

Utilities panel expanded on the **Home** ribbon

Figure 6-20

Results of the **LIST** command

```
AutoCAD Text Window - Drawing2.dwg
Edit
Select objects: 1 found, 3 total

Select objects:

              LINE      Layer: "0"
                        Space: Model space
            Handle = 19e
       from point, X=  20.8458  Y=  19.7222  Z=   0.0000
         to point, X=  50.2602  Y=  43.1372  Z=   0.0000
    Length =  37.5962,   Angle in XY Plane =     39
             Delta X =  29.4144, Delta Y =   23.4150, Delta Z =   0.0000

              CIRCLE    Layer: "0"
                        Space: Model space
            Handle = 1a1
    center point, X=  66.2366  Y=  26.1352  Z=   0.0000
       radius   16.1057
  circumference  101.1948
        area   814.9043

Press ENTER to continue:
              LWPOLYLINE  Layer: "0"
                        Space: Model space
            Handle = 1a2
          Open
  Constant width   0.0000
          area   375.2426
        length   88.6865

      at point  X=  94.1578  Y=  12.5634  Z=   0.0000
      at point  X= 106.4014  Y=  42.3915  Z=   0.0000
      at point  X= 124.4681  Y=  14.9497  Z=   0.0000
      at point  X= 131.4858  Y=  37.4699  Z=   0.0000

Command:
```

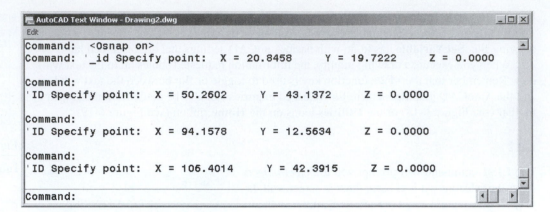

Locate Point

Figure 6-21

The **ID/Locate Point**
icon on the **Inquiry**
toolbar

Figure 6-22

Results of the **ID/Locate Point** command

Distance

The **DISTance** command (see Figure 6-23) calculates the distance between any two points selected in the drawing file. The value returned will be in the currently established drawing units and in two forms. One is the actual or true distance between the two points and the polar angles from the principal planes (**in the XY plane** or the alpha angle, and **from the XY plane** or the beta angle). Also shown will be the projected or *delta distance* (Delta X, Delta Y, and Delta Z). Along with the distance values, the command will return angle information as well (see Figure 6-24). The **Angle in XY plane** and the **Angle from XY plane** will be expressed in the current angle settings. If the **Dynamic Input** option in the status line is active at the time of the **DISTance** command, you will have a visual readout appear on the screen with a choice of options for the particular information you want to display (see Figure 6-25).

delta distance: The projected distance in the horizontal or vertical planes between two points.

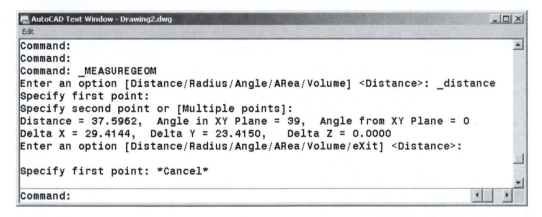

Distance

Figure 6-23

The **Distance** icon on
the **Inquiry** toolbar

Figure 6-24

Results of the **DISTance** command

Area

The **AREA** command (see Figure 6-26) calculates the area of a closed figure or series of selected points (see Figure 6-27). The value is expressed in the square of the current drawing distance units. For example, in architectural units (typically square inches) an alternative unit will typically be shown (such as square feet) in brackets. This command will also calculate the total perimeter of the selected entity or points.

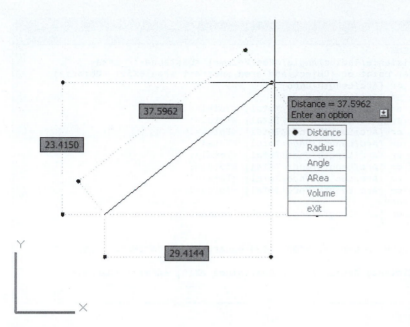

Figure 6-25

Dynamic viewing during the **DISTance** command

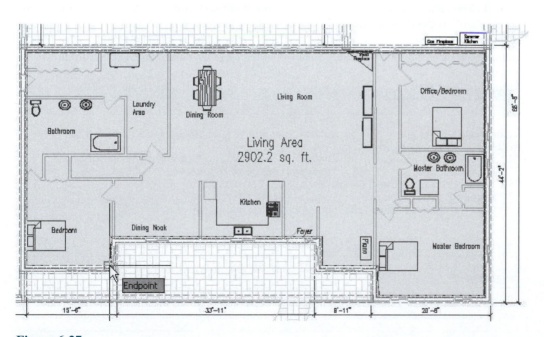

Figure 6-26

Area icon on the **Inquiry** toolbar

Figure 6-27

Dynamic window during the **AREA** command operation

The default input is to select a series of corner points. After you select the last point, you press **<Enter>** to close the figure, and the program calculates the area (see Figure 6-28). To select a closed entity such as a circle or polygon, you should exercise the **Object** option by typing **O <Enter>**. Then you will be prompted to select the object. Remember that this is a single-selection process using the pick box. The object selected should represent a closed boundary area for best results. After selecting the object, press **<Enter>** to conclude the command and see the result.

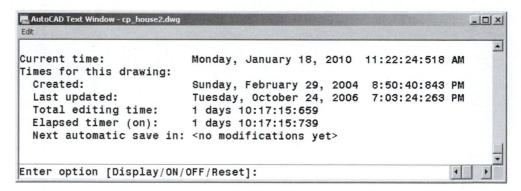

Figure 6-28

Results of the **AREA** command

Time

The **TIME** command uses the clock within your computer system to keep track of information related to the drawing file (see Figure 6-29). Information on when the drawing file was first created, when the file was last updated, and total editing and elapsed times in the file are among the information displayed. The information can be in the 24-hour time format.

```
AutoCAD Text Window - cp_house2.dwg                            _ □ ×
 Edit

Current time:              Monday, January 18, 2010   11:22:24:518 AM
Times for this drawing:
  Created:                 Sunday, February 29, 2004   8:50:40:843 PM
  Last updated:            Tuesday, October 24, 2006   7:03:24:263 PM
  Total editing time:      1 days 10:17:15:659
  Elapsed timer (on):      1 days 10:17:15:739
  Next automatic save in:  <no modifications yet>

Enter option [Display/ON/OFF/Reset]:
```

Figure 6-29

Results of the **TIME** command

JOB SKILLS

You need to log the time spent on each project. The use of the **TIME** command will allow for accurate individual session times along with total accumulated time spent on the project.

Status

The **STATUS** command displays information related to the drawing file through a variety of system variables. **Drawing Limits, GRID** and **SNAP** settings, and current **Property Settings** are included in the information displayed in the resulting text window (see Figure 6-30). The **STATUS** command also reports information about a file's size as well as disk space available (free), temporary disk space, available RAM memory, and swap file space available on the local disk drive.

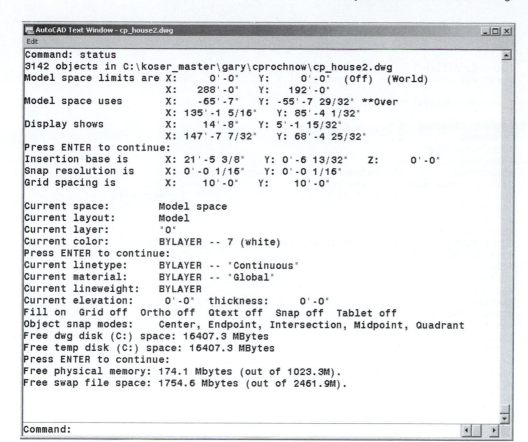

```
AutoCAD Text Window - cp_house2.dwg                                    _ □ ×
Edit
Command: status
3142 objects in C:\koser_master\gary\cprochnow\cp_house2.dwg
Model space limits are X:      0'-0"   Y:      0'-0"  (Off)  (World)
                       X:    288'-0"   Y:    192'-0"
Model space uses       X:    -65'-7"   Y:  -55'-7 29/32" **Over
                       X:  135'-1 5/16"  Y: 85'-4 1/32"
Display shows          X:     14'-8"   Y: 5'-1 15/32"
                       X:  147'-7 7/32"  Y: 68'-4 25/32"
Press ENTER to continue:
Insertion base is      X: 21'-5 3/8"   Y: 0'-6 13/32"   Z:      0'-0"
Snap resolution is     X: 0'-0 1/16"   Y: 0'-0 1/16"
Grid spacing is        X:    10'-0"    Y:    10'-0"

Current space:         Model space
Current layout:        Model
Current layer:         "0"
Current color:         BYLAYER -- 7 (white)
Press ENTER to continue:
Current linetype:      BYLAYER -- "Continuous"
Current material:      BYLAYER -- "Global"
Current lineweight:    BYLAYER
Current elevation:     0'-0"  thickness:      0'-0"
Fill on  Grid off  Ortho off  Qtext off  Snap off  Tablet off
Object snap modes:     Center, Endpoint, Intersection, Midpoint, Quadrant
Free dwg disk (C:) space: 16407.3 MBytes
Free temp disk (C:) space: 16407.3 MBytes
Press ENTER to continue:
Free physical memory: 174.1 Mbytes (out of 1023.3M).
Free swap file space: 1754.6 Mbytes (out of 2461.9M).

Command:
```

Figure 6-30

Results of the **STATUS** command

EXERCISE 6-1   **INQUIRIES ON A DRAWING**

■ Open the **Taisei Detail Plan** drawing from the **C:\Program Files\AutoCAD 2011\Sample** folder or access this drawing from the student data files.

■ Using the **TIME** command, find the total elapsed time in this file.

■ Using the **LIST** command, retrieve the name of the block that contains the bathtub and toilet.

■ Zoom in on the upper right area of the drawing.

■ What is the length of one of the red lines that form the "x" in the box?

To access student data files, go to **www.pearsondesigncentral.com.**

System Variable

The **SETVAR** command allows you to enter a *system variable* name, which in turn displays the current value as a default. Most of the system variables can be controlled through the command line by keying in the name of the variable. Options available may or may not be shown and often are just an **On/Off** or **0/1** toggle. Some variables are also set in other command prompts or command options such as **Fillet Radius** or **Linetype Scale.**

> **NOTE:**
>
> Some system variables are listed as "read only" and are not available for change.

system variable: One of a series of commands that control the settings for the operational environment.

To view all the current settings of the variables, you can execute a **SETVAR** command followed by a question mark (**?**). For a complete list of the current variables and their values, type an asterisk or star (*****) as a wildcard input (see Figure 6-31). To change the variable setting, type the variable name into the command line prompt, then change the value through alphanumeric input as directed by the variable.

Figure 6-31

Typical results of the
SETVAR command

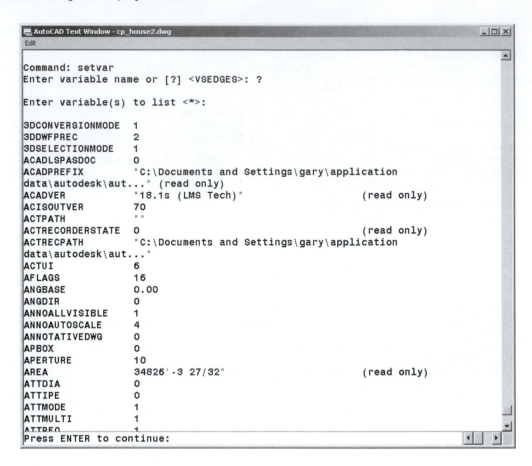

```
AutoCAD Text Window - cp_house2.dwg                                    _|□|×|
Edit

Command: setvar
Enter variable name or [?] <VSEDGES>: ?

Enter variable(s) to list <*>:

3DCONVERSIONMODE   1
3DDWFPREC          2
3DSELECTIONMODE    1
ACADLSPASDOC       0
ACADPREFIX         "C:\Documents and Settings\gary\application
data\autodesk\aut..." (read only)
ACADVER            "18.1s (LMS Tech)"              (read only)
ACISOUTVER         70
ACTPATH            ""
ACTRECORDERSTATE   0                               (read only)
ACTRECPATH         "C:\Documents and Settings\gary\application
data\autodesk\aut..."
ACTUI              6
AFLAGS             16
ANGBASE            0.00
ANGDIR             0
ANNOALLVISIBLE     1
ANNOAUTOSCALE      4
ANNOTATIVEDWG      0
APBOX              0
APERTURE           10
AREA               34826'-3 27/32"                 (read only)
ATTDIA             0
ATTIPE             0
ATTMODE            1
ATTMULTI           1
ATTREQ             1
Press ENTER to continue:
```

Chapter Summary

The viewing and inquiry commands presented in this chapter enable you to control the appearance of your drawing on the screen display regardless of how large the drawing is. We first looked at the **REDRAW** and **REGEN** (regeneration) commands, which refresh the screen display. This prepared us for the study of the viewing commands: **Zoom Realtime** and **Pan Realtime**. The **ZOOM** command and its various options allow you to modify the screen display by changing the magnification of your drawing using either the mouse wheel or left mouse button. The various **PAN** operations, controlled by the left mouse button or mouse wheel, slide the screen display in all four directions, enabling you to expose any parts of your drawing that fall outside the screen display's viewing area. Next, we examined the inquiry commands, **LIST, ID Point, DISTance, AREA, TIME,** and **STATUS.** These commands obtain and display database information about individual drawing entities as well as information regarding the complete drawing file. Finally, we introduced the **SETVAR** command. This command displays the value of an individual system variable that you specify at the text prompt. This command can also show a list of the current settings of all system variables that control the operational environment.

Chapter Tutorials

A Tutorial 6-1: *Inquiry—Architecture*

1. Open the **Wilhome** drawing file in the **Samples** folder of your AutoCAD program or access it from the student data files (see Figure 6-32).

To access student data files, go to
www.pearsondesigncentral.com.

Zoom Here

Figure 6-32

Wilhome drawing

2. **ZOOM** into the kitchen area indicated by the circle using any of the **ZOOM** command options (see Figure 6-33).

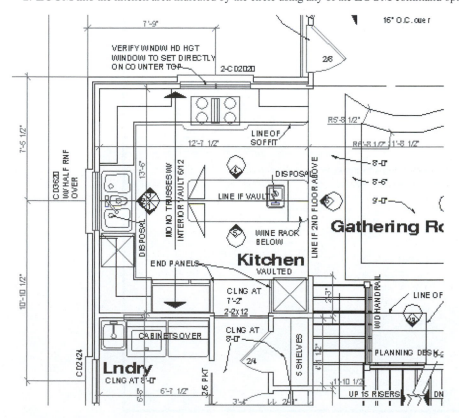

Figure 6-33

Kitchen view of Wilhome drawing

3. Invoke the **LIST** command and select the following in order and view the various information:

    a. The Sink, the Stove, the Refrigerator

    b. One of the Green Upper Cabinet Lines

      c. One of the Cyan Text entities

      d. The Magenta Dimensions

      e. Other entities you may wish to examine.

    4. Using the **AREA** command, pick points to calculate the area of the kitchen (see Figure 6-34).

```
Command: area
Specify first corner point or [Object/Add/Subtract]: end of
Specify next corner point or press ENTER for total: end of
Specify next corner point or press ENTER for total: end of
Specify next corner point or press ENTER for total: end of
Specify next corner point or press ENTER for total:
Area = 25078.4 square in. (174.156 square ft.), Perimeter = 52'-10"
Command:
```

Figure 6-34

Command line view of **AREA** command

    5. **PAN** and **ZOOM** as needed to the upper right area of the house plan to show the Grand Room. What is the area of this room? Use the **LIST** command to determine whether there are any blocks in this room. (See Figure 6-35.) Using the **ID Point** command, examine the corners of the room. What **UNITS** are in use in this drawing?

```
Edit
Select objects:

                    BLOCK REFERENCE   Layer: "MPFIXTURE"
                            Space: Model space
                    Handle = 356d
       Block Name: "KSINK-03"
                at point, X=    58'-1"  Y=    65'-3"  Z=      0'-0"
    X scale factor:       1.0
Press ENTER to continue:
    Y scale factor:       1.0
    rotation angle: 90d0'0.0000"
    Z scale factor:       1.0
   Scale uniformly: No
   Allow exploding: Yes

                    ATTRIBUTE   Layer: "MPFIXTSPEC"
                            Space: Model space
                    Handle = 356e
            Style = "STANDARD"
            Font file = txt.shx
            center point, X=59'-6 1/2"  Y=    66'-3"  Z=      0'-0"
            height      0'-1"
             value American Standard
               tag MFR
         rotation angle 90d0'0.0000"
            width scale factor       1.0
        obliquing angle 0d0'0.0000"
            flags invisible   preset
         generation normal

Press ENTER to continue:
                    ATTRIBUTE   Layer: "MPFIXTSPEC"
                            Space: Model space
Press ENTER to continue:
```

Figure 6-35

Command line view of **LIST** command

    6. Using the **DISTance** command, check a few of the dimensions to verify correctness.

    7. Close the drawing and **do not save** any changes.

M Tutorial 6-2: *Inquiry—Mechanical*

1. Open the **Welding Fixture Model** drawing file (see Figure 6-36) in the **Samples** folder of your AutoCAD program or access it from the student data files.

To access student data files, go to **www.pearsondesigncentral.com.**

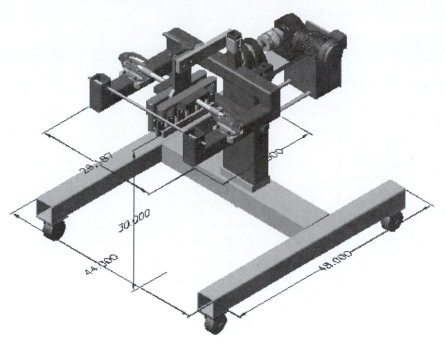

Figure 6-36

Welding Fixture drawing

2. Use the **DISTance** command to verify the dimensions shown.

3. Use the **LIST** command to determine what objects other than **3D_Solids** are in the drawing.

4. Determine the units used in this drawing with the **STATUS** command.

5. Close the drawing and **do not save** any changes.

G Tutorial 6-3: *Inquiry—Civil*

1. Open the **Lots and Roads** drawing (see Figure 6-37) file from the student data files.

2. Use the **DISTance** command to verify the lot line dimensions shown.

To access student data files, go to **www.pearsondesigncentral.com.**

3. Use the **LIST** command to determine the length of the roadway centerlines.

4. Check various lot areas using the **AREA** command. Which lot is the biggest? Which is the smallest?

5. Determine the units used in this drawing with the **STATUS** command. Change units and repeat Steps 3 and 4.

6. Close the drawing and **do not save** any changes.

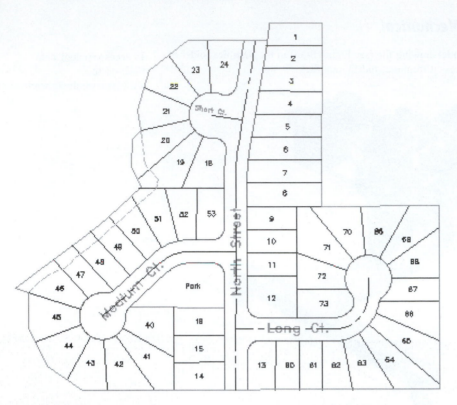

Figure 6-37

Typical subdivision layout

Chapter Test Questions

Multiple Choice

Circle the correct answer.

1. Which of the following commands will bring all objects in the drawing file into the display screen no matter where they are in space?

   a. **Zoom All**
   b. **Zoom Dynamic**
   c. **Zoom Extents**
   d. **Zoom Aerial**

2. The wheel on the mouse can perform all the following viewing commands **except**

   a. **PAN**
   b. **Zoom In**
   c. **Zoom Window**
   d. **Zoom Extents**

3. The **DISTance** command is found in the _____ menu.

   a. **Inquiry**
   b. **Format**

   c. **Modify**
   d. **Input**

4. The **CLEANSCREEN** command will

   a. Remove all lost data
   b. Refresh the drawing view
   c. Remove all drawing blips
   d. Remove all toolbars

5. The **LIST** command will **not** show information about an object's

   a. Properties
   b. Handle number
   c. Coordinates
   d. System variables

Matching

Write the number of the correct answer on the line.

a. **REGEN** _____

b. **REDRAW** _____

c. **Zoom Window** _____

d. Transparent command _____

e. **SETVAR** _____

1. Executed from within a command

2. System variable

3. Refreshes the screen

4. Recalculates the screen display

5. Defines the next area of the display

True or False

Circle the correct answer.

1. **True or False: Zoom Previous** has no limit to the number of times it can go back.

2. **True or False:** The **AREA** command will also calculate the perimeter of the zone.

3. **True or False:** The **DISTance** command requires the user to object snap each point.

4. **True or False:** The **TIME** command shows when a drawing was created.

5. **True or False:** The **STATUS** command will display information related to the drawing file through system variables.

Chapter Projects

Project 6-1 [INTERMEDIATE]

Using the **Inquiry** commands, find the "oldest" drawing in the AutoCAD **Samples** folder. Find the one with the least/most editing time. Which one has the smallest/largest file size? What are some of the block names in these drawings?

Project 6-2 [INTERMEDIATE]

Using the **Inquiry** commands, examine your drawings from Chapter 5. Which has the smallest/largest area? Which has the smallest/largest file size? Which took the least/most time to edit?

Chapter Practice Exercises

G Practice Exercise 6-1: *PAN and ZOOM* [BASIC]

1. Start AutoCAD.

2. Pick the **File** menu and choose **OPEN**.

3. Using the drop-down area at the top of the **Select File** dialog box, go to the AutoCAD **Samples** folder or access the student data files.

4. Scroll through the list of drawing files **(.dwg)** and choose one to open by picking the **OPEN** button in the lower right of the dialog box:

   a. **Architectural Drawings**—8th Floor, Hotel, Hummer, Stadium, Taisei, or Wilhome

   b. **Building Services**—8th Floor

   c. **Civil Drawings**—Hotel or SPCA Site Plan

To access student data files, go to **www.pearsondesigncentral.com.**

    d. **Facilities Management**—Db_samp
    e. **Landscaping**—SPCA Site Plan
    f. **Mechanical**—Oil Module, Welding Fixture 1, or Welding Fixture Model
    g. **Presentation**—Hotel, Hummer, Stadium, or Welding Fixture Model
    h. **Process Piping**—Oil Module
    i. **Structural**—MKMPlan or Oil Module

5. Practice using the mouse wheel, if you have one, to **ZOOM** and **PAN**.

6. Use a mixture of **ZOOM** and **PAN** as well as the **Realtime** options to move around and examine the drawing.

7. When finished, close the drawing and answer **No** to saving your changes.

8. Exit AutoCAD or return to Step 4 and repeat this exercise using another drawing.

(G) Practice Exercise 6-2: *Inquiry Commands* [INTERMEDIATE]

1. Start AutoCAD.

2. Pick the **File** menu and choose **OPEN**.

3. Using the drop-down area at the top of the **Select File** dialog box, go to the AutoCAD **Samples** folder or access the student data files.

4. Scroll through the list of drawing files **(.dwg),** choose one to open, and pick the **OPEN** button in the lower right of the dialog box:

    a. **Architectural Drawings**—8th Floor, Hotel, Hummer, Stadium, Taisei, or Wilhome
    b. **Building Services**—8th Floor
    c. **Civil Drawings**—Hotel or SPCA Site Plan
    d. **Facilities Management**—Db_samp
    e. **Landscaping**—SPCA Site Plan
    f. **Mechanical**—Oil Module, Welding Fixture 1, or Welding Fixture Model
    g. **Presentation**—Hotel, Hummer, Stadium, or Welding Fixture Model
    h. **Process Piping**—Oil Module
    i. **Structural**—MKMPlan or Oil Module

5. Use a mixture of **Inquiry** menu commands to examine the entities in the drawing and learn about the drawing.

6. When finished, close the drawing and answer **No** to the saving of changes.

7. Exit AutoCAD or return to Step 4 and repeat this exercise using another drawing.

To access student data files, go to **www.pearsondesigncentral.com.**

7 Elementary Dimensioning

CHAPTER OBJECTIVES

- Identify the items that create a dimension.
- Define and describe the basic dimensioning concepts of size and shape description.
- Demonstrate the use of the standard dimensioning methods.
- Create, justify, and edit dimension annotations.
- Construct various dimension styles.

Introduction

The general concept of dimensioning is to document the size and shape of a part or feature through the drawing file. The ultimate result of a well-dimensioned drawing is that someone can manufacture, inspect, or assemble the part; build the house; or create the design based on the dimensions. This unit covers AutoCAD's ability to create annotations and to document the size and shape of a drawing.

Dimensioning Concepts

AutoCAD has a very extensive series of commands used for the description of a drawing's shape and size within the dimensioning commands. This series of commands utilizes more than 70 system variables to control the look and placement of dimensions on a drawing. These settings form a *dimension style*. Creating the most common settings as a **DIMension STYLE** will make the dimensioning procedure quick and efficient.

dimension style: A collection of system variables that control the creation and look of a dimensional entity.

> ### JOB SKILLS
>
> AutoCAD has an outstanding series of dimensioning tools that can be useful when you understand the concepts of size and shape description. There is no magic in the dimension commands; you must understand these concepts together with the dimensioning tools to create and successfully annotate a drawing.

This flexibility allows you to accommodate changes to a dimension style that reflect the standard practices adopted in any of the engineering disciplines. A production or construction worker should never be required to calculate or assume any dimension needed to fabricate the part. Although the rules and practices of dimensioning are important in the description of a drawing's shape and size, in this chapter we are going to concentrate on the creation of the dimensioning elements. We will discuss some of the common dimensioning practices as they relate to the creation and placement of dimensions. If you need a complete description or explanation of a specific engineering's dimensioning practices, you should research the topic of dimensioning standards in an engineering graphics textbook describing the graphic language used to communicate size and shape descriptions for the engineering discipline in which you are working.

FOR MORE DETAILS   For more information on drafting standards and dimensioning, contact the American National Standards Institute (www.ansi.org) regarding Drafting Standard Y14.

Dimensioning Terminology

linear dimension: A straight-line distance between two points in space.

radial dimension: A dimension describing the center point and radius/diameter of a circle or an arc.

angular dimension: The description of the acute or obtuse angle between two lines.

ordinate dimension: A method of dimensioning describing the X, Y, and Z locations of a feature based on a fixed origin or datum.

leader: A text-based entity used to add clarification to a detail.

AutoCAD has commands (see Figures 7-1, 7-2, 7-3, and 7-4) that produce *linear, radial, angular,* and *ordinate dimensions.* Linear refers to the distance between two points, radial is a description of an arc or circle, angular depicts the acute or obtuse angle between two lines, and ordinate is a feature-based dimensioning type relating all dimensions to a datum or fixed origin. The fifth type of dimension feature is a *leader*, which is a text-based item used to add notes and other information to true dimensions. The result of a **Dimension** command is a series of lines, arrowheads, or other similar terminators along with text that relate to the points or entities selected (see Figure 7-5). These dimension entities are blocked together with an associative quality, so all parts of the dimension are treated as one entity. Furthermore, the dimension is associated with a location on the drawing. Changes made to the drawing will immediately update the dimension if any element within the dimension changes. The related elements will adjust accordingly, reflecting the new information.

Dimensioning uses several terms unique to the topic. The following definitions are related to the parts of a dimension as well as terms used in the geometric description of a drawing.

- **Dimension line** A graphic representation of the direction that is being described (see Figure 7-6). Dimension lines have related text giving the distance between the terminators attached to the ends of the dimension line. Dimension lines are offset parallel to the entities being dimensioned. When-

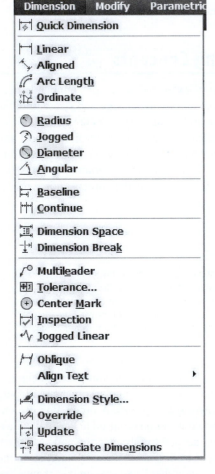

Figure 7-1

Dimension menu

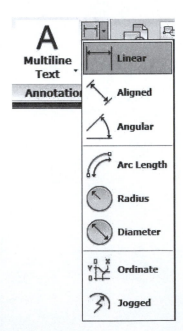

Figure 7-3

Dimension tools flyout from the **Home** ribbon

Figure 7-2

The **Dimension** toolbar

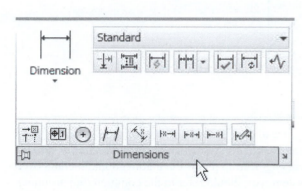

Figure 7-4

Dimension tab expanded from the **Annotate** ribbon

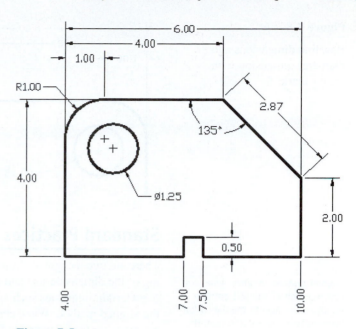

Figure 7-5

Typical dimensions in various modes

ever possible, a dimension line should be placed between the views describing the object. Clarity and legibility are two of the main issues when placing dimensions, so you should avoid placing dimensions on a drawing unless absolutely necessary. A dimension line can be one thin solid line with the text placed above the line or a line with a break with the text placed in the gap between the two parts of the dimension line. These conventions are based on the engineering discipline you are working in and controlled through the **Dimension Style Manager**.

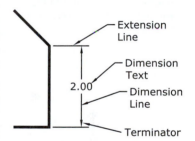

Figure 7-6

The parts of a dimension labeled with leaders

- **Extension line** A continuation of an edge or location of a feature (see Figure 7-6). An extension line should never touch the object to which it is related. An extension line offset or gap distance is programmed into the creation of a dimension to ensure clarity. Extension lines continue past the last terminator used in the dimension sequence. This offset and continuation distance are controlled through dimension variables.

- **Dimension text** The numeric readout attached to a dimension (see Figure 7-6). This text is generated at the time the dimension is created. It reads data from the entity or points selected and calculates the distance or value for the text description. The exact text style and placement are controlled through dimension system variables.

- **Terminator** A graphic representation of the intersection between the dimension line and the extension line. Terminators (see Figure 7-6) are commonly referred to as *arrowheads*. Although other symbols such as architectural ticks, squares, and dots can be used, the arrowhead is the most-often-used termination symbol.

- **Leader** An entity that points to a specific location and has a note attached allowing the addition of any text string for the description of the detail (see Figure 7-6).

- **Continuous dimension** A style of linear dimension that strings dimensions together in a continuous line (see Figure 7-7) from the end of one dimension to the beginning of the next linear dimension.

- **Baseline dimension** A style of linear dimension that uses a datum plane or baseline as a common reference point for all dimensions (see Figure 7-8).

- **Center mark** A series of lines organized as a plus sign that marks the center point of a circle or arc. The mark can be a simple plus sign (see Figure 7-8), or it can continue past the circle or arc that is selected.

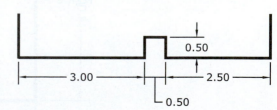

Figure 7-7

Continuous dimensioning

Figure 7-8

Baseline dimensions and
diameter dimension with
center mark

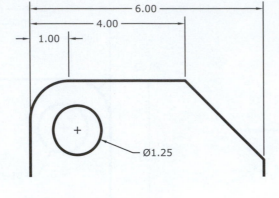

Standard Practices

aligned system: A dimensional system in which all the text entities are placed parallel to the dimension line and typically are read from the bottom or right-hand side of the document.

unidirectional system: A dimensional system in which all the text entities are written parallel to the X-axis and read from the bottom of the document.

There are two recognized forms to the practice of dimensioning. These forms relate to the reading of the dimension text and are known as the ***aligned system*** and the ***unidirectional system***.

Certain industries such as mechanical engineering prefer the unidirectional method over the aligned method. When choosing a system, you should refer to the common dimensioning practices for that industry and stay with that system's standard practices, keeping in mind that a key issue in dimensioning is clarity. Adjustments to a series of dimension variables can result in creating a dimension style used for either of these systems.

JOB SKILLS

Keep in mind the key issues in dimensioning a drawing are accuracy and clarity. The object's complete shape and size description is given through dimensional annotations and notes.

Aligned System

As the name implies, in the aligned system all dimensions are aligned with the dimension lines. The values are placed parallel to the dimension line and are read from the bottom of the drawing sheet or its right-hand edge (see Figure 7-9).

Figure 7-9

Aligned dimensions

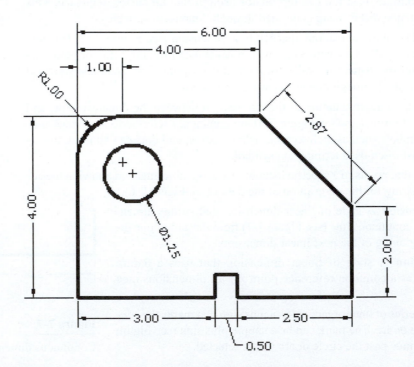

Unidirectional System

In the unidirectional system all dimensions are arranged horizontally no matter the angle of the dimension line. All dimensions are thus read from the bottom of the drawing sheet (see Figure 7-10).

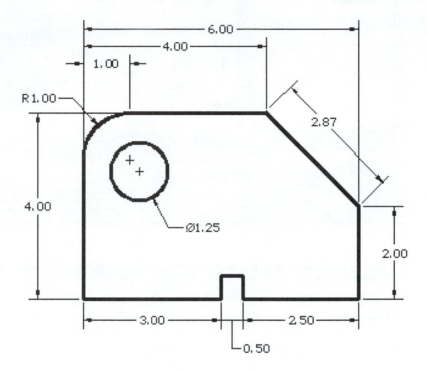

Figure 7-10

Unidirectional dimensions

Dimension Styles

AutoCAD has more than 70 dimension variables (see Appendix D) that can control the look of every part used in the creation of a dimension. You can establish values for these dimension variables; in turn, they create a look or style when placed in the drawing file. The basic AutoCAD drawing template has settings for a typical **Dimension Style** called **Standard** that works for small part drawings. This **Standard Dimension Style** provides a starting point for development of additional dimension styles to use in subsequent drawings. Some of these variables are numeric-based, such as **Text Height** or **Arrowhead Size**; others are simply **On/Off** or toggle variables; still other groups of variables control the placement of dimension features.

Dimension Style Manager

You can access the **Dimension Style Manager** (see Figure 7-11) through the **Format** menu, the **Dimension** menu, a **Dimension** toolbar icon, the expanded **Annotate** panel on the **Home** ribbon, or the **Dimensions** panel on the **Annotate** ribbon, or by typing **dimstyle** or an alias, at the command prompt. This dialog box uses a series of buttons or tabs for modifying dimension variables along with the ability to save and load different combinations of the variables under previously saved style names known as *dimension styles*. Although dimension variable settings are accessible through the command line, this dialog box gives a much more user-friendly look to altering this information. Let's take a look at the **Modify** button found on the right side of the **Dimension Style Manager** dialog box. This button produces a window with seven tabs organizing the dimension variables into categories. The following are brief descriptions of the dimension tabs within the **Dimension Style Manager**:

- **Lines** This tab has areas addressing **Dimension lines** and **Extension lines** (see Figure 7-12). The properties of color and lineweight along with physical size of the dimension and extension lines are found here. It is also possible to suppress (not show) these items.

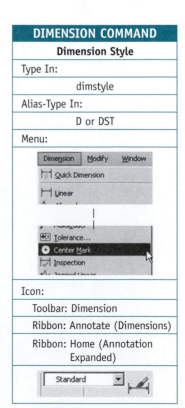

DIMENSION COMMAND
Dimension Style
Type In:
dimstyle
Alias-Type In:
D or DST
Menu:
Icon:
Toolbar: Dimension
Ribbon: Annotate (Dimensions)
Ribbon: Home (Annotation Expanded)

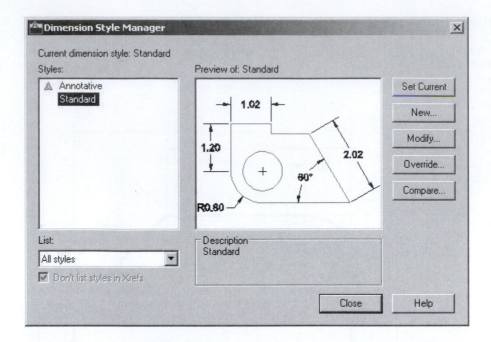

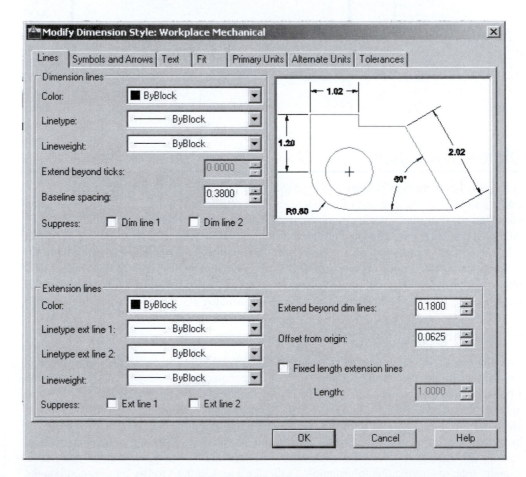

- **Symbols and Arrows** This tab (see Figure 7-13) has areas addressing **Arrowheads**, **Center marks**, **Arc length symbol**, and **Radius jog dimension**. The physical size of the symbol along with the symbol's characteristics are set and found within this tab if modifications are needed. You can view the settings in the preview window in the upper right window.

- **Text** The variables in the **Text** tab address the text appearance, including style, color, and height of the dimensional text (see Figure 7-14). A second area addresses the horizontal and

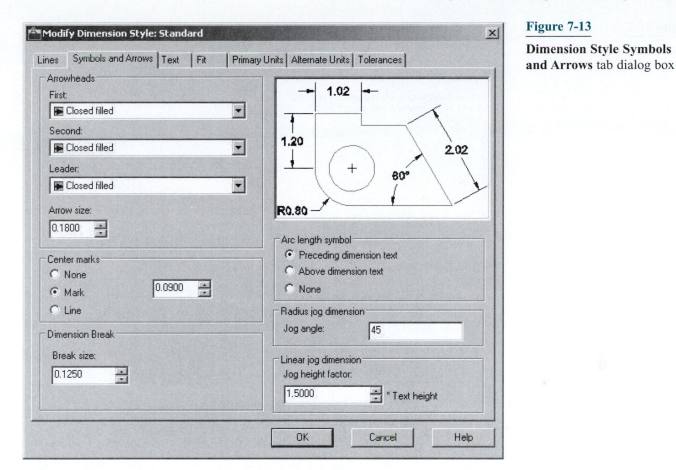

Dimension Style Symbols and Arrows tab dialog box

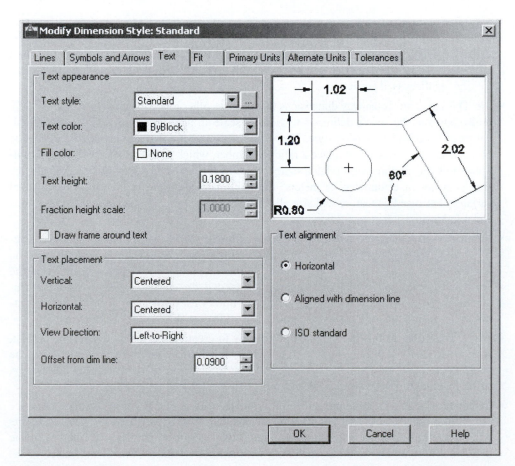

Dimension Style Text tab dialog box

NEW to
AutoCAD
2010

Figure 7-15

Dimension Style Fit tab dialog box

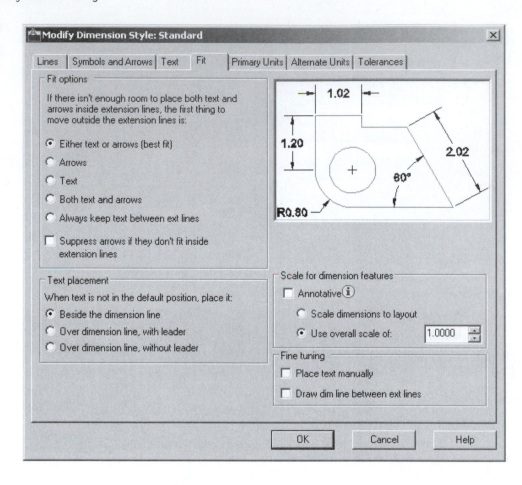

vertical placement of the text and the direction of the text, and the third area controls text alignment. This is the area that can establish an **Aligned** or **Unidirectional** form of dimensioning, as discussed earlier.

- **Fit** This tab controls the way dimensions fit as well as other related options (see Figure 7-15). It also contains the style's definition to globally scale all numeric values attached to individual variables of the dimension style. The **Scale for dimension features** area on the right side of the window allows you to place a rational number, which in turn is used as a global multiplier, to scale all dimension-related sizing values by this value. For example, you can change feet to inches or centimeters to meters. This eliminates the need to track down individual variables because this feature will size all variables at one time and maintain the proportions and relationships between entities.

- **Primary Units** This tab controls the linear output style of the dimension text (see Figure 7-16). You can specify units such as **Architectural**, **Decimal**, or **Fractional**. The control of the angle display is also housed in this tab, along with **Zero suppression**, the ability to eliminate the display of zeros not needed for clarity. Another feature, introduced in 2010, is suppression control for sub-units of a dimension. Typically, this output style of units should match the unit input style established for the drawing file.

- **Alternate Units** In this tab you have the ability to create dimensions in a second format, such as English for primary units and metric as the alternate units (see Figure 7-17). The alternate units are placed in square brackets next to or below the active dimension text. A suffix is generally needed to clarify the units of the alternate dimensions.

- **Tolerances** The final tab controls the program's ability to calculate and display tolerance dimensions (see Figure 7-18). In mechanical design, tolerances are used to ensure that parts will fit together, slide inside each other, or meet other specifications. These formats are basic to geometric tolerance methods, including symmetrical, deviation, limits, and basic.

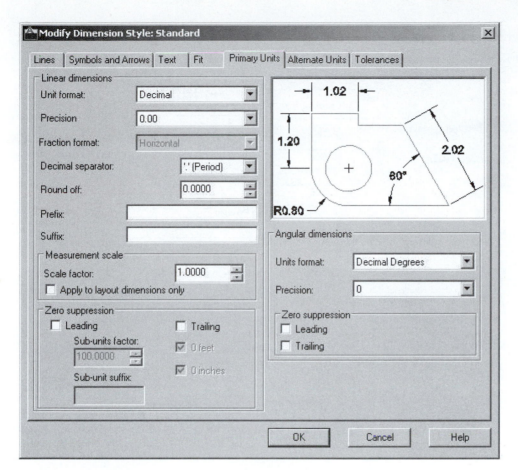

Figure 7-16

Dimension Style Primary Units tab dialog box

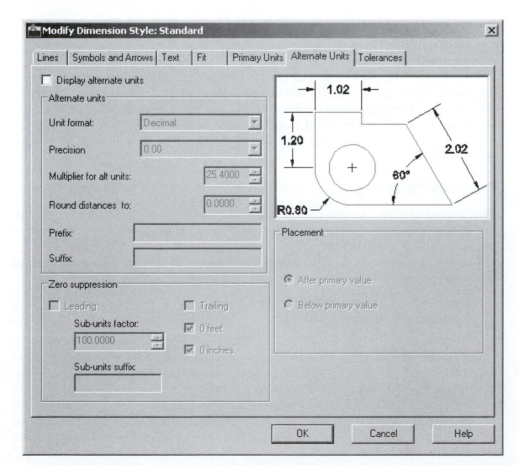

Figure 7-17

Dimension Style Alternate Units tab dialog box

Figure 7-18

Dimension Style Tolerances tab dialog box

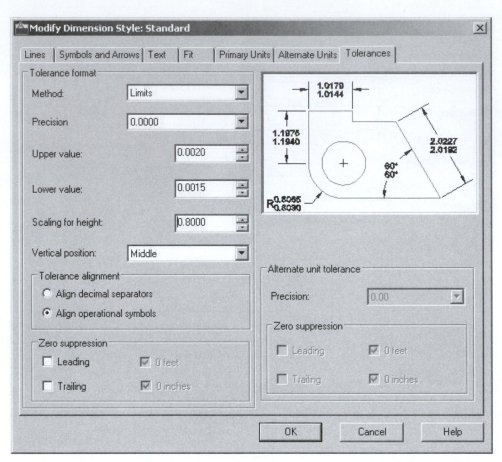

DIMENSION COMMAND
Linear Dimension
Options: Mtext, Text, Angle, Horizontal, Vertical, Rotated
Type In:
dimlinear
Alias-Type In:
DLI
Menu:

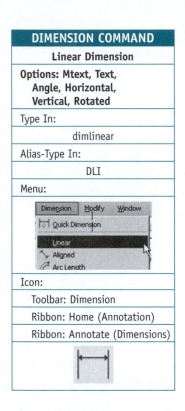

Icon:
Toolbar: Dimension
Ribbon: Home (Annotation)
Ribbon: Annotate (Dimensions)

DIMENSION COMMAND
Aligned Dimension
Options: Mtext, Text, Angle
Type In:
dimaligned
Alias-Type In:
DAL
Menu:

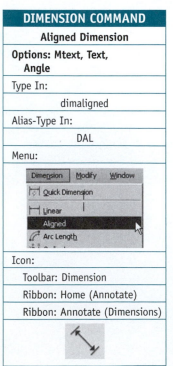

Icon:
Toolbar: Dimension
Ribbon: Home (Annotate)
Ribbon: Annotate (Dimensions)

Dimensioning Commands

AutoCAD utilizes the **Dimension** menu items, icons on the **Dimension** toolbar, or typed commands to activate all functions related to the dimensioning process. The **Dimension** menu offers a variety of techniques to create various looks to the dimensions. The four principal types of dimensions are *linear*, *radial*, *angular*, and *ordinate*.

Following is a discussion of the basic operations in creating these principal dimension types and leaders.

Linear Dimensioning

Linear dimensions are straight-line dimensions measured from one point to another. AutoCAD has two dimensional commands, **Linear** and **Aligned**, that produce this type of dimension.

With either command you will typically be prompted to define the points desired for dimensioning:

Specify first extension line origin <Select objects>
Specify second extension line origin.
Specify dimension line location.

The **Linear** command places a horizontal or vertical (projected distance on the *X*-, *Y*-, or *Z*-axis) dimension (see Figure 7-19) based on the points chosen in various methods including **Object Snap.** The dimension itself depends on the direction the mouse is dragged or where the mouse is located when the dimension line is positioned.

The **Aligned** command produces a dimension not necessarily parallel to the principal axis. It is aligned with the two points selected and shows the true length of the distance between the two points (see Figure 7-20).

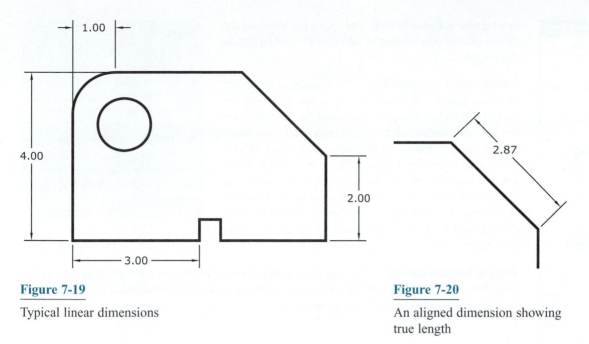

Figure 7-19

Typical linear dimensions

Figure 7-20

An aligned dimension showing true length

An option to both of these commands is to *<Select objects>*. If an object or entity is chosen, this option creates a dimension based on the length and direction of the entity selected. It is started by pressing **<Enter>** when the first command prompt message *(Select the first extension line)* is displayed and then selecting an entity in the drawing file with the following message: *Select object to dimension*. Only the single item or pick box selection is allowed, as you must place each dimension individually after choosing an object.

After the initial linear dimension is placed, there are three related linear dimension commands: **Baseline**, **Continue**, and **Jogged**. These commands can be used to create multiple dimensions quickly and are designed to be used directly following the creation of a linear or aligned dimension. Although these commands can be executed at any time, the results are more predictable when they follow the creation of a linear or aligned dimension.

Baseline Dimensioning.   **Baseline** produces a series of stacked dimensions all connected to an existing extension line. After executing the **Baseline** command, you will be prompted for the *second extension line origin*. The dimension that is created is related to the datum plane or edge of the first extension line of the initial linear dimension. To add additional dimensions you are prompted to continue picking *second extension line origin*. The result is a series of stacked dimensions as shown in Figure 7-21. If for some reason the selected dimension does not connect to the correct datum plane, you can execute an option to *Select*

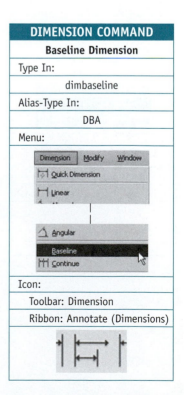

DIMENSION COMMAND
Baseline Dimension
Type In:
dimbaseline
Alias-Type In:
DBA
Menu:
Icon:
Toolbar: Dimension
Ribbon: Annotate (Dimensions)

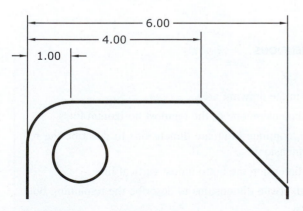

Figure 7-21

Typical baseline dimensioning

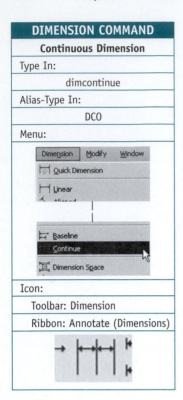

DIMENSION COMMAND
Continuous Dimension
Type In:
dimcontinue
Alias-Type In:
DCO
Menu:

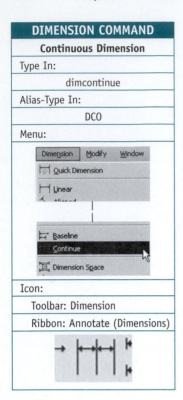

Icon:
Toolbar: Dimension
Ribbon: Annotate (Dimensions)

(and press **<Enter>**) and then specify an existing dimension line extension to serve as the initial linear dimension.

Continuous Dimensioning. The **Continue** command produces a series of dimensions in a line or string. As with the **Baseline** command you will be prompted for the *second extension line origin*, and each new linear dimension will appear on the same line as the previous linear dimension. See Figure 7-22 for an example. If for some reason the selected dimension does not connect to the correct datum plane, you can execute an option to *Select* (and press **<Enter>**) and then specify an existing dimension line extension to serve as the initial linear dimension.

Jogged Dimensioning. The **Jogged Linear** command allows for the foreshortening of the dimension line when the full length cannot be shown or would be confusing to the reader of the drawing. See Figure 7-23 for an example.

NOTE:

As with other commands in AutoCAD the location of the pick on an entity may influence the rest of the command. For example, with the **Baseline** and **Continue** dimension commands when the **Select** option is invoked, the datum selected for the basis of dimensions will be toward the closest end of the dimension line chosen.

DIMENSION COMMAND
Jogged Linear Dimension
Type In:
dimjogline
Alias-Type In:
DJL
Menu:

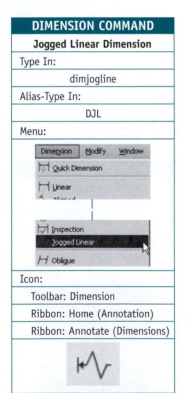

Icon:
Toolbar: Dimension
Ribbon: Home (Annotation)
Ribbon: Annotate (Dimensions)

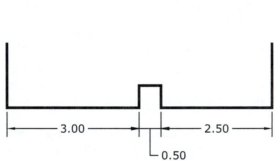

Figure 7-22

Continuous dimensions

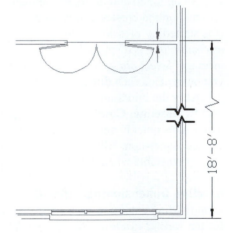

Figure 7-23

Jogged linear dimension

EXERCISE 7-1 **CREATE LINEAR DIMENSIONS**

■ Start a new drawing in AutoCAD.

■ Draw at least three rectangles in the drawing area.

■ Using the **Linear** command, dimension one of the topmost horizontal lines.

■ Using the **Baseline** command, continue to create dimensions to describe the remaining top horizontal line dimensions.

■ Using the **Linear** command, dimension the bottommost vertical line.

■ Using the **Continue** command, create dimensions to describe the remaining bottom horizontal line dimensions.

■ Repeat the preceding steps to dimension all the vertical lines.

Radial Dimensioning

Radial dimensioning displays the sizing of circles and arcs. The three commands that create radial dimensions are **Radius**, **Jogged Radius**, and **Diameter**. In all cases you will be prompted to *Select arc or circle*. Then you will be prompted for the location to place the dimension text. Depending on the type of dimension, the value of the radius or diameter of the entity selected will be displayed (see Figure 7-24). This routine also places the center mark according to the **Dimension Style** settings as shown in Figure 7-24.

The **Jogged Radius** dimension command allows for the foreshortening of the radius dimension when the full length cannot be shown or would be confusing to the reader of the drawing.

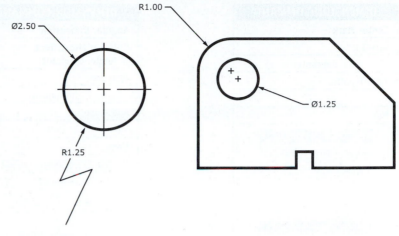

Figure 7-24

Radius, jogged radius, and diameter dimensions with center marks

Angular Dimensioning

Angular dimensioning displays and calculates the acute or obtuse angle between two entities (see Figure 7-25). To produce an angular dimension, you are prompted with the following:

Select arc, circle, line, or <specify vertex>:
Select second line.
Specify dimension arc line location.

Depending on the placement of the dimension arc line and the text, you will see a readout of the acute or obtuse angle value. Extension lines will be placed according to the dimensional arc and the entities selected. When a circle is selected along with a second point, the value can be greater than 180° depending on the placement of the dimensional arc.

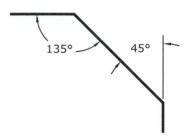

Figure 7-25

Angular dimensions

DIMENSION COMMAND
Radius Dimension
Options: Mtext, Text, Angle
Type In:
dimradius
Alias-Type In:
DRA
Menu:
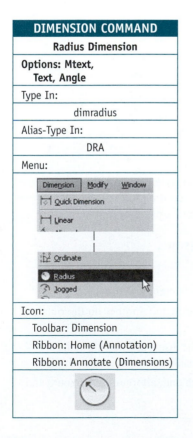
Icon:
Toolbar: Dimension
Ribbon: Home (Annotation)
Ribbon: Annotate (Dimensions)

DIMENSION COMMAND
Jogged Radius Dimension
Options: Mtext, Text, Angle, Location
Type In:
dimjogged
Alias-Type In:
DJO or JOG
Menu:
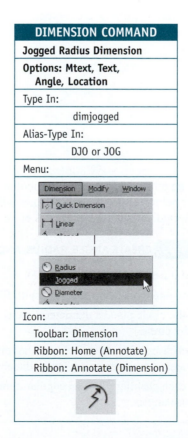
Icon:
Toolbar: Dimension
Ribbon: Home (Annotate)
Ribbon: Annotate (Dimension)

DIMENSION COMMAND
Diameter Dimension
Options: Mtext, Text, Angle
Type In:
dimdiameter
Alias-Type In:
DDI
Menu:
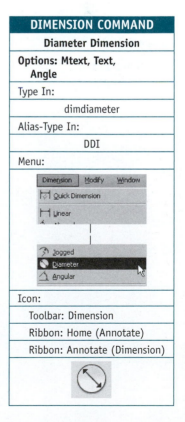
Icon:
Toolbar: Dimension
Ribbon: Home (Annotate)
Ribbon: Annotate (Dimension)

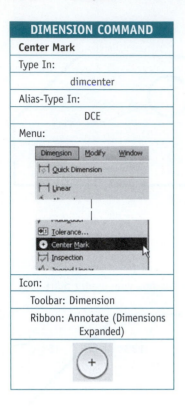

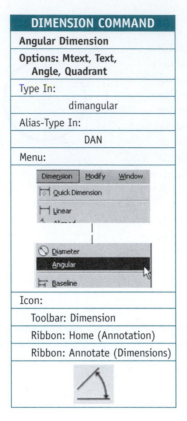

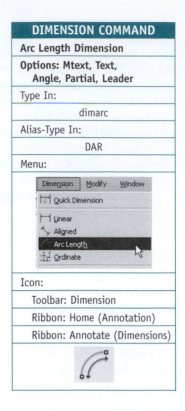

Arc Length

This dimension calculates and displays the true length of an arc entity as an object from the beginning point of the arc to its ending point (see Figure 7-26). To produce an arc length dimension, you are prompted with the following:

> Select arc or polyline arc segment
> Specify dimension arc line location

Figure 7-26

Typical arc length dimensioning

Depending on the settings of the symbol in the dimension style, you can place the dimension above or below the arc. Extension lines will be placed according to the dimension arc or the entity selected. At this time only arcs or arc segments from a polyline can be used.

EXERCISE 7-2   **CREATE ANGLE, RADIUS, AND ARC DIMENSIONS**

■ Start a new drawing in AutoCAD.

■ Draw one circle, one rectangle with fillets, and one rectangle with chamfers.

■ On the circle place a diameter dimension on the inside and another on the outside of the circle.

■ On each arc of the fillets place a radius dimension on the inside and outside in the drawing area. Also place an arc length dimension on the inside and outside of each fillet.

■ On each chamfer place an angular dimension at each end, alternating the acute and obtuse angles.

Ordinate Dimensioning

The **Ordinate** command creates a dimension that is the perpendicular distance from the current origin to the selected feature point. The dimension created will be parallel to either the *X*- or the *Y*-axis. On executing the command you will be prompted to *Specify feature location*. Although the word used is "feature," you can select any point shown in the drawing. This should be done with the aid of an **Object Snap** option to ensure accuracy. The next prompt will ask you to choose a location for text and leader placement as follows:

Specify leader endpoint or [Xdatum/Ydatum/Mtext/Text/Angle]:

The dimension produced will depend on which direction the mouse is dragged when you select the leader's endpoint. If the desired results are not seen, you can exercise an **Xdatum** or **Ydatum** option to force the dimension to the correct datum plane. The dimension text will be calculated from the current datum origin to the feature or location selected (see Figure 7-27).

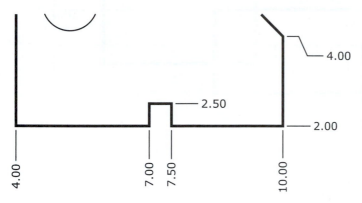

Figure 7-27

Ordinate dimension on object

EXERCISE 7-3   CREATE ORDINATE DIMENSIONS

- Start a new drawing in AutoCAD.
- Draw at least three rectangles in the drawing area.
- Place ordinate dimensions on all corners of the rectangles.

Quick Dimensioning

For placing many dimensions in a fast, single operation, AutoCAD uses a command known as **QDIM** (**Quick Dimension**). This command creates a series of dimensions based on certain parameters. You simply select—using a window, crossing window, or other selection method—the entities of the drawing you want to dimension. A series of dimensions will be created at each endpoint (see Figure 7-28) and/or center point of the entities in the selected area. These dimensions can be created with the **Continuous**, **Baseline**, **Staggered**, or **Ordinate** option (see Figure 7-29). The results of a **QDIM** command are shown in Figure 7-30. There are options available for dimensioning several circles or arcs as well as for editing previously placed strings of quick dimensions.

```
Command:  QDIM
Associative dimension priority = Endpoint
Select geometry to dimension: Specify opposite corner: 8 found
Select geometry to dimension:
```

Figure 7-28

Quick Dimension basic command prompt

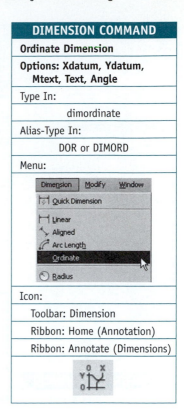

DIMENSION COMMAND

Ordinate Dimension

Options: Xdatum, Ydatum, Mtext, Text, Angle

Type In:
dimordinate

Alias-Type In:
DOR or DIMORD

Menu:

Icon:
Toolbar: Dimension
Ribbon: Home (Annotation)
Ribbon: Annotate (Dimensions)

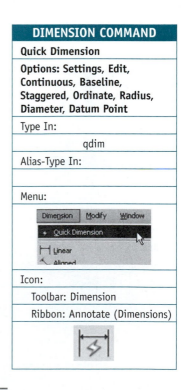

DIMENSION COMMAND

Quick Dimension

Options: Settings, Edit, Continuous, Baseline, Staggered, Ordinate, Radius, Diameter, Datum Point

Type In:
qdim

Alias-Type In:

Menu:

Icon:
Toolbar: Dimension
Ribbon: Annotate (Dimensions)

```
Specify dimension line position, or
[Continuous/Staggered/Baseline/Ordinate/Radius/Diameter/datumPoint/Edit/seTtings
] <Continuous>:

Command:
```

3.5764, 4.2181, 0.0000   SNAP GRID ORTHO POLAR OSNAP OTRACK DUCS DYN LWT MODEL

Figure 7-29

Quick Dimension style command prompts

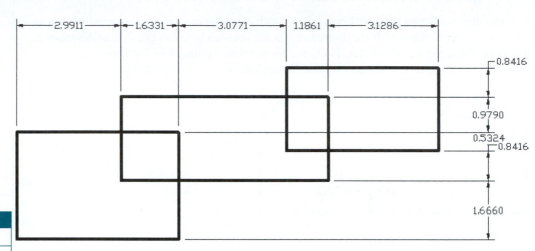

Figure 7-30

QDIM results on three overlapping rectangles

DIMENSION COMMAND
Leader Lines & Text
Type In:
leader, qleader, mleader
Alias-Type In:
LE, MLD
Menu:
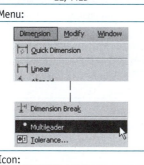
Icon:
Toolbar: Multileader
Tool Palette: Leaders
Ribbon: Home (Annotation)
Ribbon: Annotate (Multileaders)

The Leader Commands

A leader is a special object with text created through the dimensioning functions. In addition to dimensioning the shape and locations, dimensioning may include notes about the object's production, more specific information on materials, and other information needed for the proper creation of this object. These notes and directions may be connected to a particular location or may appear in the middle of an object. A leader contains four parts: an arrowhead or terminator, a leader line (straight or splined), a leader tail (sometimes called a *shoulder*), and a text or block entity. A leader (see Figure 7-31) generally starts at a specific location with the terminator (arrow, tick mark, squiggle, etc.) and continues at an angle to the object, crossing into an open area on the drawing where the text is placed. The text can be single-line or multiline depending on the user choices in the command.

LEADER and Quick Leader. The **LEADER** command is structured to create the leader line and place the text as shown by the following prompts. Only a few options are available including modifying the line from straight to splined. Text is entered in a single-line text mode and can be edited with a double click on the text or with the **Modify** commands.

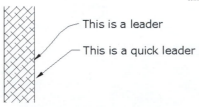

Figure 7-31

Sample of leader commands

```
Command: leader
Specify leader start point:
Specify next point:
Specify next point or [Annotation/Format/Undo]<Annotation>: f
Enter leader format option [Spline/STraight/Arrow/None]
<Exit>: s
Specify next point or [Annotation/Format/Undo] <Annotation>:
Enter next line of annotation text:  This is a leader
Enter next line of annotation text:
```

The **Quick Leader (QLEADER)** command offers more options in the form of settings (see Figures 7-32, 7-33, and 7-34), which can be set in advance to speed the creation of the leader. The command prompts enable you to modify the settings for each leader.

```
Command:  qleader
Specify first leader point, or [Settings] <Settings>:
Specify next point:
Specify next point:
Specify text width <0.0000>:
Enter first line of annotation text <Mtext>:  This is a quick leader
Enter next line of annotation text:
```

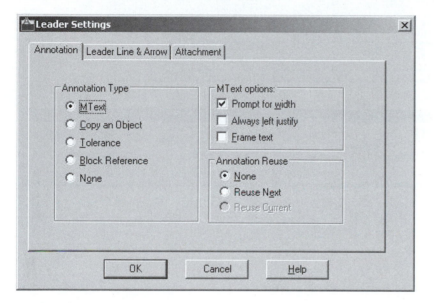

Figure 7-32

Quick Leader Settings Annotation tab dialog box

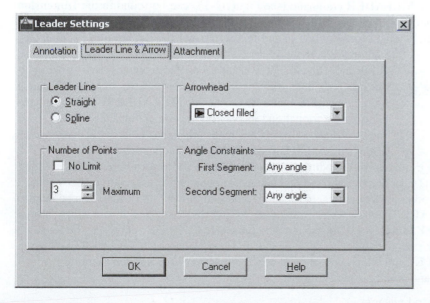

Figure 7-33

Quick Leader Settings Leader Line and Arrow tab dialog box

Figure 7-34

Quick Leader Settings
Attachment tab dialog box

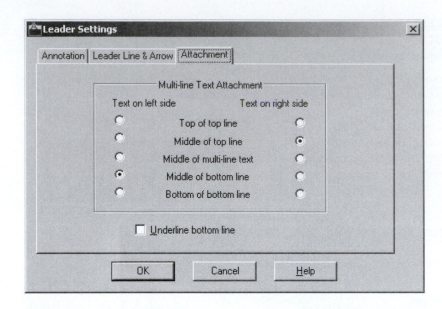

Figure 7-34

Quick Leader Settings
Attachment tab dialog box

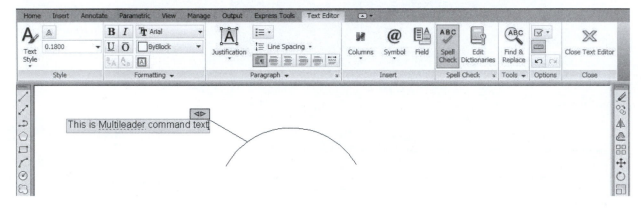

Figure 7-35

Multileader input with the **Text Editor** tab on the ribbon

MLEADER. The **MLEADER** command (see Figure 7-35) can be found in the **Dimension** menu (see Figure 7-1), on the **Multileader** toolbar (see Figure 7-36), and also on the **Annotation** panel on the **Home** ribbon or the **Leaders** panel on the **Annotate** ribbon (see Figure 7-37). You have three options to create a leader: terminator first, tail first, or content first. You can access these options through the right-click menu. Content for the leader can come from an **MTEXT** dialog box or the insertion of a **BLOCK**. The **MLEADERSTYLE** command controls the format and display options of multileaders. These styles can be created and saved much like other style editors. You can access a leader's properties through the **Modify Properties** dialog box.

Figure 7-36

Multileader toolbar

Other tools available for the editing of leaders include those for removing leader lines, creating a single leader that points to several items, and maintaining associativity between text objects and the other leader entities. In addition to these options, multileaders can be aligned with the **MLEADERALIGN** command (alias **MLA**) and collected into a single leader through the **MLEADERCOLLECT** command (alias **MLC**). These options can be found on the **Text Editor** ribbon or typed in as shown next. There is also an **MLEADEREDIT** command (alias **MLE**) with which you can add or remove leader lines and terminators.

The command prompts are as follows:

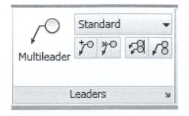

Figure 7-37

Leaders panel on the
Annotate ribbon

```
Command: mleader
Specify leader arrowhead location or [leader Landing first/Content
first/Options] <Options>: o
```

Enter an option [Leader type/leader lAnding/Content type/
Maxpoints/First angle/Second angle/eXit options] <eXit options>:l
Select a leader type [Straight/sPline/None] <Straight>:s
Enter an option [Leader type/leader lAnding/Content type/
Maxpoints/First angle/Second angle/eXit options] <Leader type>:x
Specify leader arrowhead location or [leader Landing first/Content
first/Options] <Options>:
Specify leader landing location.

The **MLEADERSTYLE** command (Figure 7-38) controls the settings of the multileader. There are three tabs (see Figures 7-39, 7-40, 7-41, and 7-42) that enable you to set the appearance for the multileader. Multileader styles can be stored and connected with an annotative scale that automatically scales objects based on layout scales for presentations or plotting.

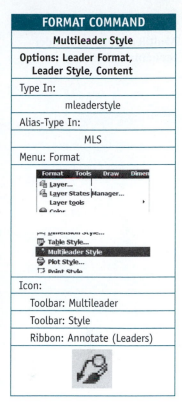

FORMAT COMMAND
Multileader Style
Options: Leader Format, Leader Style, Content
Type In:
mleaderstyle
Alias-Type In:
MLS
Menu: Format
Icon:
Toolbar: Multileader
Toolbar: Style
Ribbon: Annotate (Leaders)

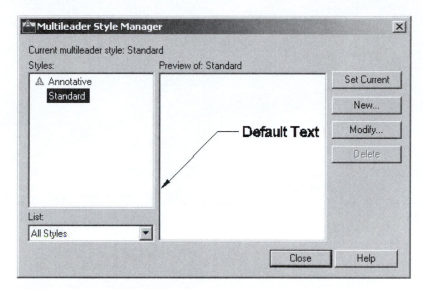

Figure 7-38

Multileader Style Manager dialog box

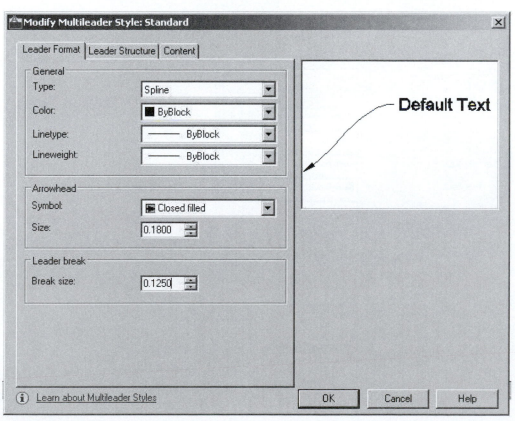

Figure 7-39

Multileader Style Leader Format tab dialog box

Figure 7-40

Multileader Style Leader Structure tab dialog box

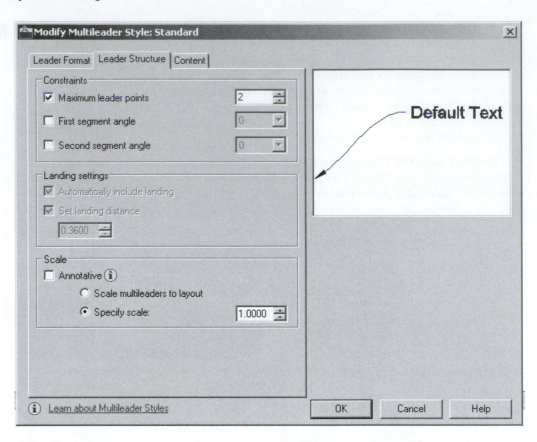

Figure 7-41

Multileader Style Content tab dialog box for horizontal alignment

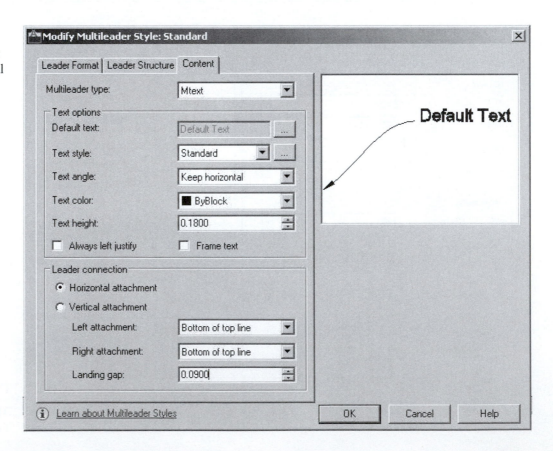

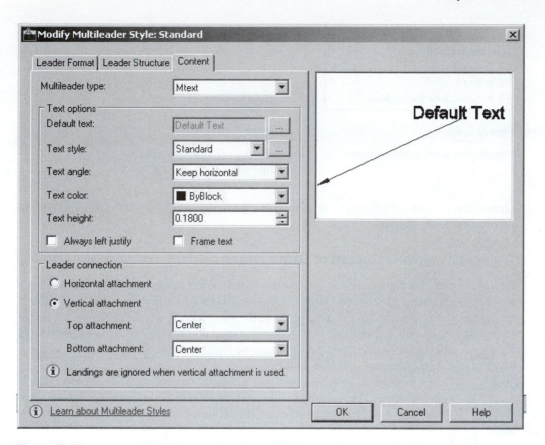

Figure 7-42

Multileader Style Content tab dialog box for vertical alignment

EXERCISE 7-4 **PLACE A LEADER**

- Start a new drawing in AutoCAD.
- Draw a rectangle from coordinates **2,2** to **6,6**.
- Type **QLEADER <Enter>** to activate the **Quick Leader** command.
- Use the midpoint of the right-side vertical line as the "First Leader Point" to start the leader to place the arrow.
- Move up and to the right (a 45° angle) a short distance to establish the "Next Point" for the leader line.
- Press **<Enter>** to end the line inputs.
- Press **<Enter>** to bypass the entry for text width.
- Type **4″ × 4″ Wood Fence Post <Enter>** to place the text in the drawing.
- Press **<Enter>** to complete the command.

Editing Dimensions

Although there are several entities within a dimension that can be changed, editing dimensions usually refers to changing the text value and related elements due to changes made to the base entity. The **Dimension Edit** menu (see Figure 7-43) and the **Dimension** toolbar (see Figure 7-44) show various edit commands. Dimensions can be modified with commands such as **STRETCH**, **SCALE**, and **ROTATE**. Dimensions can also be edited with

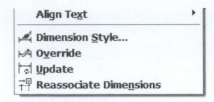

Figure 7-43

Dimension Edit menu command

Figure 7-44

Edit tools for dimensions on **Dimension** toolbar

Grips (see Chapter 11), through the **Properties** palette (see Figure 7-45), and through the **Dimension Style Manager**.

Associative/Nonassociative Dimensions

associative property: The ability to connect entities together and then make changes that will automatically be reflected in the dimension.

One of the qualities that makes editing dimensions easy is the ability to control a dimension's *associative property*. Dimensions can be linked to entities in a drawing, bringing a much higher level of intelligence to the dimension. At the same time, AutoCAD gives you the ability to flag dimensions and text that have been edited and do not reflect the current drawing's dimension style. All these controls can be found in a series of dimension variables. When a dimension has an associative property, all the dimensional entities are joined together as a single object and linked to the geometry of the object that is being selected. The system variable **DIMASSOC** has three settings that control the level of association available to a dimensional entity.

- By default this system variable is set to a value of **2**, which means that there is a full association between the dimension and the geometry. All elements of the dimension are joined as a single object, and control points are placed on the entities selected for the creation of the dimension. A no-plot layer named **Defpoints** is created to hold these control points for associativity. If the geometry changes, the dimension will also change, whether or not it is in the selected set.

- A **DIMASSOC** value of **1** creates a nonassociative relationship between the dimension and the geometry. This setting joins the elements of the dimension together, but it does not have any connection to the geometry used to create the dimension. The geometry also must be selected to have the changes affect the dimension.

- A **DIMASSOC** value of **0** constructs an exploded dimension. With this setting each element of the dimension is a separate object.

Correct use of this variable makes changing an already dimensioned drawing relatively simple. Any modification of the geometry can easily be incorporated to reflect the changed dimension value.

Updating Dimensions through Dimension Styles

All dimension (system) variables that control the look of a dimension are part of a *dimension style*. Any changes to the dimension style will affect all the dimensions currently in the drawing file that are using that particular style. The variable **DIMASSOC** controls the automatic updating of dimensions in a drawing file. As mentioned earlier, this associative property allows for changes to be passed through the geometry to the dimension. If only certain dimensions need to reflect the changes being made to the dimension style, you can use the **Update** icon (see Figure 7-44) from the **Dimension** toolbar or the **Dimension Edit** menu (Figure 7-43) to select individual dimensions for updating. This feature is currently not available on the ribbon.

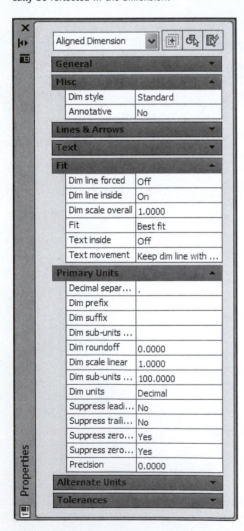

Figure 7-45

Properties palette for dimensions

Chapter Summary

This unit introduced you to the basics of dimensioning in AutoCAD, the accurate and clear documentation of the size and shape of parts or features in drawings. First, we presented the concept of dimension styles, which are groups of system variables controlling the creation and appearance of dimensional entities that enable you to generate and place dimensions on objects in your drawing quickly and efficiently. We then provided definitions of several basic terms that are used in dimensioning together with some illustrative examples. We then discussed the two standard methods of dimensioning: the aligned system, which aligns the text with the dimension line, and the unidirectional system, which arranges all dimensional text horizontally regardless of the orientation of the dimension line. We covered the features of the **Dimension Style Manager** dialog box, which allows you to select and use a dimension style from several categories of dimension variables including **Lines**, **Symbols and Arrows**, **Text**, **Fit**, **Primary Units**, **Alternate Units**, and **Tolerances**. You then learned and practiced the commands used to create linear, radial, angular, and ordinate dimensions as well as leader lines and notes. Finally, we presented the concept of editing dimensions, a process in which the text value and related elements of the dimension are altered due to changes made to the base entity, as well as the use of the **STRETCH**, **SCALE**, and **ROTATE** commands, grips, and the associative property of dimensions (controlled by the **DIMASSOC** system variable) to edit and update dimensions in a drawing.

Chapter Test Questions

Multiple Choice

Circle the correct answer.

1. Which dimension command will produce a string of in-line dimensions?
   a. **Continue**
   b. **Baseline**
   c. **Ordinate**
   d. **Linear**

2. A radial dimension is used on a
   a. Line
   b. Rectangle
   c. Circle
   d. Polygon

3. Which dimension command will produce dimensions related to a feature?
   a. **Angular**
   b. **Radial**
   c. **Linear**
   d. **Ordinate**

4. Center marks can be included with which type of dimensioning?
   a. Ordinate
   b. Radial
   c. Linear
   d. Angular

5. Which dimension command will produce a series of stacked dimensions?
   a. **Continue**
   b. **Baseline**
   c. **Ordinate**
   d. **Linear**

Matching

Write the number of the correct answer on the line.

a. Dimension style _____
b. Aligned system _____
c. Leader _____
d. Angular _____
e. Associative dimension _____

1. Used to dimension an angle
2. Set of system variables for a dimension
3. Text-based pointer
4. Link between object and dimension
5. Text parallel to the dimension line

True or False

Circle the correct answer.

1. **True or False:** Changes to a dimension style will affect only dimensions placed after the change.

2. **True or False: Quick Dimension** will create a series of linear dimensions along an object.

3. **True or False:** AutoCAD can produce dimensions in primary as well as alternate units.

4. **True or False:** The **Dimension Style Manager** controls only color and layer properties.

5. **True or False:** AutoCAD cannot produce a dimension to show an arc's length.

Chapter Projects

Project 7-1 [BASIC]

Research the various dimensioning standards as defined by the following organizations:

- ANSI (American National Standards Institute)
- ISO (International Standards Organization)
- BSI (British Standards Institute)
- ASME (American Society of Mechanical Engineers)

Project 7-2 [INTERMEDIATE]

Create a list or set of rules for proper dimensioning of a drawing. Research various engineering and architectural graphics textbooks for guidelines and standards for dimensioning.

Project 7-3 [INTERMEDIATE]

What is *overdimensioning* and why is it considered wrong? Prepare a poster with examples to compare properly dimensioned items with overdimensioned ones.

Project 7-4 [INTERMEDIATE]

Prepare a report on Geometric Dimensioning and Tolerancing (GD&T) and include the history, standards of practices, symbology, and uses. Check with area machine shops and other companies that employ GD&T practices in their operation. Do AutoCAD's dimension styles fit these operations?

Chapter Practice Exercises

Ⓜ Practice Exercise 7-1: *Dimension Styles* [BASIC]

- Start a new AutoCAD drawing based on the mechanical template you created in Chapter 4, use the standard acad.dwt template, or open a mechanical or general drawing from Chapter 5.

Creating a New Dimension Style

- Launch the **Dimension Style Manager** from the **Dimension** menu, **Format** menu, or **Dimension** toolbar, or by selecting the lower right arrow on the **Dimensions** panel on the **Annotate** ribbon (see Figure 7-46).
- Select the **New** button in the **Dimension Style Manager** (see Figure 7-47).
- Name the new style **Workplace Mechanical** and select the **Continue** button (see Figure 7-48).

Figure 7-46

The **Annotate** ribbon for dimensions and multileaders

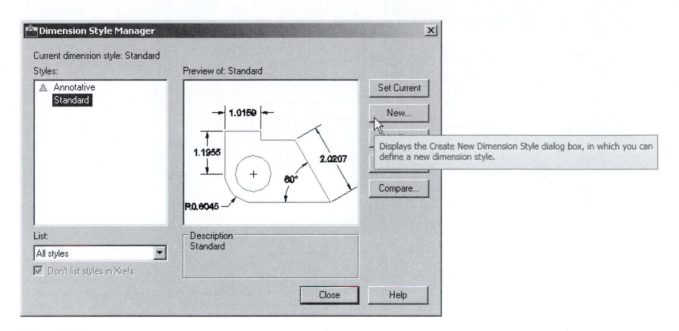

Figure 7-47

Dimension Style Manager dialog box

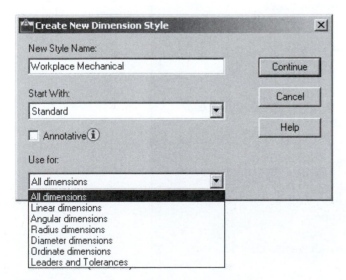

Figure 7-48

Create New Dimension Style dialog box

- Select the **Symbols and Arrows** tab and change the **Arrow size** to a value of **0.125**.
- On the same tab change the **Center marks** button to **Line** (see Figure 7-49).
- Select the **Text** tab and change the **Text height** to a value of **0.125** (see Figure 7-50).

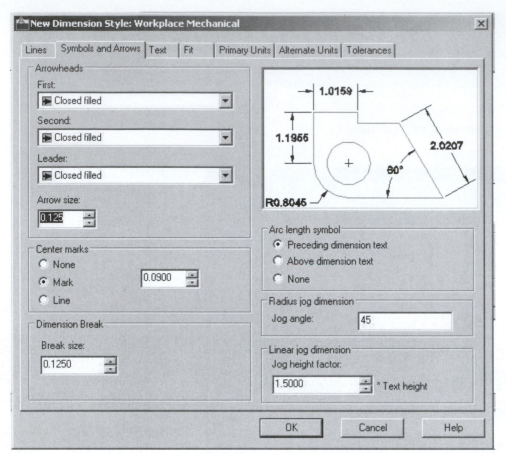

Figure 7-49

Arrowhead settings for new
dimension style

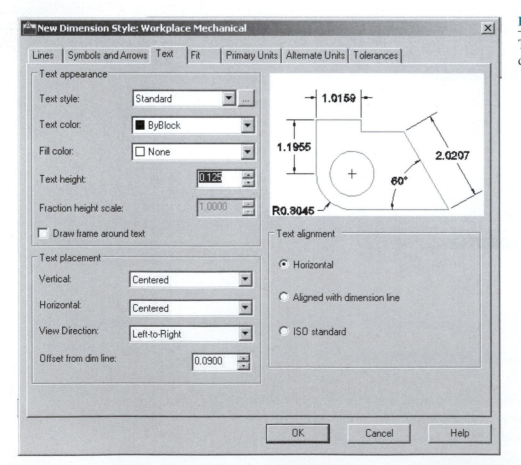

Figure 7-50

Text settings for new
dimension style

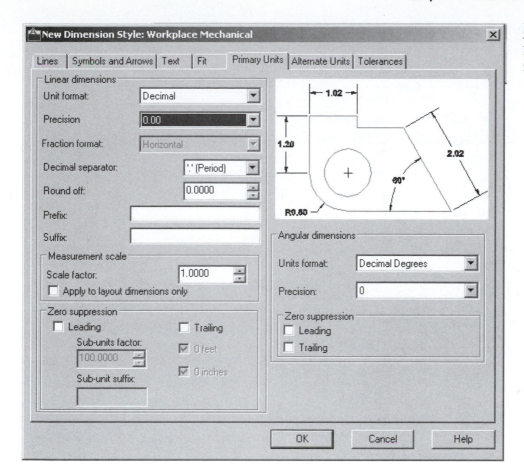

Figure 7-51

Primary Units settings for new dimension style

- Select the **Primary Units** tab and change the **Precision** setting to two-place accuracy (0.00) (see Figure 7-51).
- Select **OK** at the bottom of the dialog box to return to the **Style Manager** dialog box.
- Select **Set Current** to set the new style as current for the drawing (see Figure 7-52).
- Select **Close** to end the **Dimension Style Manager**.
- Place the dimensions on your drawings using this new dimension style.

What settings would you change to make an **Architectural** dimension style?

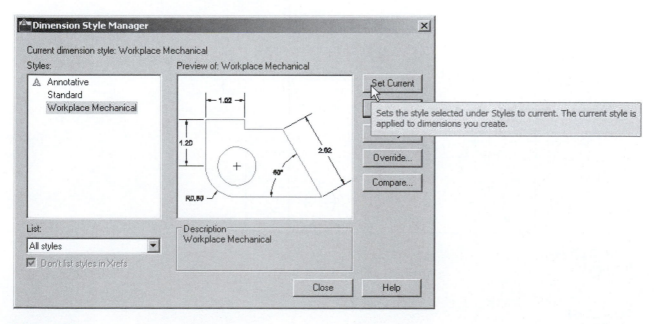

Figure 7-52

Making the new dimension style the current style

M **Practice Exercise 7-2:** *Dimensioning Linear-Angular* [BASIC]

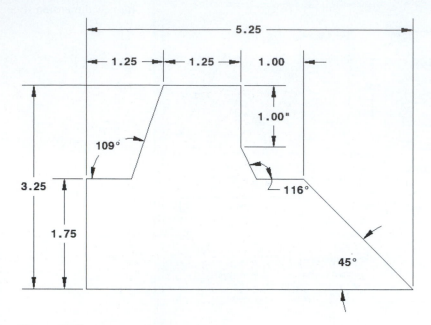

Figure 7-53

Practice Exercise 7-2 drawing and input

M **Practice Exercise 7-3:** *Dimension Ordinate* [BASIC]

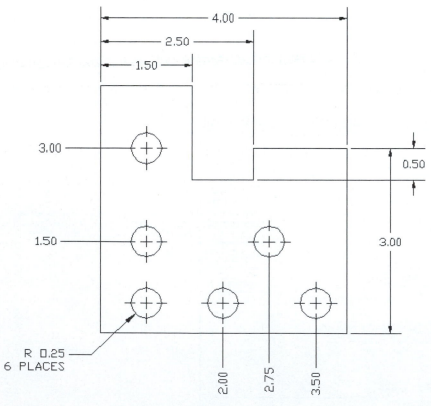

Figure 7-54

Practice Exercise 7-3 drawing and input

Practice Exercise 7-4: *Dimension-Drill Fixture* [INTERMEDIATE]

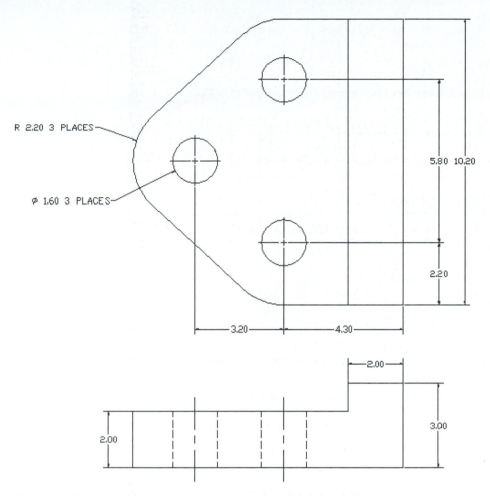

Figure 7-55

Practice Exercise 7-4 drawing and input

Ⓜ **Practice Exercise 7-5:** *Dimension-Stop Block* [INTERMEDIATE]

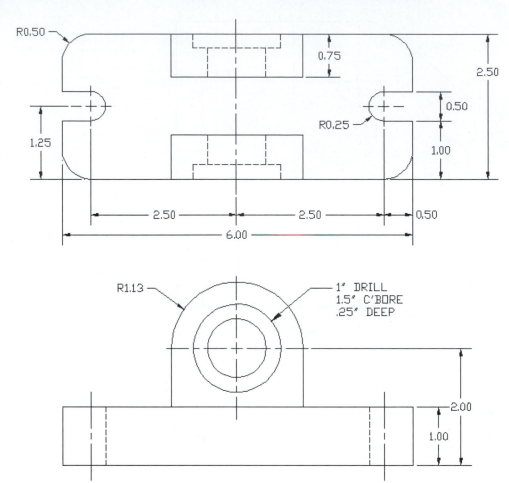

Figure 7-56

Practice Exercise 7-5 drawing and input

Fundamentals of the Printing Process

- Understand the difference between model space and layout space.
- Identify the basic plotting parameters.
- Establish plot settings for device, scale, output size, and orientation.
- Define sheet sizes and related scales.
- Create plots in both model space and layout space.

Introduction

AutoCAD software uses the term *plot* for the printing process. All the commands in the **File** menu containing the term **Plot** (see Figure 8-1) refer to the printing process needed to produce hard copies (paper versions) of the electronic drawing files created in AutoCAD.

Figure 8-1

File menu for **PLOT** command

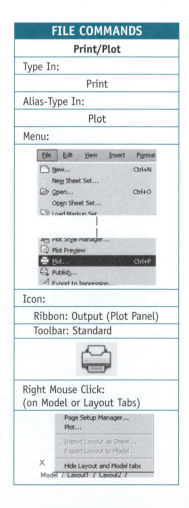

FILE COMMANDS
Print/Plot
Type In:
Print
Alias-Type In:
Plot
Menu:
Icon:
Ribbon: Output (Plot Panel)
Toolbar: Standard
Right Mouse Click: (on Model or Layout Tabs)

Plotting

plot: The process of printing through a CAD system.

Plot is synonymous with print. Plotting is the same as printing, and a plotter is the same as a printer. Prior to the boom of inkjet technology, the devices engineers used to print out their drawings were known as pen plotters. Historically, a plotter was bigger than a printer, with paper sizes up to 60″ wide. With the advancement of technology most printers are of the inkjet style. This process uses a variety of settings to control drawing data and develop a configuration understood by a plot device to print out the file on a standard engineering sheet size. What to plot, what size paper to plot on, and what drawing scale to use are questions addressed in the **Plot** process (see Figure 8-2).

> **NOTE:**
>
> Printer installation may require drivers or other additional software. An output device must be configured prior to use by AutoCAD. A network expert may be needed to assist in this process.

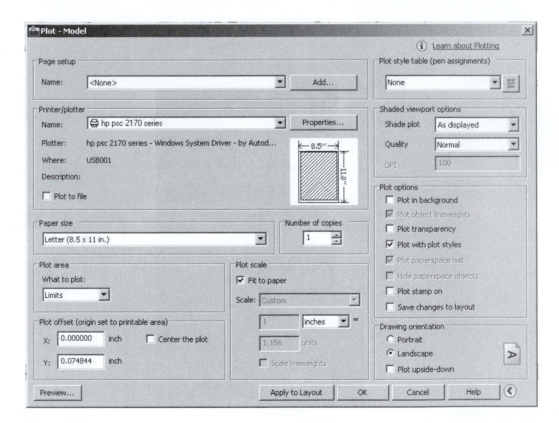

Figure 8-2

Plot settings dialog box for Model Space

Terminology Used in Plotting

There are several terms and concepts used in the plotting process that you need to be familiar with. As we look at the overall procedure, we will use terms we already know to describe the new terms needed to understand the plotting procedure.

To begin the process, a printer (plotter) needs to be configured to your system. Configuring a printer refers to the installation of the printer driver and the connection to the computer, usually through a USB cable/port, and to a power source. The last system printer used for a plot or the word "NONE" will show as the selected printer when you open the **Plot** dialog box. Other printers may be available in the selection drop-down list (see Figure 8-3). (The choices here will reflect printers configured in your Windows system.) Once your printer is listed, files can be printed from one of two worlds, model space or layout space.

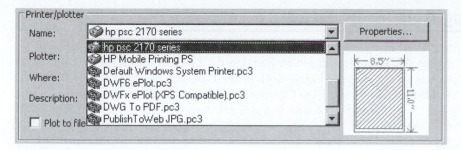

Figure 8-3

Plot device drop-down list

- *Model space* (**MSPACE** or **MS** when on a layout) is the world in which the drawing is created or produced. Model space can be unlimited in size, but as mentioned earlier, *drawing limits* produce an electronic fence that can be helpful when calculating a plotting scale.
- *Layout space* (**PSPACE** or **PS**) is a highly flexible world allowing you to create various sheet sizes and combinations of drawing views and drawing scales with annotations that are related to the final printed sheet size. The controls of the drawing to be plotted are found in the **Plot** dialog box, where you choose sheet size (Tables 8-1 and 8-2), drawing scale, and plotting style along with other plotting parameters.

model space: One of the two spaces in which entities can be created. A geometric model is created in a 3D coordinate space referred to as model space.

drawing limits: A defined area within model space used to control drawing size.

layout space: Used for creating finished views of a design with annotations and for printing or plotting, as opposed to doing design work.

TABLE 8-1	ANSI Sheet Sizes for Plotting	
Sheet Sizes Drawing Area American National Standard		
A	8.5″	11″
B	11″	17″
C	17″	22″
D	22″	34″
E	34″	44″

TABLE 8-2	ISO Sheet Sizes for Plotting	
Sheet Sizes Drawing Area (mm) International Standard		
A4	210	297
A3	297	420
A2	420	594
A1	594	841
A0	841	1189

A *plot style* is a group of settings that control the characteristics such as color, linetype, lineweight, and visibility of a drawing entity for plotting. Although this can be done in other ways, using plot styles is a convenient way to achieve uniformity in printing drawings. *Drawing scale* is the ratio between the true size of the objects to be printed in the drawing area and the sheet size for plotting.

Traditionally, this scale is 1″ = 1″ (full scale), ¼″ = 1′-0″ (architectural scale), 1 cm = 1 m (metric scale), or 1″ = 10′-0″ (civil scale). Once all the areas of the dialog box have been addressed, you can use the **Plot Preview** option to see what the results of the current configuration will produce. The image that appears in the preview window is what will be printed when the data are sent to the printer to complete the process. The AutoCAD program refers to the preview window as "what you see is what you get" (WYSIWYG), meaning the image shown will be the drawing plotted. If you do not like what you see, simply return to the **Plot** dialog box (see Figure 8-2) and make adjustments to the print configuration.

plot style: The settings that control all the parameters of a plotted file.

drawing scale: A mathematical ratio between a design's real size and the printed drawing's sheet size.

JOB SKILLS

Most engineering offices will have preestablished plot styles and plot scales based on the plotting equipment and common sheet sizes used in the office. Clients may also specify paper sizes and plot scales. Be sure the scale is appropriate before plotting.

Plotting from Model Space

When plotting from model space or **MSPACE,** you can set up one plotting scenario for the drawing. The **PLOT** command can be found in the **File** menu (see Figure 8-1), in the **Standard** toolbar as an icon (see Figure 8-4), or the **Plot** icon on the **Output** ribbon (see Figure 8-5). After executing the **PLOT** command you will establish plot settings in the **Plot** dialog box. In the simplest scenario you will select the following items from the **Plot** dialog box:

- Printer device
- Area of model space to plot
- Sheet size
- Drawing scale

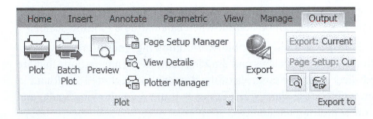

Figure 8-5

Plot icon at left end of the **Output** ribbon

Elementary Controls of Plot Settings

We will examine each area of the dialog box separately. You need to remember that at any time during the establishment of the plot settings, you can select the **Preview** button in the lower left corner of the dialog box to see a preview of your current settings.

Page Setup

All plotting scenarios can be named and saved as a **Page setup** (see Figure 8-6). By selecting a previously saved page setup, you recall a set of plotting variables as the basis or starting point of the current plotting scenario. The **Add** button on the right side will save the current plotting scenario to the list of previously saved page setups. A previously saved page setup can be selected by clicking the drop-down arrow where the name is entered.

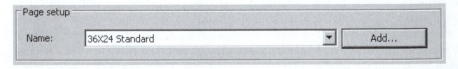

Figure 8-6

Plot Name Page setup

Printer/Plotter

The print device is selected from the **Printer/plotter** area (see Figure 8-7). The **Name** drop-down list contains all the printers currently configured to the system as well as all .PC3 printer control for other file types such as PDF, JPG, and PNG formats. If a previous page setup is not chosen, the most recently used plotter will be listed here rather than the default printer. You should always verify the plotter selection before proceeding.

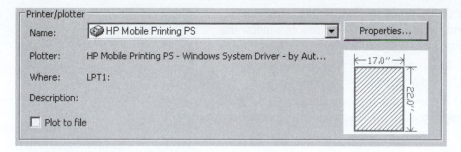

Figure 8-7

Plot device settings

In the lower left corner of the **Printer/plotter** area, there is a check box called **Plot to file**. If you check this box instead of sending the plot data to the printer, you will create a plot file with a .plt extension containing all the data needed to print the file. This file can then be printed at another location on a printer not currently connected to your system or sent via email to a plotting service.

> **NOTE:**
>
> If you are plotting to a file for offsite reproduction, you must specify a plotter. Therefore, it is important to know the plotter to be used, and it must be configured before the plot file is made.

Paper Size

The **Paper size** drop-down list contains the paper sizes available for the print device selected in the printer/plotter area. This list varies depending on the print device selected. The actual paper size is measured in length and width, with the length of the paper parallel to the X-axis and the width parallel to the Y-axis. In this area you can also specify the number of copies to be printed (see Figure 8-8).

> **JOB SKILLS**
>
> Red lines on the miniview of the paper size indicates that the drawing has entities outside the paper's edges and an adjustment is needed.

Figure 8-8

Paper size and copy information

Plot Area

The **Plot area** section specifies the area of model space to be used to calculate the print area (see Figure 8-9). There are four choices related to model space printing in AutoCAD 2011.

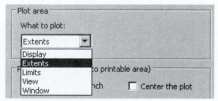

Figure 8-9

Plot area settings

1. The **Display** option calculates the current screen display for the printed area. This includes any blank or open areas around the sides of the display.

2. The **Limits** option calculates the current drawing limits (area) as the plot area. Any entities or parts of entities located outside the current drawing limits are not included in the plot calculations.

3. The **Extents** option finds all entities in the drawing file and calculates the smallest area or window that encompasses all these entities.

4. The **View** option allows you to plot any named view currently saved in the drawing file.

5. The **Window** option places you in the model space drawing screen to select an area (using a window) for the plot area.

Of all the choices mentioned you will find the most control of the plot area with the **Window** option because you can select exactly what you want to plot.

> **NOTE:**
>
> When you use the **Extents** option, the preview window may show a very small drawing as a possible print, probably because an entity was drawn way out in model space. Look around the top and edges of the preview window for any stray entities that will need to be deleted, and then reissue the **PLOT** command.

Plot Scale

Figure 8-10

Plot scale settings

The **Plot scale** area contains the information to size the plot area selected (see Figure 8-10). Traditional engineering scale factors are listed in the **Scale** drop-down list, such as $1'' = 20'$ (civil) and $\frac{1}{4}'' = 1'\text{-}0''$ (architectural). Selecting one of these scales causes the plot to be calculated based on the ratio of the model space drawing units to the plotted units. There is also a check box for scaling lineweights proportionally as well. When the box **Fit to paper** is selected, the plot scale is calculated so the plot will fit all drawing entities in the plot area to the selected paper size. You can also create a custom scale by entering your own ratio for plotting scale.

Plot Offset

All plotting instructions start from the lower left corner of the selected paper size, which is designated the origin of the plot. **Plot offset** allows you to shift the start point along the X- or Y-axis as needed. These values can be negative or positive based on the direction you need to shift the plot. You can select the **Center the plot** check box to automatically center the drawing on the current paper size based on the plot scale and paper sheet size (see Figure 8-11). When these areas of the **Plot** dialog box have been addressed, you have an option to preview the results of the page setup. The preview window shows the current results based on the parameters entered. Remember WYSIWYG, and if you like the preview, then pick the right mouse button to see a menu with the **PLOT** command to immediately send the plot to the specified printer from the Preview window. You can also press **<Enter>** or **<Esc>** to return to the **Plot** dialog box. This allows you to reset information and preview again or pick **OK** to accept the settings and send the data to the print device. If you do not like the preview, you can use **<Esc>** or **<Enter>** to return to the **Plot** dialog box to make adjustments in the settings and then produce another preview until the plot is correct.

> **NOTE:**
>
> When the annotation scale established in model space does not match the plot scale, you will receive the Plot scale annotation warning message (Figure 8-12). This mismatch will result in the plotting of any annotations using only the current plot scale and no other.

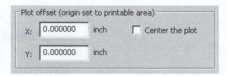

Figure 8-11

Plot offset/center settings

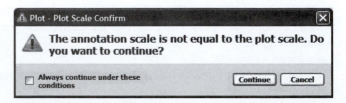

Figure 8-12

Plot scale annotation warning

EXERCISE 8-1   **PLOT FROM MODEL SPACE**

- Either open the **Quick-Start Tutorial Drawing QS-1** (see Figure 2-16 in Chapter 2) or access the **QS-1** drawing from the student data files.
- Verify that the **Model** tab at the bottom left of the drawing is selected.
- Add your name by creating a piece of text; place the text in the upper right area of the drawing.
- Select the **PLOT** command from the **File** menu.
- Plot the drawing in model space and choose the following: a valid printer, **8.5 × 11** paper size, **Landscape** orientation, scale: **1″ = 1″**, **Extents** for plot area.
- Preview the plot. If it is OK, proceed to plot the drawing. If not, return to the **Plot** dialog box and modify the settings as needed.

To access student data files, go to **www.pearsondesigncentral.com.**

Relationship between Drawing Limits and Plot Scale

In the initial setup of the drawing file, you can establish the drawing limits of the area that you will be working in. If you know the size of the paper the drawing will be printed on and the scale at which the drawing will be printed, you can include this information. For example, if you know your file will be printed on an 11″ × 17″ sheet at a scale of 1:1 (one drawing unit = one plotted unit), drawing limits can then be established with the lower left corner at 0,0 and the upper right corner at 11,17. Since paper sizes and engineering scale factors have established standards and are consistent, drawing limits can be calculated for all combinations. Here's another example. A floor plan that is being plotted on a 24″ × 36″ sheet of paper at a scale factor of ¼″ = 1′-0″ (1:48) will have drawing limits of 0,0 for the lower left and 144′,96′ for the upper right. As long as the floor plan fits into the established drawing limits at full size, the entities will fit on the sheet at the calculated scale. See Tables 8-1 and 8-2 earlier in the chapter for lists of sheet sizes. Given scale factors and sheet sizes, drawing limits can be calculated. Although this list is not all-inclusive, it does cover the most common scenarios for the three major engineering disciplines.

Layout Space

Layout space (also known as *paper space*) is an alternative area of the program where finished views of a design can be arranged, annotations can be created, and various scaled plots can be located and plotted on the same sheet. Layout space is far more flexible for documenting a design. Layout space utilizes *viewports* to display a particular view of the drawing. Zoom magnification can be used to adjust the drawing's scale based on the size of the sheet on which it will be plotted. Therefore, each viewport can have its own scale assignment (as opposed to model space plotting, where everything in the drawing is plotted at the same scale). There is virtually no limit to the number of layout space tabs that can be created in a drawing file; it depends on available memory. Although entities can be created in either model space or layout space, you can work with entities only in the space in which they were created. The exception is certain transmodal dimensions (drawn in layout space and associated to locations in model space). **Object Snap** positions can be determined from model space and used in layout space.

The simplest way to establish layout space is to begin a drawing session with a predefined AutoCAD template such as **ANSI-A**, **ANSI-B**, or **Architectural**. When you use the template option, the template includes a sheet size and sheet orientation. This process also places the selected title block and border on a layer named **Title Block**. A viewport is created at the same time and placed on its own layer named **Viewport**.

JOB SKILLS

A thorough understanding of printing from layout space is advantageous when it comes to outputting drawing files. You have an array of options to choose from; as you become familiar with those options, you will begin to understand the potential of layout space.

EXERCISE 8-2 **PLOT FROM LAYOUT SPACE**

To access student data files, go to **www.pearsondesigncentral.com.**

■ Open the **QSLayout 1** drawing from Chapter 8 of the student data files.

■ Select the **ANSI A Title Block** tab at the bottom left area of the screen.

■ Add your name by creating a piece of text, and place the text in the title block area.

■ Set the following parameters: paper size: **8.5 × 11**; orientation: **Portrait**; scale: **1″ = 1″**; and What to Plot?: **Extents**.

■ Preview the plot. If it is OK, proceed to plot the drawing. If not, return to the **Plot** dialog box and modify the settings as needed.

■ Save the file as **HO8-2** in your **Workskills** folder.

Creating and Managing Viewports

A viewport can be considered a screen on which your drawing is displayed (see Figure 8-13). You can divide the screen into smaller screens by establishing the viewport configuration using the **VIEWPORTS** command or other command options. Viewports can be created after the start of a drawing through the **View** menu (see Figure 8-14) or from the **Viewport** panel on the **View** ribbon (see Figure 8-15). A typical viewport configuration might consist of two vertical displays or four screens of equal area. Each of the viewports can have its own display configuration, such as a **View**, **Pan**, **Zoom**, **Layer** display, **Visual Style, Plot Scale**, and **Plot Style**. Once a configuration is established, the display can be *locked* to preserve the values established.

Figure 8-13

Viewports dialog box

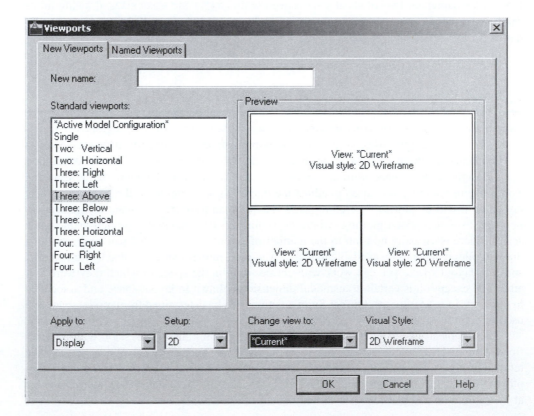

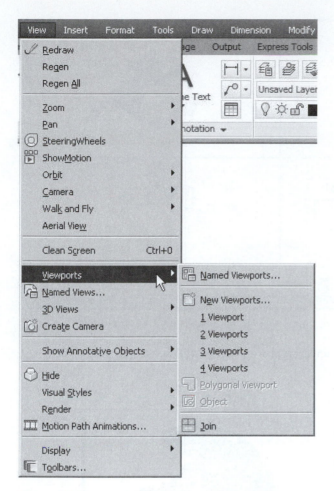

Figure 8-14

View menu showing **Viewport** submenu

Figure 8-15

Viewport panel on the **View** ribbon

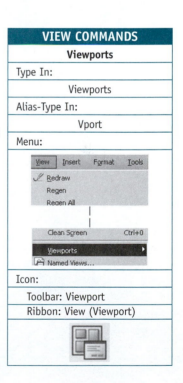

VIEW COMMANDS
Viewports
Type In:
Viewports
Alias-Type In:
Vport
Menu:
Icon:
Toolbar: Viewport
Ribbon: View (Viewport)

JOB SKILLS

Demonstrate your understanding of customizing the viewport scale list to minimize the choice of scale options. This list can be unique to the primary plotting scales currently used in the office.

Model space viewports are "tiled"; that is, they must fill the display area, are rectangular, cannot overlap, and cannot have gaps in covering the screen area. You will notice a thick line or border around the active viewport. When using multiple viewports in model space, you switch from one viewport to another by moving the cursor into a viewport and clicking with the left mouse button to activate the new viewport.

Even though you may divide the model space world into multiple viewports, model space will print only the current or active viewport (see Figure 8-16). You will only be able to print multiple viewports through layout space (see Figure 8-17).

To view a design through layout space, you will need to have at least one viewport created. The actual viewport object holds the scale along with other information for the purpose of plotting. As mentioned earlier, only the entities created in layout space are eligible for selection and modification.

NOTE:

You can switch viewports in the middle of the command without interrupting the active command.

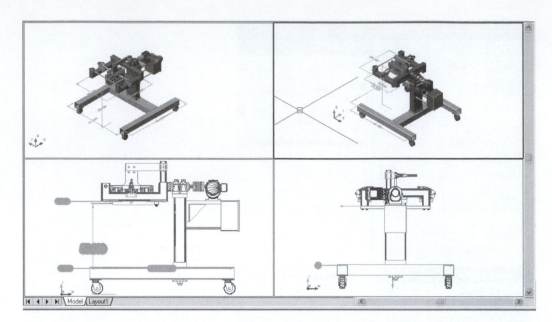

Figure 8-16

Four tiled viewports in model space; upper right is active and will be the only one plotted

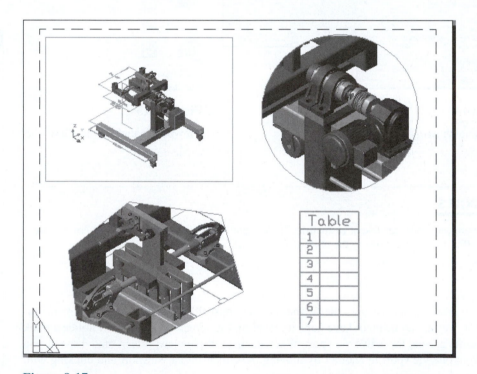

Figure 8-17

Four viewports in layout space. All four will be on plot

When a viewport is created in layout space, you can double-click inside the viewport and enter the world of floating model space. This alternative method of accessing model space makes the objects created available while in the traditional layout space world. You will notice a thick line or border around the active viewport that is currently in floating model space. To switch back and forth between the two worlds, toggle the button in the status bar labeled **Model** or **Paper**.

EXERCISE 8-3   **CREATE LAYOUT SPACE PLOTS**

- Open drawing **HO8-2** from the student data files.

- Click on the **Layout1** tab at the bottom of the drawing area.

- Right click on the **Layout1** tab and select **Page setup manager** from the menu.

- Establish the layout page settings for the current plot device, paper size, plot area, plot scale, and drawing orientation similar to Figure 8-18.

- Using the **Layer manager**, create a new layer named **3-Viewports**. Establish the **No Plot** value and set the layer to be the current layer (see Figure 8-19).

- Using the **VIEWPORT** command in the **View** menu, create a three viewport layout (see Figure 8-20).

- Set the scale of the right viewport to **1:2** scale (see Figure 8-21).

- Activate the other viewports and adjust the views in each viewport by using **PAN** and **ZOOM** to match the views in Figure 8-22.

- Double-click in each of the other viewports and establish a **1:1** scale (see Figure 8-22) for the viewport using the scale list.

- Preview the plot (see Figure 8-23). If it is OK, proceed to plot the drawing. If not, return to the **Plot** dialog box and modify the settings as needed.

- Save the drawing as **HO8-3** in your **Workskills** folder.

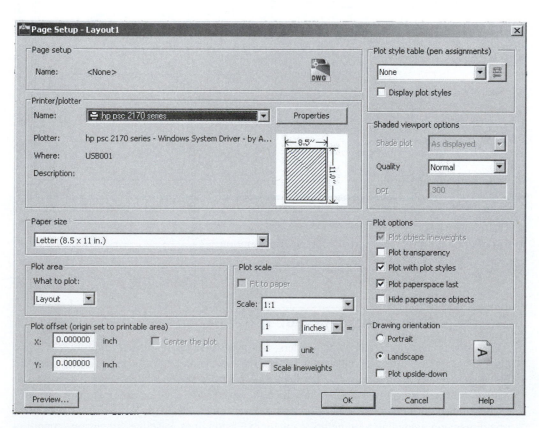

Figure 8-18

Page setup for **Layout1**

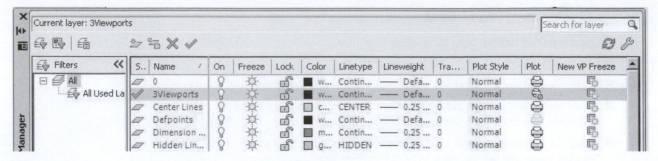

Figure 8-19

Layer palette for new **3-Viewports** layer

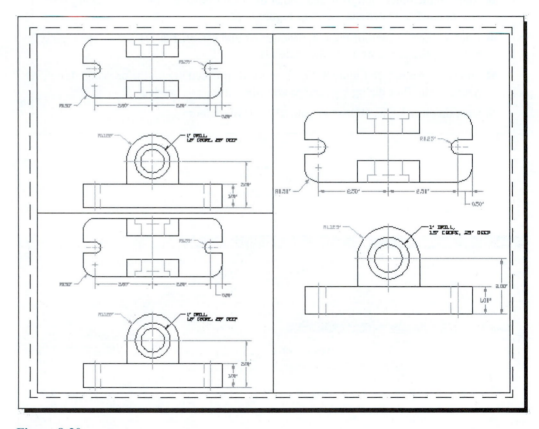

Figure 8-20

Result of creating three viewports using the **Right** option

Creating Annotations in Layout Space

Annotations consist of dimensions, leaders, and general notes that describe an object's size and shape. These entities can be created in either model space or layout space. Remember that objects created as a dimension- or text-based object have physical sizes. These objects will have to be sized based on the world in which they were created. For example, text that is ⅛″ high would be difficult to read in a floor plan describing a 60′ wall. This is true for all parts of a dimension, including terminators, gaps for extension lines, baseline dimension separation distance, and so on. Often, it is better to use multiple dimension styles to reflect annotations in viewports of varying scale than to modify individual parts of dimensions. The option **Scale**

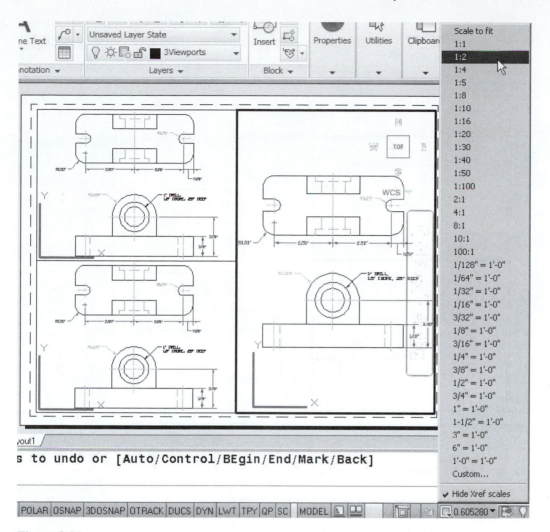

Figure 8-21

Right viewport active for setting the scale at 1:2

dimensions to layout in the **Fit** tab of the **Modify Dimension Style** dialog box is a quick way to factor the size of all parts of the annotations (see Figure 8-24).

JOB SKILLS

Applying all annotations in layout space allows you to control the sizes related to the sheet layout and not the model size.

When creating annotations in layout space, you must click the button next to **Scale dimensions to layout** under the **Fit** tab in the **Modify Dimension Style** dialog box (see Figure 8-24).

JOB SKILLS

An organized office uses an established series of plot styles defining the office's lineweight, color, and other standards. Understanding plot style concepts from both the setup and application point of view will ensure a uniform look to all plotted files.

Figure 8-22

Lower left viewport active for setting the scale at 1:1

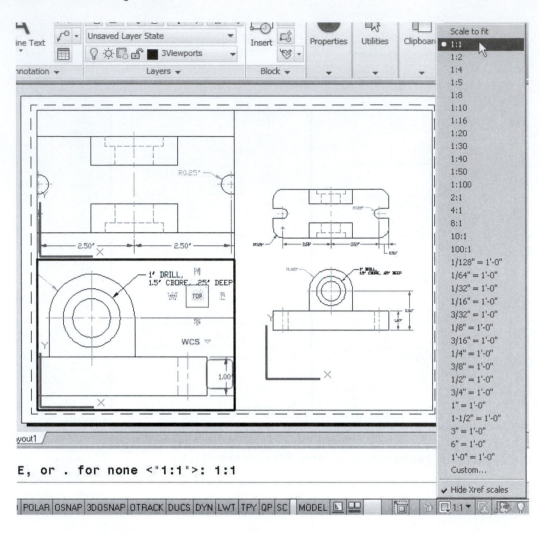

Figure 8-23

Plot preview of Exercise 8-3

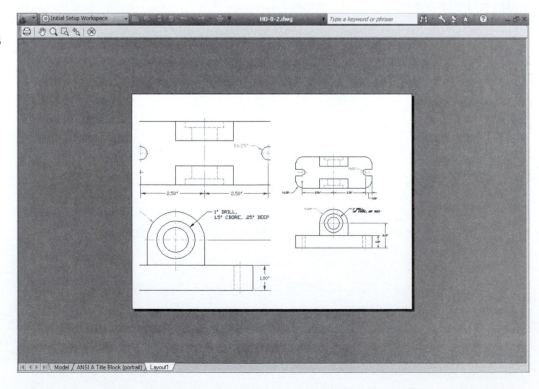

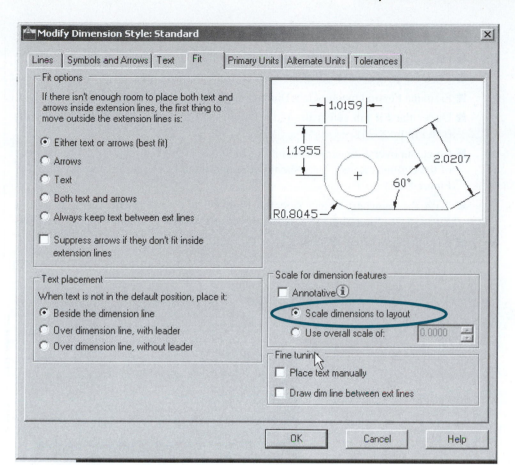

Figure 8-24

Scale dimensions to layout option in the **Dimension Style Manager**

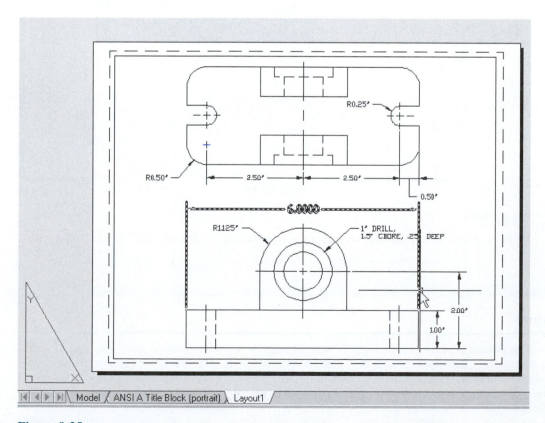

Figure 8-25

Placing dimensions in layout space

To access student data
files, go to
www.pearsondesigncentral.com.

EXERCISE 8-4 **CREATE ANNOTATIONS IN LAYOUT SPACE**

■ Open drawing **HO8-3** from Exercise 8-3 or from the student data files.

■ Click on the **Layout1** tab at the bottom of the drawing area.

■ From the **Format** menu, select **Dimension Style** and the **Modify** button on the right.

■ Under the **Fit** tab select the radio button next to **Scale dimensions to layout** (see Figure 8-24).

■ Create an overall linear dimension for both the X and Y directions. Note the sizes of the entities created. They should be proportionally correct for the drawing (see Figure 8-25).

■ With the viewport object selected, right-click to get to the menu shown in Figure 8-26. From this menu select the **Display Lock** command and set it to **Yes**.

■ Save the drawing as **HO8-4** in your **Workskills** folder.

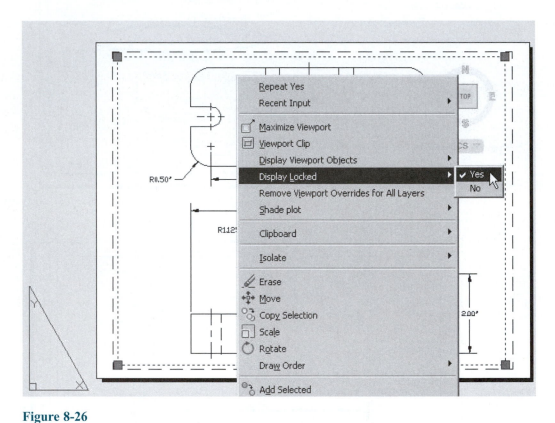

Figure 8-26

Right-click cascading menu for **Viewport** settings (locking the **Display** window) in layout space

Chapter Summary

The topic of this chapter was the process of plotting or printing a hard copy of an electronic drawing using AutoCAD software. We first defined and distinguished the concepts of model space, the world in which the drawing is created for purposes of design, and of layout (paper) space, the space in which the design drawing is given a finished view with annotations that is suitable for plotting on a given sheet layout and size. You then learned and practiced plotting from model space using the **PLOT** command and the

settings (page setup, printer/plotter, paper size, and plot area, scale, and offset along with other plotting parameters) in the **Plot** dialog box. After the relationship between drawing limits and plot scale in a drawing was explained, you learned about the use of multiple viewports in model and layout space to display particular views of your drawing and practiced plotting a drawing from layout space. Table 8-3 summarizes the printing options for both model space and layout space.

TABLE 8-3	AutoCAD Plotting Methods
Model Space	**Layout Space/Paper Space**
One model space plot per drawing	Many layouts using unique names per drawing
WYSIWYG—"What you see is what you get"	Multiple viewports per layout possible; each viewport has one view of any orientation
Pick plotter	Pick plotter per layout
Pick paper size	Pick paper size per layout
Pick area to plot	"Layout" is area to plot
Pick plot scale	"Layout plot scale" is 1:1
Pick offsets	Each viewport has scale relative to layout
Pick paper orientation	Pick orientations of paper for each layout
Pick plot style	Each layout can use a different plot style
	Each layout can hold model dimensions or annotations related to model
Preview plot	Preview each layout
	Viewport Controls
	Can be any shape and can overlap or have gaps
	Each viewport has individual layer control and settings that can be retained **(Visretain)**
Pick visual style and quality	Each viewport can have a different visual style and quality
	Each viewport can be locked
	Each viewport is directly related to the model
	A viewport can be clipped
	Viewport frame can be placed on **No Plot** layer

Chapter Test Questions

Multiple Choice

Circle the correct answer.

1. The plot device refers to the
   a. Paper
   b. File type
   c. Printer
   d. Port to send the information to

2. Multiple viewports can be printed only
   a. In model space
   b. In layout space
   c. Through the **Plot** dialog box
   d. Through a .pc3 file format

3. To print all objects on the selected paper, which scale option should you use?
   a. **All**
   b. **1 = 1**
   c. **Fit**
   d. **Full**

4. **Plot offset** will move the plot's
   a. Title block
   b. Edges
   c. Dimensions
   d. Origin

5. **Plot style** will control at least which two properties?
   a. Color and lineweight
   b. Layers and lineweight
   c. Linetype and visibility
   d. Layers and colors

Matching

Write the number of the correct answer on the line.

a. Display _____

b. Window _____

c. Extents _____

d. View _____

e. Limits _____

1. Print the objects within the defined drawing area

2. Print a named drawing view

3. Print a user-defined window selection

4. Print the current screen

5. Print all objects regardless of where they are

True or False

Circle the correct answer.

1. **True or False:** What you see in the preview is what you get on the print.

2. **True or False:** Sheet size and drawing area mean the same thing.

3. **True or False:** Plot style will control the color of the objects.

4. **True or False:** Page setup will save the current configuration for future use.

5. **True or False:** AutoCAD can make only one plot at a time.

Chapter Projects

Project 8-1 [INTERMEDIATE]

Visit a local consulting engineer, government office, manufacturing plant, or blueprinting company and see what type of plotter is used. What size paper is used most often? What are the typical scales used for plotting?

Project 8-2 [INTERMEDIATE]

Create a poster or chart showing the various architectural, engineering, metric, and mechanical scales related to the various paper sizes and showing the maximum size of the drawing object. For example: A scale of $\frac{1}{4}'' = 1'$ on a D sheet can fit a $136' \times 88'$ model.

Chapter Practice Exercises

(G) Practice Exercise 8-1: *Plot from Model Space* [BASIC]

To practice plotting, use the drawings you created in the Quick-Start Tutorials, in Chapter 5, or in Chapter 7, and plot each of the mechanical drawings at a scale of $1'' = 1''$, the architectural drawings at a scale of $\frac{1}{4}'' = 1'\text{-}0''$, and the civil drawings at a scale of $1'' = 10'\text{-}0''$. Be sure the tab at the lower left is set to **Model**.

Preview each drawing to be sure it is ready to plot.

(G) Practice Exercise 8-2: *Plot from Model Space with Different Parameters* [INTERMEDIATE]

To practice plotting, use the drawings you created in the Quick-Start Tutorials, in Chapter 5, or in Chapter 7, and plot each of the drawings by varying the parameters regarding plot scale, plot area, offsets and centering, and orientation. Be sure the tab at the lower left is set to **Model**. If possible, vary the paper size and output device to gain more understanding of the possibilities for output.

Preview each drawing to be sure it is ready to plot.

(G) Practice Exercise 8-3: *Plot from Layout Space* [INTERMEDIATE]

To practice plotting, use the drawings you created in the Quick-Start Tutorials, in Chapter 5, or in Chapter 7, and plot each in layout space using at least two viewports per sheet. Be sure the tab at the lower left is set to **Layout1** or **Layout2**. The viewports should have different settings for the parameters regarding plot scale, plot area, offsets and centering, and orientation. If possible, vary the paper size and output device to gain more understanding of the possibilities for output.

Preview each drawing to be sure it is ready to plot.

9 Intermediate Drawing and Modifying

Introduction

In Chapters 4 through 8 we covered a series of commands that encompass one of this textbook's core concepts. The draw-modify-dimension-print cycle is a standard approach to the completion of a drawing in a basic AutoCAD system with most engineering disciplines.

In the first chapters, we covered a series of commands at an elementary level, trying to focus on a small amount of information needed to work through the draw-modify-dimension-print cycle. At this time you should feel comfortable with the various input methods available: creating lines, circles, and arcs; selecting objects and making simple modifications to these objects; creating size and shape descriptions with dimensions; and plotting. It is understood that a complete mastery of these concepts and commands will take some practice.

Now it is time to revisit the draw-modify-dimension-print cycle not only to practice what we have learned but also to look at an intermediate level of commands in each of these areas. By expanding your knowledge of the commands, you will have the opportunity to practice previous information covered at the elementary level while learning new methods and procedures linked to your productivity in the workplace.

Building Intermediate Entities

As we cover the creation of other types of entities, it is time to recognize that the **Draw** menu is not the only place to create more geometry. You will learn in this chapter that the **Modify** menu has several commands for making more geometry out of existing geometry. Let's first look back at the **Draw** menu (see Figure 9-1), **Draw** toolbar (see Figure 9-2), and **Draw** panel on the **Home** ribbon (see Figure 9-3) and cover a few options from commands we are already using, along with a few new commands to create other types of geometry.

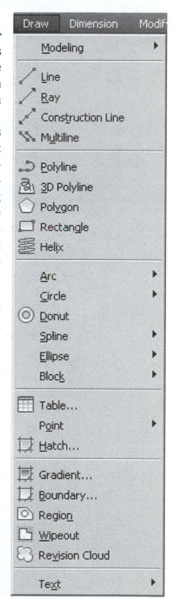

Figure 9-1

Draw menu

Figure 9-2

Draw toolbar

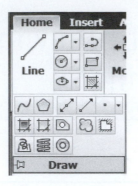

Figure 9-3

Draw panel on the
Home ribbon expanded

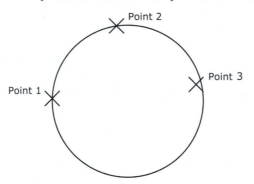

Figure 9-4

Circle created with **2 Points** option

Creating Circles

circle: A geometric shape with a constant radius.

There are four other options for creating a *circle* beyond the **Center/Radius** or **Center/Diameter** commands.

DRAW COMMAND
Circle
Options: Radius, Diameter, 2 Points, 3 Points, Tan-Tan-Rad, Tan-Tan-Tan
Type In:
Cirlce
Alias-Type In:
C
Menu:

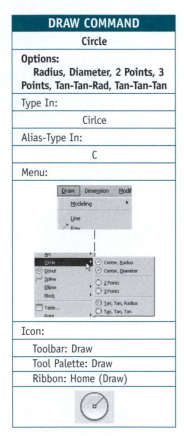

Icon:
Toolbar: Draw
Tool Palette: Draw
Ribbon: Home (Draw)

tangent: A place on a circle touched at only one point by an object and where the radius is perpendicular to the object.

- The **2 Points** option (see Figure 9-4) allows you to select any two points on the screen and create a circle between the two points selected. Note that the distance between the two points selected is the diameter value of the circle created. Using this option you have no control over the placement of the center point for the circle.

- Much like the previous method, the **3 Points** option (see Figure 9-5) allows you to select three points, through which the circle is constructed. Once again, there is no control over the placement of the center point for the circle created.

Figure 9-5

Circle created with **3 Points** option

- The **Tan**, **Tan**, **Radius** (see Figure 9-6) option is similar to the **2 Points** option. You select two points, one on each of the objects to which you want the circle to be tangent, and then the system prompts you for a radius to complete the circle. The difference is in the addition of the *tangent* object snap override to the cursor during the selection of the initial two points. This means that instead of selecting two points in space (X,Y,Z location), you select two pieces of existing geometry that will be tangent to the circle. The objects the circle is tangent to should be selected close to the final tangent points, although the exact tangent point will be calculated when the circle's radius is entered.

NOTE:

When you use either of these methods, it is strongly suggested that you select the points with some form of object snap assistance.

- The final option for creating a circle is **Tan**, **Tan**, **Tan** (see Figure 9-7). With this option you select three existing entities to which the circle will be tangent. As with the **Tan**, **Tan**, **Radius** option, you should select the entities close to the final tangent points. The actual value of the radius is calculated after the third entity is selected. The circle is then created tangent to all three objects selected.

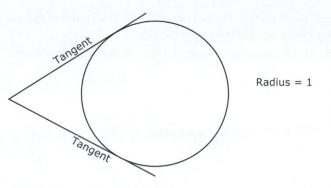

Figure 9-6

Circle created with **Tan, Tan Radius** option

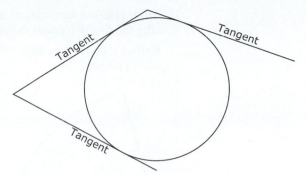

Radius = 1

Figure 9-7

Circle created with **Tan, Tan, Tan** option

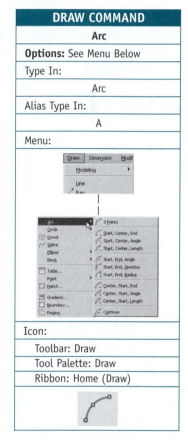

DRAW COMMAND
Arc
Options: See Menu Below
Type In:
Arc
Alias Type In:
A
Menu:
Icon:
Toolbar: Draw
Tool Palette: Draw
Ribbon: Home (Draw)

| EXERCISE 9-1 | CREATE A CIRCLE WITH TANGENTS |

- Start a new drawing.
- Using the **LINE** command, create three line segments in the drawing area.
- In the **Draw** menu select the **Circle** command and then the **Tan**, **Tan**, **Radius** option from the cascading menu.
- Now select two of the line segments and enter a radius value of **1.** Select the lines approximately where you want the circle to be tangent. Notice that the **Tangent** object snap override will be loaded to the cursor automatically. The actual location of the circle's center point and tangent points will be calculated on entry of the radius value (see Figure 9-6).
- In the **Draw** menu select the **Circle** command and then the **Tan**, **Tan**, **Tan** option from the cascading menu.
- Now select each of the line segments. Select the lines approximately where you want the circle and lines to be tangent. Notice that the **Tangent** object snap override will be loaded to the cursor automatically. The actual location of the circle's center point and tangent points will be calculated on selection of the third entity (see Figure 9-7).

Arcs

There are 11 individual options for the construction of an *arc*. In Chapter 5 we discussed the **3 Points** option (see Figure 9-8). The remaining 10 options are a combination of various terms to describe the three points needed to construct an arc. By understanding the definition of the terms used to define the three points, you will be able to construct arcs using a variety of methods.

- **Start** refers to the first endpoint of the arc, and **End** describes the second endpoint of the arc (see Figure 9-9).
- **Center** defines the X,Y,Z location for the center point of the arc with the distance between the center position and the start position defining the radius value of the arc (see Figure 9-9).

arc: A portion of a circle.

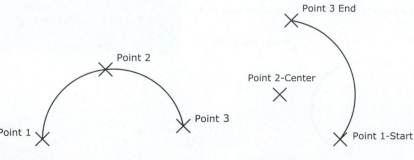

Figure 9-8

Arc created with **3 Points** option

Figure 9-9

Arc created with **Start, Center, End** option

- **Angle** refers to the included angle (see Figure 9-10) that describes the final point of the arc after the first two points define a line or leg of the included angle.
- **Radius** prompts you for a value of the radius (see Figure 9-11) to be used to describe the size of the arc.

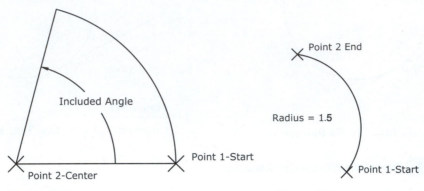

Figure 9-10

Arc created using the **Angle** option

Figure 9-11

Arc created using the **Radius** option

- **Length** (see Figure 9-12) uses a value as defined by the chord distance or length of the arc. This input determines the included angle used to locate the final position of the arc.
- **Direction** uses the starting tangent direction (see Figure 9-13) as indicated by the pointing device to specify the direction of travel between the two points selected. Moving the cursor up from the start point to the endpoint draws a concave arc between the two points; moving the cursor down draws a convex arc between the two points selected.

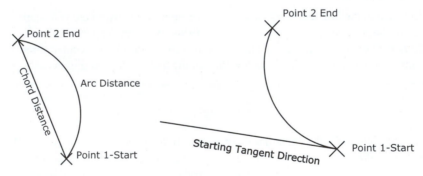

Figure 9-12

Arc created using the **Length** option

Figure 9-13

Arc created using the **Direction** option

- **Continue** creates an arc tangent to the previous entity constructed (see Figure 9-14). This method needs only an endpoint to complete the construction of the new arc.

NOTE:

Arcs are produced in a counter-clockwise direction from the start point to the endpoint.

Figure 9-14

Continued arc

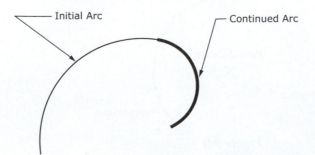

As you look at the different combinations available in the **Draw** menu to create arcs, you can select the appropriate combination to define the arc for its precise construction, given the information available.

EXERCISE 9-2 **CREATE AN ARC WITH START, END, RADIUS**

- Start a new drawing.
- Draw two line segments at any given angle to each other, similar to those in Figure 9-6.
- In the **Draw** menu select the **ARC** command and then the **Start, End, Radius** option from the cascading menu.
- Select an endpoint of the first line as the start point.
- Select the closest endpoint of the second entity to establish the endpoint of the arc.
- Drag the mouse to establish the radius value (see Figure 9-11).

Ellipse

An *ellipse* is typically defined by a major and a minor axis. These axes are the longest and shortest line segments between the quadrant points of the shape. AutoCAD defines the axes for an ellipse from the center point of the ellipse in both the major (long) and minor (short) axis directions. The points for an ellipse can be entered using one of three methods.

- The **Center** method uses three points. The first point selected is the center point of the ellipse, the second point describes the distance and orientation of one axis, and the third point sets the distance for the remaining axis, which is perpendicular to the orientation of the first axis (see Figure 9-15).

ellipse: A geometric shape with a varying radius.

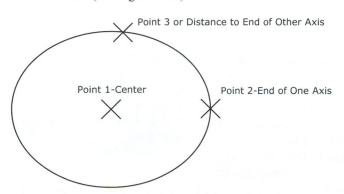

Figure 9-15

Ellipse created with the **Center** option

- The **Axis, End** method uses the first two points to describe the complete length of one axis and then uses the third point selected to define the distance as a radial distance or half the length for the remaining axis of the ellipse. This radial distance is the length of the line calculated from the location of the third point projected back to and perpendicular to the first axis created (see Figure 9-16).

> **NOTE:**
> The total axis length described by the **Axis, End** method is determined by a radius value for the distance of the axis, which in essence is half the axis distance, not the total length of the major or minor axis.

DRAW COMMAND
Ellipse
Options: Center, Axis End, Rotation, Arc
Type In:
Ellipse
Alias-Type In:
EL
Menu:
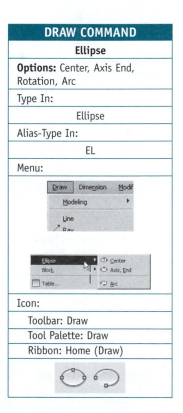
Icon:
Toolbar: Draw
Tool Palette: Draw
Ribbon: Home (Draw)

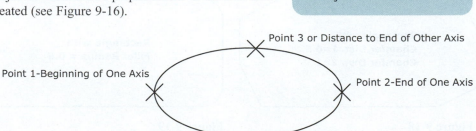

Figure 9-16

Ellipse created using the **Axis, End** option

Figure 9-17

Points needed to create an ellipse arc

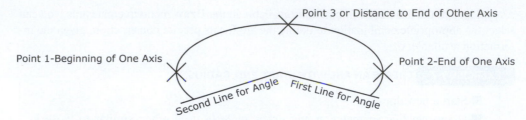

Point 3 or Distance to End of Other Axis

Point 1-Beginning of One Axis   Point 2-End of One Axis

Second Line for Angle   First Line for Angle

• The **Arc** option is used to create a portion of an arc on an elliptical path or shape. You first input information to size the ellipse, following the **Axis, End** method. You select two points that define one complete length of an axis followed by a third point to define the radial distance for the second axis. After these three points are established, you will be prompted for the start angle position and then for the end angle position or included angle. The elliptical arc is created in a counterclockwise direction from the start angle position to the end angle position (see Figure 9-17).

EXERCISE 9-3	CREATE AN ELLIPSE

■ Start a new drawing.

■ In the **Draw** menu select the **ELLIPSE** command and the **Center** option from the cascading menu.

■ Select any point on the screen as the center point of the ellipse.

■ Drag a line out in any direction to specify half the distance of the first ellipse axis.

■ Drag a second line out of the center point to specify half the distance of the second axis for the ellipse (see Figure 9-16).

rectangle: A four-sided geometric shape with equal opposite sides.

polyline: Multiple-line or arc segments joined as one entity.

Rectangle

The *rectangle* command (**RECTANG**) creates a four-sided figure, through a two-point input, based on the opposite corners or a diagonal of the shape. This command results in the creation of a *polyline*. You are prompted for the *First corner point* and then for the *Other corner point*.

Prior to picking the first point, you can choose any of the following options: **Chamfer**, **Elevation**, **Fillet**, **Thickness**, and **Width** and execute them by entering the capital letter of any one of them. After you pick the first point, the additional options **Area**, **Dimension**, and **Rotation** appear to aid in setting the second point or diagonal point.

The following are brief descriptions of each of the options:

> **NOTE:**
>
> A rectangle must be exploded to select the individual entities for modification. See Chapter 10 for more details on the **EXPLODE** command.

• **Chamfer** creates straight-line beveled corners based on the distances entered at the prompts. Only one value is entered for each of the chamfer distances and applied to all four corners (see Figure 9-18).

• The **Fillet** option creates rounded corners. After executing the **Fillet** option you can establish the **Radius** value. Only one value for radius is input and applied to all four corners (see Figure 9-19).

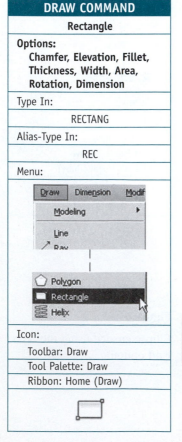

DRAW COMMAND
Rectangle

Options:
  Chamfer, Elevation, Fillet,
  Thickness, Width, Area,
  Rotation, Dimension

Type In:
RECTANG
Alias-Type In:
REC
Menu:
Icon:
Toolbar: Draw
Tool Palette: Draw
Ribbon: Home (Draw)

Rectangle with Chamfer Dist. 1=0.5 Chamfer Dist. 2=1

Rectangle with Fillet Radius = 0.5

Figure 9-18

Rectangle with chamfers

Figure 9-19

Rectangle with fillets

- The **Elevation** option is used to create rectangles at some distance above or below the XY plane, which is typically given as an elevation of 0. This value allows you to establish a start position on the Z-axis.

- The **Thickness** option establishes the end position on the Z-axis, or gives a height to the rectangle. For example, **Thickness** is used to create the look of a building, as walls are created by this variable (see Figure 9-20).

Figure 9-20

Rectangle with fillets and thickness in a 3D isometric view

- The **Width** option establishes a value for the polyline width of the segments that make up the rectangle. This width can vary for the entities involved. This option is similar to adding a lineweight property value to the rectangle that results in a constant width per entity.

- The **Area** option aids in creating a precise area for the rectangle when you input the value of the desired **Area** and either a **Length** (or X-direction value) or **Width** (or Y-direction value) to complete the needed information.

- **Dimension** requests the input of a **Length** (or X-direction value) and **Width** (or Y-direction value), leading to a request for the second point. The second point essentially becomes a directional pointer for the location of the rectangle.

- The **Rotation** option allows you to specify or pick a location at any angle, which will rotate the rectangle to that orientation.

DRAW COMMAND
Hatch (Filling an Area with a Pattern)
Options: Pattern, Scale, Angle, Location, Islands, Origin, Associative, Gap
Type In:
Hatch or BHatch
Alias: Type In:
H or BH
Draw   Dimension   Modif Modeling ▸ Line Ray ... Point ▸ Hatch... Gradient...
Icon:
Toolbar: Draw
ToolPalette: Draw
Ribbon: Home (Draw)

EXERCISE 9-4   **CREATE A RECTANGLE**

- ■ Start a new drawing.
- ■ From the **Draw** menu access the **RECTANG** command.
- ■ Type an **F** to set the **Fillet Radius** for the corners of the rectangle.
- ■ Enter **.5** as the **Radius** value and press **<Enter>**.
- ■ Pick a point in the drawing area for one corner of the rectangle.
- ■ Move the mouse and see the temporary view of the rectangle as the mouse is moved.
- ■ Pick a second point for the rectangle that will be diagonally across the rectangle from the first point (see Figure 9-19).

Hatching

The **HATCH** command fills an enclosed area with a vector-based pattern of lines, circular shapes, or a solid fill color with gradient. There are four items on the **Hatch** ribbon (see Figure 9-21) or in the **Hatch** dialog box (see Figure 9-22) that need to be addressed in the creation of a hatched area. If we look at the simplest form of hatching, it includes the selection of a *hatch* pattern, the selection of a boundary area, and the scale and/or rotation of the hatch pattern in the hatch area.

hatch: Using a pattern of lines and shapes to fill a closed area of a drawing.

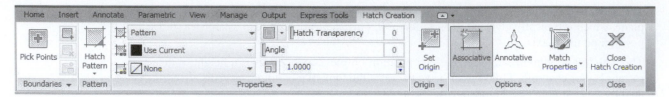

Figure 9-21

Hatch Creation ribbon

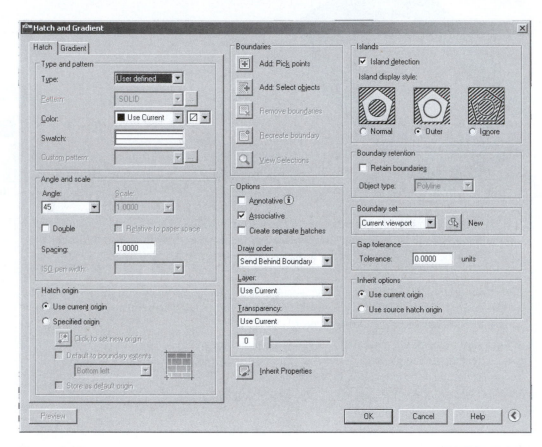

Figure 9-22

Hatch dialog box

Hatch patterns can be linked with the boundary entities through an associative property. After this link has been established through the **Hatch** ribbon **Options** panel the hatch pattern will adjust if the boundary changes.

Patterns come from one of three sources. The **Type** drop-down list (see Figure 9-23) or on the ribbon (see Figure 9-24) in the **Hatch** dialog box allows you to choose from a library of patterns from one of the three sources listed. Let's first take a look at the general types of hatch patterns.

Figure 9-23

Type drop-down list in **Hatch** dialog box

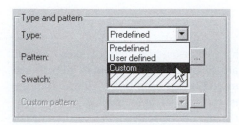

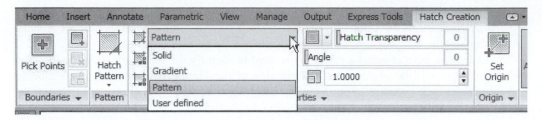

Figure 9-24

Setting the type of patterns available on the **Hatch Creation** ribbon

User-defined patterns (see Figure 9-25) are based on a simple line and a rotational and spacing value. The value input in **Angle** field in the dialog box establishes the rotational value of the pattern. A value of 0° creates a lined pattern parallel to the X-axis. Any positive value rotates the pattern in a counterclockwise direction; a negative value rotates the pattern clockwise. The **Spacing** field is the distance between lines in the pattern. This value is expected to be a positive numerical input. When the check box for **Double** is checked, the pattern is created at a 90° angle to the initial pattern.

Patterns (see Figures 9-26 and 9-27) come in several categories. These include definitions of lines, circles, and arcs that are created through computer code to repeat the pattern until the designated closed areas are filled. Some of these patterns are based on ANSI or ISO drafting standards that have established cross-sectional symbols related to identifying materials; other predefined patterns have an architectural theme based on actual materials (e.g., block, brick, earth, grass, roof, and concrete).

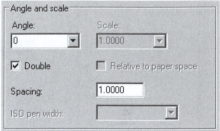

Figure 9-25

User-defined hatch scale and angle

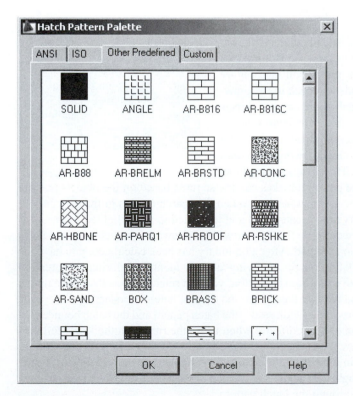

Figure 9-26

Other Predefined tab on the **Hatch Pattern Palette**

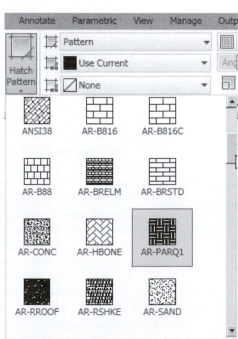

Figure 9-27

Choosing patterns on the **Hatch Creation** ribbon

Figure 9-28

Boundaries area of the
Hatch dialog box

Custom patterns are defined by the user. These are often created in a computer language such as Visual Basic or AutoLISP. You can create a pattern using any series of lines or symbols defined through a programmable language.

Once you have selected a pattern, you need to identify the boundary area in which the hatch pattern will be placed. On the right side of the **Hatch** dialog box is a box labeled **Boundaries** (see Figure 9-28) or from the ribbon (see Figure 9-29). There are two options for creating a boundary area and one option for removing objects selected that define a boundary area. The easiest way to define a hatch boundary is to select an object or objects that define the boundary of the area. When you select the **Add: Select objects** button, the program sends you back to the drawing screen to select objects to make up the boundary area. Keep in mind that the hatch pattern needs a closed area to define the boundary, and the pattern created will touch all parts of the objects selected. If the objects do not make up a clearly defined area, the hatch pattern may leak out of the closed boundary area to try to touch all parts of the objects selected.

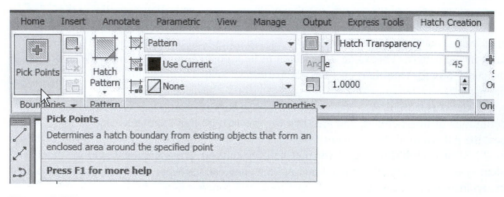

Figure 9-29

Pick Points panel on the **Hatch Creation** ribbon

The second way to define a hatch boundary is to select the **Add: Pick points** button from the **Boundaries** area (see Figure 9-28) or from the ribbon (see Figure 9-29). This selection again sends you back to the drawing screen to select an internal point among objects defining an area. The program then calculates a closed boundary area based on the closest object to the point selected and travels in a counterclockwise direction until a closed loop has been defined. The objects selected may not be the complete object. The program makes clockwise turns based on the objects that are encountered when searching the area in question. When the search returns to the original object it started with, the boundary area is calculated and identified in a highlighted form.

NOTE:

If no boundary can be defined or calculated, the error message "Valid boundary not found" will appear and circles will outline the errors (see Figure 9-30).

If no boundary is found (see Figure 9-30), you will be allowed to select a second point or alternative boundary definition method. After a boundary has been calculated, you have the option to edit the boundary definition by removing objects identified during the creation process. By selecting the **Remove boundaries** button, you can select objects that make up the current boundary definition and remove them from the current hatch boundary.

Now that two hatch issues have been addressed—the hatch pattern and the hatch boundary—you can use the **Preview** button or see it directly when using the ribbon in the lower left corner of the dialog box to preview the current hatching scenario. At this time you may choose to adjust two remaining areas in the **Hatch** dialog box. The **Scale** field adjusts the size of the pattern (see Figure 9-31), the **Angle** field adjusts the rotation of the pattern, and the **Transparency** field adjusts the ability to see through the hatch pattern.

In the **Scale** field a scale of 1.0 represents the pattern in its original defined size. A larger number enlarges the pattern, whereas a smaller number reduces the size of the pattern. In the

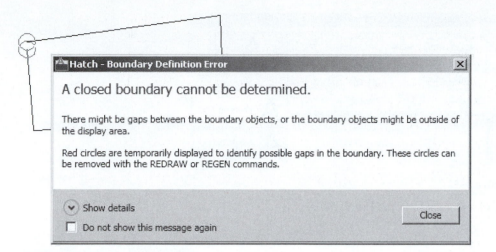

Figure 9-30

The **Hatch Boundary** error message

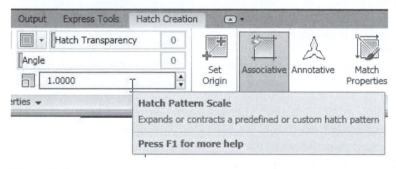

Figure 9-31

Hatch properties control settings on the **Hatch Creation** ribbon

Angle field, the number and slide bar represent a rotational value, where 0 points East, positive numbers rotate counterclockwise, and negative numbers rotate clockwise.

EXERCISE 9-5   **CREATE AND HATCH ITEMS**

- Start a new drawing.
- From the **Draw** menu, place a rectangle and a circle in the drawing area so that these entities intersect.
- From the **Draw** menu, access the **HATCH** command and place a different hatch pattern in each enclosed area.

Text Commands

Creating Text

There are two methods for creating text with AutoCAD. Because this program is a vector-based system, creating text is slightly different than when using a typical word processor. The first method is referred to as **Single Line Text** or **Dynamic Text**. This command is found in the **Draw** menu (see Figure 9-1) or on the ribbon (see Figure 9-32) and creates a string of text characters that act as one object. To execute this command from the command line, you type in **TEXT** or **DTEXT**. Although the command sounds as if it creates only a

DRAW COMMAND
Single Line or Dynamic Text
Options:
Style, Justification, Height, Rotation, Annotative
Type In:
Text or Dtext
Alias-Type In:
DT
Menu:

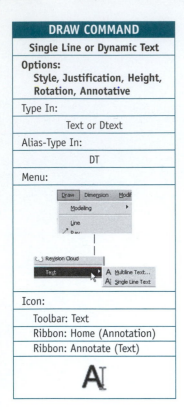

Icon:
Toolbar: Text
Ribbon: Home (Annotation)
Ribbon: Annotate (Text)

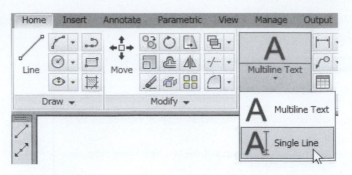

Figure 9-32

TEXT commands on the **Home** ribbon

single line of text, this is misleading. You can produce more than one line of text during a command sequence, with each line being treated as a single object regardless of how many characters are used. The procedure for **Single Line Text** will prompt you for three pieces of information. The text start position, the text height, and the text rotation all need to be established prior to typing the actual text string.

> **NOTE:**
>
> Keep in mind that the text will not be justified to the selected style until the command is completed and placement is calculated.

We now take a closer look at this sequence of prompts for **TEXT**. On entering the command, you are prompted to *Specify start point of text [Justify/Style]*. By default, the insert or control point selected is the lower left corner of the first line of text. This is referred to as *left justification*. If you want to use the point selected with a different type of justification, you can execute the option *justify* and select from a series of predefined justifications based on the point selected as the start point. Refer to Figure 9-33 for a description of each of the basic justification codes and the corresponding locations.

justify: A method used to place text.

Figure 9-33

Text justification locations

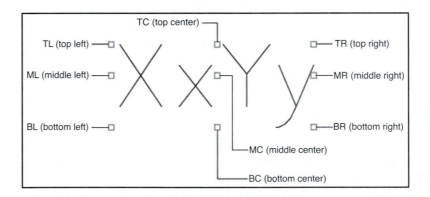

Additional methods of text justification include the following:

- **Align** With this option you select two points on the screen, and the text is placed between the two points. The actual height and width of the text will depend on how many characters are in the string of text and the distance between the points.

- **Fit** With this option you select two points on the screen, and the text is placed between the two points. The height of the text remains fixed, but the width of the characters depends on how many characters are in the string of text and the distance between the two points.

- **Center** This option calculates the center of the text string and places the bottom center of the text string on the point selected.

- **Middle** This option calculates the center of the text string along with the middle of the text height and places the text string on the point selected.
- **Right** This option places the lower right point on the end of the text string on the point selected.

The text **Style** is another option in the command prompt and is used to establish the link to the numerous type fonts, special codes, letter width, and other special items. **TEXTSTYLE** in the **Format** menu, or from the expanded **Annotation** panel on the **Home** ribbon (see Figure 9-34), is the command used to create, view, and modify these items (see Figure 9-35).

Figure 9-34

Text Style access from the expanded **Annotation** panel on the **Home ribbon**

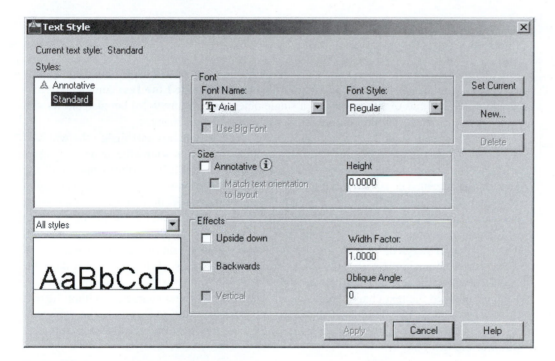

Figure 9-35

Text Style dialog box

After you select the starting point, the command prompts you to *Specify height <0.2000>*. The current height is shown in the default brackets. This value can be accepted by pressing **<Enter>** or changed by keying in a different value followed by **<Enter>**.

Once the height is established, you are prompted to *Specify rotation angle of text <0>*. The default angle of **0** produces a text string parallel to the *X*-axis, moving from left to right. A positive angle rotates the text around the insert point counterclockwise. A negative angle rotates the text around the insert point clockwise.

After these three pieces of information are established, a text box with a flashing cursor appears at the position selected for the start point. At this time you can input the characters for the string of text. If multiple lines of text are needed, you simply press **<Enter>** to start a new line of text. The new line of text uses all the same parameters established earlier in the command sequence. To end the command, you press **<Enter>** twice (once to end the current line of text and once to end the command). This completes the single line text command.

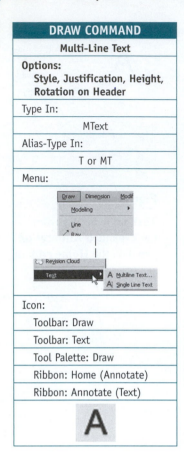

DRAW COMMAND
Multi-Line Text
Options:
Style, Justification, Height, Rotation on Header
Type In:
MText
Alias-Type In:
T or MT
Menu:
Icon:
Toolbar: Draw
Toolbar: Text
Tool Palette: Draw
Ribbon: Home (Annotate)
Ribbon: Annotate (Text)

EXERCISE 9-6 **PLACE TEXT IN A DRAWING**

- Start a new drawing.
- From the **Draw** menu, access the **TEXT** command and choose **Single Line Text** from the cascading menu.
- Pick a location for the text with the mouse, enter **.5 <Enter>** for the text height, and accept **0** for the angle by pressing **<Enter>** after each entry.
- Type in your name and address on three or four lines.
- Press **<Enter>** twice to complete the command.

Creating Multiline Text

The second method for creating text is called **Multiline Text** or **MTEXT**. This command is more closely related to a word processing format than the **Single Line Text** command. It manipulates all the lines of text entered as a single object (see Figure 9-36) but also allows you to select any characters within the sequence for unique format changes.

This command starts by having you create a *text box*. The box establishes the width of the text line and is expandable in the downward direction as shown by the arrow in the box at the bottom. Once the text box has been established, the multiline editor ribbon will appear on the screen. The ribbon has all the traditional text format options, such as text style, character font, height, bold, italicized, underlined, color, justification, and areas addressing several special characters. You can address any of these options during the creation of text or highlight previously created text and alter the properties of the selected text as needed. The *rule* can be toggled on or off through an icon on the main multiline ribbon and is used to establish tab positions within the text window and the width of the text. When the ruler is pulled wider, the text box will widen, and all text will adjust to the new width. After you have established the text characteristics needed, you type all text characters within the text box. When all text is typed in, you can select the **Close** button to complete the command and place the contents of the text box into the file at the location established by the first point of the text box.

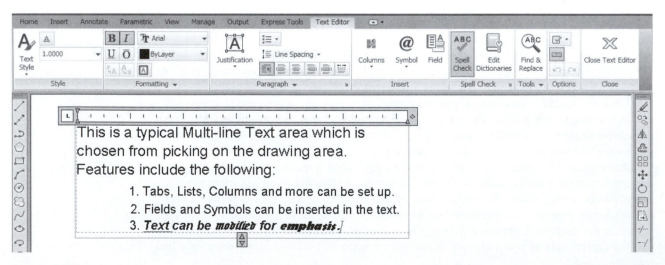

Figure 9-36

Multiline text input window on the **Text Editor** ribbon

EXERCISE 9-7　**CREATE MULTILINE TEXT**

- Start a new drawing.
- From the **Draw** menu, access the **TEXT** command and choose **Multiline Text** from the cascading menu.
- Pick two points on the screen to represent the width of the text in your drawing.
- Enter your name and address using three or four lines for the information.
- Pick **OK** to complete the command.

Editing Text

To edit text that has been placed within a drawing, you can double-click on the text object. Depending on the method used to create the text, this double-click action produces one of two results. If the text was created with a **Single Line Text** command, a text edit window appears as shown in Figure 9-37 with the selected string of text inside the edit window. At this time you can place the cursor anywhere within the text string and alter the characters as needed. This method does not allow you to change text height, color, and font or style—only the characters of the text string. To change the other text characteristics, you have to use the **PROPERTIES** command or **Properties** palette in the **Modify** menu (see Figure 9-39) or from the right-click menu when the text is selected. This palette is shown in Figure 9-38.

This is an example of Single Line Text

Figure 9-37

Text edit window for single line text

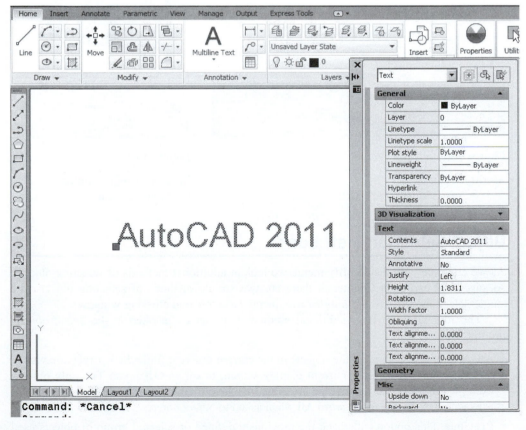

Figure 9-38

Properties palette for modifying single-line text

Figure 9-39

Modify menu

If the text selected for editing was produced with the **Multiline Text** command, the double-click produces the multiline text box (see Figure 9-36) with the text selected in it. At this time you can place the cursor anywhere within the box and make the changes needed. This method also allows you to highlight any series of characters and alter the properties of the selected contents such as text height, color, font, or style. To complete the editing session, select the **OK** button on the toolbar, and all changes will then be placed back into the drawing file.

Modify Commands

Now it is time to look at a few more commands found in the **Modify** menu (see Figure 9-39) that will help produce more geometry based on objects already in the drawing file. Most of the following commands can also be found on the **Modify** toolbar (see Figure 9-40) or on the **Modify** panel on the **Home** ribbon (see Figure 9-41). Keep in mind that during the execution of these commands you will be prompted to *Select objects*. You have to establish which objects you want to work with; the options available were discussed in Chapter 5 and are further explained in the next section.

Figure 9-40

Modify toolbar

Figure 9-41

Modify panel expanded on the **Home** ribbon

Object Selection Methods

As we continue with the **Modify** menu, we look at additional methods of selecting objects. As discussed earlier in Chapter 5, there are two simple methods of selecting objects, the single-selection *pick box* and *implied windowing* (window and crossing window).

The following are four additional methods that can be invoked at the *Select objects* prompt message.

- **All** This option selects all the objects in the current drawing file, whether they are visible on the screen, outside the current display screen, or on an **Off** layer. The only objects exempted in this selection method are those on a layer that is currently frozen. This option is executed by typing in the word **All** when asked to *Select objects.*

- **Previous** This option calls back the previously defined or selected group of objects used in the last completed **Modify** command. This option is executed by typing in the letter **P** when asked to *Select objects.*

- **Last** This method selects only the last object added to the drawing file or highlighted in a previous command. It is executed by typing in the letter **L** when asked to *Select objects*.

- **Fence** This option allows you to create a temporary line that acts in the same manner as a crossing window. Any object that comes in contact with the fence will be in the selected set. This option is executed by typing in the letter **F** when asked to *Select objects*.

Although these methods are not used often, they are good to know when you are faced with a tricky selection set of objects to be made for a **Modify** command. A little practice with each of these methods will help you see their value.

Modifying Commands

To this point we have covered the basic commands within the **Modify** menu that will **MOVE, COPY,** or **ERASE** an object. We have discussed a series of commands that will produce more geometry from existing objects such as **OFFSET, MIRROR,** and **ARRAY.** Now it's time to look at a series of commands in the **Modify** menu that will alter the selected geometry in some form. As with most of the **Modify** commands, you are prompted to *Select objects* at the beginning of the command. The following commands will ask you to select objects that have a special function pertaining to the execution of the command. Novice users should pay particular attention to the command prompt line, where extra information is displayed regarding the type of objects to be selected, the method of selection to be used, or the proper procedure and options for the command.

Fillet

A **FILLET** command creates an arc that is tangent to two other entities at a specified radius. The simple concept of a fillet is to specify a radius and then *Select two objects*. The command produces an arc based on the radius entered that is tangent to the objects selected, typically trimming off any extra portions of the selected objects to form a clean intersection at the tangent points (see Figure 9-42). When you first enter the **FILLET** command (see Figure 9-43), the current trim mode setting and radius value are listed in the prompt line.

To establish the value of the radius, you exercise the **Radius** option by entering an **R** and pressing <**Enter**>. The program then prompts you for a radius value. After you enter a value and press <**Enter**>, the command resumes with the request to *Select objects*.

To change the **Trim** mode, you follow a similar action. By entering a **T**, you can adjust the trim mode from **Trim** to **No Trim**.

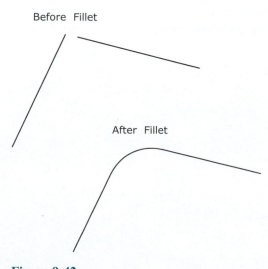

Before Fillet

After Fillet

Figure 9-42

Fillet result

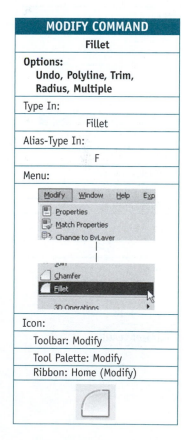

MODIFY COMMAND
Fillet
Options:
Undo, Polyline, Trim, Radius, Multiple
Type In:
Fillet
Alias-Type In:
F
Menu:
Icon:
Toolbar: Modify
Tool Palette: Modify
Ribbon: Home (Modify)

Figure 9-43

FILLET command prompt

```
Command:
Command: _fillet
Current settings: Mode = TRIM, Radius = 0.5000
Select first object or [Undo/Polyline/Radius/Trim/Multiple]:
Select second object or shift-select to apply corner:

Command:
```

After addressing the desired options, you are prompted to *Select first object* and then *Select second object*. You must keep in mind that the portion of the object selected is the portion retained after the command has completed trimming the entities. Once the second object is selected, the arc is constructed, and the objects are trimmed if this mode is set to the **Trim** value. At this time the command is complete, and you are returned to the command prompt.

If you would like to create additional fillets, you can use an option within the **FILLET** command called **Multiple**. This option allows you to select multiple sets of entities to fillet; you press **<Enter>** to complete the command.

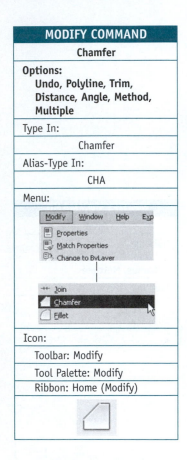

MODIFY COMMAND
Chamfer
Options: **Undo, Polyline, Trim,** **Distance, Angle, Method,** **Multiple**
Type In:
Chamfer
Alias-Type In:
CHA
Menu:
Icon:
Toolbar: Modify
Tool Palette: Modify
Ribbon: Home (Modify)

EXERCISE 9-8 **CREATE A FILLET ON TWO OBJECTS**

- Start a new drawing.
- From the **Draw** menu place two lines in the drawing that are roughly perpendicular.
- From the **Modify** menu pick the **FILLET** command.
- Type **R** and press **<Enter>** to set the radius at **0.5**.
- Select each of the lines at the end to be modified. After you pick the second object, the fillet is created (see Figure 9-42).

Chamfer

The **CHAMFER** command creates an angled line that connects two other objects. The simplest way to create a chamfer is to specify a distance for each object and then select two objects. The command produces a line based on the distance entered from an intersection point between the two objects. It trims off any extra portions of the selected objects to form a clean intersection at the intersecting points (see Figure 9-44). When you first enter the **CHAMFER** command, the current settings are shown in the prompt line. There are two methods used to calculate a chamfer—distance and angle. By default the distance method is active with the two values for distance set to **0** (see Figure 9-45). You need to establish values for distance on each object. These values de-

Figure 9-44

Chamfer results

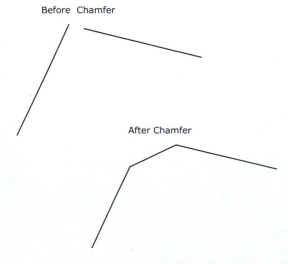

Before Chamfer

After Chamfer

```
Command: _chamfer
(TRIM mode) Current chamfer Dist1 = 0.0000, Dist2 = 0.0000
Select first line or [Undo/Polyline/Distance/Angle/Trim/mEthod/Multiple]: d
Specify first chamfer distance <0.0000>: 1
Specify second chamfer distance <1.0000>: 1.5
Select first line or [Undo/Polyline/Distance/Angle/Trim/mEthod/Multiple]:
Select second line or shift-select to apply corner:

Command:
```

Figure 9-45

CHAMFER command prompts

termine the distance calculations for the chamfer placement. The connecting line is then generated. You can establish the values for distance by entering a **D** at the first prompt, which is *Select first line or <Undo/Polyline/Distance/Angle/Trim/mEthod/Multiple>*.

Once the values for distances are established, you select the two objects. After the second object is selected, the chamfer is produced. Keep in mind that the portion of the object selected is the portion retained after the command has completed trimming the entities.

The **Angle** option uses the **Distance1** value and an angle value to generate the connecting line. You still need to select two objects. The distance is calculated on the first object selected, and the angle line then continues until it intersects the second object selected. Values for the distance and angle can be established through the **Angle** option. As with the **FILLET** command, the **Trim** option controls the cleanup of the objects selected, and the **Polyline** option applies the **Chamfer** values to all vertices capable of creating angle lines with the current settings.

EXERCISE 9-9 | **CREATE A CHAMFER**

- Start a new drawing.
- From the **Draw** menu place two lines in the drawing that are roughly perpendicular.
- From the **Modify** menu pick the **CHAMFER** command.
- Type a **D** and enter the distances **0.75** and **0.5**.
- Select each of the lines at the end to be modified. After you pick the second object the chamfer will be created (see Figure 9-44).

Trim

Unlike the **ERASE** command, which removes an entire object, the **TRIM** command uses other pieces of geometry to act as a cutting edge or knife when you are removing only a portion of an object (see Figure 9-46). When starting the command, you select objects referred to as the *cutting edges*. In the command line you will see the following prompt:

> Select cutting edges . . .
> Select objects or <select all>:

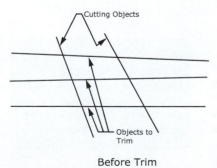

Before Trim   After Trim

Figure 9-46

The **TRIM** command

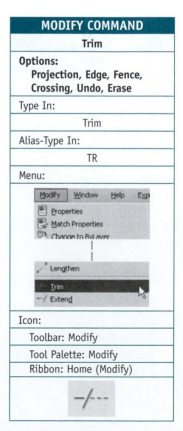

MODIFY COMMAND
Trim
Options:
Projection, Edge, Fence, Crossing, Undo, Erase
Type In:
Trim
Alias-Type In:
TR
Menu:
Icon:
Toolbar: Modify
Tool Palette: Modify
Ribbon: Home (Modify)

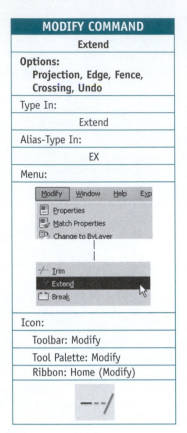

MODIFY COMMAND
Extend
Options:
Projection, Edge, Fence, Crossing, Undo
Type In:
Extend
Alias-Type In:
EX
Menu:
Icon:
Toolbar: Modify
Tool Palette: Modify
Ribbon: Home (Modify)

Any objects selected under this prompt are considered the "knife," or the objects that will do the cutting. The geometry selected as the cutting edge has to come in contact with the object that will be trimmed. You can select several objects, or up to **All** objects, to act as cutting edges. You may even choose to press **<Enter>**, which will select all the objects in the drawing file as cutting edges. To end this selection process, press **<Enter>**.

After selecting the cutting edges, you then select the objects or parts of objects to trim away or remove. Keep in mind that the location used to touch the object will be the part of the object trimmed or removed. You can select the **Objects to trim** with a single-selection pick box, or you can choose to select multiple objects with the **Fence** or **Crossing** options. These two methods will select multiple objects to **TRIM** only at one time.

Extend

The **EXTEND** command is basically the opposite of the **TRIM** command. **EXTEND** uses other pieces of geometry to act as a boundary edge when extending an object. When starting the command, you select objects referred to as *boundary edges* (see Figure 9-47). The command line shows the following prompt:

> Select boundary edges . . .
> Select objects or <select all>

The objects selected while this prompt message is active are considered the stop entity, the limit, or the objects to cause the extension to end. The geometry selected has to be in a direct path with the object that is extended. You can select several objects to act as boundary edges. You may even choose to press **<Enter>**, which will select all the objects in the drawing file to act as boundary edges. To end this selection process for the boundaries, you must press **<Enter>**.

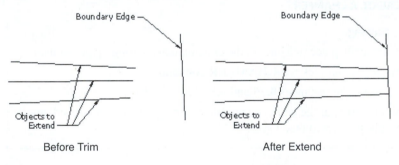

Before Trim   After Extend

Figure 9-47

The **EXTEND** command

After selecting the boundary edges, you then select the objects to extend. Keep in mind the objects touched are the objects extended. The program does not add an additional entity for the extension, but it repositions the closest endpoint to intersect the new position defined by the extension. You can select the **Objects to extend** with a single-selection pick box, or you can choose to select objects with the **Fence** or **Crossing** options. These two methods will select multiple objects to extend at one time.

Break

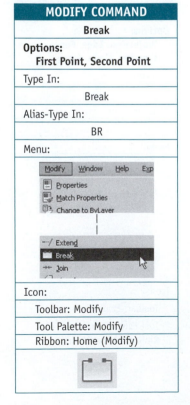

MODIFY COMMAND
Break
Options:
First Point, Second Point
Type In:
Break
Alias-Type In:
BR
Menu:
Icon:
Toolbar: Modify
Tool Palette: Modify
Ribbon: Home (Modify)

Much like the **TRIM** command, **BREAK** removes a portion of an existing object. The difference between the two commands is that **BREAK** does not need other pieces of geometry to act as cutting edges. **BREAK** prompts you to *Select objects.* The object selected is the object that will be broken. The object's selected location automatically becomes the *first break point.* To complete the command, you are prompted for a *second break point.* After the selection of the second break point, the portion of the object that lies between the two break points is removed. If you choose not to use the initial object selection point as the first break point, you

> **NOTE:**
>
> When you use the **BREAK** command on arcs, the break will occur in a counterclockwise direction from the first selected point to the second selected point.

can invoke a **First Point** option by typing in an **F** at the command prompt line after selecting the object (see Figure 9-48). This allows you to reposition the first break point to a new location and continue to select the second break point, thus completing the command. The **Object Snaps** such as **ENDpoint**, **INTersection**, and **MIDpoint** are available in the **BREAK** command to aid in the proper location of the break.

```
Command:
BREAK Select object:
Specify second break point or [First point]:
Command:
```

Figure 9-48

BREAK command prompts

EXERCISE 9-10   **CREATE A BREAK IN A LINE**

■ Start a new drawing file.

■ Draw a line.

■ From the **Modify** menu select the **BREAK** command.

■ Pick the line in any location.

■ Move to a second location along the line and select that location. The line should have been removed between the two selected points (see Figure 9-49).

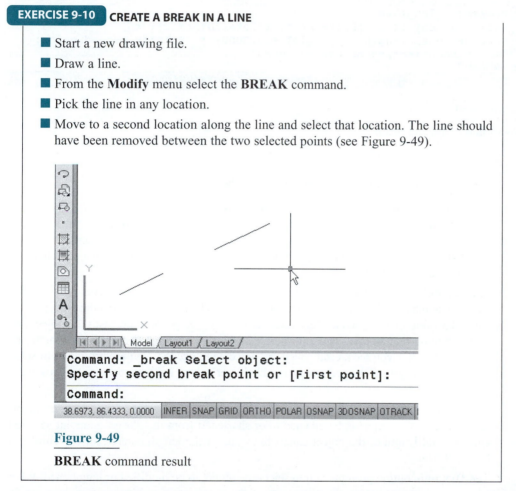

Figure 9-49

BREAK command result

Lengthen

Much like the **EXTEND** command, the **LENGTHEN** command increases (and may also decrease) the distance end to end of a selected object. After you select the object, the following options are displayed (see Figure 9-50).

```
LENGTHEN
Select an object or [DElta/Percent/Total/DYnamic]:
Current length: 3.2715
Select an object or [DElta/Percent/Total/DYnamic]: t
Specify total length or [Angle] <1.0000)>: 4
Select an object to change or [Undo]:
Select an object to change or [Undo]:
Command:
```

MODIFY COMMAND
Lengthen
Options: Dynamic, Total, Percent, Delta, Undo
Type In: Lengthen
Alias-Type In: LEN
Menu:
Icon: Ribbon: Home (Modify Expanded)

Figure 9-50

LENGTHEN command prompts

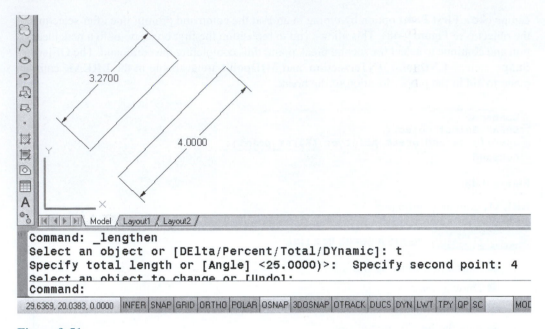

Figure 9-51

Lengthen command result

The following four options determine how much the object is to be lengthened:

- The **Delta** option is executed by typing **DE** at the prompt line. This option allows you to select any two positions on the screen as a length value or enter a value at the command prompt. Next, you are prompted to select the object to be lengthened. After the object is selected, the distance calculated between the first two points is added to the end closest to the object end that was selected.

- The **Percent** option is invoked by typing **P** at the command line. This option uses a percent value to increase or decrease the length of an object. The current length of the object is considered a value of 100 percent. Any value larger than 100 percent increases the object proportionally by that amount, and any value less than 100 percent decreases the length proportionally. After you have established the percentage needed, you are prompted to select the object to lengthen; the percentage is added to or subtracted from the closest chosen end of the object.

- The **Total** option uses the number entered as the new, current value of the length of the object selected. The object is lengthened to or shortened from the closest endpoint selected, and the total length of the object equals the value of the length entered for the **Total** (see Figure 9-51).

- The **Dynamic** option prompts you to select the object to be modified or lengthened. When you see a dynamic link to the movement of the mouse, you can increase or decrease the length of the object simply by moving the mouse position to a desired location. This chosen length is then adjusted to the end closest to the original selection point.

Stretch

The **STRETCH** command allows you to select objects and relocate the endpoints, vertices, or control points of those objects so that the objects are lengthened or shortened in any direction. You can also change the rotation angle of the objects. When using the **STRETCH** command, you must select the objects with a crossing window or a crossing polygon. Any other method of selecting the objects will result in a **MOVE** command, not a **STRETCH** command.

Once the object selection process (including hatches and dimensions) is complete, you are prompted to *Specify a base point or displacement*. You can enter a displacement value directly, and the objects will **STRETCH** the corresponding distance and direction. If a base

MODIFY COMMAND
Stretch
Options:
Base Point, Undo
Displacement
Type In:
Stretch
Alias-Type In:
S
Menu:
Icon:
Toolbar: Modify
Tool Palette: Modify
Ribbon: Home (Modify Expanded)

```
Command: _stretch
Select objects to stretch by crossing-window or crossing-polygon...
Select objects: Specify opposite corner: 1 found
Select objects:                                              I
Specify base point or [Displacement] <Displacement>:
Specify second point or <use first point as displacement>:
Command:
```

Figure 9-52

STRETCH command prompts

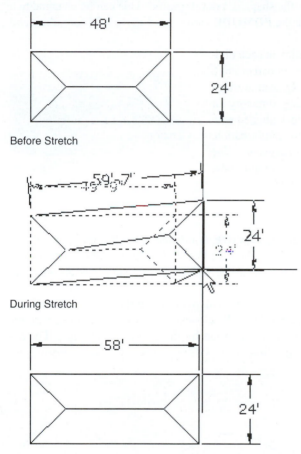

Before Stretch

During Stretch

After Stretch

Figure 9-53

Stretch the house 10' or @10',0.

point is chosen, the command requests that you *Specify a second point* (see Figure 9-52). The objects selected are dynamically stretched to the new location prior to the selection of the second point (see Figure 9-53).

Divide

The **DIVIDE** command allows you to create points or insert blocks at equal spaces along a selected object. Although the command may sound as if it will break the main objects into smaller objects, this is not true. The command places reference objects along the selected object that can be used as geometric references. The **DIVIDE** command is essentially a **Modify** command but is found in the **Draw** menu as one of the **Point** menu cascade options.

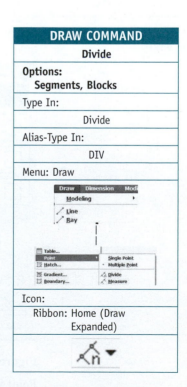

DRAW COMMAND
Divide
Options:
Segments, Blocks
Type In:
Divide
Alias-Type In:
DIV
Menu: Draw
Icon:
Ribbon: Home (Draw Expanded)

On entering the command, you are prompted to *Select object to divide.* After the selection has been made, you are prompted to *Enter the number of segments or [Block].* If you enter a numeric value, the program places a point node at each proportioned location along the object. The actual shape of the symbol at the divided point node is controlled by the **PDMODE** system variable. By default the shape is a dot or period. This can be changed to a more recognizable symbol by changing the **PDMODE** value. See Figure 9-54 for values and related symbol results.

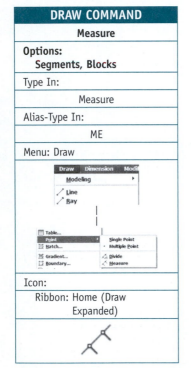

DRAW COMMAND
Measure
Options: **Segments, Blocks**
Type In: Measure
Alias-Type In: ME
Menu: Draw
Icon: Ribbon: Home (Draw Expanded)

If you want to insert a block definition at each division location, you need to enter a **B** at the second prompt, *Enter the number of segments or [Block].* You are then prompted for the block name including directory or folder path and whether you want the block aligned with the selected object. After entering the block information, you are prompted to *Enter the number of segments.* The symbol is placed along the object and at the proportional or division location as shown in Figure 9-55.

NOTE:

A complete explanation of **BLOCKS** can be found in Chapter 10.

Measure

The **MEASURE** command is similar to the **DIVIDE** command. The difference is that the **MEASURE** command allows you to specify a distance that will be measured off as equal intervals from one end of a selected object. As with the **DIVIDE** command, this distance can be identified with points or blocks.

The starting point for the measurement will vary depending on the object selected. On lines or arcs, the distance will be measured from the closest endpoint of the line or arc selected. For circles, the starting point will be identified by the current snap angle. For example, if the snap angle is set to 90°, the first point will be at the 12 o'clock position on the circle.

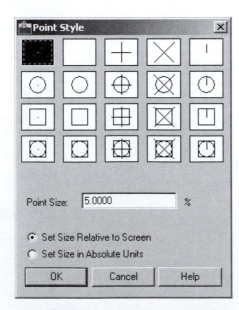

Figure 9-54

Point Style dialog box for default symbol

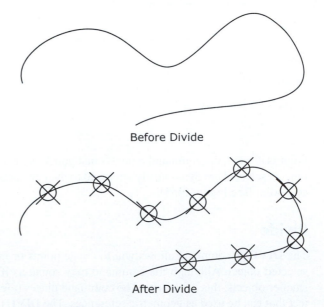

Figure 9-55

Point symbol placement

Join

The **JOIN** command joins selected objects into a single unbroken object. Depending on the type of objects selected, you see one of several prompts. There are certain restrictions to the objects eligible for this operation, as follows:

- If you select lines for the objects to join, the lines must be collinear, although they may have gaps between the objects.
- If you select arcs, the arcs must lie on the same imaginary circle, although they may have gaps between the objects. If you want a series of arcs to form a closed circle, you need to invoke the **Close** option from the command line.
- If you select polylines, the polylines must be in the same XY plane, and there can be no gaps between the vertices of the polylines.
- Finally, if you select a series of splines, they must be one continuous spline joined end to end.

The **JOIN** command results in the creation of a single object of the same nature as the source objects selected, as shown in Figure 9-56.

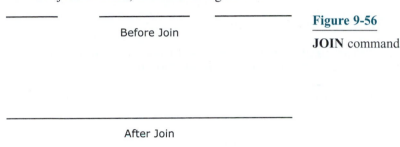

Before Join

After Join

Figure 9-56

JOIN command

MODIFY COMMAND
Join
Options: Select Objects
Type In:
Join
Alias-Type In:
J
Menu:
Icon:
Toolbar: Modify
Tool Palette: Modify
Ribbon: Home (Modify Expanded)

Matching Properties

Proper drawing techniques use layers, colors, linetypes, and so on, for specific definitions and meanings. In the process of creating and modifying entities in an AutoCAD drawing, object properties may not be properly defined, since an object may be drawn on the wrong layer or have the incorrect linetype. The **MATCH PROPERTIES** command lets you quickly change properties to match a properly defined object that already exists in the drawing.

The properties of an object as shown in Figure 9-57 include **Color**, **Layer**, **Linetype**, **Lineweight**, and others as shown. If a source object with the correct settings is already in the

MODIFY COMMAND
Match Properties of a Source Object
Options: Color, Layer, Linetype, Linetype Scale, Lineweight, Thickness, Plot Style
Type In:
MatchProp
Alias-Type In:
MA
Menu:
Icon:
Toolbar: Standard
Ribbon: Home (Properties Expanded)

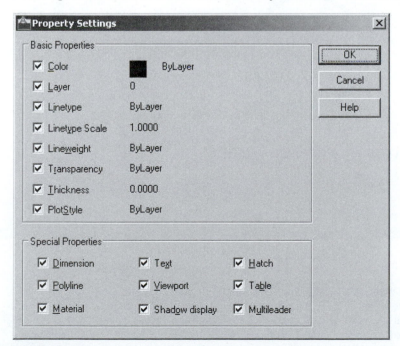

Figure 9-57

Property settings for the **MATCH PROPERTIES** command

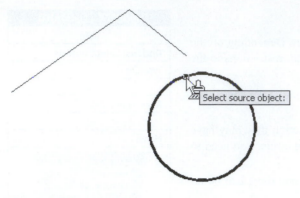

Figure 9-58

Selecting the source or original object for matching

drawing, it is easier to **Match Properties** than to **Modify Properties** within the **Modify** palette. Through the **MATCH PROPERTIES** command, all changes are made at the same time. If not all the properties are to be transferred, you can deselect or select the correct combination from the **Property Settings** dialog box (see Figure 9-57) while processing the command.

When the **MATCH PROPERTIES** command is invoked, you are requested to select a source object. Only one source object is allowed, and therefore the only selection method is the pick box (see Figure 9-58). After the original or source object is chosen, the command prompt displays the active settings and prompts you to type an **S** to modify the current match settings if desired (see Figure 9-59). Once the settings have been verified, destination objects or entities to be modified can then be chosen with any of the selection methods. The result is properly modified entities, as shown in Figure 9-60.

```
'MATCHPROP
Select source object:
Current active settings:  Color Layer Ltype Ltscale Lineweight Transparency
Thickness PlotStyle Dim Text Hatch Polyline Viewport Table Material Shadow
display Multileader
Select destination object(s) or [Settings]:
Select destination object(s) or [Settings]:
Command:
```

Figure 9-59

The **MATCH PROPERTIES** command prompt

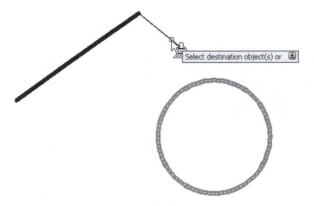

Figure 9-60

The result of the **MATCH PROPERTIES** command

Chapter Summary

In this chapter you advanced from using elementary AutoCAD commands in the draw-modify-dimension-print cycle to an intermediate skill level acquired through practice of what you have previously learned as well as an expansion of your knowledge of the **DRAW** and **MODIFY** commands. First, you learned some additional commands and options for creating various entities: circles

(**2 Points; 3 Points; Tan, Tan, Radius; Tan, Tan, Tan**); arcs (using various combinations of values for **Start** [first endpoint], **End** [second endpoint], **Center** [center point], **Angle** [included angle], **Radius, Length** [chord or arc distance], **Direction** [starting tangent direction], and **Continue** [endpoint]); ellipses (**Center** method, **Axis, End** method, and **Arc** method); rectangles

(RECTANG command with **Chamfer**, **Fillet**, **Elevation**, **Thickness**, **Width**, **Area**, **Dimension**, and **Rotation** options); and predefined and user-defined hatch patterns (**HATCH** command). Next, you learned how to create and edit **Single Line (Dynamic) Text** using the **TEXT** or **DTEXT** command, and **Multiline Text (MTEXT)** using the **MULTILINE TEXT** command. Finally, you were introduced to additional methods of object selection (**All**, **Previous**, **Last**, and **Fence**) and additional modifying commands (**FILLET**, **CHAMFER**, **TRIM**, **EXTEND**, **BREAK**, **LENGTHEN**, **STRETCH**, **DIVIDE**, **MEASURE**, **JOIN**, and **MATCH PROPERTIES**) from the **Modify** menu, **Modify** toolbar, and **Modify** panel on the **Home** ribbon.

Chapter Test Questions

Multiple Choice

Circle the correct answer.

1. Which is **not** an option for creating a circle?
   a. **Tan, Tan, Tan**
   b. **3 Points**
   c. **2 points** and a **Radius**
   d. **Tan, Tan, Radius**

2. Which is **not** a valid selection option?
   a. **Last**
   b. **Layer**
   c. **All**
   d. **Previous**

3. Hatching will fill a boundary area with
   a. Solid color
   b. Gradient
   c. Patterns
   d. All the above

4. Single-line text produces text that will act as
   a. Individual letters
   b. A paragraph
   c. A single line
   d. Individual words

5. The **STRETCH** command requires the objects to be selected with what method?
   a. Fence
   b. Window
   c. Crossing
   d. Previous

Matching

Write the number of the correct answer on the line.

a. **Join** _____

b. **Break** _____

c. **Trim** _____

d. **Lengthen** _____

e. **Last** _____

1. Removes a portion of an object

2. Changes the endpoint distance

3. Connects multiple objects

4. Requires cutting edges

5. Selects the most current object created

True or False

Circle the correct answer.

1. **True or False:** Multiline text acts more like word-processor text than does single-line text.

2. **True or False: Offset** will copy the properties of the selected object.

3. **True or False:** A fillet radius cannot have a zero value.

4. **True or False:** The **Rectangle** command will allow you to insert fillets on the corners of the rectangle.

5. **True or False:** You can use only a single object as a cutting edge.

Chapter Projects

Project 9-1 [INTERMEDIATE]

Research the size and create a top view of a 54-tooth 8″ spur gear.

Project 9-2 [INTERMEDIATE]

Develop a reflected ceiling plan for a 20′ × 20′ room using a traditional 2′ × 4′ fluorescent light fixture.

Project 9-3 [INTERMEDIATE]

Develop a site plan of your campus showing buildings, parking, sidewalks, and so on.

Chapter Practice Exercises

Ⓖ Practice Exercise 9-1: *Direct Distance Input* [BASIC]

1. Start a new drawing with the **NEW** command in the **File** menu.

2. Enter **0,0** and **11,8.5** as **Drawing Limits** in the **Format** menu.

3. In the **View** menu pick **ZOOM/ALL** to reset the drawing area to the limits.

4. Create two layers, one for the part drawing and one for dimensions.

5. Draw a rectangle starting at **1,1** that is **5.5** units in the X direction and **4.0** units in the Y direction.

6. Using the **OFFSET**, **TRIM**, **EXTEND**, and other commands in this chapter, modify the rectangle to create the plate shown in Figure 9-61.

7. Using the **STRETCH** command, expand the right half of the drawing units to the right. Be sure to include all the dimensions in this operation.

8. Save the drawing in your **Workskills** folder as **EX9-1**.

> **NOTE:**
> You can use the template created in Chapter 4 or establish each of these settings in a new file.

Figures 9-62 through 9-73 represent typical architectural, civil, and mechanical drawings (and include dimensions, text, and other information) that can be created using the techniques and commands explained in this chapter.

1. To begin the drawing process for each drawing, access the **File** menu and pick **NEW**. (Use the acad.dwt template if this is requested.) You may choose to use one of your previously created templates from Chapter 4. Select the appropriate template as it relates to the drawing discipline.

2. Set the **Units** for the drawing if the drawing will use feet and inches or **Architectural** as units for the input. Set the **Length** units to **Architectural**. This command is found in the **Format** menu.

3. Set **LIMITS** for the drawing to resize the screen to hold the drawing. This command is in the **Format** menu. The lower left corner should be set to **0,0** with the upper right set to numbers just beyond the maximum X,Y of the figure.

4. Process the **ZOOM ALL** command using the keyboard, **View** menu, or icon. This resizes the screen to view the complete drawing as described by the limits.

5. Create layers for dimensions, notes, text, and other information as well as layers for object lines, centerlines, hidden lines, and other linetypes that may be used.

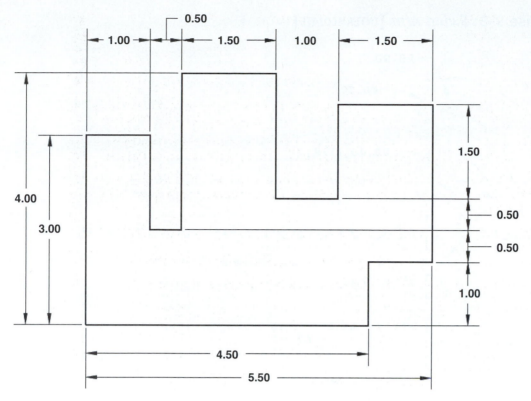

Figure 9-61

Drawing EX9-1

6. Access the **LINE** command to begin drawing the figure.

7. Add dimensions, leaders, text, and other information to the drawings to make them complete.

8. Remember to save your drawing every 10 to 15 minutes to avoid losing your work. Save the drawing in your **Workskills** folder with the figure number as the file name.

Ⓜ **Practice Exercise 9-2:** *Bracket* [INTERMEDIATE]

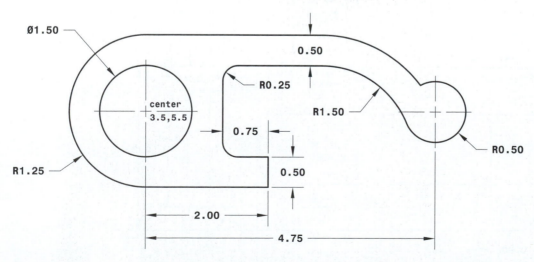

Figure 9-62

Drawing EX9-2

Ⓜ **Practice Exercise 9-3:** *Swing Arm* [INTERMEDIATE]

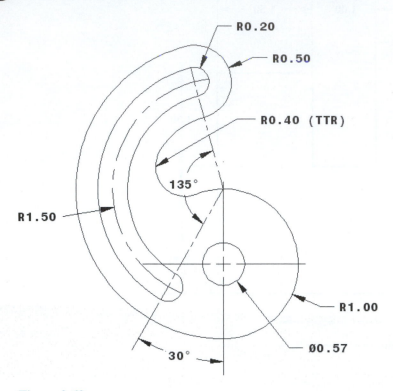

Figure 9-63
Drawing EX9-3

Ⓜ **Practice Exercise 9-4:** *Gasket* [INTERMEDIATE]

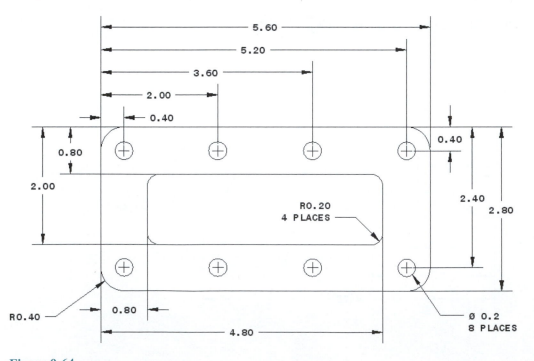

Figure 9-64
Drawing EX9-4

ⓜ Practice Exercise 9-5: *Angle Bar* [INTERMEDIATE]

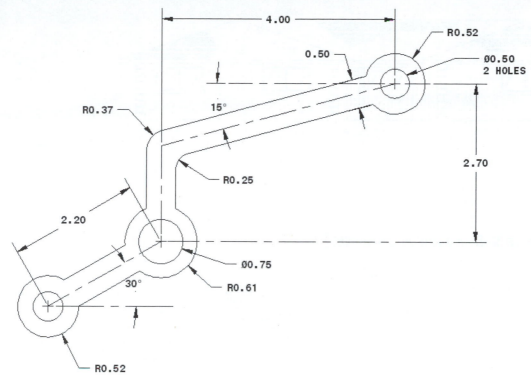

Figure 9-65

Drawing EX9-5

ⓜ Practice Exercise 9-6: *Polar Array* [INTERMEDIATE]

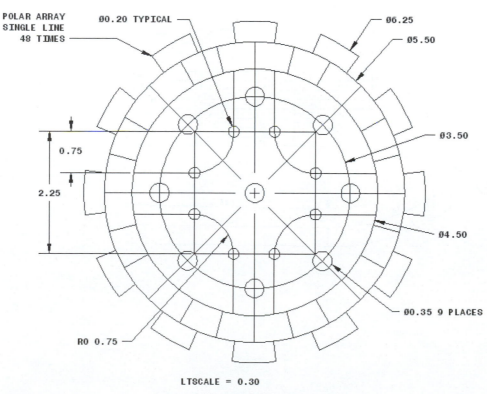

Figure 9-66

Drawing EX9-6

A **Practice Exercise 9-7:** *Front Elevation* [ADVANCED]

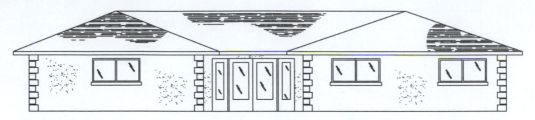

Figure 9-67

Drawing EX9-7

C **Practice Exercise 9-8:** *Roadway* [ADVANCED]

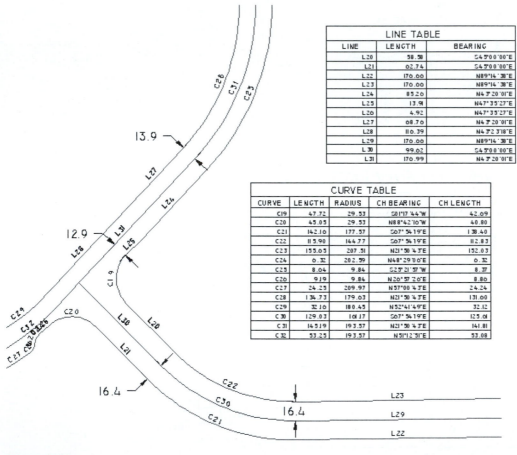

LINE TABLE		
LINE	LENGTH	BEARING
L20	58.58	S45°00'00"E
L21	62.74	S45°00'00"E
L22	170.00	N89°14'38"E
L23	170.00	N89°14'38"E
L24	85.20	N43°20'01"E
L25	13.91	N47°35'27"E
L26	4.92	N47°35'27"E
L27	68.70	N43°20'01"E
L28	110.39	N43°23'18"E
L29	170.00	N89°14'38"E
L30	99.62	S45°00'00"E
L31	170.99	N43°20'01"E

CURVE TABLE				
CURVE	LENGTH	RADIUS	CH BEARING	CH LENGTH
C19	47.72	29.53	S01°17'44"W	42.09
C20	45.03	29.53	N88°42'16"W	40.80
C21	142.10	177.57	S67°54'19"E	138.40
C22	115.90	144.77	S67°54'19"E	112.83
C23	155.65	207.51	N21°50'43"E	152.03
C24	6.32	202.59	N48°29'06"E	6.32
C25	8.04	9.84	S23°21'57"W	8.37
C26	9.19	9.84	N20°57'20"E	8.80
C27	24.25	209.97	N57°00'43"E	24.24
C28	134.73	179.63	N21°50'43"E	131.00
C29	32.10	180.45	N52°41'49"E	32.12
C30	129.03	161.17	S67°54'19"E	125.61
C31	145.19	193.57	N21°50'43"E	141.81
C32	53.25	193.57	N51°12'51"E	53.08

Figure 9-68

Drawing EX9-8

Ⓜ **Practice Exercise 9-9:** *Ellipse-Hatching* [ADVANCED]

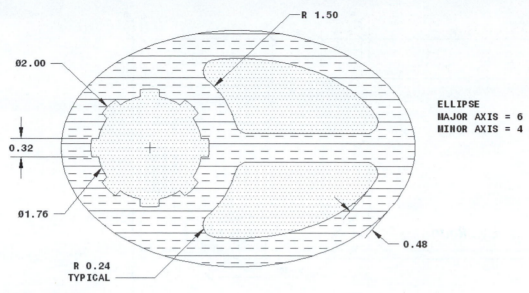

Figure 9-69

Drawing EX9-9

Ⓜ **Practice Exercise 9-10:** *Calipers* [ADVANCED]

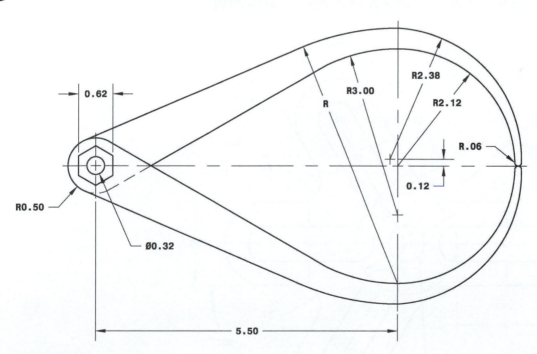

Figure 9-70

Drawing EX9-10

Ⓐ **Practice Exercise 9-11:** *Kitchen* **[ADVANCED]**

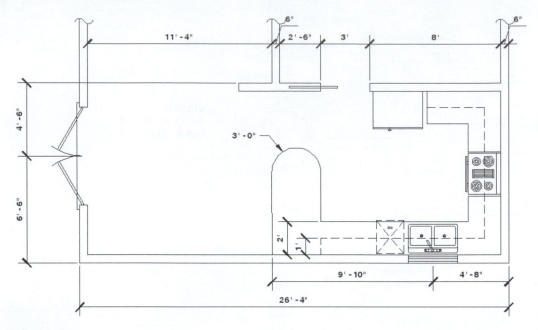

Figure 9-71

Drawing EX9-11

Ⓜ **Practice Exercise 9-12:** *Adjustable Arm Bracket* **[ADVANCED]**

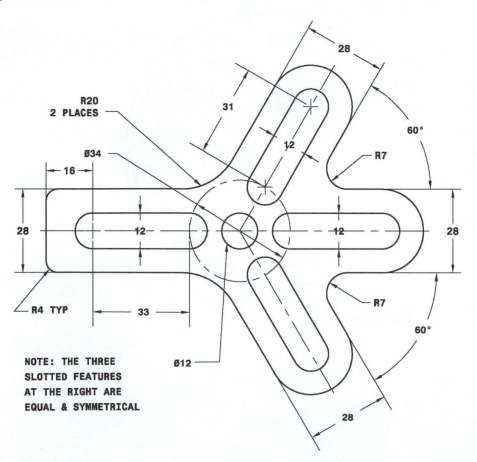

Figure 9-72

Drawing EX9-12

Practice Exercise 9-13: *Curb Section* [ADVANCED]

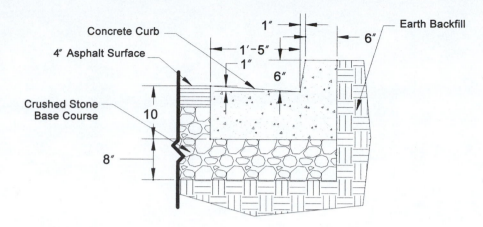

Figure 9-73

Concrete curb detail with hatch patterns; EX9-13

10 Fundamentals of Layers, Groups, and Blocks

CHAPTER OBJECTIVES

- Define layer properties.
- Create and manage groups.
- Create block definitions.
- Insert and manipulate blocks and external references.
- Use the **DesignCenter** for blocks and online objects.
- Use layers in the plotting process.

Introduction

In Chapter 4 we presented an introduction to the topic of layers. The general concept of layers was to use them to organize a drawing file. Commands such as **GROUP** and **BLOCK** will further these concepts of organization within a drawing file.

Layers

When layering was introduced as an object's property, the organization of a drawing suggested that similar objects are placed on individual layers. This discussion focuses on the creation of a layer and the explanation of a layer's properties and display controls. As already mentioned, the AutoCAD program does not automatically create layers in a drawing file. It is up to you to establish a *layering scheme*. In some cases, the layering scheme is part of a defined series of office standards or standards set by a permitting agency. In other cases, it is simply personal preference based on experience.

    The following discussion focuses on the implementation of a layering scheme and the fundamental practice operators use during a drawing session. You may want to revisit Chapter 4 to review the explanation of the various options and display controls found in the **LAYER** command.

layering scheme: A plan to create and manage a series of layers within a complex design.

FOR MORE DETAILS The U.S. National CAD Standards used by the Department of Defense and others establish a layering scheme that uses the American Institute of Architects (AIA) Layering Guidelines. For more information, check www.aia.org, www.nationalcadstandard.org, or the Building Smart Alliance (www.buildingsmartalliance.org), a Council of the National Institute of Building Science, for more details.

Layer Functions

You will address the layering topic in several types of commands. The definition of a series of layers and the ongoing placement of objects onto layers during a drawing session are the most basic command concerns of beginning users. As you learn to display a layer's content and control plotting through layers, you will discover the power of using layers. Keep in mind that the actual organization of specific objects on specific layers is governed by the type of drawing and the discipline involved.

Palette Versus Toolbars

There are two general ways to organize information when you create a layering scheme. You can define a series of layers that are property-based, or you can organize information according to topic. Property-based layers can be defined by object lines, hidden lines, centerlines, dimensions, or text. A layering scheme using drawing topics might contain information for foundation plans, electrical plans, elevations, section views, or contour lines. In either case new layers are created with the **Layer Properties Manager** palette (see Figure 10-1). The Manager is a palette that can be launched from the **Format** menu, the command line, the **Layers** toolbar (see Figure 10-2), or the **Layers** panel on the **Home** ribbon (see Figure 10-3). When you create a layer, you will give it a unique name, you will define the layer properties, and you may establish it to be the *current layer*.

current layer: The layer that is active to receive all newly created entities.

After the layering scheme is created, all other **Layer** command options can easily be executed through the **Layers** toolbar. When dealing with layers, it is important to have the correct *current layer* when creating new objects, because objects take on the current layer as a property. Although this property can be changed after an object is created, it is better to pay attention to the current layer to make sure it is the correct one for your objects. You can change the current layer by clicking on the down arrow in the **Layers** toolbar and simply

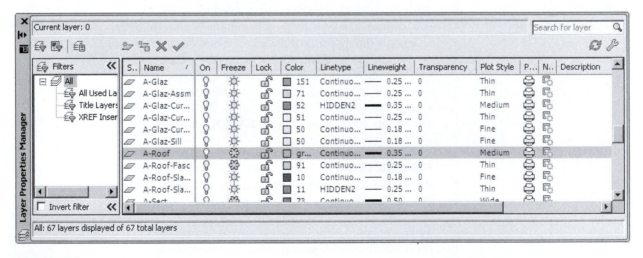

Figure 10-1

Layer Properties Manager palette

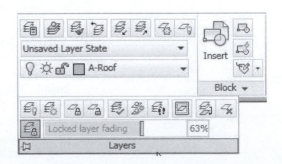

Figure 10-2

Layers toolbar

Figure 10-3

Layers panel on the **Home** ribbon

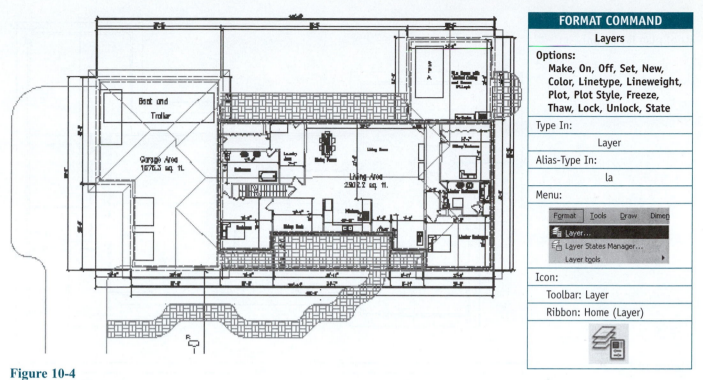

FORMAT COMMAND
Layers
Options: **Make, On, Off, Set, New, Color, Linetype, Lineweight, Plot, Plot Style, Freeze, Thaw, Lock, Unlock, State**
Type In: Layer
Alias-Type In: la
Menu: Format Tools Draw Dimen   Layer...   Layer States Manager...   Layer tools ▸
Icon:
Toolbar: Layer
Ribbon: Home (Layer)

Figure 10-4

All layers are on and visible

selecting another layer name to be the next current layer. The visibility controls for a layer's content are found in this same drop-down list, represented by a lightbulb, a sun, and a padlock. Clicking on these icons executes the **On/Off** toggle options (see Figures 10-4, 10-5, 10-6, and 10-7) as well as the **Freeze/Thaw** and **Lock/Unlock** toggles. These options are referred to as the *display-based* options. Although these same options are available in the **Layer Properties Manager**, access through the toolbar or ribbon can be faster. If you want to change one of the layer's properties (linetype, color, lineweight, or plot style), you have to do this in the **Layer Properties Manager**.

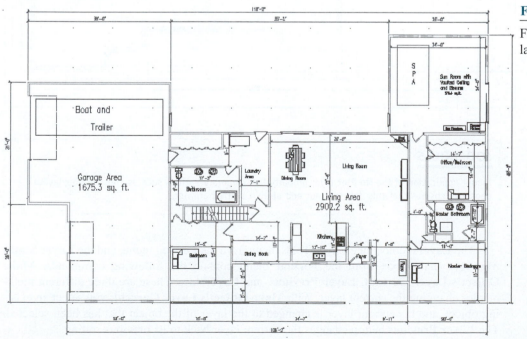

Figure 10-5

Floor plan with furniture layers on

Figure 10-6

Roof plan layers only on

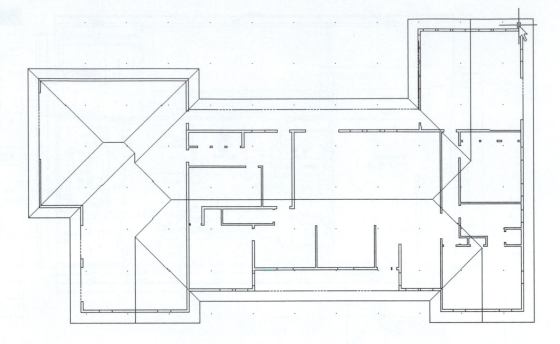

Figure 10-7

Foundation layers only on

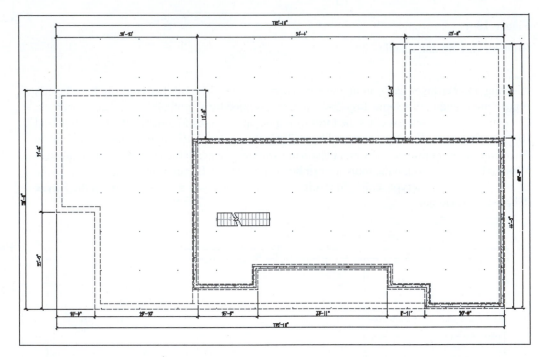

JOB SKILLS

Proper application of the **No Plot** layer property for temporary entities such as construction/layout geometry ensures that this data will not end up in a plotted drawing.

The **Layers** toolbar, the **Layer Tools** menu from the **Format** menu, and the **Layer States Manager** dialog box from the **Format** menu contain the following commands: **Make Object's Layer Current**, **Layer Previous**, and **Layerstate**. These are three different methods for changing the current layer. With **Make Object's Layer Current**, you select an existing object, and the current layer is changed to the layer of the object that has been selected. The **Layer Previous** button changes the current layer back to its previous setting.

The **Layerstate** button displays a list of layer states saved within the drawing file. The **Layer States Manager** dialog box (see Figure 10-8) allows you to create, rename, edit, or delete layer states. Layer states are a snapshot of the current conditions of the drawing layer's organization and display properties (see Figure 10-9). These snapshots or what is called the *current layer state* can be saved for future reference to adjust layer settings quickly (see Figure 10-10) or exported to other drawings (see Figure 10-11).

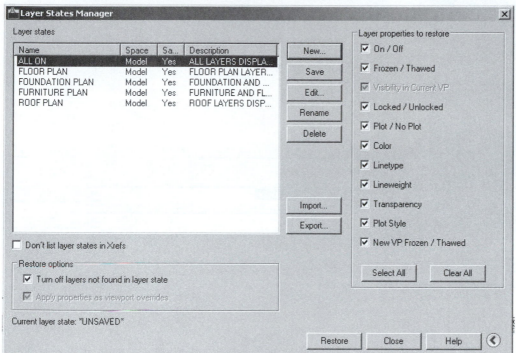

Figure 10-8

Layer States Manager dialog box

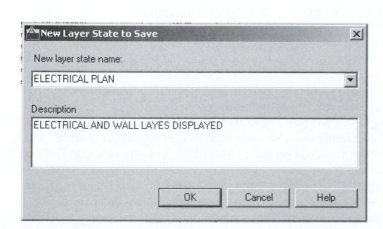

Figure 10-9

Creating a **New Layer State** dialog box

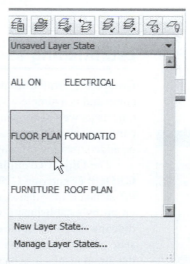

Figure 10-10

Layer State drop-down list on the **Layers** panel on the **Home** ribbon

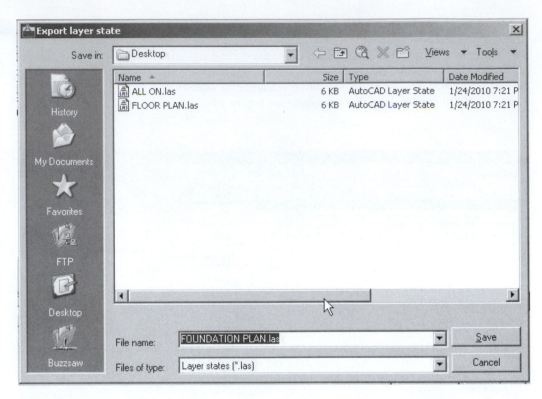

Figure 10-11

Exporting a Layer State dialog box

Paying attention to the current layer will make it easier to maintain an organized drawing file. As mentioned earlier, if needed, objects can be reassigned to other layers. If an object is placed on an incorrect layer, you simply select the object with the command prompt present (grip the object), then move the cursor to the drop box in the **Layers** toolbar or in the ribbon. Then, from the list, select the layer on which you want to place the object. Again, it is to your benefit to maintain an organized drawing. Using a logical layering scheme is a major factor in a drawing's organization.

Establishing and Working with Object Groups

groups: A command used to manipulate a group of objects as if it were one.

Groups are formed from a selected set of objects and can be saved into a named set. This command is a simple way to organize objects into subsets that can be used to select multiple objects as well as to manipulate those same objects as a single unit. Groups can be adjusted continuously. Objects assigned to a group can be removed at any time, and new objects can be added, making this an alternative method for drawing organization.

The **Object Grouping** dialog box (see Figure 10-12) is launched by typing in the word **GROUP** or entering **G** at the prompt line. (No menu item or icon options are available with the standard installation of the AutoCAD program.) This dialog box allows you to define a group by establishing a **Group Name**. Selecting the **New** button places you back into the drawing file to select the objects to be placed in the group. When a group is defined, you must state whether the group is **Selectable**. If a group is labeled **Selectable**, selecting any object in the group results in selecting the entire group. The second option in the creation of a group is designating whether the group will be named. This option, when active, assigns a generic name to each group created if no name is input.

Once a group is defined, the same dialog box is used to adjust the members of the group. All defined groups are listed in the top area of the dialog box. Selecting a name from this area

COMMAND
Group
Options: **Add, Remove, Rename,**   **Re-order, Description,**   **Selectable, Explode**
Type In:
Group
Alias-Type In:
G
Menu:
Icon:

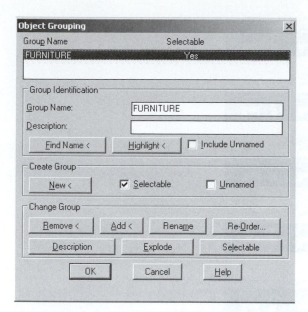

Figure 10-12

Object Grouping dialog box

activates the lower portion of the dialog box, where you can edit the group definition. Editing of the group can include adding or removing objects as well as exploding the entire group definition. Groups that are created are saved with the drawing file and are available from one drawing session to another. The one disadvantage of groups is that the group definitions are not available to move from one drawing file to another drawing file to be used again. However, groups can be made into blocks, as detailed next.

block: A series of objects in a drawing controlled as one entity.

Fundamentals of Making Blocks

Blocks are similar to groups. A ***block*** is a series of objects that is saved under a unique name in a drawing. The block definition consists of the objects and their relationship at the time the objects are selected for the subset.

When the block is created, the individual objects combine into one new object, which results in a smaller and more efficient object than the individual entities. Merging many objects into one block reduces the size of a set of objects by one-third to half (see Figure 10-13). The result is a more compact drawing that allows for faster selection of objects, faster pans and zooms, and an overall productivity improvement with every command. Also, any block can be exported and saved as a drawing, and any existing drawing can be used as a block and placed in other drawings. The use of blocks increases consistency in a drawing file and throughout the organization, as more consistent symbols, details, and libraries are used.

Selection of the **BLOCK Make** command launches the **Block Definition** dialog box (shown in Figure 10-14). You need to do at least three things to define a block. You enter a **Name** for the block definition. This name should follow the same naming standards as for other item definitions or standards you use related to AutoCAD drawings. After establishing the name, you select the objects to be part of the definition. Selecting the **Select objects** icon in the upper right area of the **Block Definition** dialog box shifts you back into the drawing file to use any of the **Select objects** methods discussed previously. The next item of the definition is to select a **Base point** to control the location for future insertion of this series of objects in this block definition. The base point should be chosen with an object snap drawing aid to ensure accuracy and should be on or near the block. Figure 10-15 shows the possible locations of the base point based on grips. Using the typical default base point with 0,0,0 as the coordinates is not recommended, as the base point should be on or near the block to aid

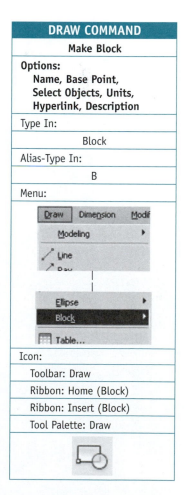

DRAW COMMAND
Make Block
Options:
Name, Base Point, Select Objects, Units, Hyperlink, Description
Type In:
Block
Alias-Type In:
B
Menu:
Icon:
Toolbar: Draw
Ribbon: Home (Block)
Ribbon: Insert (Block)
Tool Palette: Draw

Figure 10-13

Classroom of 25 desks; drawing is 42% smaller when desks are blocks (33 kB versus 57 kB)

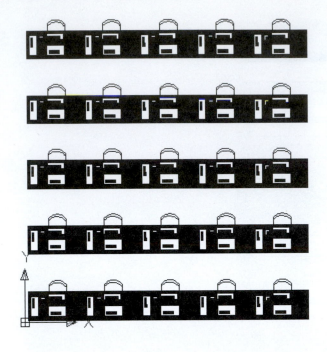

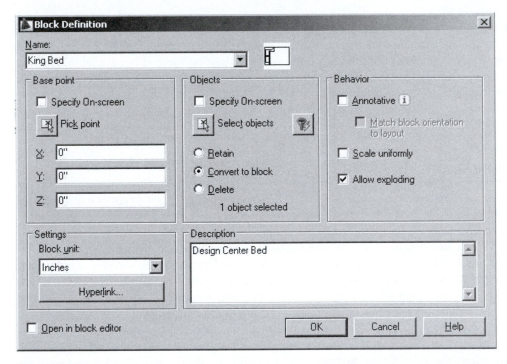

Figure 10-14

Block Definition dialog box

in placement. The blocks are created in the drawing units currently active. If you need to select a different type of unit, you can change the unit type in the **Block unit** area of the **Block Definition** dialog box.

After entering all the information in the dialog box, you finish the process by clicking on the **OK** button (see Figure 10-16). This writes the definition into the current drawing file for use and further placement in this drawing. Depending on the setting in the **Select objects** area of the dialog box, the objects selected may be treated as follows:

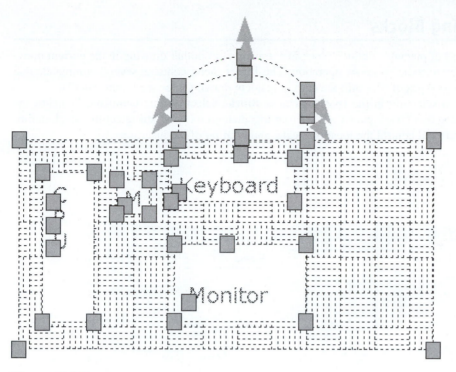

Figure 10-15

Computer desk as 16 objects

- **Converted** Selected entities become the new block definition.
- **Retained** Entities keep current form as separate objects.
- **Deleted** Objects are removed from the drawing file as individual entities and retained only as a block in the drawing; with this option, the new block may be inserted in the drawing, if needed.

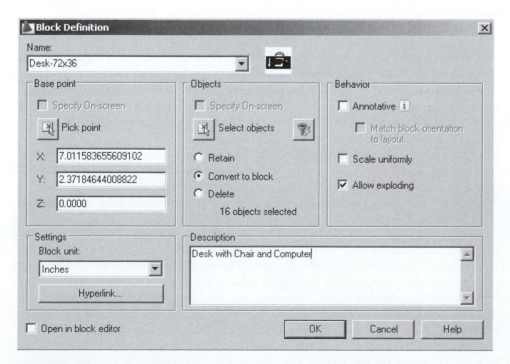

Figure 10-16

Block definition completed

Inserting Blocks

insert: The process of merging a drawing file into the resident drawing file.

The process of placing a defined block in a drawing, or another drawing in the current drawing, is referred to as an *insert* operation. The **Insert** menu contains several commands that place various types of files into the current resident drawing file (see Figure 10-17).

The top selection in the **Insert** menu is **Block**. Selecting this command launches the **Insert** dialog box (see Figure 10-18). From this dialog box, you can select the block definition to insert and control the location, scale, and rotation of the insertion.

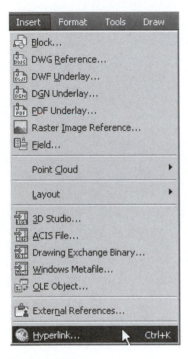

Figure 10-17

Insert menu

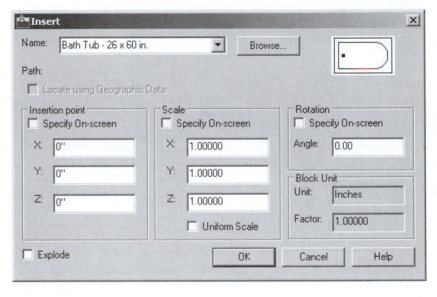

Figure 10-18

Insert Block dialog box

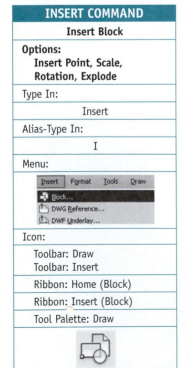

INSERT COMMAND
Insert Block
Options:
Insert Point, Scale,
Rotation, Explode
Type In:
Insert
Alias-Type In:
I
Menu:
Icon:
Toolbar: Draw
Toolbar: Insert
Ribbon: Home (Block)
Ribbon: Insert (Block)
Tool Palette: Draw

To begin the insertion process, you select a block definition from the **Name** drop-down list at the top of the dialog box. All the block definitions that have been created in this drawing file or previously inserted into the drawing file will be found in this list. You may select to insert a complete drawing into the resident drawing file. To do this, you click on the **Browse** button. This launches the **Select Drawing File** dialog box (see Figure 10-19), allowing you to select any AutoCAD drawing file for insertion.

Once you have selected the block definition, you must supply three pieces of information to complete the process. You must specify the **Insertion point**, **Scale**, and **Rotation** through the dialog box fields (see Figure 10-18), the command line, or on the drawing screen. A check mark in any of the **Specify On-screen** boxes will cause this information to be entered on the drawing screen or in the command line (see Figure 10-20).

The insertion point, which can be an absolute coordinate, is specified through the X, Y, and Z coordinate location. Use your cursor and an object snap override or other location method to specify the point on the drawing screen. The block definition can be scaled on any one of the three axes (*X*, *Y*, or *Z*) by inputting a value in the **Scale** field. The default value or current scale of the definition is 1.0. To increase the size, you use a number larger than 1.0. To decrease the size, you input a number less than 1.0. Scale can vary on one or more directions on insertion. If you select the **Uniform Scale** check box, the value placed in the X scale field is applied to all scale fields. **Rotation** of the block definition is specified in the third area. A value of zero inserts the block in the same orientation it was created in. Positive values rotate the block definition counterclockwise, and negative values cause a clockwise rotation.

When all the fields in this dialog box have been addressed, click on the **OK** button. The block definition will be inserted into the drawing file. If the insertion point is to be specified

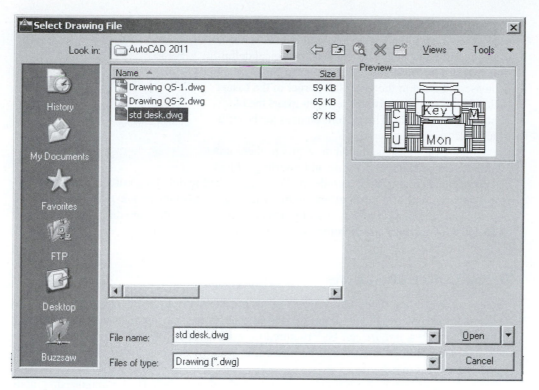

Figure 10-19

Browse dialog box for selecting a drawing file to insert as a block

```
Command:
Command: _insert
Specify insertion point or [Basepoint/Scale/X/Y/Z/Rotate]:

Command:
```

Figure 10-20

Command line options for insertion of a block

on-screen, you will see a ghost image of the block definition attached at the cursor control point in the drawing screen. The block will be placed in the file when the location is selected. This ghost image could take a few moments to appear depending on the complexity or size of the block.

MODIFY COMMAND
Explode
Options: **Select Objects**
Type In:
Explode
Alias-Type In:
X
Menu:
Icon:
Toolbar: Modify
Ribbon: Home (Modify)
Tool Palette: Modify

JOB SKILLS

Creating blocks, maintaining symbol libraries, and applying the various insertion options are daily activities for CAD operators. When you can demonstrate an understanding of these fundamental concepts, you will gain the productivity benefits offered by these commands.

The EXPLODE Command

As mentioned earlier, a block definition is imported into a file as one object regardless of how many objects make up the definition. By using the **EXPLODE** command, found in the **Modify** menu, Modify toolbar, **Home** ribbon, or Modify Panel, you can choose to explode the block definition into the original objects. This breaks up only the block or blocks selected; it does not affect other similar blocks already in the drawing and does not destroy the original block definition. Exploding a block definition allows you to select the individual objects within a definition.

Keep in mind that the block will no longer act as one object, but you will be able to insert additional versions of the definition when needed, since the original definition will still be valid and stays as part of the drawing database. A button in the lower left corner of the **Insert** dialog box (see Figure 10-18) lets you insert the block in an exploded format. This action removes the benefits of a block.

> **NOTE:**
> Blocks have additional advantages. You can attach attributes to block definitions, apply data-based searches for blocks, and edit blocks through dynamic global editing functions.

Although a block is similar to a group, there are significant advantages to defining and inserting a block as opposed to a group. These include smaller size; exploding only one, not all, selectable control points; nonuniform scaling; and more. The biggest advantages are that blocks can be copied from drawing file to drawing file and can also become a drawing directly (through the **WBLOCK** command) and therefore stored in a library for all to use.

DesignCenter Operations

DesignCenter: A tool palette that allows you to drag and drop entities from other AutoCAD files into the current file.

An alternative method for block insertion is available through the *DesignCenter*. The **DesignCenter** palette allows definition-based objects to be copied, inserted, or dragged from file to file. A *palette* can be structured to open when active and close when inactive (through Auto-Hide). Palettes can be resized, moved, or docked. Some palettes can also have a level of transparency.

palette: A special window that can access drawings, blocks, and commands in the AutoCAD environment.

The **DesignCenter** allows you to search through other AutoCAD files and use drag-and-drop techniques to copy information from the selected file into the resident file. The following types of information are available for this operation:

- Blocks
- Dimstyles
- Layers
- Layouts

- Linetypes
- Tablestyles
- Textstyles
- External references

The **DesignCenter** palette (see Figure 10-21) is split into two sections, much like the Windows Explorer environment. The section on the left allows you to navigate directly to the category of interest in an AutoCAD drawing file or on the **Autodesk Seek Design Content** network. The three tabs at the top show the areas available in **DesignCenter**. With the first tab, you can select the type of information you are interested in from the various storage devices and network drives that can be accessed by your computer. You can quickly examine any currently open drawings or drawings recently accessed with the second and third tab, respectively. The fourth option leads to **Autodesk Seek** (in the upper right corner), an Internet-based service (Internet access must be available for this option) from Autodesk containing symbols, blocks, manufacturer materials, and more.

> **NOTE:**
> From **DesignCenter**, items of interest can also be dragged and dropped onto a tool palette. Tool palettes have many of the same properties as **DesignCenter**. Although tool palettes cannot be used to find items, they can be taken from drawing to drawing as part of a template and also exported for others to use. See Chapter 13 for more information.

After the type of information is selected, the definitions found in the selected drawing file are listed on the right side of the dialog box. When an object is chosen, a detail view is available in the middle right area, and descriptive data are shown in the lower right window. You can select the items with the left mouse button depressed and drag them into the current drawing file, releasing the left mouse button when the cursor is over the resident drawing file for a 1:1 scale placement. Multiple items can be selected and copied at the same time, by adhering to the multiple selection methods of the Windows environment. If a different scale is desired, using the right mouse button will provide the menu shown in Figure 10-22 to allow changes before placement. The **Insert Block** item shown leads to the **Insert** dialog box as

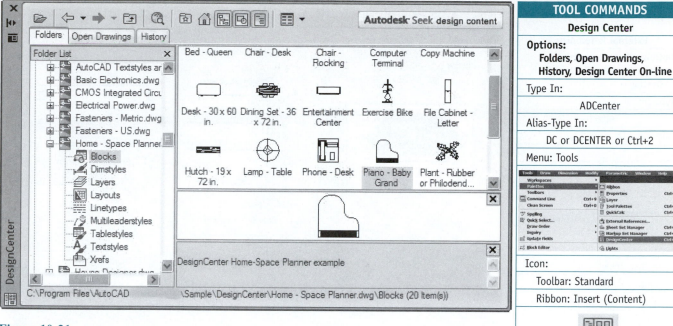

TOOL COMMANDS

Design Center

Options:
Folders, Open Drawings, History, Design Center On-line

Type In:

ADCenter

Alias-Type In:

DC or DCENTER or Ctrl+2

Menu: Tools

Icon:

Toolbar: Standard

Ribbon: Insert (Content)

Figure 10-21

Autodesk Seek in the **DesignCenter**

seen in Figure 10-18, which allows precision placement, nonuniform scaling, rotation, and change of units.

External or DWG References

External references, sometimes referred to as *Xrefs*, are an alternative for inserting a selected drawing file into the resident drawing file. When a block is inserted into a drawing file, the process stores all the information regarding the definition in the active file, enlarging the resident file accordingly and thus maintaining no link to the original file. Therefore, if the original block file changes, the block insertions in the active drawing will not.

The use of an external reference has two distinct advantages. First, the externally referenced file is attached through a file-linking process from any location available to the computer (see Figure 10-23). This file-linking process does not import the entire contents of the definition into the resident file, but rather, it maintains a link to the file location and merely displays the file's content in the resident drawing file when it is opened. This file-linking process leads to the second advantage. If the referenced original file changes, the changes will be reflected in all the locations to which the external reference is attached on the next reload.

A single external reference can simultaneously be attached to multiple drawings, and multiple external references can be attached to a single drawing file as well. Maintaining this link is important because it ensures that you are using the most current version of a related drawing file (see Figure 10-24). This process also increases uniformity throughout an office when multiple operators use the same and most current version of the drawings.

Another advantage of Xrefs is the ability to access layers, to make changes in visibility and color that can be assigned to that attachment or overlay (see Figure 10-25). For example, this allows the first floor to be easily screened into a gray state, showing the second floor in the active colors to locate doors, walls, and windows more easily, or allows changing colors of existing contour lines from proposed lines for easier editing.

> **NOTE:**
>
> Blocks and external references can be edited by following their links through the drawing in which they reside back to the original or master, if you have the rights to access and edit these items.

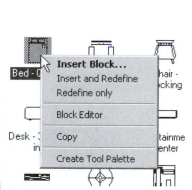

Figure 10-22

Insert Block right-click menu from **DesignCenter** palette

external reference: A special block that creates and maintains a live link between drawing files.

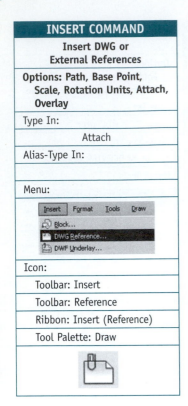

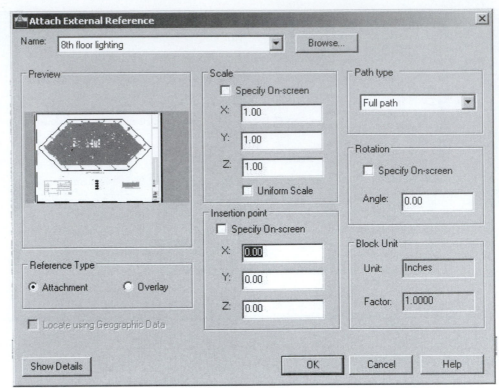

Figure 10-23

Attach External Reference dialog box

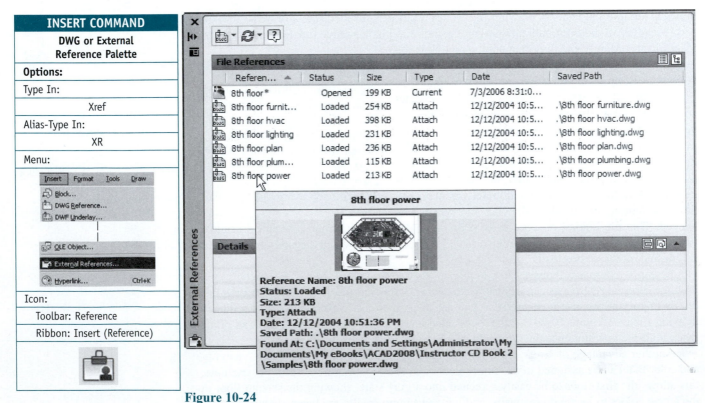

Figure 10-24

File References in **External References** palette

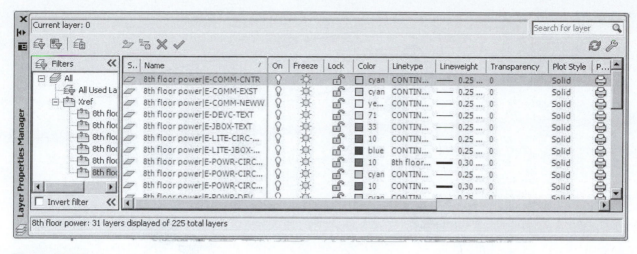

Figure 10-25

Layer Properties Manager showing externally referenced layers with the drawing name as a prefix

An external reference is attached through the **Insert** menu. In this menu you find the **EXTERNAL** or **DWG REFERENCE** command. When you select this command, you will be prompted to *Select the referenced file* through a dialog box similar to the **Select Drawing File** dialog box (see Figure 10-19). Once the file is selected, the **External Reference** dialog box appears. This box displays the file name along with the file location path at the top of the dialog box. To maintain the intelligence of the external reference, the **Reference Type** should be an **Attachment**, and the **Path type** should be **Full path**.

As shown in Figure 10-24, a quick preview of information about the drawing will appear as the cursor crosses the information row on the palette.

When you attach an external reference, you have all the same options you had with block insertion. **Insertion point**, **Scale**, and **Rotation** act in the same manner as they did with the block insertion. When the command is complete, the externally referenced drawing file is displayed at the insertion point location. This sequence is shown in Figures 10-26, 10-27, and 10-28.

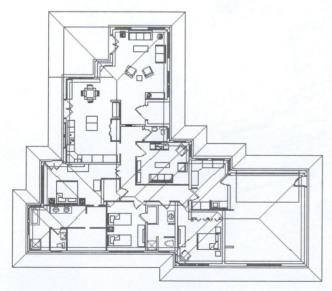

Figure 10-26

The house plan

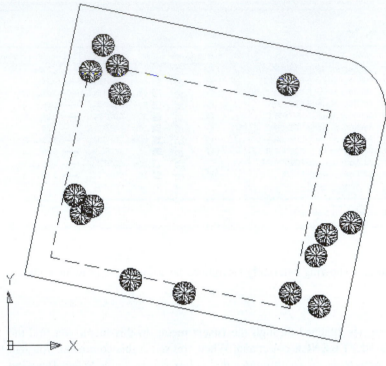

Figure 10-27

The site plan

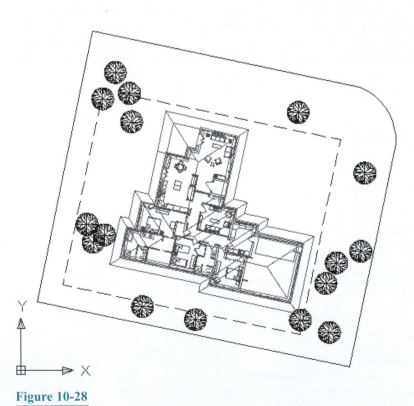

Figure 10-28

The site plan with the house plan as an external reference

Chapter Summary

This chapter introduced you to the use of layers, groups, and blocks for organizing AutoCAD drawings. First, you learned how to implement a layering scheme by creating layers with the **Layer Properties Manager,** giving them unique names and defining their properties, as well as how to modify layers with the **Layers** toolbar or the **Layers** panel on the **Home** ribbon and its commands (drop-down menu icons, **Make Object's Layer Current**, **Layer Previous,** and **Layerstate**). Then, you learned how to organize selected sets of objects into groups using the **Object Grouping** dialog box, a process that enables you to manipulate the objects as a single unit. Subsequently, you were introduced to the creation and manipulation of blocks using the

Block Definition and **Insert** dialog boxes, the **EXPLODE** command, and the **DesignCenter** palette. Blocks are series of objects, saved under unique names, that may be used repeatedly in a drawing. Using blocks results in more compact, consistent drawings that allow commands to be executed quickly, improving productivity. Finally, you learned how to attach external references (Xrefs) from the **Insert** menu (**EXTERNAL** or **DWG REFERENCE** command). Xrefs are special blocks that create and maintain live links between drawing files, enabling the contents of externally referenced file(s) to be displayed in the resident file and providing multiple operators with the same and most current version of drawing files.

Chapter Tutorials

A Tutorial 10-1: *Bedroom Drawing*

1. Start a new drawing.

2. **Drawing Units Length Type** should be set to **Architectural** (see Figure 10-29).

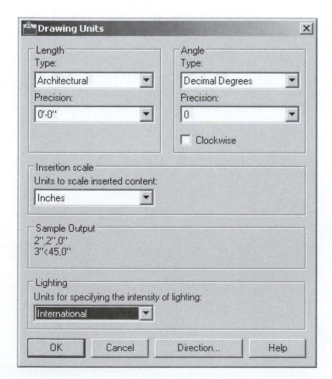

Figure 10-29

Drawing Units dialog box

3. Draw a rectangle that is **15′ × 13′** and save the drawing as **My Bedroom** in your **Workskills** folder (see Figure 10-30).

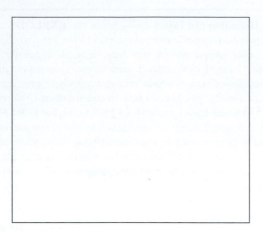

Figure 10-30

Your bedroom drawing

4. Start **DesignCenter** and navigate to the following folders: **C:\Program Files\AutoCAD 2011\Sample\ DesignCenter\Home-Space Planner.dwg, HouseDesigner.dwg**, or **Kitchen.dwg**.

5. To complete the drawing, drag and drop your bedroom furniture (see Figure 10-31). Remember to show a door and windows and more to create your bedroom layout.

6. Save your drawing in your **Workskills** folder.

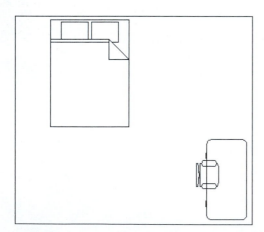

Figure 10-31

Start of dream bedroom

ⓒ Tutorial 10-2: *Creating a Site Plan*

1. Open the **Site** drawing from the student data files.

2. **Zoom Extents** to fill the screen with the display (see Figure 10-32).

3. From the **Format** menu, pick **Drawing Units** and be sure the **Insertion scale** is set to **Feet**, as the **Site** drawing from the surveyor team is in feet (see Figure 10-33).

To access student data files, go to
www.pearsondesigncentral.com.

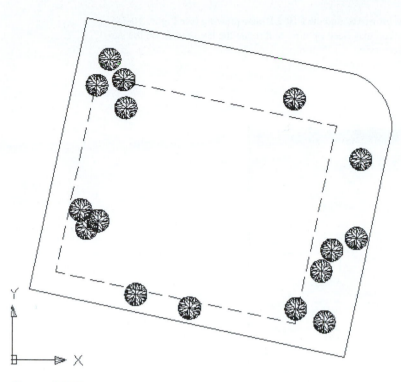

Figure 10-32

Site drawing

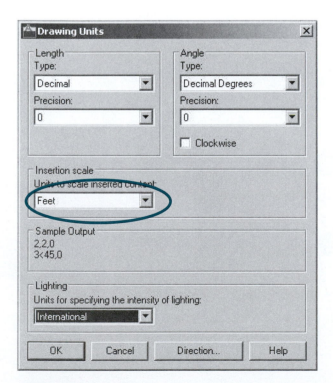

Figure 10-33

Drawing Units dialog box

4. From the **Insert** menu, select the **Block** dialog box, browse to find the **F10-2 House** drawing (see Figure 10-34), and insert it in a good location (see Figure 10-35). You may need to move and rotate the house to fit on the site plan inside the dashed lines (setbacks) and away from trees.

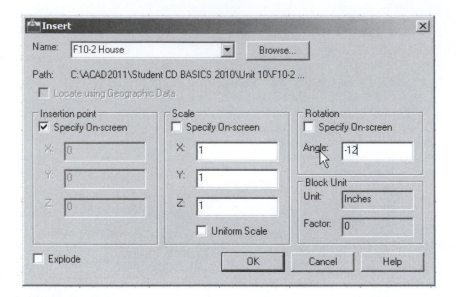

Figure 10-34

Insert dialog box for the house

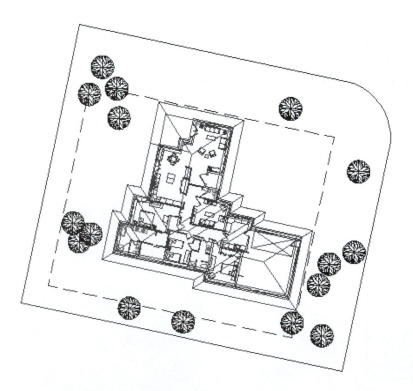

Figure 10-35

House inserted as block into site plan

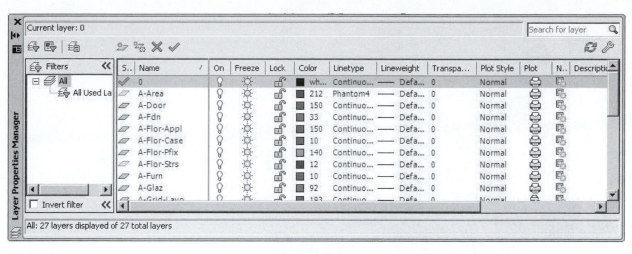

Figure 10-36

Layer palette for Tutorial 10-2

5. Examine the **Layer Properties Manager** (see Figure 10-36) and see what layers are available for control.

6. Save the drawing as **Site1** in the **Workskills** folder and exit AutoCAD.

7. Repeat Steps 1–3 in this tutorial.

8. Insert the "house" as an external reference (DWG Reference) (see Figure 10-37) to produce basically the same image (see Figure 10-38) as Figure 10-35.

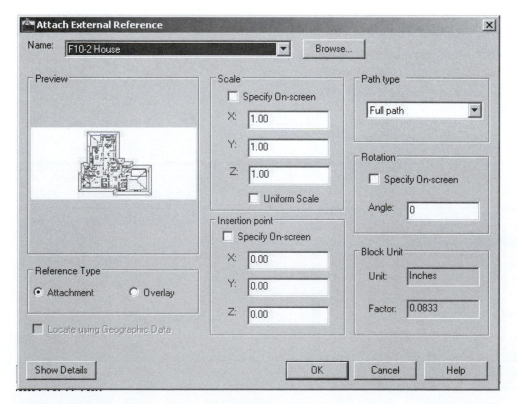

Figure 10-37

Attach External Reference dialog box for Tutorial 10-2

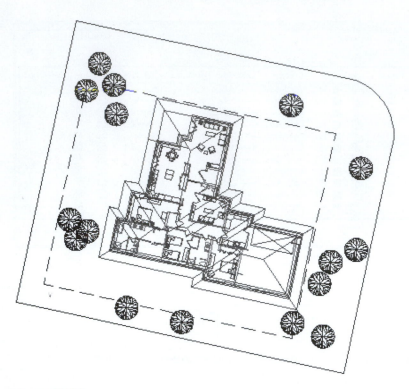

Figure 10-38

House as Xref in the site plan

9. Examine the **Layer Properties Manager** (see Figure 10-39) and notice the difference in the layer names, control, and visibility.

10. Save your drawing as **Site2** in the **Workskills** folder.

11. Turn various layers **On/Off** and change the colors of the externally referenced layers and watch the change to the drawing.

12. Close the drawing, do not save the drawing, and end the work session.

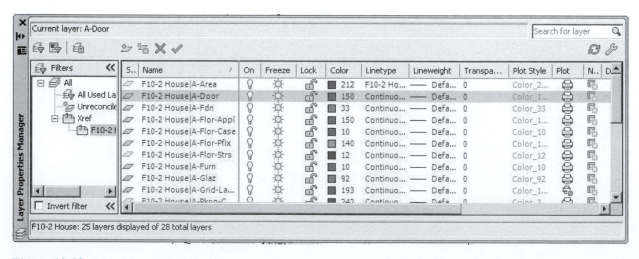

Figure 10-39

Layer palette for external reference

ⓔ Tutorial 10-3: *Creating a Basic Circuit*

The following tutorial creates the basic circuit drawing shown in Figure 10-40. The process for creating this drawing is as follows:

- First, make three block definitions.

- Insert the symbols in the drawing.

1. Open the **Electrical Block Tutorial** drawing (see Figure 10-41) from the student data files.

To access student data files, go to **www.pearsondesigncentral.com.**

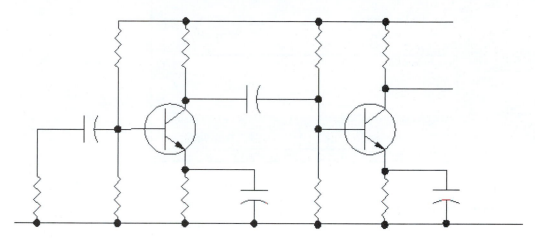

Figure 10-40

The completed tutorial drawing

Figure 10-41

The initial drawing

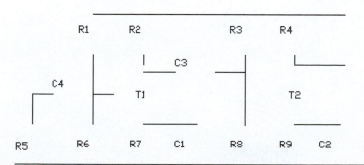

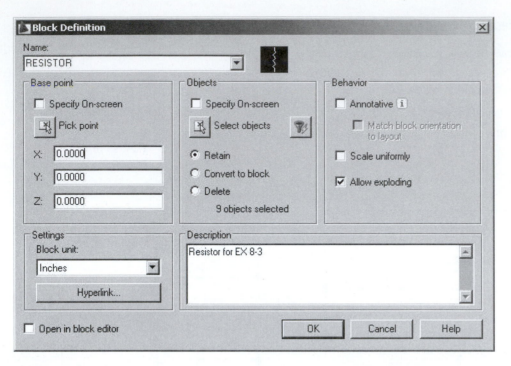

Figure 10-42

The **Block Definition** or **Block Make** dialog box

2. In the **Draw** menu, select the **Block** cascading menu and choose the **Make** command.

3. In the **Block Definition** dialog box (see Figure 10-42), enter the word **RESISTOR** in the **Name** field.

4. Click on the **Select objects** icon (see Figure 10-43). This sends you back to the drawing screen to select the entities that make up the block. Place a selection window, either a crossing or window version, around the entities that form the resistor (see Figure 10-44). Press **<Enter>** to complete the selection process and return to the **Block Definition** dialog box.

5. Select the **Pick point** icon (see Figure 10-45). This sends you back to the drawing screen to select a control point for the block. Select the point marked with the **X** in Figure 10-44. Be sure to use the **ENDpoint Object Snap** when selecting the control point. This increases accuracy when inserting the block.

6. Finish the block definition procedure by clicking on the **OK** button near the bottom of the dialog box. Although there are a few other areas to the **Block Definition** dialog box, the default values for these other areas will work fine for this tutorial. Now, let's repeat these steps to make two other blocks.

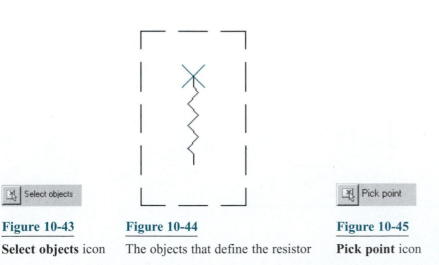

Figure 10-43

Select objects icon

Figure 10-44

The objects that define the resistor

Figure 10-45

Pick point icon

7. In the **Draw** menu, select the **Block** cascading menu and choose the **Make** command.

8. In the **Block Definition** dialog box, enter the word **CAPACITOR** in the **Name** field.

9. Click on the **Select objects** icon. This sends you back to the drawing screen to select the entities that make up the block. Place a selection window, either a crossing or window version, around the entities that form the capacitor (see Figure 10-46). Press **<Enter>** to complete the selection process and return to the **Block Definition** dialog box.

10. Select the **Pick point** icon. This sends you back to the drawing screen to select a control point for the block. Select the point marked with the **X** in Figure 10-46. Be sure to use **ENDpoint Object Snap** when selecting the control point. This increases accuracy when inserting the block.

11. Finish the block definition procedure by clicking on the **OK** button near the bottom of the dialog box.

12. In the **Draw** menu, select the **Block** cascading menu and choose the **Make** command.

13. In the **Block Definition** dialog box, enter the word **TRANSISTOR** in the **Name** field.

14. Click on the **Select objects** icon. This sends you back to the drawing screen to select the entities that make up the block. Place a selection window, either a crossing or window version, around the entities that form the transistor (see Figure 10-47). Press **<Enter>** to complete the selection process and return to the **Block Definition** dialog box.

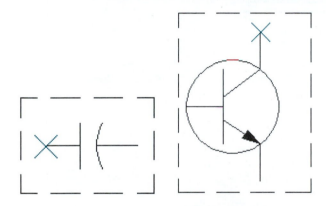

Figure 10-46

The objects that define the capacitor

Figure 10-47

The objects that define the transistor

15. Select the **Pick point** icon. This sends you back to the drawing screen to select a control point for the block. Select the point marked with the **X** in Figure 10-47. Be sure to use **ENDpoint Object Snap** when selecting the control point. This increases accuracy when inserting the block.

16. Finish the block definition procedure by clicking on the **OK** button near the bottom of the dialog box.

With the blocks defined, the next steps are to place the blocks in the drawing as shown in Figure 10-48.

17. From the **Insert** menu, select **Block** (see Figure 10-49). This brings up the **Insert** dialog box (see Figure 10-50).

18. From the **Name** drop-down list, select **RESISTOR**.

19. Select the **OK** button to return to the drawing screen.

20. Using the **ENDpoint Object Snap**, insert the **R1** resistor into the circuit drawing as shown in Figure 10-48. Make the connection based on the control point and the correct endpoint of the lines in the tutorial file.

21. Repeat Steps 18–20 to insert the remaining eight resistors. Keep in mind there are endpoints in the locations where the resistors will be connecting, too.

22. From the **Insert** menu, select **Block** (see Figure 10-49). This brings up the **Insert** dialog box (see Figure 10-50).

23. From the **Name** drop-down list, select **CAPACITOR**. In the **Rotation** area of the dialog box, enter a value of **−90** for the **Angle**.

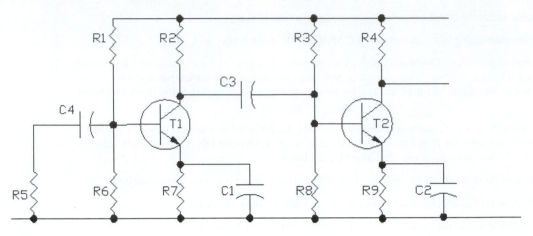

Figure 10-48

The completed drawing; the text represents ID tags to aid in placement of the blocks

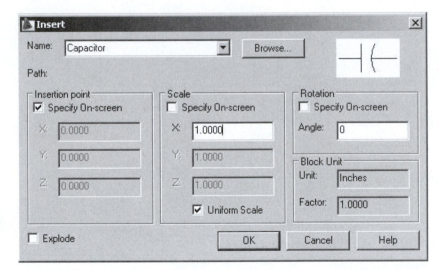

Figure 10-49

Insert Block menu

Figure 10-50

The **Insert** dialog box

24. Select the **OK** button to return to the drawing screen.

25. Using the **ENDpoint Object Snap**, insert the **C1** capacitor as shown in Figure 10-48. Make the connection based on the control point and the correct endpoint of the lines in the tutorial file.

26. Repeat Steps 22–25 to insert the **C2** capacitor. Keep in mind there are endpoints in the locations where the capacitors will be connecting.

27. From the **Insert** menu, select **Block** (see Figure 10-49). This brings up the **Insert** dialog box (see Figure 10-50).

28. From the **Name** drop-down list, select **CAPACITOR**.

29. Select the **OK** button to return to the drawing screen.

30. Using the **ENDpoint Object Snap**, insert the **C3** capacitor as shown in Figure 10-48. Make the connection based on the control point and the correct endpoint of the lines in the tutorial file.

31. Repeat Steps 27–30 to insert the **C4** capacitor.

32. From the **Insert** menu, select **Block** (see Figure 10-49). This brings up the **Insert** dialog box (see Figure 10-50).

33. From the **Name** drop-down list, select **TRANSISTOR**.

34. In the **Scale** area of the dialog box, turn on the **Uniform Scale** option by placing a check mark in the box; enter a value of **.75** for the **X** value.

35. Select the **OK** button to return to the drawing screen.

36. Using the **ENDpoint Object Snap**, insert the **T1** transistor as shown in Figure 10-48. Make the connection based on the control point and the correct endpoint of the lines in the tutorial drawing file. Keep in mind there are endpoints in the locations where the transistors will be connecting, too.

37. Repeat this process (Steps 32–36) to insert the remaining **T2** transistor.

38. The solder joints can be created by using a **DONUT** command. From the **Draw** menu, select the **DONUT** command.

39. Enter a value of **0** for the inside diameter and a value of **.05** for the outside diameter. Then object snap to the locations that show a solder joint symbol. Refer to Figure 10-51 for the solder joint locations.

40. Save your drawing as **T10-3** in your **Workskills** folder.

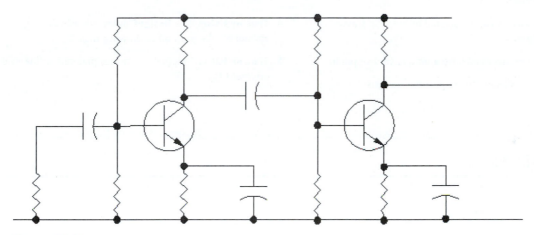

Figure 10-51

The completed drawing with blocks and donuts

Chapter Test Questions

Multiple Choice

Circle the correct answer.

1. Properties of a layer can include all the following except
   a. Color
   b. Linetype
   c. Coordinates
   d. Lineweight

2. Which of the following is not a display control for a layer?
   a. **On/Off**
   b. **Freeze/Thaw**
   c. **Lock/Unlock**
   d. **Plot/No Plot**

3. A group is a named set of
   a. Entities
   b. Menu commands
   c. System variables
   d. Layers

4. To place a block in a drawing file, which command would you use?
   a. **Import**
   b. **Open**
   c. **Merge**
   d. **Insert**

5. Which of the following cannot be brought in through the **DesignCenter**?
   a. Layers
   b. Blocks
   c. Dimension styles
   d. System variables

Matching

Write the number of the correct answer on the line.

a. Block _____

b. Base point _____

c. Overlay _____

d. Layer _____

e. Bind _____

1. A way of using an external reference

2. To make an external reference a permanent part of a drawing file

3. A form of a drawing's organization

4. The control point of a block

5. The result of combining many entities into one object

True or False

Circle the correct answer.

1. **True or False:** Layers can be created only in the **Layer Manager** dialog box.

2. **True or False:** Groups must have a unique control point.

3. **True or False:** Blocks are the opposite of groups.

4. **True or False:** The **DesignCenter** allows you to grab layers and blocks from other drawing files.

5. **True or False:** External references maintain a link to the original file.

Chapter Projects

Project 10-1 [INTERMEDIATE]

Interview various consultants, government agencies, manufacturing companies, architects, and other CAD users about the following:

1. Storage of drawings and naming conventions

2. Storage of blocks and naming conventions

3. Use of external references

4. Use of layer standards

Project 10-2 [BASIC]

Make a presentation to the class on "How I Store and Back Up My Drawings and Blocks."

Project 10-3 [INTERMEDIATE]

Download various items from the **Autodesk Seek** to add to your library and show the class. Explain why you chose these items.

Chapter Practice Exercises

Ⓐ Practice Exercise 10-1: *Classroom Design* [BASIC]

1. Create a classroom similar to the one in Figure 10-13 by first building a block consisting of a 60″ × 30″ desk that holds a computer system and books with a chair using new or existing blocks from the **DesignCenter** library at **C:\Program Files\AutoCAD_2011\Sample\DesignCenter\Home-Space Planner.dwg**.

2. Save the desk block as **Desk6030**.

3. Save your drawing as **Classroom1** in the **Workskills** folder.

Ⓒ Practice Exercise 10-2: *Site Plane Elevation Contours* [INTERMEDIATE]

1. Open the drawing **Civil1** from the student data files (see Figure 10-52).

2. Attach as external references the drawings **Pond Contours, Roads,** and **Existing Contours** to make the complete drawing (see Figure 10-53).

To access student data files, go to **www.pearsondesigncentral.com.**

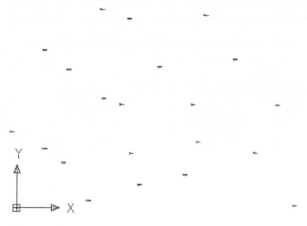

Figure 10-52

The **Civil1** drawing

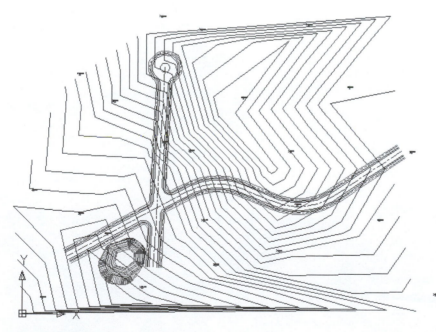

Figure 10-53

The **Civil1** drawing with external references attached

3. Review the layers to avoid color conflicts and change as needed (see Figure 10-54).

4. Save the drawing as **Civil Complete** in your **Workskills** folder.

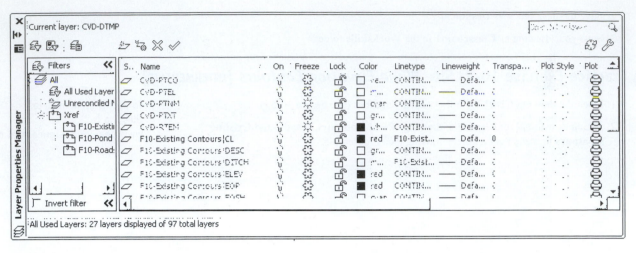

Figure 10-54

Layer palette for external referenced drawings for Practice Exercise 10-2

11 Editing with Grips

CHAPTER OBJECTIVES

- Demonstrate grip editing techniques.
- Identify grip options.
- Recognize the grip control points for all objects.
- Improve productivity with grips.
- Edit object properties through grips.
- Identify additional right-click options.

Introduction

Grips are often referred to as automatic editing. The AutoCAD program, in general, is command-driven. This means you pick a command first (verb), and then the object for the operation (noun). Grips reverse the process, allowing you to choose the object first (noun) and then select the action or command (verb).

grips: Editing points that appear at key locations on drawing objects. Once grips are activated, you can directly modify drawing objects by selecting their grips.

Elementary Concept of Grip Editing

Through the **Grips** series of commands, you can execute the five basic editing commands: **STRETCH**, **MOVE**, **ROTATE**, **MIRROR**, and **SCALE**. The **Copy** and **Basepoint** options can accompany any of these commands. This series of commands expedites the traditional commands through the use of predefined control points known as grips. The execution of a grip command presents you with a series of predefined control point boxes.

> **JOB SKILLS**
>
> The advent of the **Grips** series of commands greatly increased the productivity of the basic modify commands. An understanding of their accessibility and simple execution is a job skill that will increase speed, accuracy, and consistency within a drawing file.

Each entity has the same predefined grips, which can be shown as colored boxes. **GRIPS** is a system variable that will enable grips (if set to **1**) or disable grips (if set to **0**). It is reflected in the check mark next to **Enable grips** in the **Options** dialog box under the **Selection** tab (see Figure 11-1). The color of grips is shown by accessing the button in the center of Figure 11-1 and can be set as shown in Figure 11-2.

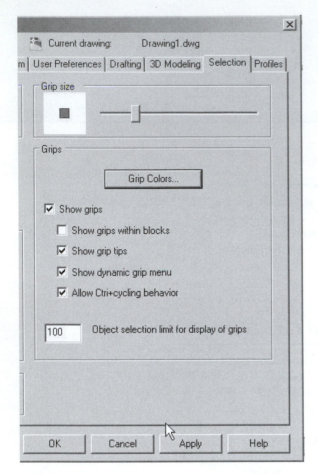

Figure 11-1

Grips dialog area of the **Selection** tab in the **Options** dialog box

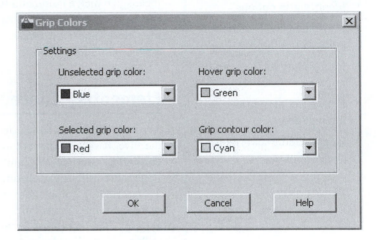

Figure 11-2

Grip Colors dialog box

NOTE:

There are three graphic symbols used to identify grips. The square box represents a grip used to execute a modifying command, and the triangle grip represents a grip used to resize an object. The dash allows for subobject modifications.

NEW to AutoCAD 2011

grip box: Graphic symbol used to show grip control points.

grip control points: Predefined locations on an entity used to modify the selected object.

Figure 11-3

View of grips on line, arc, circle, and single-line text

Grip Control Points

Grip boxes are shown at the same location for each of the entities. A line has three *grip control points*—each endpoint and the midpoint of the line (see Figure 11-3). An arc has three grip control points—at the endpoints of the arc and the midpoint of the arc—plus three directional control points and a center control point for a total of seven (see Figure 11-3). A circle has five grip control points—one at each quadrant point and one at the center point of the circle (see Figure 11-3). Single-line text has a grip control point at the insertion point of the text (see Figure 11-3), and **MTEXT** has control points at three locations, plus subobject grips (see Figure 11-4). The polylines (see Figure 11-4) and splines have a control point on each vertex. Dimensions have five grip control points—two control the extension line locations, two control the dimension line locations, and one controls the dimension text location (see Figure 11-4). Leader lines have three grip control points (see Figure 11-5). Finally, a block definition can have a single control point at the insertion point of the block (see Figure 11-6), or all the grips can be shown for each object that makes up the block definition (see Figure 11-7). This option is controlled through the **Options** dialog box in the **Selection** tab as seen in Figure 11-1. The maximum number of grips that can be displayed is set by the **GRIPOBJLIMIT** system variable, and its default value is 100.

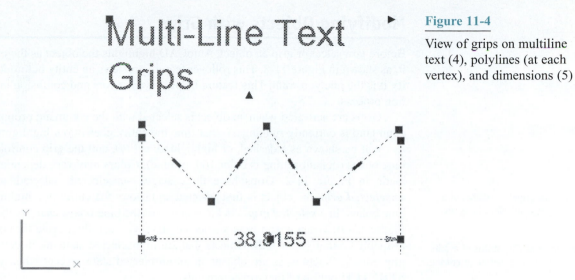

Multi-Line Text Grips

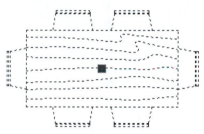

38.0155

▶

Figure 11-4

View of grips on multiline text (4), polylines (at each vertex), and dimensions (5)

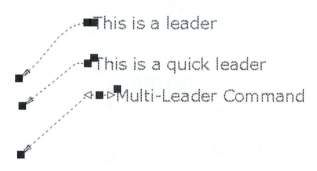

This is a leader

This is a quick leader

Multi-Leader Command

Figure 11-5

Grips on the various leader lines

Figure 11-6

Basic grip on a block set at the insert point

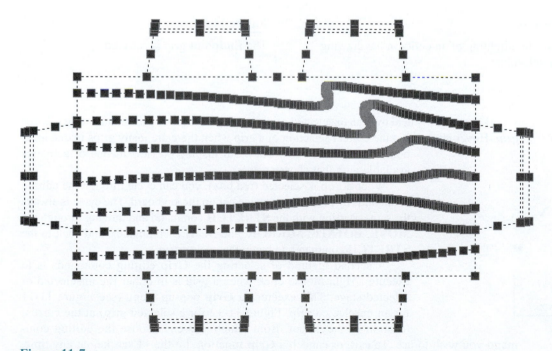

Figure 11-7

View of the Figure 11-6 block with internal grips displayed

Modifying Objects with Grips

Before you select or grip an object, AutoCAD highlights the object as the cursor passes over it, as shown in Figure 11-8. This rollover feature previews an entity before it is chosen to verify it is the one you want. This feature helps prevent errors and confusion in the object selection process.

Grips are activated when an object is selected with the command prompt in place and no command is currently running. At that time the entity goes into a highlighted mode (the object will be shown as a dashed, or highlighted, entity), and the grip control points appear as blue boxes (default setting is color 160, or blue). Colors may vary depending on the choices made in Figure 11-2. Grips have three stages—unselected, selected, and hover. In an **unselected grip**, the object is first selected and shows the entity in a highlighted mode with blue boxes. In a **selected grip**, clicking on one of the blue boxes changes its color to red (see Figure 11-9). When a grip is in a selected state, you can then cycle through the choices of available editing commands. Objects that are in a selected state are directly affected by the grip editing function, as are objects in an unselected state, except when you are using the **STRETCH** option of the grip commands.

unselected grip: The status of a grip control point identifying an object.

selected grip: The status of a grip control point involved in an editing function.

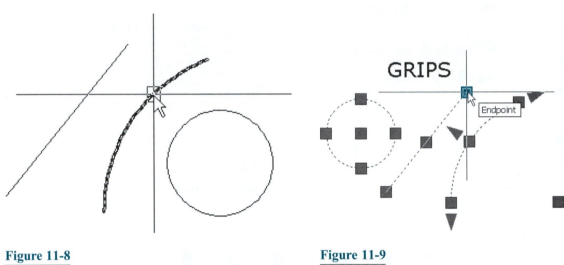

Figure 11-8

Rollover highlighting of an entity in the drawing before selection

Figure 11-9

The **Endpoint** grip is selected

hover grip: The status of a grip control point when there are multiple choices in a grip location.

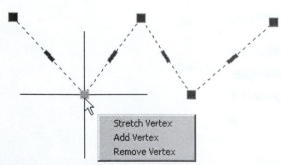

Figure 11-10

The cursor is placed over a grip and hovers on a polyline

If the cursor is held over an unselected grip, its color changes to green, indicating a **hover grip**. Hover grips aid in the correct selection of a grip when there are many grips in one location (see Figure 11-10). They can display preview menus of activities available with that chosen grip.

When a grip is selected (red box), you can cycle through the editing commands by pressing the space bar on the keyboard. The cycle is always the same, starting with the **STRETCH** command and moving through the **MOVE**, **ROTATE**, **MIRROR**, and **SCALE** commands, and back to the **STRETCH** command, to begin the cycle again.

A second method of selecting the **Grip** editing commands is to execute a right mouse click when a grip is in either the unselected or selected stage. This executes a **Grip** pop-up menu (see Figure 11-11 for an unselected grip, Figure 11-12 for a selected grip) at the current location of the cursor, from which you can choose the editing command you wish to use. To exit, or cancel, a **Grip** function, hit the <Esc> key at any time, use the **Exit** or **Deselect** menu items, or begin another AutoCAD command from a menu or toolbar.

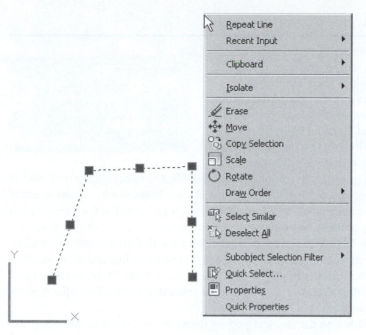

Figure 11-11

The right-click menu when grips are present

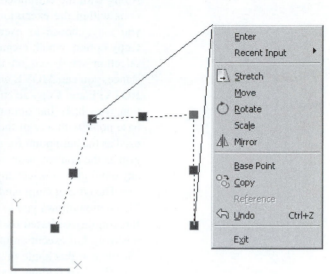

Figure 11-12

The right-click menu when a grip is selected

Objects, Grips, and Hovering for Menus and More

As more software is developed using object technology, grips are becoming more intelligent, as shown in Figure 11-13 from the Autodesk Architecture software.

    Notice that the door object has the basic three grips of a line. The two ends show directional operations, and the other two directional grips are used to flip the hinge point and thus the door. When you hover over an object's grip, tip boxes may appear to explain its operation. Some object-oriented grips have menus of operations as shown in Figures 11-10 and 11-14 from the Autodesk Architecture program.

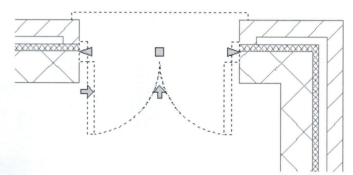

Figure 11-13

A door object showing grips (from Autodesk's Architecture software)

Figure 11-14

A door object showing grips and the menu (from Autodesk's Architecture software)

Grip Options

Along with the editing commands, there are a few options within the execution of the grip commands that you may choose to exercise. Each command has a **Copy** option, which creates a new entity of the current selection set, based on the editing function. For instance, you can **MOVE** and **Copy** an entity, or you can **ROTATE** and **Copy** an entity. Along with the **Copy** option, you have the option to redefine the operation's base point with any of the grip editing commands. By default, the selected grip (red box) is used as the base point for the execution of the command. If you choose not to use this selected grip as the control point, you can select the **Base Point** option and redefine the base point to any other grip or select any point by coordinates, object snap, or other methods on the screen.

The editing commands **ROTATE** and **SCALE** also have the **Reference** option available. This option allows you to select two points on the screen that define a line and then specify a rotation degree based on the AutoCAD 360° increment (0° is east, and counterclockwise is positive). On execution of the command, the objects are rotated, pointing the defined reference line at that angle in space.

The final options available on the shortcut pop-up menu are always available. They are **Undo**, to reverse the previous function; **Properties**, which launches the **Properties** panel displaying the properties of the selected entities; and **Exit**, or **Cancel**, which returns you to the command prompt.

The following operations are available with each grip editing command.

- **STRETCH** When a grip is selected, it can be moved to a new location, changing the dimension of the entity (see Figure 11-15). When a midpoint grip, a centerpoint grip, a text grip, or a block reference grip is selected, the resulting action is a **MOVE** command instead of a **STRETCH** command.

Figure 11-15

The **Grip** mode showing **STRETCH** command line prompts

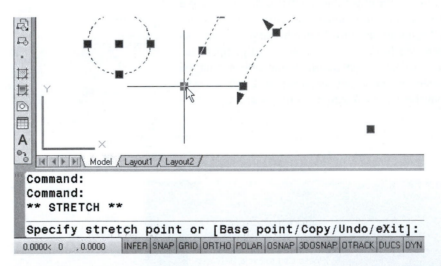

- **MOVE** This option moves the selected entity, using the selected grip as a base point (see Figure 11-16), to a new location specified by a second selected point. This command also moves all entities that are currently in the unselected state. If you want the original entities to remain in the original location, you can select the **Copy** option, which creates a second set of entities at the new location. If you choose not to use the selected grip as the base point, you may select the **Base Point** option to select a different point as the control point.
- **ROTATE** The **ROTATE** command (see Figure 11-17) rotates the entity around the selected grip point by selecting a new point for the direction of rotation that you specify. An alternative method to the dragging operation is to specify the amount of rotation through a keyboard entry. As in the previous commands, the options **Base Point** and **Copy** are available for the selection of a new control point or the creation of multiple copies of the entities around the rotation point.

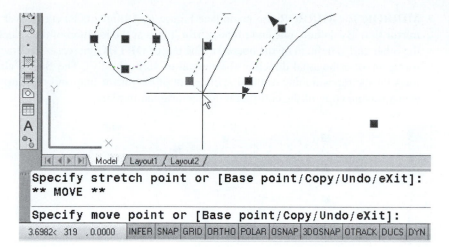

Figure 11-16

The **Grip** mode showing **MOVE** command line prompts

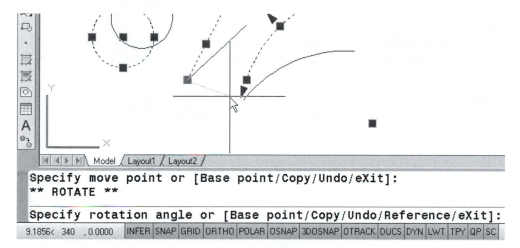

Figure 11-17

The **Grip** mode showing **ROTATE** command line prompts

- **SCALE** This command changes the size of an entity, or entities, relative to a base point (see Figure 11-18). If you move a grip control point outward, the entity increases in size, whereas if you move the point inward, the entity decreases in size. You can also choose to enter a relative scale factor through the keyboard. The original object size has a value of 1.0. Entering a 2.0 doubles the size of the object. Entering a 3.0 triples the size. To decrease size, you put in a decimal value such as 0.5, which decreases the object by half. The **SCALE** command uses the selected grip (red box) as the base point. All scaling operations are relative to that base point. You can choose a different base point through the **Base Point** option and then execute a **Copy** option, leaving the original entities unchanged but still scaling the copied entities.

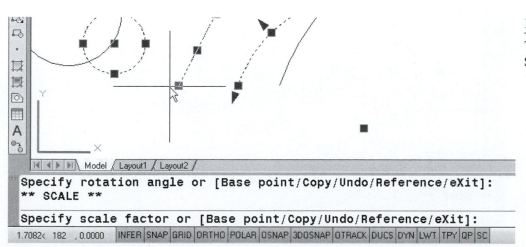

Figure 11-18

The **Grip** mode showing **SCALE** command prompts

- **MIRROR** The **MIRROR** command (see Figure 11-19) inverts an entity over a temporary mirror line. By default, one end of the mirror line is at the location of the selected grip, and the other end is defined by the operator. The use of **ORTHO** increases accuracy when mirroring in an orthogonal direction (horizontal or vertical only). The **Base Point** option allows for the repositioning of the first endpoint of the mirror line, and the **Copy** option creates a second copy of the entity, leaving the original in place.

Figure 11-19

The **Grip** mode showing **MIRROR** command prompts

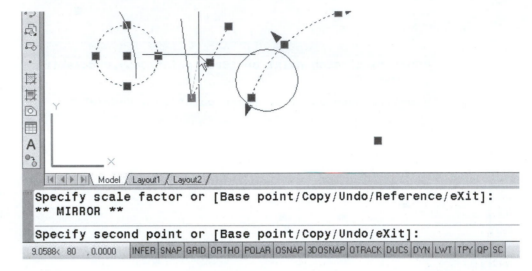

- **Delete** When using grips to delete entities, you will not encounter questions about deleting source objects. They will simply be deleted when the **<Del>** key is pressed.
- **Grip Snap Setting** Grips have the ability to create a temporary snapping distance based on the first copy's input when it is created. To activate the snapping distance, simply hold down the **<Shift>** key when placing additional copies. The future copies will be controlled in the same fashion as with the **SNAP** function in the status line. The snapping distance is equal to the original distance made from the first copy and has the same value in all directions.

As shown in Figures 11-20 and 11-21, a circle is to be located 10 units away from its current location. You enter **C** for copies of the entities and **@10,0** to establish the distance for the **Grip SNAP** as shown in Figure 11-20. The result is shown in Figure 11-21. Holding down the **<Ctrl>** key and picking locations with the pick button on the mouse places the copies 10 units apart in the X and/or Y directions.

Control of most grip system variables is located in the **Options** dialog box under the **Selection** tab shown in Figure 11-1. Here you can turn grips on or off, change the size of grip boxes, and alter the color of grips at the different stages.

Figure 11-20

Command line prompts for **MOVE** command with Copy and specific distance establishing a temporary **SNAP** distance

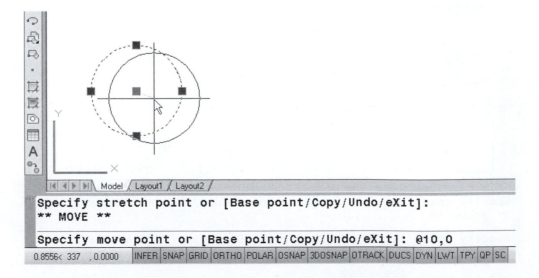

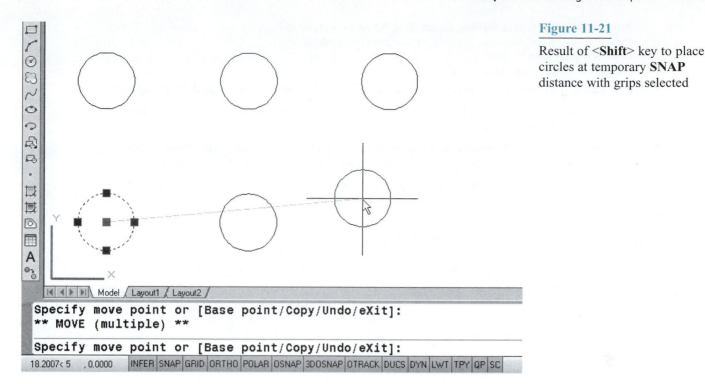

Figure 11-21

Result of <**Shift**> key to place circles at temporary **SNAP** distance with grips selected

Chapter Summary

The editing of objects in AutoCAD is usually command-driven, requiring the user to pick a specific editing command first, and then the object(s) to be edited. Grips, which consist of predefined control points, reverse this process, allowing the user to pick the object first, then select one of the five basic editing commands (**STRETCH, MOVE, ROTATE, MIRROR,** and **SCALE**) from a preview or a pop-up (right mouse button) menu. In this chapter you learned how to use grip control points to modify objects such as lines, arcs,

circles, single-line and multiline text, polylines and splines, dimensions, leader lines, and block definitions. You also learned about the increasingly intelligent nature of grips (e.g., tip boxes and menus that appear when the mouse cursor hovers over an object's grips) with improvements in software technology. Finally, you learned about the options (**Copy, Base Point, Undo, Properties, Exit,** and **Cancel**) you can use together with the grip editing commands as well as the **Delete** and **Grip snap setting** operations.

Chapter Tutorials

Tutorial 11-1: *Basic Operations with Grips*

1. Start AutoCAD.

2. Pick the **File** menu and choose **Open**.

3. Using the drop-down area at the top of the **Select File** dialog box, maneuver to the **C:\Program Files\AutoCAD 2011\Samples** folder or access the sample folder from the student data files.

4. Scroll through the list of drawing files (.dwg) and choose one to open by picking the **Open** button in the lower right of the dialog box:

   a. **Architectural Drawings**—8th Floor, Hotel, Hummer, Stadium, Taisei, or Wilhome
   b. **Building Services**—8th Floor
   c. **Civil Drawings**—Hotel or SPCA Site Plan
   d. **Facilities Management**—Db_samp
   e. **Landscaping**—SPCA Site Plan

To access student data files, go to **www.pearsondesigncentral.com**.

f. **Mechanical**—Oil Module, Welding Fixture 1, or Welding Fixture Model

g. **Presentation**—Hotel, Hummer, Stadium, or Welding Fixture Model

h. **Process Piping**—Oil Module

i. **Structural**—MKMPlan or Oil Module

5. Practice placing grips on various entities in these drawings. Remember that **<Esc>** will cancel the grips.

6. Access the various **Grip** command options with these entities and watch the command line for instructions. Feel free to press **<Esc>** to cancel any operation.

7. To end your work session on a drawing, go to the **File** menu and pick **Close**. Pick the answer **No** so no modifications are saved at this time. If you want to open and examine another drawing go back to Step 4.

8. To end your AutoCAD session, go to the **File** menu and pick **Exit**. If a drawing is active, pick the answer **No** so no modifications are saved at this time. The program will then end.

Ⓐ Tutorial 11-2: *Creating a Storage Warehouse Plan*

Create a storage warehouse plan that has six rows of 10′ × 10′ storage spaces that are in 160′-long buildings.

1. Start a new drawing or use the architectural template created in Chapter 4, Practice Exercise 4-3.

2. In the **Format** menu set the following parameters:

a. **LAYERS:** Current: WALLS—color = **cyan**
DOORS—color = **red**
DIMS—color = **magenta**

b. Drawing **UNITS:** Length = **Architectural**

c. Drawing **LIMITS:** Lower Left—**0′,0′**
Upper Right—**200′,200′**

3. Process a **ZOOM ALL** command to reset the display screen to the above drawing limits.

4. Draw a rectangle by choosing the icon (see Figure 11-22) (or using another method) with the first point at **10′,10′** and the other corner at **20′,20′**, as shown in Figure 11-23. This unit represents the lower left storage area for the site.

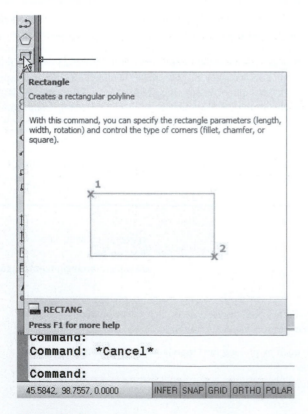

Figure 11-22

The **Rectangle** command

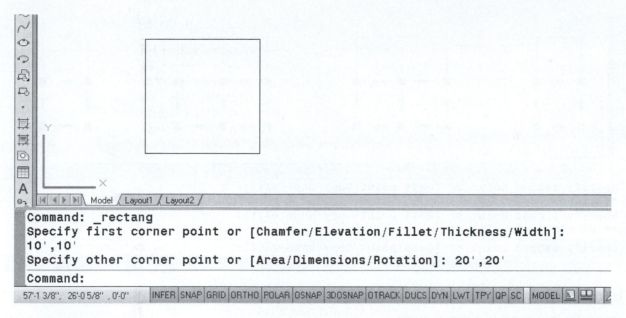

Figure 11-23

Rectangle command prompts

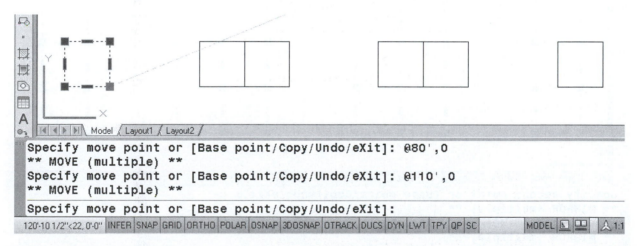

Figure 11-24

First row of the warehouse plan

5. Using the **Grip MOVE** with **Copy** option and **Grip SNAP**, copy the first unit at 30′, 40′, 70′, 80′, and 110′ to the right to make the first row of the storage units as shown in Figure 11-24.

6. Using the **Grip MIRROR** with **Copy** option on all the rectangles, create a second row of units (see Figure 11-25).

7. Using the **Grip MIRROR** with **Copy** option on all the rectangles, create the third and fourth rows of units (see Figure 11-26).

8. Using the **Grip MIRROR** with **Copy** option on all the rectangles, create the fifth, sixth, seventh, and eighth rows of units.

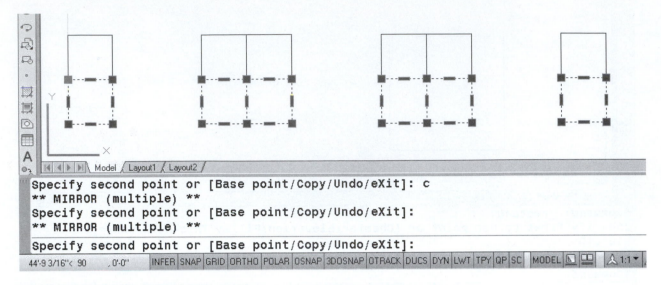

```
Specify second point or [Base point/Copy/Undo/eXit]: c
** MIRROR (multiple) **
Specify second point or [Base point/Copy/Undo/eXit]:
** MIRROR (multiple) **
Specify second point or [Base point/Copy/Undo/eXit]:
```

Figure 11-25

Creating the second row of warehouse units

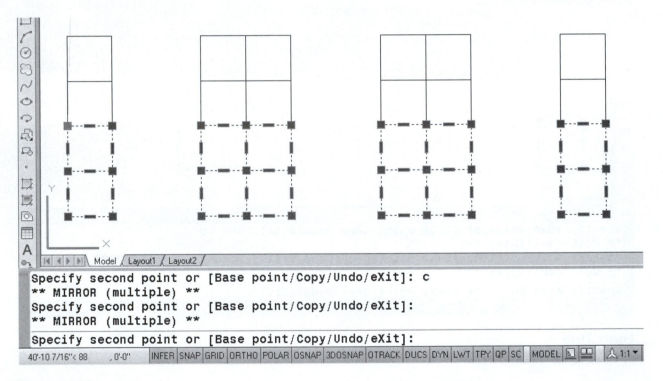

```
Specify second point or [Base point/Copy/Undo/eXit]: c
** MIRROR (multiple) **
Specify second point or [Base point/Copy/Undo/eXit]:
** MIRROR (multiple) **
Specify second point or [Base point/Copy/Undo/eXit]:
```

Figure 11-26

The plan after the creation of rows 3 and 4

9. Using the **Grip MIRROR** with **Copy** option on all the rectangles, create the final eight rows of units. After this operation, the basic layout is complete for the storage center as shown in Figure 11-27.

10. Add some overall dimensions to complete this basic drawing. Remember to change to the correct layer for dimensions.

11. Save the drawing as **T11-2**.

There are at least two other methods using grips and grip commands to create this drawing. What are the other procedures? Which do you think is the most efficient? Why?

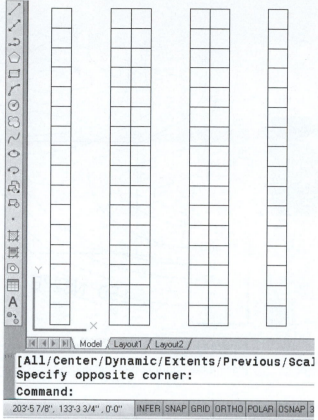

Figure 11-27

Completed warehouse plan

Figure 11-28

Drawing **T11-3**

c Tutorial 11-3: *Modifying Contour Lines with Grips*

Create a final grading plan (contour map) for a 100' by 100' building pad that is set back 30' from the front lot line (the property line that is labeled with the distance and bearing).

1. From the **File** menu pick **Open** and load the **T11-3** drawing from the student data files.

2. Examine the contour lines as shown in Figure 11-28.

3. From the **Modify** menu pick the **OFFSET** command and enter **30** for the offset distance.

4. Pick the front lot line, and the line will go to highlight mode.

5. Pick anywhere above the front lot line to establish the setback line as shown in Figure 11-29.

6. Change the color of this line to red by gripping the new line (see Figure 11-30) and then moving to the **Object Properties** color drop-down menu to choose **Red** (see Figure 11-31).

To access student data files, go to **www.pearsondesigncentral.com.**

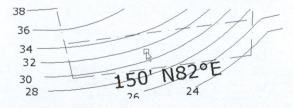

Figure 11-29

Creating the setback line from the property line

Figure 11-30

Gripping the setback line

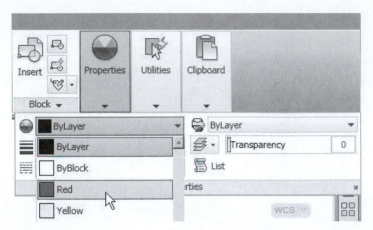

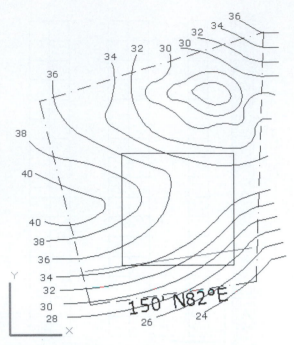

Figure 11-31

Choosing the new color

Figure 11-32

Placing the building pad rectangle

7. Press <**Esc**> to clear the grips.

8. Draw a rectangle and with the mouse pick one corner on the red setback line. Type in **@100,100** for the second corner of the rectangle and end the command, as shown in Figure 11-32.

9. Grip the rectangle, select the lower left grip to make it hot, and use the space bar to proceed to the **Rotate** option (see Figure 11-33).

10. Enter **8** for the rotation angle because this will align the building area to the front lot line. The result should look like Figure 11-34.

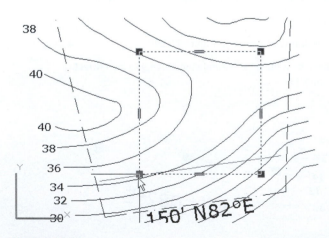

Figure 11-33

Gripping for rotation of building pad

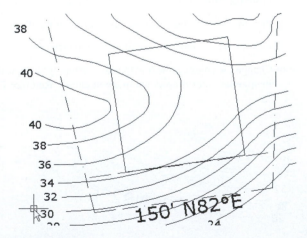

Figure 11-34

Lot with rotated rectangle

11. If the building area is not centered, grip it and move it to a position similar to that shown in Figure 11-34.

12. Based on the drawing in Figure 11-34, a decision is made to put the building area at an elevation of 35'. Grip each contour line (see Figure 11-35) and move the vertices appropriately to create the new contours (see Figure 11-36). Remember that contour lines *do not cross* because no location can have two elevations.

13. Continue gripping and stretching the contour lines to finish the drawing similar to the one in Figure 11-37.

14. Save the drawing in your **Workskills** folder as **T11-3A**.

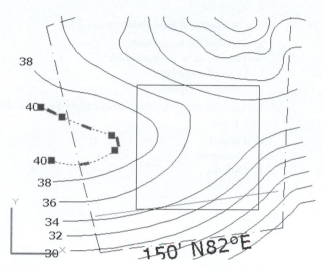

Figure 11-35

Grips on the 40′ contour line before modifications

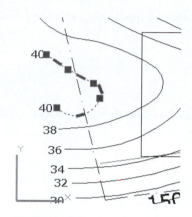

Figure 11-36

Grips on the 40′ contour line after movement

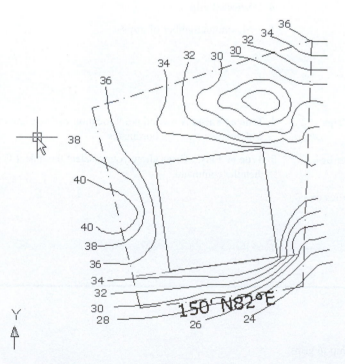

Figure 11-37

Drawing **T11-3A**

Chapter Test Questions

Multiple Choice

Circle the correct answer.

1. Which of the following is **not** a type of grip?
   a. Hover
   b. Selected
   c. Unselected
   d. Floating

2. To continually copy a gripped object, which key would you use?
   a. **<Alt>**
   b. **<Shift>**
   c. **<Ctrl>**
   d. Space bar

3. To cycle through the automated editing options, which key would you use?
   a. **<Alt>**
   b. **<Shift>**

   c. **<Ctrl>**
   d. Space bar

4. The function of a **Base Point** option is to
   a. Redefine the base point
   b. Measure from the base point
   c. Delete the symbol
   d. Launch an **Options** menu

5. Settings for the **Grip** commands can be found in what dialog box?
   a. **Format**
   b. **Configure**
   c. **Options**
   d. **SetVAR**

Matching

Write the number of the correct answer on the line.

a. Hot grip _____

b. Reference _____

c. **GRIPOBJLIMIT** _____

d. Hover grip _____

e. Unselected grip _____

1. An aid in the correct placement of objects

2. Unselected grip

3. Scale option

4. Selected grip

5. Maximum number of grips

True or False

Circle the correct answer.

1. **True or False:** A right mouse click will access the **Grips** shortcut menu.

2. **True or False:** Grips are on all the time and can never be shut off.

3. **True or False:** Grips have no control over the properties of an object.

4. **True or False:** A second point location can be established with relative (@x,y) coordinates.

5. **True or False:** Grips allow you to select the object first, then the command.

Chapter Projects

Project 11-1 [BASIC]

Explain the following setting variables and their relationship to grips:

1. PICKFIRST
2. GRIPBLOCK

3. GRIPSIZE

4. GRIPOBJLIMIT

5. GRIPTIPS

6. GRIPCOLOR

7. GRIPHOT

8. GRIPHOVER

Project 11-2 [BASIC]

List three production advantages of using grips.

Project 11-3 [BASIC]

List three disadvantages of using grips.

Chapter Practice Exercises

ⓖ Practice Exercise 11-1: *Using Grips with Stretch, Grip Snaps, and OSNAPs* [BASIC]

1. From the **File** menu pick **New** to start a new drawing, or use one of your templates.

2. Verify that **SNAP**, **GRID**, **ORTHO**, **POLAR**, **OSNAP**, and **OTRACK** are **Off** in the status line.

3. Check to be sure that **Grips** are **enabled** in the **Options** dialog box with the **Selection** tab.

4. Draw a line with **1,2** and **4,7** as coordinates.

5. Grip this line and select the upper right point to make it active or hot (red box).

6. Move the mouse and see how the line moves with the cursor.

7. Type in **6,10**, and this endpoint of the line will move to this location.

8. Press **<Esc>** to remove the grips.

9. Draw a circle with center at **8,5** and a radius of **2**.

10. Grip the circle and select the center grip to make it active or hot (red box).

11. Move the mouse and see how the circle moves with the cursor and stays the same size.

12. Press **<Esc>** to remove the grips.

13. Grip the circle and select the north quadrant point to make it active.

14. Move the mouse and see the circle changing radius but not location.

15. Type in **8,9**, and the circle will enlarge. What is the radius?

16. Press **<Esc>** to remove the grips.

17. Grip the line and the circle. Select the north quadrant point on the circle to make it active.

18. Move the cursor to the upper-right line grip and pick. Notice that the quadrant point and the endpoint snap together.

19. Press **<Esc>** to remove the grips.

20. Grip the line and select the upper right end to make it active.

21. Type in **CEN** and press **<Enter>**, then move across the circle. The centerpoint **Osnap** will appear. Move the mouse to the center and pick. The line will connect to the center of the circle.

22. Save your drawing as **EX11-1** in your **Workskills** folder.

(G) Practice Exercise 11-2: *Using Grips with Move, Copy, and Auxiliary Grids* [BASIC]

1. From the **File** menu pick **New** to start a new drawing, or use one of your templates.

2. Verify that **SNAP**, **GRID**, **ORTHO**, **POLAR**, **OSNAP**, and **OTRACK** are **Off** in the status line.

3. Check to be sure that **Grips** are **enabled** in the **Options** dialog box with the **Selection** tab.

4. Draw a line with **2,1** and **7,4** as coordinates.

5. Draw a circle with the center at **5,2** and a radius of **1**.

6. Grip the line and the circle.

7. Make the middle grip on the line active and press **<Enter>** to get to the **Move** option in the **Grips** command series.

8. Type in **@1<135** and press **<Enter>** to move the entities **1** unit at an angle of **135**.

9. Make the middle grip on the line active and press **<Enter>** to get to the **Move** option in **Grips**.

10. Type a **C** and press **<Enter>** to use the **Copy** mode.

11. Type in **@2<315** and press **<Enter>** to copy the entities **2** units at an angle of **315**. Now a second line and the circle should appear.

12. Repeat Step 11 three more times, typing in **@2<45**, **@2<135**, and **@2<225**.

13. Draw an arc in the center area of the drawing.

14. Grip the arc and select a triangular grip on one end to activate. As you move the mouse, the arc is extended or shortened, keeping the same radius.

15. Make each grip on the arc active and test the action under the **STRETCH** mode.

16. Press **<Enter>** and see the different actions under the **MOVE** mode.

17. Save the drawing as **EX11-2** in your **Workskills** folder.

(G) Practice Exercise 11-3: *Using Grips with Rotate, Scale, and Mirror* [BASIC]

1. From the **File** menu pick **New** to start a new drawing, or use one of your templates.

2. Verify that **SNAP**, **GRID**, **ORTHO**, **POLAR**, **OSNAP**, and **OTRACK** are **Off** in the status line.

3. Check to be sure that **Grips** are **enabled** in the **Options** dialog box with the **Selection** tab.

4. Draw a line with **2,2** and **2,7** as coordinates.

5. Grip the line and make the bottom or lower grip active.

6. Press **<Enter>** twice to access the **ROTATE** mode.

7. Type a **C** to go to the **Copy** operation.

8. Enter **15** at the command prompt to create a line 15° on the counterclockwise rotation.

9. Continue by entering **30**, **45**, **60**, **75**, and **90** to complete lines in this quadrant.

10. Grip the second, fourth, and sixth lines and make the base grip active.

11. Press **<Enter>** three times to be in **SCALE** mode.

12. Enter **.7** as the scale factor to reduce these lines to 70 percent of their original size.

13. Press **<Esc>** to clear the grips.

14. Grip all lines and make the bottom of the first line active.

15. Press <**Enter**> four times to be in **MIRROR** mode.

16. Type a **C** to go to the **Copy** operation.

17. Move the mouse to the grip box farthest to the west or left. This defines a mirror line for the reflection.

18. Grip all lines and make the bottom of the first line active.

19. Press <**Enter**> four times to be in **MIRROR** mode.

20. Type a **C** to go to the **Copy** operation.

21. Move the mouse to the grip box, to the grip farthest down. This defines a mirror line for the reflection.

22. Save your drawing as **EX11-3** in your **Workskills** folder (see Figure 11-38).

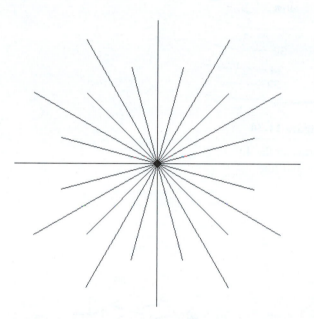

Figure 11-38

Drawing **EX11-3**

○c Practice Exercise 11-4: *Using Grips to Modify Object Properties* [ADVANCED]

1. From the **File** menu pick **Open** and load drawing **T11-3** from the student data files (see Figure 11-39).

2. Verify that **SNAP**, **GRID**, **ORTHO**, **POLAR**, **OSNAP**, and **OTRACK** are **off** in the status line.

3. Check to be sure that **Grips** are enabled in the **Options** dialog box in the **Selection** tab.

4. Grip the **40′** contour line as shown in Figure 11-40.

5. Go to the **Home** ribbon, **Properties** panel, **Color** drop-down menu, and pick **cyan** as the new color for this object as shown in Figure 11-41.

6. Proceed with the same operation (Steps 4 and 5) on the 30′ contour lines.

7. When completed, the drawing should look like Figure 11-42.

8. **Save** your drawing as **EX11-4** in your **Workskills** folder.

To access student data files, go to **www.pearsondesigncentral.com.**

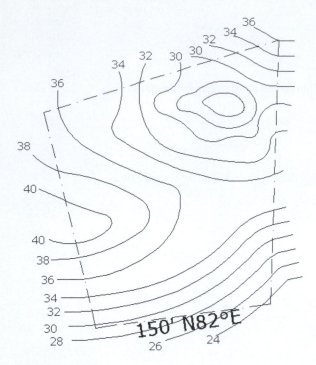

Figure 11-39

Drawing **T11-3**

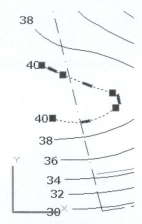

Figure 11-40

Grips on the 40′
contour line

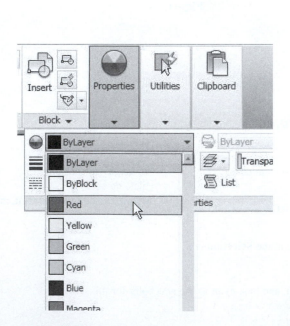

Figure 11-41

Properties panel expanded for **Color**
drop-down menu

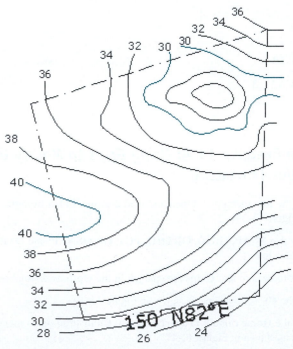

Figure 11-42

Drawing **EX11-4**

Ⓐ Practice Exercise 11-5: *Using Grips to Complete the GROFFICE Plan* [ADVANCED]

1. Open the **GROFFICE** drawing as shown in Figure 11-43 from the student data files.

2. Using only **Grips** and the related commands, complete the drawing approximately as shown in Figure 11-44.

3. Save your completed drawing in your **Workskills** folder as **EX11-5**.

To access student data files, go to **www.pearsondesigncentral.com.**

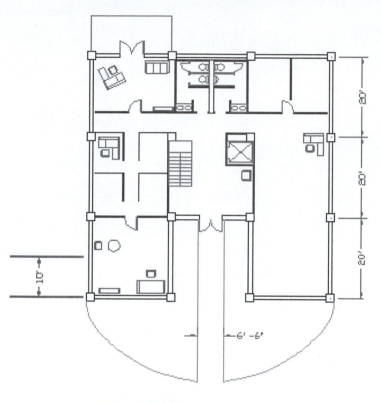

Figure 11-43

Initial office drawing

Figure 11-44

Completed office drawing

12

Parametric Constraints

Introduction

Parametric constraints are drawing controls that allow the designer to apply relationships between objects in a drawing file. *Constraints* are a series of controls that govern the position, slope, tangency, and/or the dimensions of the drawing elements. Normally, constraints are applied in the design stage of a project and can be maintained throughout the drawing process. Applying constraints removes an object's degrees of freedom and thus places logical controls on a design's intent. Thereafter, any changes made to one object will result in the adjustment of the other object. The applications of constraints provide a way to test out ideas and make changes to a design in an efficient manner while maintaining the constrained relationships and distances.

Parametric controls are based on two styles: geometric constraints and dimensional constraints. Either style will control a drawing element in a defined manner that will ensure that the relationship and/or measurements will remain consistent even as the design is modified. *Geometric constraints* place one or more objects into a fixed relationship such as making a line horizontal or two lines parallel. *Dimensional constraints* apply a value related to the size or location of an entity, for example, the length of a line, the diameter of a circle, or the location of the circle off an edge. Applying either style of constraint adds a level of intelligence to your design that will allow you easily to adjust your design at a later time while creating predictable, stable models.

Geometric Constraints

Geometric constraints establish a relationship between 2D elements. These constraints can be defined in both model space and layout space. See the Parametric menu in Figure 12-1, the toolbar in Figure 12-2, and the ribbon in Figure 12-3 for access to the **Constraint** commands. You will want to apply geometric constraints in a drawing file for consistent exchange of the design's intent. Once a constraint is applied, the constraint will not allow any changes to the geometry that would violate the defined constraints. AutoCAD has 12 types of geometric constraints: **Horizontal, Vertical, Perpendicular, Parallel, Tangent, Smooth, Coincident, Concentric, Collinear, Symmetric, Equal,** and **Fix**. Refer to Table 12-1 for a definition of each type of constraint.

Geometric constraints can be applied to a single point on an object or to a pair of points that lie on or between two objects. Geometric constraints can also be applied to a

parametric constraints: Drawing controls that allow the designer to apply relationships between objects in a drawing file.

constraints: A series of controls that govern the position, slope, tangency, and/or the dimensions of the drawing elements.

geometric constraints: Controls that place one or more objects into a fixed relationship such as making a line horizontal or two lines parallel.

dimensional constraints: Controls that apply a value related to the size or location of an entity, for example, the length of a line, the diameter of a circle, or the location of the circle off an edge.

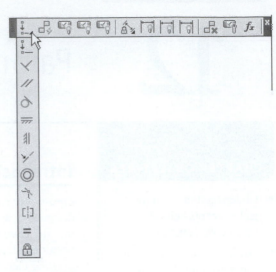

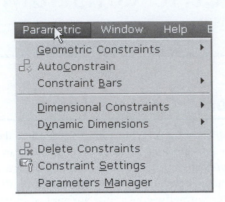

Figure 12-1

Parametric menu

Figure 12-2

Geometric Constraints toolbar

Figure 12-3

Parametric ribbon

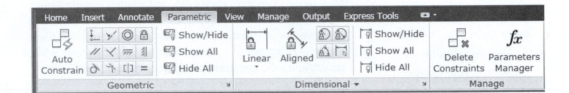

TABLE 12-1	Geometric Constraint Types	
〰	Horizontal	Causes lines or pairs of points to lie parallel to the *X*-axis of the current coordinate system.
⫴	Vertical	Causes lines or pairs of points to lie parallel to the *Y*-axis of the current coordinate system.
∠	Perpendicular	Causes selected lines to lie at a 90° angle to one another.
//	Parallel	Causes selected lines to lie parallel to one another.
↺	Tangent	Causes curves (lines, arcs, plines, or circles) to be tangent to other curves. One curve can be tangent to another even if they do not physically share a point (e.g., line or arc tangent to a circle).
⤳	Smooth	Creates a continuous curvature condition between two splines or between a spline and a line, arc, or polyline. A spline curve must be coincident with the endpoint of the other object. The coincident constraint is automatically applied.
⊥	Coincident	Constrains two points together or a point to a curve (or extension of a curve). Any constraint point on an object can be coincident with any constraint point on another object.
◎	Concentric	Constrains two arcs, circles, or ellipses to the same center point. The result is the same as that of a coincident constraint applied to the center points of the curves.
⟋	Collinear	Causes two line segments to lie along the same line.
[]⋮	Symmetric	Causes selected lines or circles to become symmetrically constrained about a selected line. For lines, the line's angle is made symmetric (not the endpoints); for circles, the center and radius are made symmetric. Points can also be selected to be symmetric.
=	Equal	Resizes selected arcs and circles to the same radius, or selected lines to the same length.
🔒	Fix	Fixes points and curves relative to the coordinate system. When applied to a curve, it fixes the angle of the line or fixes the center point and radius of arc, but allows changing the endpoints (length) of the curve. Fixing a circle fixes the center point and radius.

single object as well as to a pair of objects. Once a constraint is applied, AutoCAD displays an icon to denote the type of constraint for each object.

Applying Geometric Constraints

To apply a geometric constraint, you first select the desired type of constraint from the **Parametric** ribbon, from the **Parametric** menu, or from the **Geometric Constraints** toolbar. Next, you will be prompted to *Select Object*. As you are selecting the objects to which to apply the constraint, you will notice that an icon appears next to the cursor as a reminder of which constraint has been put in place, as shown in Table 12-2.

TABLE 12-2	Geometric Constraint Icons
Constraint Type	**Cursor Icon**
Horizontal	⟂
Vertical	⫞
Perpendicular	⊻
Parallel	//
Tangent	♂
Equal	=
Smooth	⟲
Coincident	⊡
Concentric	◎
Collinear	↘
Symmetric	⊏⫶⊐
Fix	🔒

In general, the second object selected will relocate in relation to the first object based on the type of constraint applied. AutoCAD uses predefined points on an object as constrainable points. This process is shown in Figures 12-4, 12-5, and 12-6.

These points are similar to the object snap positions you are already familiar with. Keep in mind that not all object snap positions are available for use with constraints. Refer to Table 12-3 for a description of the points available for use with specific object types. Once

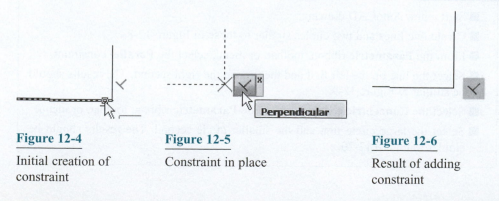

Figure 12-4

Initial creation of constraint

Figure 12-5

Constraint in place

Figure 12-6

Result of adding constraint

TABLE 12-3	Geometric Constraint Points
Object Type	**Valid Constraint Points**
Point	Node
Line	Endpoints, midpoint
Arc	Center, endpoints, midpoint
Circle, ellipse	Center
Spline	Endpoints
Polyline	Endpoints, midpoints of line and arc segments, center of arc segments
Block, Xref, text, Mtext, attribute, table	Insertion point

a relationship has been defined, either object will be updated if the other object is modified. It is not unusual to have multiple constraints applied to a single object. If the constraints being applied will conflict, the program will issue a warning message and not accept the proposed constraint. Constraints can be active or inactive. The setting to control this is found in the **Constraint Settings** dialog box (see Figure 12-7). This dialog box also contains the controls for a constraint bar's transparency and visibility.

Figure 12-7

Geometric Constraint Setting dialog box for geometric tab

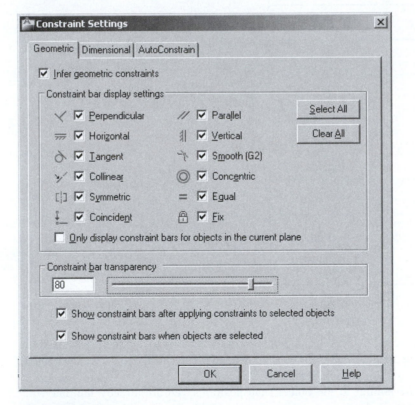

EXERCISE 12-1   **APPLYING GEOMETRIC CONSTRAINTS**

- Start a new AutoCAD drawing.
- Create two lines and two circles similar to those in Figure 12-8.
- From the **Parametric** ribbon, toolbar, or menu, select the **Parallel** constraint.
- Select the line on the left first and the line on the right second. The results should be similar to Figure 12-9.
- Select the **Concentric** constraint from the **Parametric** ribbon, toolbar, or menu.
- Select the large circle first and the smaller circle second. The results should be similar to Figure 12-10.

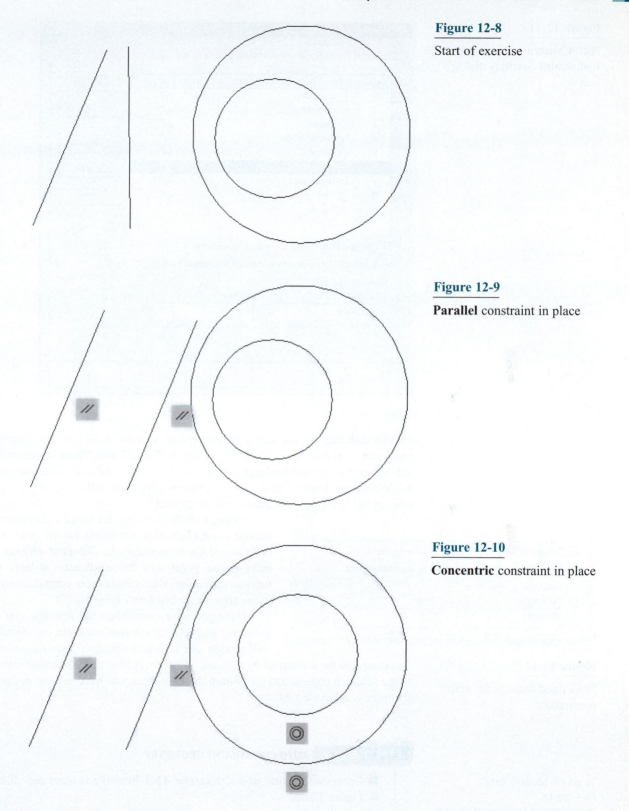

Figure 12-8

Start of exercise

Figure 12-9

Parallel constraint in place

Figure 12-10

Concentric constraint in place

Auto Constraints

The **AutoConstrain** command (see Figures 12-1 and 12-3) applies predefined constraints to objects that fall within the tolerances established through the **AutoConstrain** tab in the **Constraint Settings** dialog box (see Figure 12-11).

You start this process by selecting the constraints that you want to apply to the selected geometry through the **AutoConstrain** tab. The check mark indicates an active auto constraint

Figure 12-11

AutoConstrain tab in the
Constraint Settings dialog
box

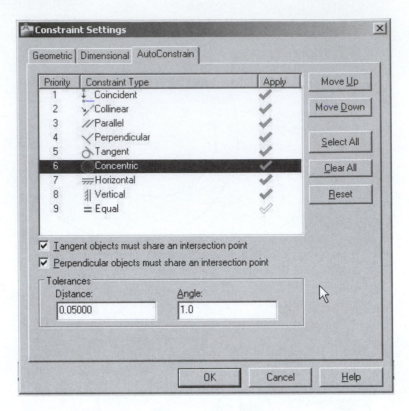

for this drawing. As you select the constraints to work with, you also prioritize them in the
order you want them to be applied by using the **Move Up** or **Move Down** buttons on the right
side of the **Constraint Settings** dialog box. Next, you establish a tolerance for **Distance** and
a tolerance for **Angle**. These values are the range or zone within which an object or point will
have to fall before the constraint will be applied.

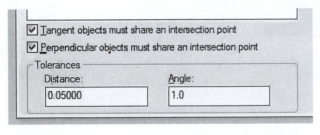

Figure 12-12

Predefined settings for auto
constraints

Along with the type and tolerance information, you may also
choose to establish other conditions for the geometry. The two predefined conditions available are **Tangent objects must share an
intersection point** and **Perpendicular objects must share an
intersection point.** You activate these conditions by placing a check
in the appropriate box (see Figure 12-12).

Once you have established the settings, you can create your
geometry and select the **AutoConstrain** command. The command
will prompt you to *Select Objects.* Once the objects are selected,
you complete the command by pressing <**Enter**>. At that time the constraints will be applied
to the selected objects that fall within the tolerances you have set and in line with the priority order you have established.

EXERCISE 12-2   **AUTO CONSTRAINT GEOMETRY**

To access student data
files, go to
www.pearsondesigncentral.com.

■ Open the drawing named **Exercise 12-2** from the student data files as shown in
Figure 12-13.

■ From the **Parametric** ribbon, select the **Constraint Settings** command.

■ Establish the following **AutoConstrain** settings and priority. Your settings should
be similar to Figure 12-14. Be sure to establish the tolerance distance and angle
settings as well.

■ Select the **AutoConstrain** command.

■ Select all the geometry. The results should be similar to Figure 12-15.

Figure 12-13
Exercise 12-2 starting drawing

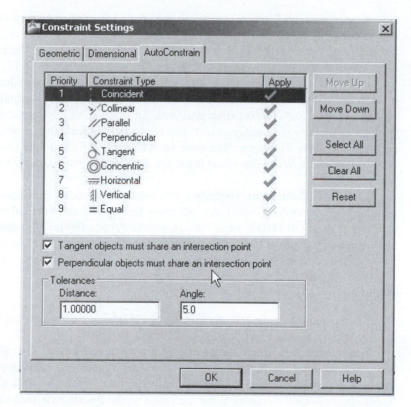

Figure 12-14

Exercise 12-2 **AutoConstrain** settings

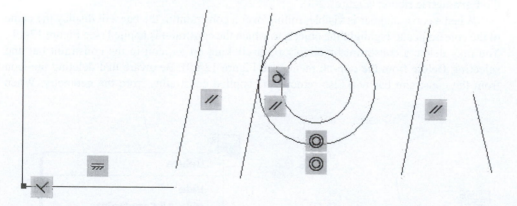

Figure 12-15

Results of the **AutoConstrain** process

Infer Geometric Constraints

New to AutoCAD 2011 is the **INFER** constraint button on the status bar. You will also find a check box for **Infer geometry constraints** in the **Constraint Settings** dialog box (see Figure 12-16). **Infer** constraints are similar to **Auto Constraints**. When turned on, a constraint can be

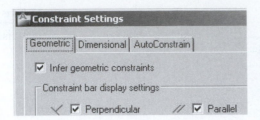

Figure 12-16

Infer check box for **Geometric Constraints**

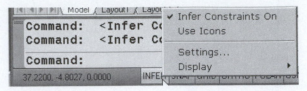

Figure 12-17

INFER button on status line with right-click menu visible

automatically inferred, which means you can create and apply a constraint to geometry. This can be done during the creation or modification of the geometry when object snaps are used. The **INFER** button on the status bar will allow you to turn on or off the **Infer** constraint the same way you can turn on and off **GRID** and **OSNAP** (see Figure 12-17).

The most common constraints that will be created are the **Coincident** constraints. The object snaps connected to inferring this constraint are **Endpoint, Midpoint, Center, Node, Insertion point**, and **Nearest snap** positions. An example of this would be when you create two circles and use the **Center** object snap command to create the second circle at the same center point as the first circle. The program will apply a **Coincident** constraint to both circles' center points. When one circle is moved, copied or mirrored, the other circle will be edited as well.

Along with **Coincident** constraints, you can infer that other constraints be applied based on other object snap functions. **Infer** will apply **Horizontal** and **Vertical** constraints to an object drawn when **ORTHO** is turned on, as well as **Perpendicular, Parallel,** or **Tangent** constraints if you use any of those object snap functions. The object snap positions not supported by the **Infer** command are **Intersection, Quadrant, Apparent Intersection,** and **Extension**.

Displaying Geometric Constraints

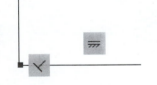

Figure 12-18

Typical constraint bar display

Once a constraint is applied to an object, AutoCAD uses a constraint bar to display the constraints applied to the object (see Figure 12-18).

You may choose which constraints to display through the **Constraint Settings** dialog box. By default the constraint bar will be visible at all times. You will have a choice to change this setting to **Hide All Constraints** or **Show** only the constraints of a selected object. The display options for the constraint bar are found on the **Parametric** menu (Figure 12-1) or on the **Parametric** ribbon (Figure 12-3).

When a constraint bar is visible, rolling over a constraint in the bar will display the name of the constraint and highlight the objects to which the constraint is applied (see Figure 12-19). You may delete a constraint by simply right-clicking on an icon in the constraint bar and selecting **Delete** from the pop-up menu (see Figure 12-20). Be aware that deleting the icon from the constraint bar will also remove the applied constraints from the geometry. When

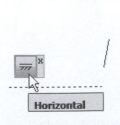

Figure 12-19

Rollover constraint bar display

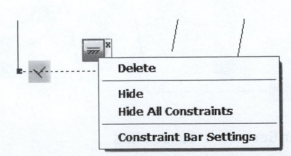

Figure 12-20

Right-click menu for constraints

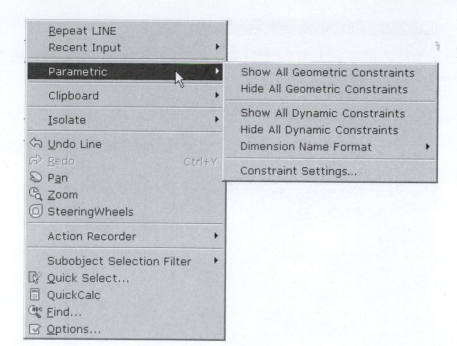

Figure 12-21

Right-click menu for con-
straints are active in a drawing

constraints are active, you can also control the display of the constraint through a right-click menu (see Figure 12-21). New to AutoCAD 2011 is the ability to relax constraints temporarily through the use of the <**Ctrl**> key when editing constrained objects.

Dimensional Constraints

Dimensional constraints create a relationship based on a measurement. A dimensional constraint can specify the length of a line, the diameter of a circle, or the distance between two parallel lines. In all cases the constraint applies a value that controls the size or location of an object. Changing the value of the constraint will cause a change in the geometry. There are six types of dimensional constraints that can be applied to objects or points along objects, namely, **Aligned, Horizontal, Vertical, Angular, Radial,** and **Diameter.**

The constraint types available resemble the typical dimension types used in AutoCAD. Once a constraint is applied, the constraint will include a name and a value. Refer to Table 12-4 for a definition of each dimensional constraint type.

TABLE 12-4	Dimensional Parametric Constraints
Aligned	Controls the distance between two points on an object or objects, between a point and an object, or between two line segments.
Horizontal	Controls the delta X distance between two points on an object or between objects.
Vertical	Controls the delta Y distance between two points on an object or between objects.
Angular	Controls the angle between two lines, polyline segments, or the angle of an arc.
Radial	Controls the radius of a circle, arc, or polyline arc segment.
Diameter	Controls the diameter of a circle, arc, or polyline arc segment.

Applying Dimensional Constraints

You access dimensional constraints through the **Parametric** menu (Figure 12-1), the **Parametric** ribbon (Figure 12-3), or the toolbar shown in Figure 12-22.

Dimensional constraints can be applied to a single point on an object or to a pair of points that lie on or between two objects. Geometric constraints can also be applied to a single object

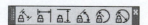

Figure 12-22

Dimensional Constraint toolbar

Figure 12-23

Dimensional Constraint Settings dialog box

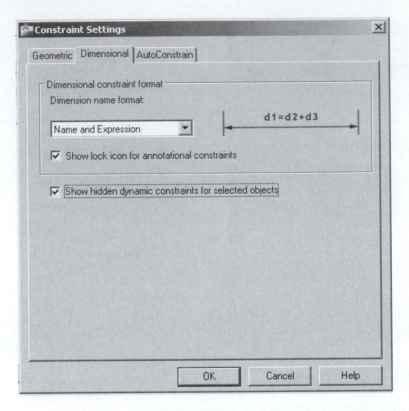

as well as to a pair of objects. Once any type of constraint is applied, AutoCAD will display an icon to denote the type of constraint for each object (see Figure 12-23).

To apply a constraint, you select the style of constraint from the **Parametric** command. Next, you select the objects that you want to constrain. Be sure to read the prompt line to select the correct objects related to the constraint you are attempting to define.

EXERCISE 12-3 **APPLYING DIMENSIONAL CONSTRAINTS TO GEOMETRY**

■ Continue with the drawing from Exercise 12-2.

■ From the **Parametric** ribbon or from the menu, select the **Linear** constraint.

■ When prompted to select the first constraint point, press **<Enter>** to select the *OBJECT* suboption of the command.

■ Select the horizontal line at the lower left.

■ Select a location for the dimensional constraint display. The results should be similar to Figure 12-24.

■ Enter **14** as the new dimension, as shown in Figure 12-25.

■ Press **<Enter>** to complete the command, and the line will extend to 14 units, as shown in Figure 12-26.

■ Select the **Aligned** constraint icon from the **Parametric** ribbon.

■ Select the bottom endpoint of the vertical line on the right side, then select the top point of the vertical line on the right side.

■ Select the location for the dimensional constraint and enter **10** for the new constraint distance. The results should be similar to Figure 12-27.

■ Select the **Diameter** constraint.

■ Select the inner circle in the center of the drawing and set the constraint dimension to **7**. The results should be similar to Figure 12-28.

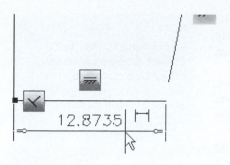

Figure 12-24

Placing the **Linear** dimensional constraint

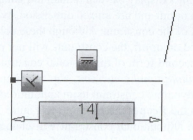

Figure 12-25

Entering **14** as the constraint

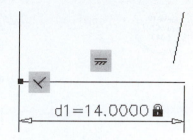

Figure 12-26

Completed constraint

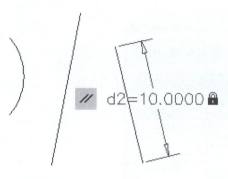

Figure 12-27

Applying the **Aligned** dimensional constraint

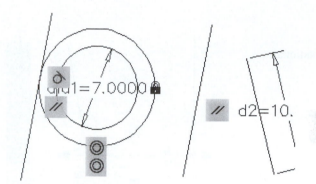

Figure 12-28

Applying the **Diameter** constraint

Displaying Dimensional Constraints

Dimensional constraints can be displayed in three different formats. By default an applied dimensional constraint will first be displayed in the name = formula/value style. Constraints can also be displayed as a numeric value or an expression. Once a constraint has been applied, the constraint will be displayed as a value. In expression format, the constraint can be in the name = formula/value style or a valid math equation that may use variable names or values in combination. For example, a dimensional constraint named *Length* could be defined as *Width/3*. This would constrain the length of the object to one-third the width of an object. The display settings of dimensional constraints are controlled in the **Constraint Settings** dialog box under the **Dimensional** tab (see Figure 12-29) or by the **CONSTRAINTNAMEFORMAT** system variable. By default a dimensional constraint is dynamic by nature. A dynamic

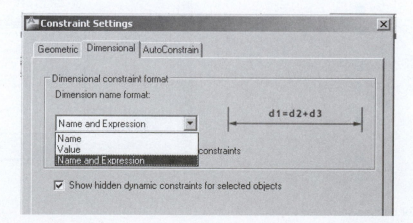

Figure 12-29

Drop-down menu for dimensional constraints options

constraint's display bar will remain the same size as you zoom in or out and use a fixed dimension style to control the look of the constraint. Although these constraints can be turned on or off, the constraints will not print.

A second form of dimensional constraint is known as an *annotational constraint*. You can change the form from a dynamic constraint to an annotational constraint through the **Properties** palette (see Figure 12-30).

The annotational constraint will change in size as you zoom in and out. This type of constraint will be displayed in the current dimension style and will also be displayed on a plot of your drawing file. Rolling over a constraint bar will identify the style of the constraint and highlight the objects defined by the constraint.

> **NOTE:**
>
> New to AutoCAD 2011 is the **Convert** option when creating dimensional constraints. This option will convert associative dimensions to dimensional constraints.

Figure 12-30

Creating an annotational constraint

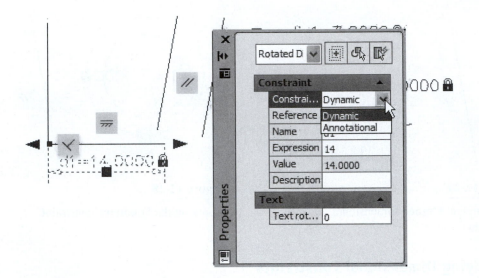

Modifying Parametric Constraints

Constraint geometry can be modified through several methods. Keep in mind that modifications to the geometry will be restricted by the constraints applied. Modifications made to geometry that is not fully constrained may reveal some interesting results. You can make changes to your constrained geometry by accessing any of the standard editing commands, by executing any of the grip editing commands, through the **Properties** palette, and through the **Parameters Manager**, as shown in Figure 12-31.

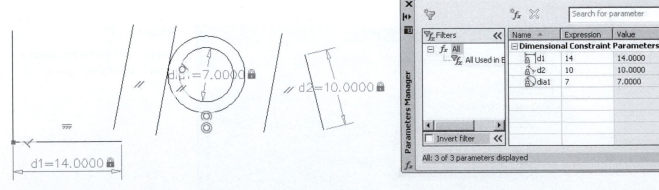

Figure 12-31

Parameters Manager palette for completed Exercise 12-3

Chapter Summary

In this chapter we introduced the concept of using parametric constraints to create relationships between points and/or objects. You learned there are two styles of constraints: geometric and dimensional. The 12 geometric constraints are **Horizontal, Vertical, Perpendicular, Parallel, Tangent, Smooth, Coincident, Concentric, Collinear, Symmetric, Equal,** and **Fix**. You access geometric constraints through the **Parametric** ribbon, the **Parametric** menu, or the appropriate toolbars. You found out that geometric constraints can be applied to a single point on an object or to a pair of points that lie on or between two objects. You also learned that geometric constraints can be applied to a single object as well as to a pair of objects.

Dimensional constraints are applied to control the size, shape, or location of geometry. The six types of dimensional constraints are **Aligned, Horizontal, Vertical, Angular, Radial,** and **Diameter**. You learned that dimensional constraints can be displayed in three different formats: name = formula/value, numeric value, or an expression, and that constraints are displayed on a constraint bar. Once a constraint is defined, a visual glyph will appear near the object to show an icon that defines the type of constraint applied to the object. When you roll the cursor over the icon, a tooltip will appear giving the name of the constraint, and the objects being constrained will be highlighted.

You learned there are two styles for displaying a dimensional constraint. A standard dynamic constraint's display bar will remain the same size as you zoom in or out and use a fixed dimension style. This style of constraint will not show on a printed drawing. The annotational display of a constraint will change in size as you zoom in and out. This style of constraint will be displayed in the current dimension style and will display on a print of your drawing file. You also learned how to **Infer** constraints to apply a constraint automatically to geometry when object snaps are used.

Finally, you learned that parametric constraints can be edited with any of the standard modify commands as well as by executing any of the grip editing commands. Furthermore, constraints can be edited in the **Properties** palette as well as in the **Parameters Manager**.

Chapter Test Questions

Multiple Choice

Circle the correct answer.

1. Which of the following is **not** a geometric constraint?

   a. Fixed
   b. Position
   c. Parallel
   d. Perpendicular

2. Parametric constraints will

   a. Aid in consistent design modifications
   b. Control the size and location of objects
   c. Create relationships between objects
   d. All the above

3. Two styles of dimensional constraints are

   a. Dynamic and annotational
   b. Dynamic and visible
   c. Annotational and editable
   d. Editable and consistent

4. An applied parametric constraint can be viewed in the

   a. **Parameters Manager**
   b. Constraint bar
   c. **Properties** palette
   d. **Parametric** panel on the ribbon

5. To modify a parametric constraint, you can use

   a. A grip command
   b. The **Properties** dialog box
   c. The **Parameters Manager**
   d. All the above

Matching

Write the number of the correct answer on the line.

a. Collinear _____

b. Concentric _____

c. Fixed _____

d. Coincident _____

e. Perpendicular _____

1. Merges two points together in one location

2. Causes two line segments to lie along the same line

3. Constrains two arcs, circles, or ellipses to the same center point

4. Causes selected lines to be at a 90° angle to each other

5. Causes a point or an object to be locked in its position

True or False

Circle the correct answer.

1. **True or False:** Dimensional constraints cannot be applied to points on separate objects.

2. **True or False:** Parametric constraints can be applied in layout space.

3. **True or False:** Modify commands will ignore the parametric constraint applied to an object.

4. **True or False:** Constrainable points will match up with all object snap positions.

5. **True or False:** The constraint bar can be turned on and off on the **Parametric** ribbon.

Chapter Practice Exercises

(M) Practice Exercise 12-1: *Parametric Constraints—Mechanical* [BASIC]

1. Open the drawing named **Part Shape** from the Chapter 12 folder of the student data files, as shown in Figure 12-32.

To access student data files, go to **www.pearsondesigncentral.com.**

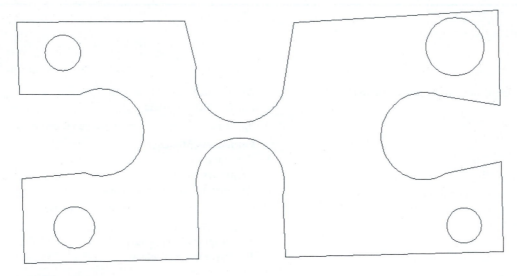

Figure 12-32

Start shape for Parametric problem

2. Go to the **Constraint Settings** dialog box and on the **AutoConstrain** tab, establish the settings found on Figure 12-14. Once those settings are established, **AutoConstrain** all of the objects in the drawing file.

3. Apply the **Horizontal, Vertical, Concentric, Tangent, Equal, Coincident,** and **Collinear** geometric constraints to the appropriate objects. Your final results should look like Figure 12-33.

4. Apply the following dimensional constraint to establish the size and location of the geometry. Your final results should look like Figure 12-34.

5. Save the drawing in your **Workskills** folder as **Part-New**.

Figure 12-33

Shape after geometric
constraints are applied

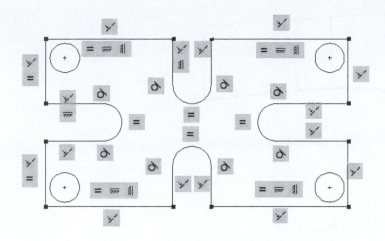

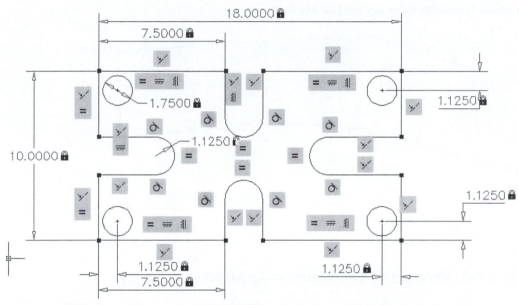

Figure 12-34

Shape after dimensional constraints are hidden

c Practice Exercise 12-2: *Parametric Constraints—Civil* [BASIC]

1. Open drawing **CIVIL LOTS** from the Chapter 12 folder of the student data files, as shown in Figure 12-35.

2. Using parametric constraints, establish the interior relatively vertical property lines as parallel to the leftmost property line. The result is shown in Figure 12-36.

To access student data
files, go to
www.pearsondesigncentral.com.

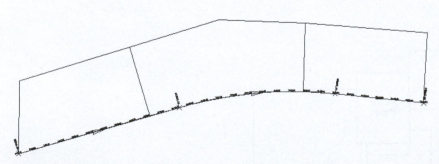

Figure 12-35

Initial lot drawing

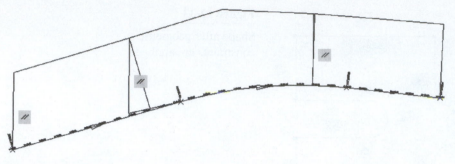

Figure 12-36

After the constraints are applied

  3. Edit the polylines to complete the lot layout as shown in Figure 12-37.

  4. Save the drawing in your **Workskills** folder as **Civil Lots Fixed**.

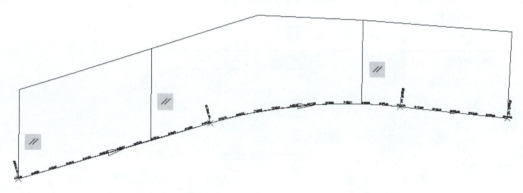

Figure 12-37

Completed lot layout

Ⓐ **Practice Exercise 12-3:** *Parametric Constraints—Architectural* [BASIC]

  1. Open the drawing named **House** from the Chapter 12 folder of the student data files, as shown in Figure 12-38.

  2. Assign the parametric constraints as shown in Figure 12-39.

To access student data files, go to **www.pearsondesigncentral.com.**

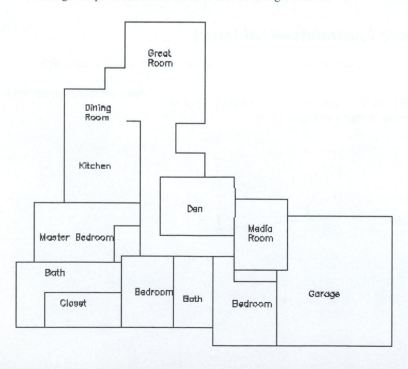

Figure 12-38

Drawing for start of exercise

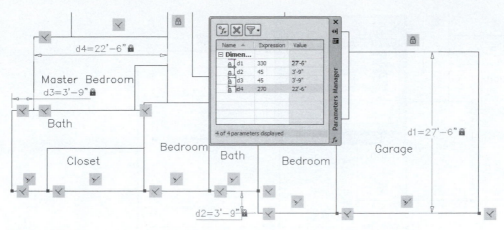

Figure 12-39

Parameters added to floor plan

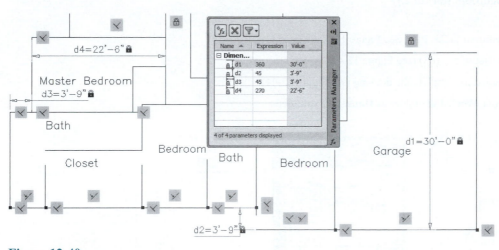

Figure 12-40

Expanding the garage to 30′

3. Expand the Garage dimension (d1) to 30′. With the top line fixed, the expansion will be toward the bottom of the screen (see Figure 12-40).

4. Modify the wall offset (d2) to 54″. Owing to the 30′ constraint (d1) the wall on the left will move up (see Figure 12-41).

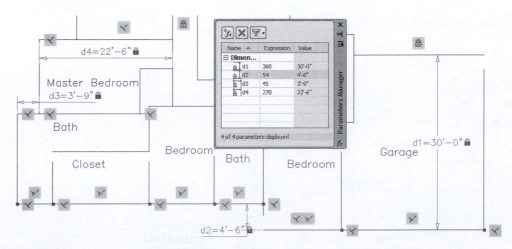

Figure 12-41

Modifying the wall offset (d2) to 54″

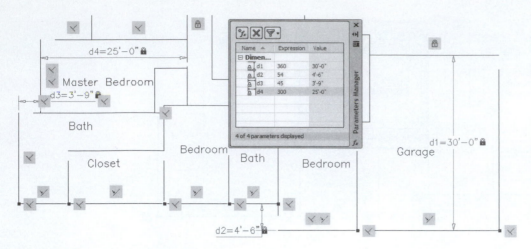

Figure 12-42

Expanding the Master Bedroom (d4) to 25′

5. Expand the Master Bedroom to 25′ (d4). See Figure 12-42.

6. Modify the left wall offset to 54″ (d3) (see Figure 12-43).

7. Extend the lines as needed to complete the drawing (see Figure 12-44).

8. Save the drawing in your **Workskills** folder as **House12 Expanded**.

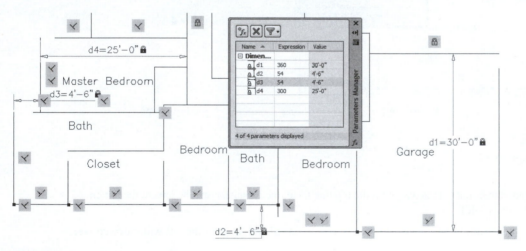

Figure 12-43

Modifying the wall offset (d3) to 54″

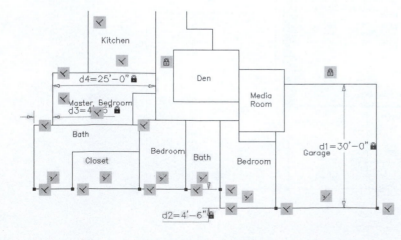

Figure 12-44

Final modified floor plan

13

Tables, Cells, and Fields Fundamentals

- Create a table using table styles.
- Edit table elements.
- Edit cells in a table.
- Create and edit table styles.
- Distinguish the categories related to fields.
- Insert fields in a drawing.
- Update fields in a drawing.
- Use fields across drawings.

Introduction

Drawings show the size and shape of an object. In many cases more information is needed. One such way to present an enhanced version of the information is by adding text to the drawing, which was discussed in Chapter 9. Another way to present this additional information is in the form of a table, schedule, or spreadsheet. *Cells* are the individual items of data in the table. *Fields* are information taken from the drawing such as area or attribute data. Fields can also be a direct input.

AutoCAD Tables

Tables are used to present information in an organized, efficient, and easy-to-read format (see Figure 13-1). Schedules and spreadsheets are additional examples of tables. In many cases there are many options or pieces of information to describe an object in a drawing, and it is not possible to place this information as text or attribute data near the object. To avoid confusion and increase understanding, a key code or symbol is placed near the object to be described. This code or symbol is then placed in the table to create the connection of the information or data to the object.

cell: The box at the intersection of a table row and column that contains the table data or a formula. A cell is typically referenced using its column letter and row number separated with a colon. For example, the cell in column A and row 1 is referenced as A:1

field: A specialized text object set up to display data that may change during the life cycle of the drawing. When the field is updated, the latest value of the field is displayed.

> **JOB SKILLS**
>
> All engineering disciplines make use of a table format when displaying certain types of information. Whether it be a door and window schedule, a room finish schedule, or a bill of materials/parts list, these items will be easier to create and maintain if they are developed using the table, cells, and field commands offered in AutoCAD.

Tables have rows and columns that form cells, which can contain repetitive or similar information. For example, a plant table (see Figure 13-1) shows quantities, names of plants, size, and more. A door schedule (see Figure 13-2) typically has columns showing the door dimensions, finish, lock and key, and more. A dimension table (see Figure 13-3) shows the dimension relationships of a part, based on parametric modeling procedures.

Figure 13-1

Typical plant table

Plant Table

Broadleaf Deciduous

Quantity	Symbol	Scientific Name
1		Cercis canadensis

Broadleaf Evergreen

Quantity	Symbol	Scientific Name
13		Grevillea 'Noellii'
1		Grevillea 'Noellii'
36		Nandina domestica 'Nana'
10		Podocarpus macrophyllus
11		Raphiolepis indica
15		Rhododendron indicum
6		Thevetia peruviana

Perennial

Quantity	Symbol	Scientific Name
12		Heuchera sanguinea
60		Heuchera sanguinea

Shrub

Quantity	Symbol	Scientific Name
5		Camellia japonica

Figure 13-2

Typical architectural door schedule

DOOR SCHEDULE				
Code	Height	Width	Finish	Handle
D101	8'	3'	Exterior Glazed	Bar with Lock
D102	6'-8'	8'	Exterior Sliding	Locking
D103	6'-8"	3'	White	Locking

Figure 13-3

Typical parametric dimension table

Case Dimensions						
Shaft Size	A	B	C	D	E	F
3/8"	4-1/2	3-3/4	2-1/8	5-5/8	1-1/2	6-3/4
1/2"	4-3/4	3-3/4	2-1/4	5-7/8	1-3/8	7
5/8"	4-7/8	4	2-3/8	6	1-1/4	7-1/4
3/4"	5	4	2-1/2	6-1/8	1-1/8	7-1/2
7/8"	5-1/8	4-1/4	2-5/8	6-3/8	1	7-3/4

Tables use a row and column layout to create the basic layout size. A column header row and a title row can be added to enhance the table. Tables are set up based on the table styles defined in the current drawing template or defined by the user. The numbers of rows and columns can be defined when they are inserted. The row-and-column format creates a matrix of the information in cells.

Inserting a Table

If a table is to be used, the style will dictate the look of the table. You select the size of the table (the number of rows and columns) as well as the column width and row height when you insert the table. If a title row and column header row are desired, the style should reflect this choice.

To place a table in the drawing, choose **Table** from the **Draw** menu. The dialog box shown in Figure 13-4 will appear. After specifying the needed information, you can specify an insertion point or choose the opposite corners of the window to fit the table based on the setting in the upper right. The table appears with the **Text Editor** tab displayed above it as shown in Figure 13-5. The tools on the **Text Editor** ribbon help you with the placement, size, font, color, emphasis, and other parameters of the text in the table.

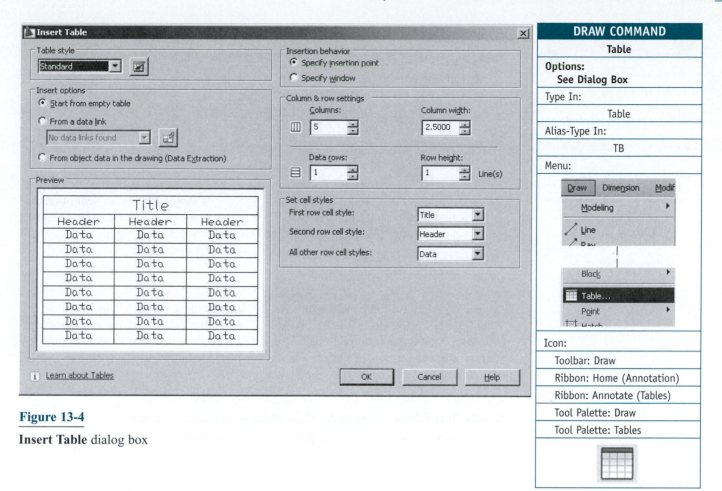

Figure 13-4

Insert Table dialog box

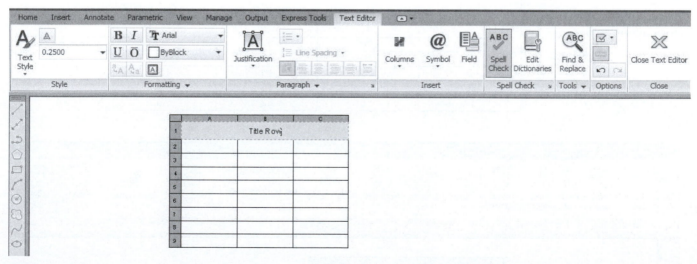

Figure 13-5

Table with **Text Editor** active for entering information

To move around the table, you may use any of the following methods:

- Use the left mouse button to choose the cell for input of information.
- Use the arrow keys to move around the table from cell to cell.
- Use the **<Enter>** key to move to the next cell (moving to the right or down depending on the initial style setting).

To access student data files, go to **www.pearsondesigncentral.com.**

EXERCISE 13-1 **TABLE OPERATIONS**

- Start AutoCAD and open the **CHAPTER 13** drawing from the student data files.
- Verify that the current layer is **TABLE** and that all other layers are off.
- Access the **Draw** menu and choose **Table**.
- Insert a table with the following specifications:
  Rows: **7**
  Columns: **6**
  Column Width: **2"**
  Row Height: **2 lines**
- Put your name in the Title Area (i.e., _____'s Table). Place your year of graduation as the center column header. Place the years before this date as column headers to the left and after this date as column headers to the right.
- Save the drawing in your **Workskills** folder as **CHAPTER 13**.

The cells in a table can contain alphanumeric text, numeric data, symbols, blocks, fields, and attribute data (see Figure 13-6). Information in a cell can be rotated using the standard AutoCAD angles. Information will word-wrap if two or more lines are needed because the column width will not change. Once the table is placed in the drawing, there are five ways to modify the table and its content:

- Use the tools on the **Table Cell** ribbon by gripping a cell (see Figure 13-7).
- Use the **Text Editor** ribbon by double-clicking in a cell (see Figure 13-8).
- Use the slide-out panels from the panels on the **Text Editor** ribbon (see Figure 13-9).

Figure 13-6

Typical AutoCAD table with sample information

Title Area				
Header 1	Header 2	Header 3	Header 4	Header 5
A	1	2	3	4
B	5	6	7	8
C	9	10	11	12
D	13	14	15	16
E	17	18	19	20
F	21	22	23	24

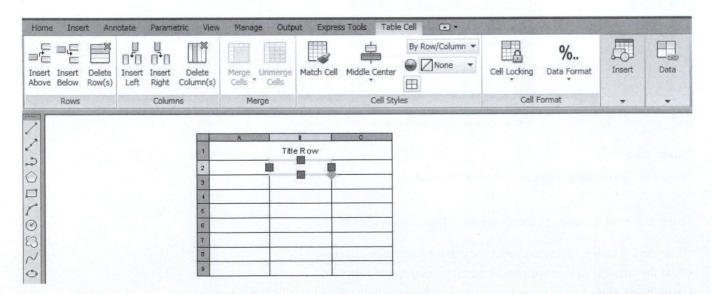

Figure 13-7

Cell modifications with **Table Cell** ribbon active

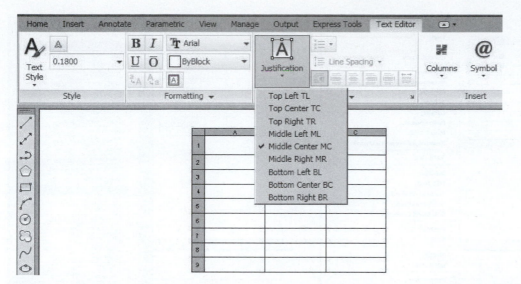

Figure 13-8

Text Editor ribbon option for cell text justification

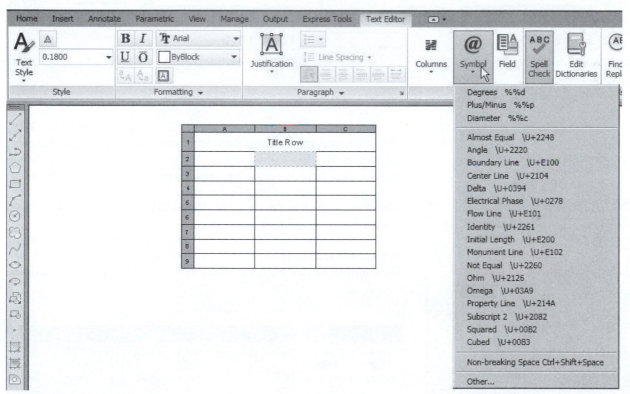

Figure 13-9

Insert Symbol panel on the **Text Editor** ribbon

- Use the right mouse button menu (see Figure 13-10).
- Use the **Properties** palette (see Figure 13-11).

When you touch the keyboard to enter information into a cell, the **Text Editor** ribbon appears to aid in entering the information in the correct format. To enter information into a cell or to edit information, choose the cell to make it active (with grips) and enter the new text or data.

JOB SKILLS

An understanding of Quick Calc and transparent CAL command will allow you to work out complicated calculations and copy the results to the table cell as expressions. Engineering formulas are often needed in the design process. The application of these commands increases a drawing's accuracy.

Figure 13-10

Edit cell right-click menu

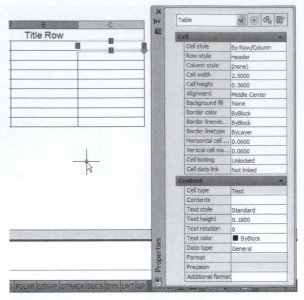

Figure 13-11

Cell Properties palette

You can also right-mouse-click to display a menu (see Figure 13-10) with more options, or display these other options by clicking on the symbol icon in the **Text Editor** ribbon, as shown in Figure 13-9. Although some of these menu items are the same, many are different and offer additional options as well. Many of these items and actions are straightforward to understand such as **Insert Field**, **Delete**, **Justification**, **Change Case**, **Find & Replace**, and **Cell Borders**.

Further formatting of the cells in a table can include single and double line borders (see Figure 13-12) and various data formats (see Figure 13-13). These formats include currency, whole numbers, angles, percentages, dates,

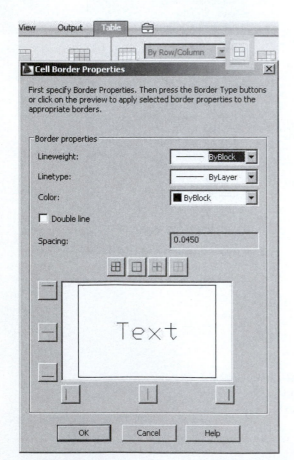

Figure 13-12

Edit cell borders dialog box

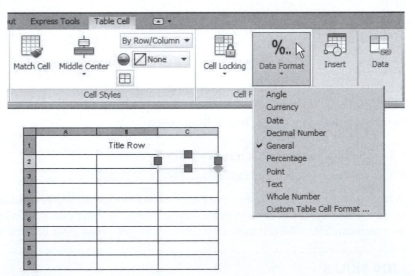

Figure 13-13

Cell formats on the **Table Cell** ribbon

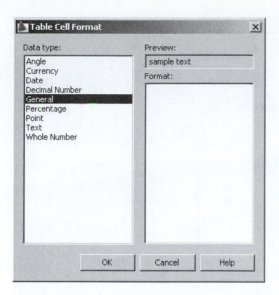

Figure 13-14

Edit cell format customize menu

and text. These formats can be further customized as shown in Figure 13-14. The table can contain and have a dynamic link with other files such as Excel spreadsheets, Word documents, and other similar objects that can be embedded and linked. The link is named and established using the **Select a Data Link** dialog box as shown in Figure 13-15. You can insert blocks in a cell as shown in Figure 13-16.

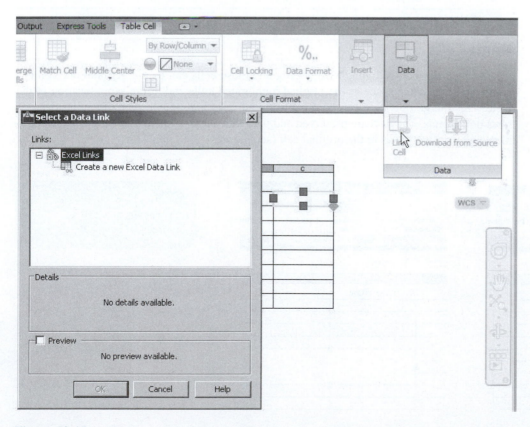

Figure 13-15

External data link setup dialog box

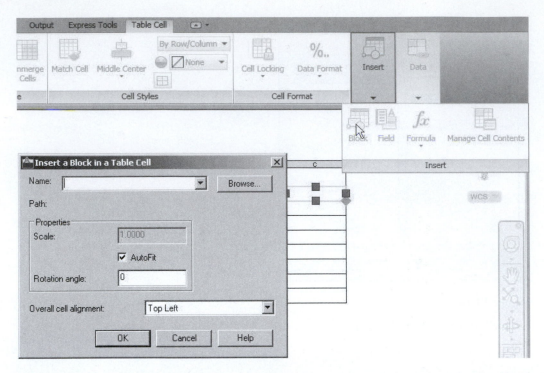

Figure 13-16

Block Insert dialog box from **Table Cell** ribbon

FOR MORE DETAILS   The insertion of fields in a cell of a table is discussed later in this chapter.

Merge Cells

If more than one cell is highlighted by gripping, those cells can be merged into one cell encompassing the same space as the original highlighted cells and in the same location in the table. This merge operation can be done using all cells highlighted or by merging them as rows or columns. The data are preserved and placed in the merged cell using the same alignment and justification as in the original cell (see Figures 13-17 and 13-18).

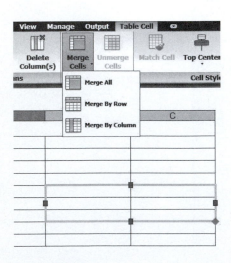

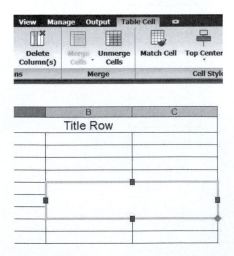

NOTE:

Only merged cells can be unmerged.

Figure 13-17

Merge cells menu

Figure 13-18

Cell after merge

Symbols

The ability to add special symbols to information in a cell is available through the @ symbol or through the **Options** slide-out panel, both of which are on the **Text Editor** ribbon. The list of symbols available in the menu is shown in Figure 13-9. The chosen symbol is placed at the current location of the blinking cursor.

Insert Formula

When you highlight a cell (see Figure 13-19), you can use the right mouse button menu to assign various mathematical operations to that cell. For these operations you pick inside the range of cells to be considered for this action. You can also type the operation and the range with relative or absolute locations (using a $ sign). The result is a formula similar to that in an Excel spreadsheet when in **Edit** mode, and the answer to the formula appears in normal view (see Figures 13-20, 13-21, and 13-22). In the **Formula** option (Figure 13-23), the equation must begin with an equals sign (=). Formulas can use addition (+), subtraction (−), multiplication (×), division (/), and exponent (^). Parentheses "( )" can be used to show hierarchy in the formula, and a colon is used to define a range of cells. A comma can be used to list individual cells.

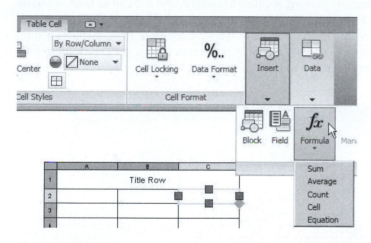

Figure 13-19

Cell formula options on the **Table Cell** ribbon

C
Title Area
Header 3
2
6
10
14
18
=Sum(C3:C7)]

Figure 13-20

Sum formula example

D
Header 4
3
7
11
15
19
=Average(D3:D7)

Figure 13-21

Average formula example

E
Header 5
4
8
12
16
20
=Count(E3:E7)]

Figure 13-22

Count formula example

B
Header 2
1
5
9
13
17
]=(C8+D8)*E8

Figure 13-23

Another formula example

To access student data
files, go to
www.pearsondesigncentral.com.

> **EXERCISE 13-2** **TABLE WITH FORMULAS**
>
> ■ Continue with the **CHAPTER 13** drawing or open this drawing from the student data files.
> ■ Make the **TABLE2** layer current and on. Turn off any other layers.
> ■ Randomly enter numbers between **1** and **50** in the empty cells except for the bottom row.
> ■ In the bottom row of cells, use the following formulas:
>   • Column 2—use the **Sum** of the column
>   • Column 3—use the **Average** of the column
>   • Column 4—use the **Count** of the column
>   • Column 5—use the formula "= (B8+C8)*D8/2"
>   • Column 6—use the same as cell **E8**
> ■ Save the drawing in your **Workskills** folder as **CHAPTER 13**.

Table Styles

As with many objects in the AutoCAD program, tables can be predefined as a style. The initial style in the AutoCAD template drawing is called **Standard**, and this can be used as a basis for other styles. From the **Format** menu you can access the **Table Style** dialog box (see Figure 13-24) or call on another method. Initially the standard-style table includes a title, column headers, and data cells. To **Modify** the table or to create a **New** style, pick the appropriate tab on the right side of the dialog box.

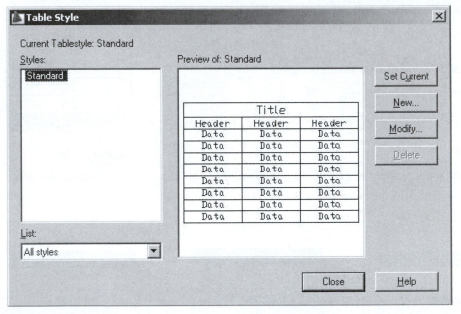

Figure 13-24

Table Style dialog box

For a new table, choose a name as well as a base table to begin the design. Toggles are available to include the title row and the column header row in a new table.

The **Modify Table Style** dialog box (see Figure 13-25) allows you to change any of the variables regarding the format of a table. You can change the table direction in the **General** area; change the style of a cell that contains data, header information, or title information in the **Cell styles** area (see Figure 13-26); or select one of the three tabs dealing with the

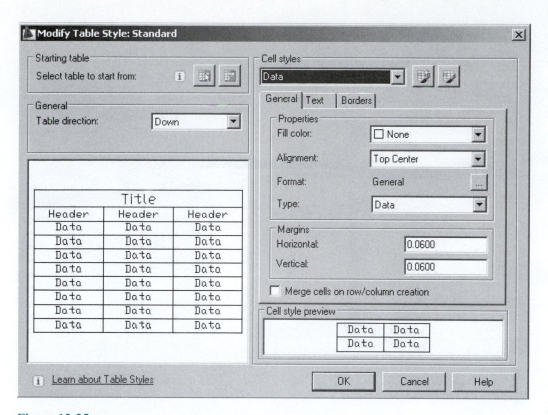

Figure 13-25

Modify Table Style dialog box

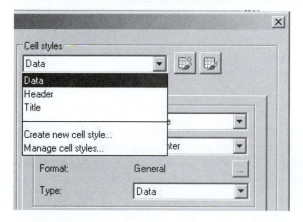

Figure 13-26

Cell Styles drop-down menu in **Table Style** dialog box

properties of the table in the right side of the dialog box. The three tabs in this area are **General** for color, alignment, format, and type; **Text**, which addresses text characteristics; and **Borders**, which allows you to change the lineweight, linetype, and color of lines along with line spacing. This dialog box also contains two preview windows where you can see what effect your change(s) will have on the table.

Fields

Fields are an enhancement to multiline text or tables and allow for use of information contained in the drawing. These data can be placed as part of text or can stand alone if so desired (see Figure 13-27). For example, a field can display the current date in a title block,

INSERT COMMAND
Field
Options: **Various Categories**
Type In:
Field
Alias-Type In:
Menu:
Icon:
Ribbon: Insert (Data)
Ribbon: Table Cell (Insert)

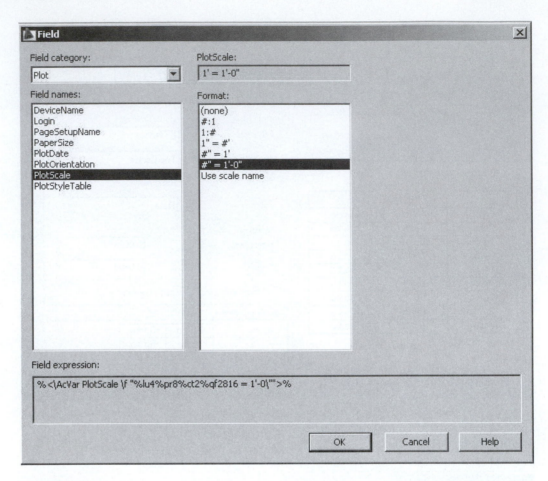

Figure 13-27

The **Field** dialog box

show the area of a closed polyline, or show the current plot scale of a layout window on the paper. There are hundreds of options in creating a freestanding field or using it in a multiline text environment. If the drawing information changes, fields can be automatically updated to reflect the current level of data. Fields can also come from drawings in a sheet set.

Categories of Fields

Owing to the many possibilities available as fields, categories have been developed to aid in quickly locating the appropriate field to insert. The categories (see Figure 13-28) are as follows:

- **All** Shows all fields available (see Figure 13-29)
- **Date & Time** (see Figure 13-30)
- **Document** Keywords, title, author, etc. (see Figure 13-31)
- **Linked** Hyperlinks (see Figure 13-32)
- **Objects** Entities in the drawings, formula equation, and blocks (see Figures 13-33, 13-34, and 13-35)
- **Other** System variables and Diesel expressions (see Figure 13-36)
- **Plot** Plot scale, plot date, paper size, and others (see Figure 13-37)
- **SheetSet** Current sheet set data and placeholders (see Figure 13-38)

Figure 13-28

Insert field categories

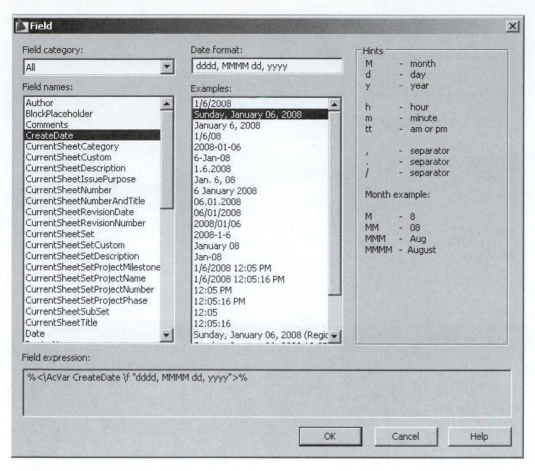

Figure 13-29

The field category list

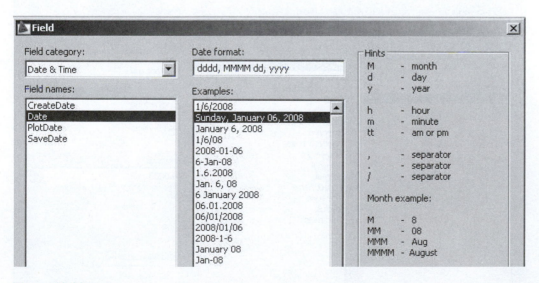

Figure 13-30

Field Date dialog box

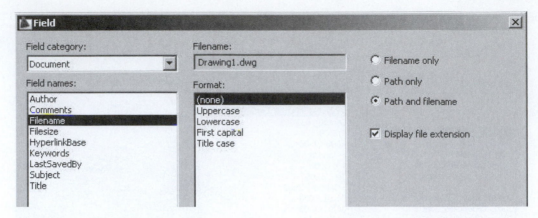

Figure 13-31

Field document options

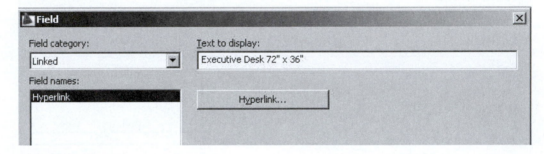

Figure 13-32

Field linked option

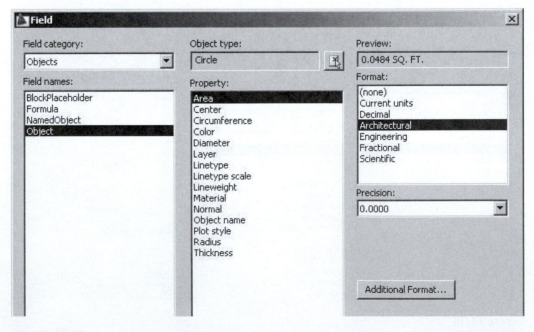

Figure 13-33

The **Field** dialog box for objects

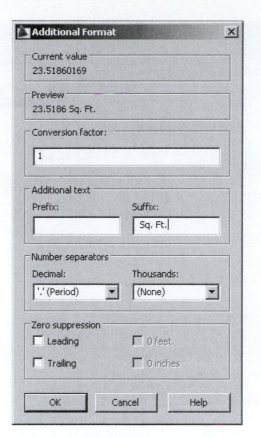

Figure 13-34

Field Additional Format
dialog box

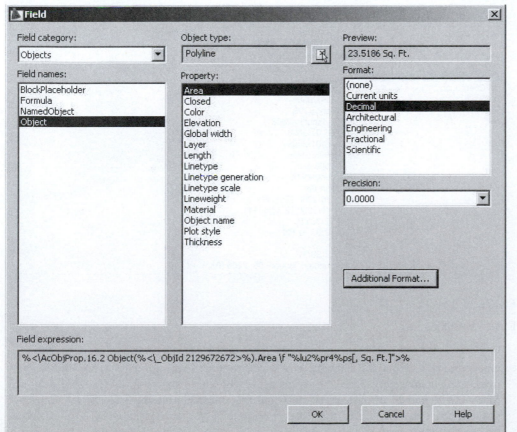

Figure 13-35

Field Object Polyline
dialog box

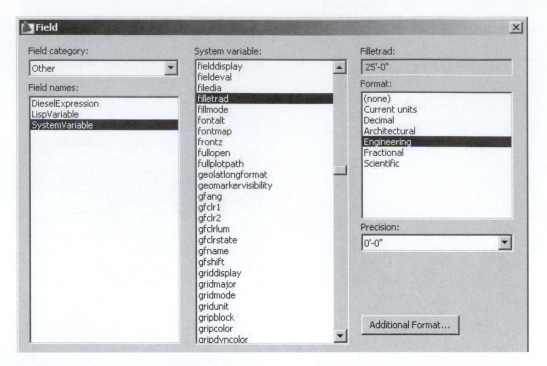

Figure 13-36

Field Other dialog box

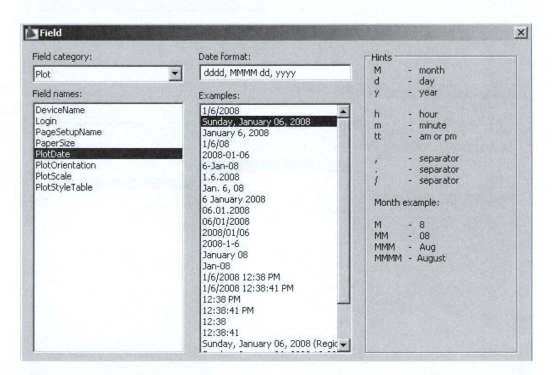

Figure 13-37

Field Plot dialog box

Once you have chosen the category, you select from the **Field name** list below the category field. Field names vary based on the category chosen as shown in the following figures. Many of the names are self-explanatory and are entered in various parts of the AutoCAD program or set by the profile, template, or options. A further explanation of some field categories follows.

Date & Time. In the **Data & Time** category (see Figure 13-30), many examples are presented for the four field names available. Hints are provided to aid in picking the correct format for the field to be inserted. Except for the **CreateDate** of the drawing, the other options update to the current date of the activity involved.

Document. Most of these fields (see Figure 13-31) are defined in the **Drawing Properties** dialog boxes from the **File** menu. Various formats are available to display this information as a field.

Linked. Hyperlinks can connect an object in a drawing to an Internet website, an intranet site, or another object to further define the object or to be used as an aid in specifying the correct item. This link can also connect to a graphic, picture, or video file. For example, in Figure 13-32, the desk identified can link to an office supply website that shows the desk desired, its price, and other specifications.

Objects. Various objects in the drawing have properties that can be accessed and used as fields (see Figure 13-33). Typically, you choose the precise object via the pick box that will supply data to the inserted field.

The list of objects is extensive; you can choose virtually any entity currently in the drawing. You cannot choose an object type directly because it must exist in the drawing for entity properties to be available. For example, in Figure 13-33, a circle is the object selected using the pick symbol at the top right of the middle column. Once the object is chosen, the properties available are displayed in the middle column. After you choose a property value to display, the value is shown in the third column, and you can choose the proper format of those shown. The **Additional Format** button leads to options regarding conversion factors, zero suppression, numerical separators, the prefix phase, and the suffix phase (see Figure 13-34). For Figure 13-35, the object chosen is a polyline. Some of the properties available are the same as for the circle, and some are different. You should examine numerous objects and review the properties available for fields in various formats.

Other. The **Other** category focuses on system variables and Diesel expression values (see Figure 13-36). The **System variable** values are set in the drawing template, workspaces, customized programming, and other locations throughout the AutoCAD program. These fields can be used to inform others of certain "standard" values used in the current drawing. If this value has differing formats available, the third column will display the possibilities for format. You should examine various options and see the current values and format options.

Plot. The **Plot** category (see Figure 13-37) displays fields that relate to layout and plotting settings. These values can be used to inform others of the settings needed for the proper plotting and presentation of the drawing. The device name present for these items is based on the current default printer. It is not possible to change the device name in this dialog box; this needs to be changed before accessing this command.

Sheet Sets. The **SheetSet** category (see Figure 13-38) displays values that can be used related to sheet sets. Sheet sets allow the organization of multiple drawings and their corresponding layouts into a set for plotting, view control, and the relationship of details.

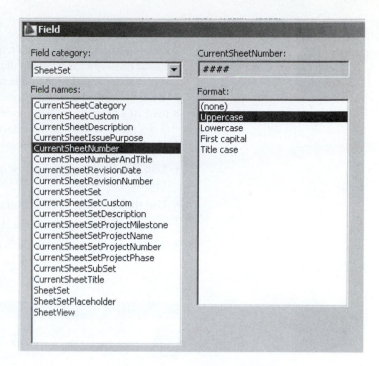

Figure 13-38

Field SheetSet dialog box

JOB SKILLS

To determine who has locked a sheet set, simply hover the mouse over the icon, and the user's name will appear in a tooltip box.

Using Fields in Tables

As shown earlier in this chapter, tables can be used to present a large amount of data in an organized form. Fields showing drawing information can also be inserted in a table using various methods. A cell in the table must be active to place a field as part of the table. Using the **FIELD** command does not place a field inside the cell, but the command can be used to place a field in a location on the drawing, which can be in the table.

To place a field in the drawing, you can activate the cell by clicking in it. The **Insert Field** dialog box can be accessed by the following methods:

- Use the **Insert** panel arrow at the right end of the **Text Editor** ribbon as shown in Figure 13-39.
- Use the right-click menu as shown in Figure 13-40 when the **Text Editor** ribbon is active.
- After gripping a cell, use the right-click menu as shown in Figure 13-41.
- After gripping a cell, use the icon in the **Table Cell** ribbon as shown in Figure 13-42.

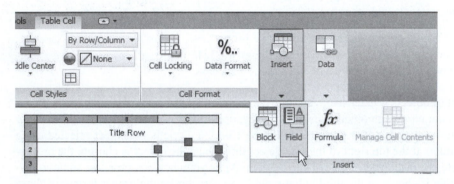

Figure 13-39

Insert Field panel on **Text Editor** ribbon

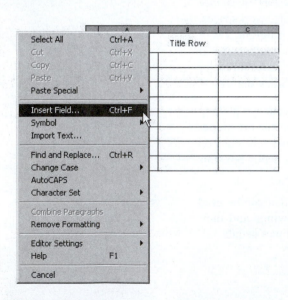

Figure 13-40

Inserting a field in a table from the right-click menu

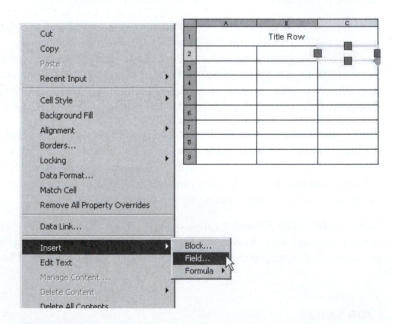

Figure 13-41

Inserting a field from the right-click menu when a table cell is gripped

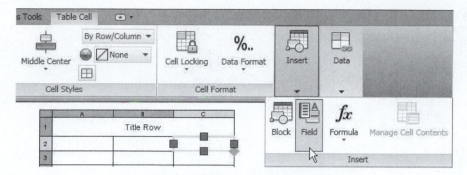

Figure 13-42

Insert Field panel on **Table Cell** ribbon

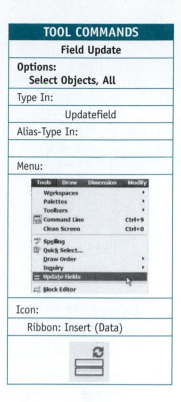

After you choose **Insert Field** using one of the preceding methods, the **Field** dialog screen will appear. This allows you to pick the field category and proceed as discussed previously in this chapter to complete the field placement in the cell of the table. Be careful in placing fields in tables so that updates to field information do not modify the table disproportionately by adjusting cell size; you don't want to make the table difficult to read and understand.

Update Fields

As field information changes, it may be necessary to update the fields with current information. This is done with the **UPDATE FIELDS** command found on the **Tools** menu. You can select a cell for updating or use the **ALL** option to update all the current fields to current values. Data may be updated automatically depending on the setting of the **FIELDEVAL** system variable.

Chapter Summary

Often, more information than the size and shape of an object is needed in an AutoCAD drawing. In this chapter, you learned how to incorporate tables, cells (individual items of data in tables), and fields (information taken from the drawing) into AutoCAD drawings to supply additional information. After being introduced to the basic layout of AutoCAD tables (including schedules and spreadsheets), you learned how to insert a table into a drawing (using the **Table** item from the **Draw** menu) and modify and format the table and the contents of its cells (**Table Cell** and **Text Editor** ribbons, right mouse button menu, and **Properties**

palette). Then you learned how to perform various operations on table cells (merging, adding special symbols to information, and inserting mathematical formulas). Next, you were introduced to the topic of defining and modifying table styles using the various options available in the **Table Style** and **Modify Table Style** dialog boxes. Finally, you learned the advantages and use of automatically updatable data fields (either freestanding or in a multiline text environment), some of their various categories (**Date & Time**, **Document**, **Linked**, **Objects**, **Other**, **Plot**, and **SheetSet**), and their use in tables.

Chapter Tutorials

Ⓐ Tutorial 13-1: *Creating Tables for Doors and for Windows*

1. Start AutoCAD.

2. Open drawing **T13-1** (shown in Figure 13-43) from the student data files.

3. From the **Draw** menu insert a **Table** with four rows and six columns as shown in Figure 13-44 to be the **Door Schedule**. Fill in the information as shown.

To access student data files, go to **www.pearsondesigncentral.com**.

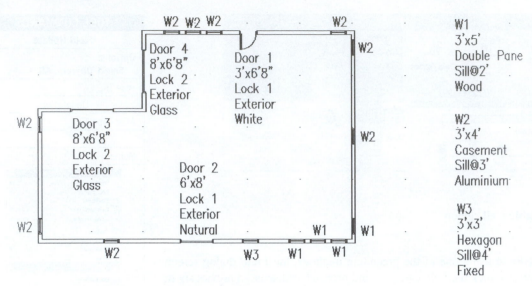

Figure 13-43

Drawing **T13-1**

Door Schedule					
Description	**Height**	**Width**	**Type**	**Finish**	**Lock #**
Door 1	6' - 8"	3' - 0"	Exterior	White	1
Door 2	8' - 0"	6' - 0"	Exterior	Natural	1
Door 3	6' - 8"	8' - 0"	Exterior	Glass	2
Door 4	6' - 8"	8' - 0"	Exterior	Glass	2

Figure 13-44

The completed table for the door schedule

Window Schedule					
Code/ID	**Height**	**Width**	**Type**	**Finish**	**Sill Height**
W1	5' - 0"	3' - 0"	Double Pane	Wood	2' - 0"
W2	4' - 0"	3' - 0"	Casement	Aluminum	3' - 0"
W3	3' - 0"	3' - 0"	Hexagon	Fixed	4' - 0"

Figure 13-45

The completed table for the window schedule

4. From the **Draw** menu insert a **Table** with three rows and six columns as shown in Figure 13-45 to be the **Window Schedule**. Fill in the information as shown.

5. Modify the drawing to reflect the addition of the tables, erase the unwanted text, and save as **T13-1A** in your **Workskills** folder (see Figure 13-46).

c Tutorial 13-2: *Adding Fields to Properties*

1. Start AutoCAD.

2. Open drawing **T13-2** (see Figure 13-47) from the student data files.

3. Add multiline text to the drawing, including the **Area** field for each lot (these are polyline objects). See Figure 13-48.

To access student data files, go to **www.pearsondesigncentral.com**.

4. The field to insert is an object (using the polyline that defines the lot) in the **Object** category. After choosing the polyline, the property is **Area**, the **Format** is **Decimal**, and **Precision** should be **0**. The preview box should show **24000** as the value. See Figure 13-49.

5. Repeat this procedure to label the other lots as shown in Figure 13-50.

6. Save the finished drawing as **T13-2A** in your folder.

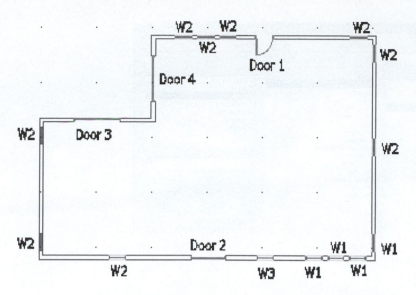

Window Schedule

Code/ID	Height	Width	Type	Finish	Sill Height
W1	5' - 0"	3' - 0"	Double Pane	Wood	2' - 0"
W2	4' - 0"	3' - 0"	Casement	Aluminum	3' - 0"
W3	3' - 0"	3' - 0"	Hexagon	Fixed	4' - 0"

Door Schedule

Description	Height	Width	Type	Finish	Lock #
Door 1	6' - 8"	3' - 0"	Exterior	White	1
Door 2	8' - 0"	6' - 0"	Exterior	Natural	1
Door 3	6' - 8"	8' - 0"	Exterior	Glass	2
Door 4	6' - 8"	8' - 0"	Exterior	Glass	2

Figure 13-46

Drawing **T13-1A**

Figure 13-47

Drawing **T13-2**

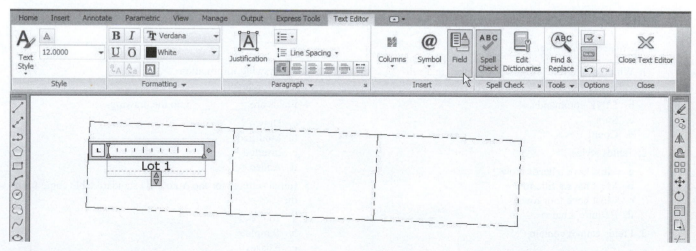

Figure 13-48

Field Insert on **Text Editor** ribbon for Tutorial 13-2

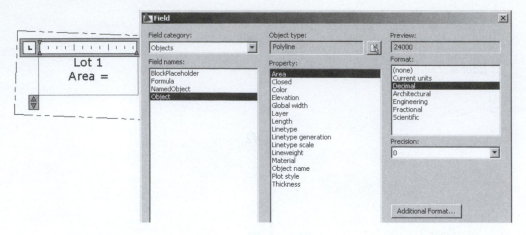

Figure 13-49

Field Objects dialog box for Tutorial 13-2

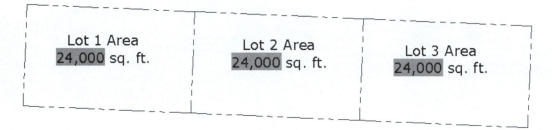

Figure 13-50

Text with **Area** fields for the completed drawing

Chapter Test Questions

Multiple Choice

Circle the correct answer.

1. Which of the following is **not** allowed in a cell?
   a. Formula
   b. **LINE** command
   c. Sum
   d. Count

2. Tables styles
   a. Must have a header row
   b. Must have a title row
   c. Must have four rows
   d. Require a name

3. Fields cannot contain
   a. Commands
   b. Dates

   c. Drawing information
   d. Hyperlinks

4. Fields are _____ into the drawing.
   a. Drawn
   b. Modified
   c. Inserted
   d. Added

5. Initial settings for the AutoCAD standard table come from the
   a. Toolbars
   b. Template
   c. Aliases
   d. Standards

Matching

Write the number of the correct answer on the line.

a. Table _____

b. Cell _____

c. Table styles _____

d. Formulas _____

e. Field _____

1. Can contain alphanumeric characters
2. Can contain entity property data
3. Can be created in a cell
4. Contains rows and columns
5. Can be established in the drawing

True or False

Circle the correct answer.

1. **True or False:** Fields are updated automatically.

2. **True or False:** Tables can contain only numeric data.

3. **True or False:** Cells can be merged.

4. **True or False:** Fields can contain symbols.

5. **True or False:** Using a $ in a cell formula means the formula is using absolute cell locations.

Chapter Projects

Project 13-1 [INTERMEDIATE]

Measure your house on a room-by-room basis and create a chart showing the dimensions, color, wall coverings, and so on.

Project 13-2 [BASIC]

Create a chart of your class schedule. Is each day different? What does this mean in making a table?

Project 13-3 [INTERMEDIATE]

Visit a home development center or home construction company and ask to see a set of plans. Examine the plans, especially the schedules of doors, finishes, and windows. Report to the class on the information shown.

Chapter Practice Exercises

Practice Exercise 13-1: *Basic Table Creation 1* [BASIC]

Create a table of information related to cars such as gas mileage, length, wheelbase, engine size, or interior size. Use the Internet, magazines, or other sources for this information. See Figure 13-51.

Car Comparison					
Description	Ford	Chevrolet	Dodge	Honda	Toyota
Item 1					
Item 2					
Item 3					
Item 4					
Item 5					
Item 6					

Figure 13-51

Sample table for Practice Exercise 13-1

Ⓖ Practice Exercise 13-2: *Basic Table Creation 2* [BASIC]

Create a table based on information collected from people around you (family, friends, instructors, fellow students, etc.) based on their current age. With a formula cell, calculate the year of birth for all in the table. See Figure 13-52.

Birth Year Table				
	Friend 1	Friend 2	Friend 3	Friend 4
Current Age				
Current Year				
Year of Birth				

Figure 13-52

Sample table for Practice Exercise 13-2

Ⓐ Practice Exercise 13-3: *Table Creation for Room Finishes* [INTERMEDIATE]

Assume a house has three bedrooms, two bathrooms, a kitchen, a dining room, a living room, and a family room. Create a table showing room finishes for each wall in each room.

Ⓜ Practice Exercise 13-4: *Table Creation for Machine Equipment* [INTERMEDIATE]

Create a table showing information on lathes such as speed, bar sizes, number of tools, horsepower, and torque. Information can be found on the Internet regarding the various manufacturers and models.

Ⓒ Practice Exercise 13-5: *Table Creation for Volume Calculations* [ADVANCED]

Create a table that summarizes and calculates the earthwork volume of cut and fill for the 20′ × 20′ grid shown in Figure 13-53. The number in each grid area is the average depth in feet for cut (C) or for fill (F). The table should calculate the final volumes in cubic yards.

C=1.6	C=0.4	C=1.5	C=0.6	F=0.3	F=0.6	C=0.3	C=0.5	C=1.4	C=0.5
C=2.1	C=0.8	F=1.2	F=2.3	F=3.1	F=3.2	F=2.9	F=1.2	C=0.3	C=1.2
C=3.3	C=2.5	C=0.5	F=2.1	F=3.9	F=3.8	F=3.5	F=1.4	F=0.6	C=1.5
C=4.2	C=3.6	C=1.3	F=1.5	F=3.2	F=4.1	F=3.8	F=1.2	C=0.4	C=1.8
C=4.1	C=3.9	C=1.5	C=0.5	F=1.4	F=1.7	F=1.2	F=0.6	C=1.2	C=1.4
C=4.6	C=4.2	C=5.1	C=3.1	C=2.3	C=1.8	C=2.2	C=1.7	C=2.3	C=2.1

Figure 13-53

Cut-and-fill grid for earthwork volume calculations

14 More about AutoCAD Screens and Commands

Introduction

In the previous chapters of this book, the focus has been on commands and their operations. This chapter focuses on additional ways to become a more efficient and productive user of AutoCAD. The topics presented can improve your operation of the program and create a more consistent workspace. The use of customized toolbars and palettes can add uniformity throughout your office by convenient placement of often-used commands and blocks for quick access and production.

Using Commands

As you have seen from the command graphics, there are generally six ways to activate a command. For example, the **LINE** command is available by using the following methods:

- Type **LINE** in the command prompt area and press **<Enter>**.
- Type the alias, **L**, in the command prompt area and press **<Enter>**.
- Choose the **Draw** menu drop-down and then choose **LINE** from the menu.
- Pick the **LINE** command icon in the **Draw** toolbar.
- Pick the **LINE** command icon from the **Draw** tab of the Tool palette.
- Pick the **LINE** command icon from the **Draw** panel on the **Home** ribbon.

In addition, if a **LINE** command has just been processed, three more options are available:

- Press **<Enter>** to repeat the **LINE** command just completed.
- Use the right mouse button menu to repeat the **LINE** command just completed.
- Use the right mouse button's **Recent Input** menu to access the previous **LINE** command.

This gives you much flexibility to work in the most efficient way by using any or all of the preceding methods and to develop a flow in drawing creation and modification. In addition, commands can be customized, scripted together to form a process, and moved around in the menus.

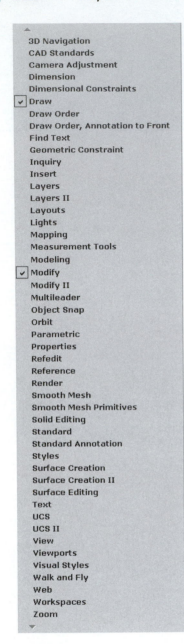

Figure 14-1

Toolbar list

Toolbar Organization

Toolbars offer single-click icons of various commands, thereby providing quick access to the command desired. Some toolbars (see Figure 14-1) are typically placed around the AutoCAD workspace or docked; others can float around the screen (see Figure 14-2). As mentioned in Chapter 3, floating toolbars can be docked in a location around the edge, or they can be pulled off the edge to float with the double bars at the end of the icons. When toolbars are shown floating at that edge, their shape can be changed by grabbing an edge and moving as shown by the double arrow.

The standard list of toolbars (see Figure 14-1) contains commands that are generally related. Toolbars already in view have a check mark present in the list, and this list acts as a toggle to turn the toolbars on and off. The **Draw** toolbar contains many of the **DRAW** commands; the **Modify** toolbar contains many of the **MODIFY** commands. Typically, the toolbars offer only one option of the command and do not have every command in that category. For example, in the **Draw** toolbar, the **Circle** icon defaults to the **Center**, **Radius** option, the **Arc** icon defaults to the **3 Point Arc**, and the **Point** icon defaults to the **Multiple Points** option. In the same regard, the **Draw** toolbar does not contain **Multiline**, **Donut**, and **Ray**, which are found in the **Draw** menu.

Toolbars can also be customized to maximize productivity by mixing various commands on a new toolbar. This can aid the access to commands by putting your most frequently accessed commands together and closer to the area of the drawing activity.

EXERCISE 14-1   **INSERT A TOOLBAR**

- Start AutoCAD and open the **CHAPTER 14** drawing from the student data files.   To access student data files, go to **www.pearsondesigncentral.com.**
- Right-click on any icon in a toolbar to bring up the toolbar list (Figure 14-1).
- Left-click on **Render** to put the **Render** toolbar in the drawing area.
- Hold the left mouse button while pointing at the left end of the toolbar. Move around the screen. Dock and undock the toolbar.
- Save as **CHAPTER 14-1** in your **Workskills** folder.

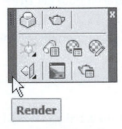

Figure 14-2

Render toolbar in floating mode

Tool Palettes

Tool palettes were initially established as a way to store blocks and hatch patterns for quick access, review, and insertion. When the **Tool Palettes** window is activated, various named tabs are present to expedite finding the block or hatch you want (see Figure 14-3). These can be named Doors, Tables, Bolts, Kitchen, Plants, Trees, and so on. You can easily add new palettes. Then you can drag blocks from the **DesignCenter** and other sources onto the appropriate palette or create the correct hatch settings.

Tool palette items can be assigned properties as shown in Figure 14-4; these will be put into play when the palette item is placed in the drawing. This allows presetting of layers, color, and more as you select an object or hatch from the palette. These

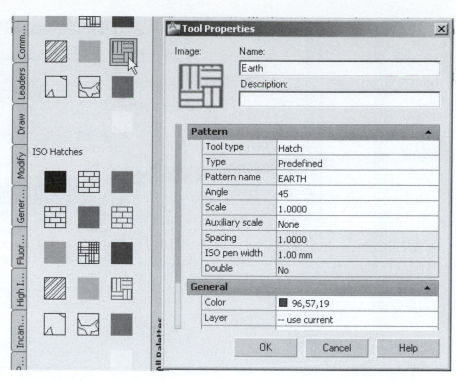

Figure 14-4

Tool Properties dialog box for **Hatch**

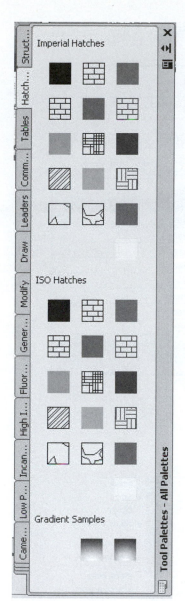

Figure 14-3

Basic **Hatch** palette
showing tabs

TOOL COMMAND
Tool Palette
Options:
Properties, AutoHide
Type In:
Toolpalettes
Alias-Type In:
TP or Ctrl+3
Menu:
Icon:
Toolbar: Standard
Toolbar: Standard Annotate
Ribbon: View (Palettes)

properties must be set in advance and already be defined
to work properly. For example, if a hatch pattern is to go
on the **Steel** layer in the color **Red**, the layer **Steel** must
be defined in the **Layer** set. Then it can be assigned to
the palette item properties. The resulting icon displays
the color, scale, pattern, and other settings.

NOTE:

You can access the **Tool Properties** dialog box by a right mouse click on the symbol and make the changes desired.

In addition to blocks and hatches, tool palettes can
also host commands for quicker access (see Figure 14-5).
As with a toolbar, single-clicking the icon activates the command. The appropriate prompts
and requests for information are displayed as with any other method to access that command.
As already mentioned, properties can also be preset so that a line or text placed on the predefined and/or preset layer has a preset linetype, a preset color, and other attributes as shown in
Figure 14-6.

You can arrange the order of the tool palettes as shown in Figure 14-7. This menu also
allows for the creation of new palettes, the renaming of palettes, and the removal of palettes.
A right mouse click on the menu symbol at the bottom of the title bar on the tool palette brings
up the menu shown in Figure 14-8. Some of the same options appear along with others. For

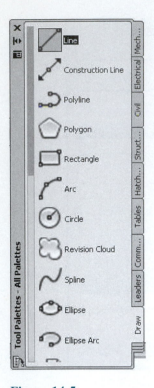

Figure 14-5
Draw palette

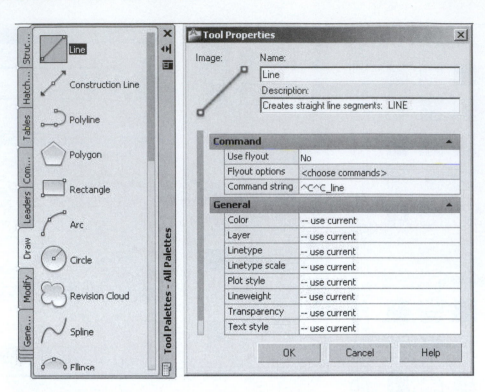

Figure 14-6
Tool Properties dialog box for a tool palette command

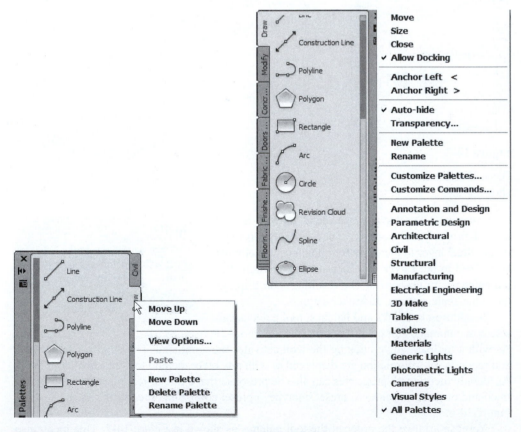

Figure 14-7
Tool Palettes tab right-click menu

Figure 14-8
Tool Palettes title right-click menu

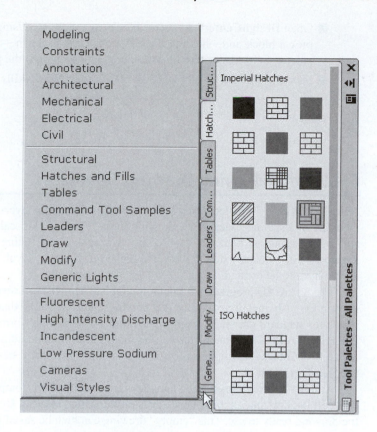

Figure 14-9

Tool palette list

example, one menu item is for hiding (opening and closing of the window), another for the transparency (being able to see through the palette), and a third for docking. Tool palettes can also be exported and imported through the **Customize** option in this menu by assigning names with an .xtp extension. Figure 14-9 shows an example of a tool palette list. This list will vary based on the current workspace.

JOB SKILLS

The use of customized toolbars and tool palettes will simplify the screen layout. You will benefit by organizing the commands used most often within these custom toolbars and palettes. This will also allow you to close the traditional toolbar and palettes to maximize the screen drawing area to its largest possible size.

EXERCISE 14-2 **CREATE A PALETTE AND ADD COMMANDS AND BLOCKS**

- Start AutoCAD and open the **CHAPTER 14** drawing from the student data files.
- Type **TP** to access the **Tool Palettes** window. Right-click on one of the tabs of a tool palette to bring up the menu.
- Left-click to create a new palette and enter your name as the name of the palette.
- With the new palette active, right-click and choose **Customize Commands** from the menu.
- In the **Customize User Interface** dialog box, pick and drag the **Copy** command icon onto the palette. Add two other command icons to the palette. Close the **Customize** window.
- In the drawing pick the **Motor** and copy it to the clipboard. Move the mouse to the palette and right-click to paste the block into the palette. Select two other blocks to copy and paste onto the palette.

To access student data files, go to **www.pearsondesigncentral.com**.

■ Open **DesignCenter** and access blocks in a drawing. Using the left mouse button, pick a block and—holding the left mouse button down—drag the block onto the palette. Select two other blocks to drag and drop onto the palette.

■ Save the drawing as **CHAPTER 14-2** in your **Workskills** folder.

Creating and Using Drawing Templates

AutoCAD drawing templates are empty drawings with all the layers, linetypes, text styles, dimension styles, table styles, units, drawing limits, layouts, plot scales, toolbars, tool palettes, and other settings in place, as detailed in Chapter 4. By initiating the proper template (see Figure 14-10), you are ready to draw at a higher productivity level, since the preceding items do not have to be created.

The AutoCAD program has a default template named **acad.dwt**. This file is empty of the items previously mentioned. AutoCAD provides a special folder that contains predefined templates for standard drawings, along with various international formats recognized by the engineering world. These templates can be modified to include additional items and saved as .dwt files (AutoCAD template files) in this special folder with descriptive names for future use (see Figure 14-11).

Another approach to creating templates is to begin with a completed project drawing and erase all the drawing entities. This leaves all the defined layers, styles, layouts, and so on, in the drawing ready to use. This "empty" drawing can then be saved in the template folder (see Figure 14-12) as a .dwt file. It can then be accessed by anyone starting a new drawing through the **Create New Drawing** dialog box as shown in Chapter 4 of this book.

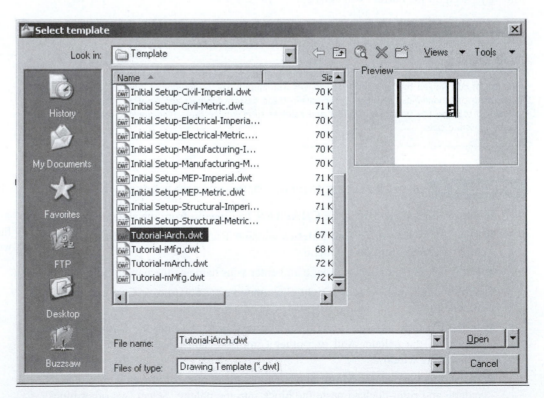

Figure 14-10

Using a template to begin a new drawing

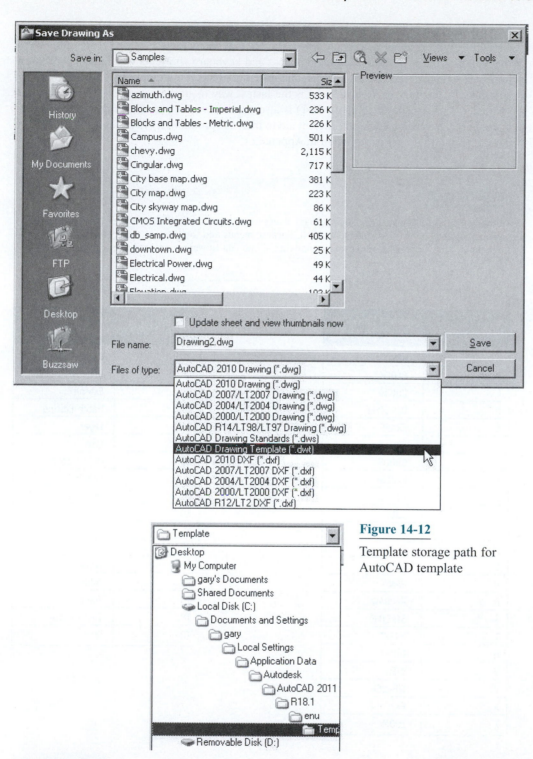

Figure 14-11

Saving as a template

Figure 14-12

Template storage path for AutoCAD template

EXERCISE 14-3 **SAVE AS A TEMPLATE**

- Start AutoCAD and open the **CHAPTER 14-Template** drawing from the student data files.

- Examine the drawing for layers, text styles, and dimension styles. Add two more linetypes to this drawing.

- From the **File** menu, pick **Save As** and change the **File type** to **AutoCAD Drawing Template (.dwt)** at the bottom of the window. Notice the **Save in:** folder change at the top of the dialog box.

- Save as **AATemplate.dwt** in your **Workskills** folder.

To access student data files, go to **www.pearsondesigncentral.com.**

More Alias and Keyboard Shortcuts

In Chapter 3 the concept of command aliases and keyboard shortcuts was introduced. These items are designed to increase your productivity by giving you a quicker method to initiate a command. Generally, the toolbar icon is the fastest way to start a command. Using a single-character alias (as shown in Table 14-1) is also a quick way to start a command. Many two-character aliases can also be an efficient aid to increase productivity (see Table 14-2). A more complete list of aliases is presented in Appendix C.

> **JOB SKILLS**
>
> Experienced users generally employ keyboard shortcuts and command aliases because these have been very consistent in every version of AutoCAD. Because menus and toolbars are usually modified in new versions of the program, learning these shortcuts allows you to work more easily on any version of the AutoCAD program.

TABLE 14-1	Single-Character Aliases (Typical)
A	ARC
B	BLOCK
C	CIRCLE
D	DIMSTYLE
E	ERASE
F	FILLET
G	GROUP
H	HATCH
I	INSERT
J	JOIN
L	LINE
M	MOVE
O	OFFSET
P	PAN
R	REDRAW
S	STRETCH
T	MTEXT
U	UNDO
V	VIEW
W	WBLOCK
X	EXPLODE
Z	ZOOM

TABLE 14-2	Two-Character Aliases (Typical)
DC	DesignCenter
DL	Dimension Linear
EX	Extend
HE-1	Hatch Editing
LA	Layer
LI, LS	List
OS	Object Snap
PL	Polyline
QC	Quick Calc
RO	Rotate
SC	Scale
SP	Spell
ST	Style
TB	Table
TO	Toolbar
TP	Tool Palette
TR	Trim

Action Recorder

Many actions in the production of a drawing are repetitive. Blocks offer one method of reusing drawing entities again and again in the same drawing or in a new drawing, increasing the productivity in completing the drawing. In some cases the actual drawing sequence can be used many times. Examples include laying out the floor plan of a house, building a machine case of varying sizes, or developing a landscape layout. AutoCAD allows for the capturing of commands and inputs as the drawing is created. This sequence can be saved with a name, allowing the re-creation of that drawing object by running the named recorded file.

Access the **ACTRECORD** command or pick the **Record** icon in the **Action Recorder** panel on the **Manage** ribbon (see Figure 14-13). The result is a new window that shows the

Figure 14-13

Action Recorder panel on the **Manage** ribbon

commands and input as they are captured from the user's actions (see Figure 14-14) as they are completed. A red dot near the crosshairs indicates that the recording of the steps is underway. The result of the inputs and commands to make three rectangles is shown in Figure 14-15.

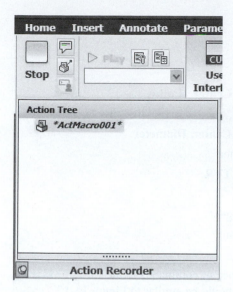

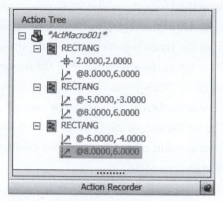

Figure 14-14

Beginning the recording

Figure 14-15

Completed input for recording

The **Record** icon becomes the **Stop** button. At the end of the steps to be recorded, you "stop" by picking the icon. A dialog box then appears in which you enter the name of the stored steps and their location, plus other information (see Figure 14-16). The name may contain no more than 31 characters with no spaces or special characters.

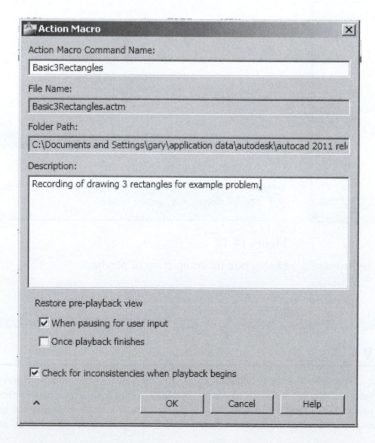

Figure 14-16

Action recording dialog box to name and save actions

Once the file is named and stored, you can "play" the file to create the same objects or drawing.

EXERCISE 14-4   **RECORD ACTIONS**

- Start a new AutoCAD drawing.
- Start the **Action Recorder**.
- From the **Draw** menu choose **Circle**, then **Center, Radius**.
- Enter **4,4** as the center and **3** for the radius.
- From the **Draw** menu choose **Circle**, then **Center, Diameter**.
- Enter **8,8** as the center and **5** for the diameter.
- From the **Draw** menu choose **Circle**, then **TTR**.
- Choose the first circle as the first tangent.
- Choose the second circle as the second tangent.
- Enter a radius of **4** to complete the command.
- Stop the recording.
- Enter the name **3Circles** to save the sequence of commands in the **Action Macro** dialog box (see Figure 14-16). The result should be similar to Figure 14-17.
- Start a new AutoCAD drawing.
- From the **Action Recorder** panel, pick the **Play** icon with the name **3Circles** showing in the drop-down name panel to draw the circles in the new drawing. When the circles have been completed, the message in Figure 14-18 will appear.

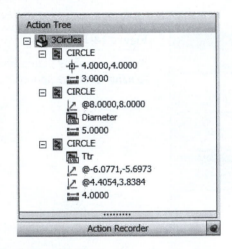

Figure 14-17

The saved example action recording

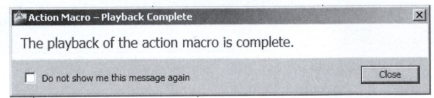

Figure 14-18

Dialog box for completion of playback

Chapter Summary

In the final chapter of this text, we presented various methods that will enable you to use the AutoCAD program more efficiently and productively. First, you learned how to use the <**Enter**> key, the right mouse button menu, and the right mouse button's **Recent Input** menu to repeat previously executed commands, thereby saving time in drawing creation and modification. You also learned how to customize the organization and arrangement of floating and docked toolbars and tool palettes; this eases access to frequently used commands by placing them closer to the area of the drawing activity and makes the use of drawing space more efficient. Then you reviewed the use and creation of AutoCAD drawing templates (empty drawings with predefined layers, linetypes, text styles, etc.) for saving the drawing time that otherwise would be consumed in the creation of these items. Keyboard shortcuts and command aliases were then presented to allow you to work more quickly on any version of the AutoCAD program. Finally, we presented the **Action Recorder,** which allows you to capture commands and inputs as you create a drawing, so you can use them again to re-create the drawing object.

Chapter Tutorials

Ⓖ Tutorial 14-1: *Creating a Toolbar*

- From the **File** menu, pick **New** to begin a new drawing.

- From the **Tools** menu, pick **CUSTOMIZE** and then pick **INTERFACE** from the menus that appear. The result should be the **Customize User Interface** dialog box as shown in Figure 14-19. Be sure the **Customize** tab is active.

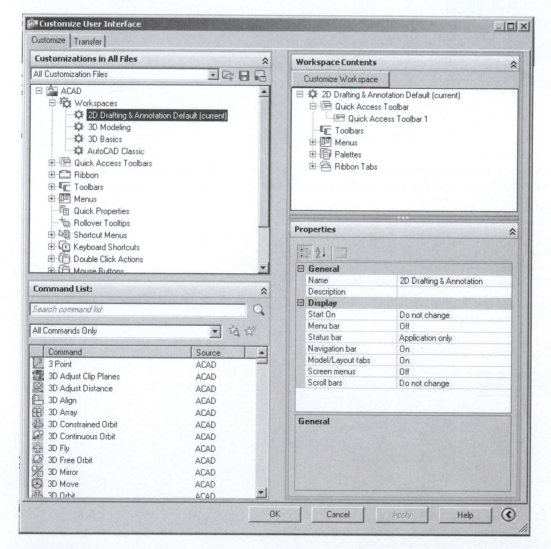

Figure 14-19

Customize User Interface dialog box

- Using the right mouse button, pick on the word **Toolbars** in the upper left area of the dialog box and pick **New Toolbar** (see Figure 14-20) to create a new toolbar for this interface.

- Right-click on the new toolbar and **Rename** it **14Special** (see Figure 14-21).

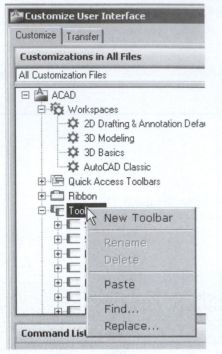

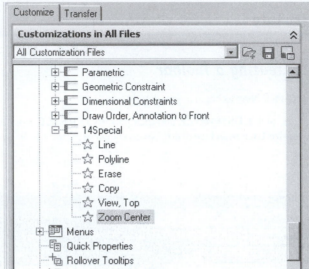

Figure 14-20

Creating a new toolbar

Figure 14-21

Tools added to the new toolbar

- From the lower left of the **Customize User Interface** dialog box, find the following commands and drag and drop them to the new toolbar. The upper right area will show the icons as the toolbar is constructed (see Figure 14-21).

  - **LINE** command
  - **POLYLINE** command
  - **ERASE** command
  - **COPY** command
  - **VIEW, TOP** command
  - **ZOOM CENTER** command

- Close the **Customize User Interface** dialog box. The new toolbar created should be on the list of toolbars as well as on the screen (see Figure 14-22).

- Save the drawing in your **Workskills** folder as **T14-1**.

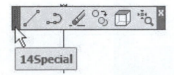

Figure 14-22

Completed toolbar

Ⓖ **Tutorial 14-2:** *Creating a Tool Palette*

- From the **File** menu, pick **New** to begin a new drawing.

- From the **Tools** menu, pick **Palettes** and then pick **Tool Palettes** to bring the tool palettes forward into the drawing area.

- Right-click on one of the tabs of **Tool Palettes** to generate the **New Palette** menu item (see Figure 14-23).

- Rename the new tool palette **14Special**.

- Right-click on the new palette to access the **Customize Commands** menu item (see Figure 14-24).

- With the **Customize User Interface** dialog box open, drag and drop the following commands from their location on the various toolbars around the drawing area as shown in Figure 14-25:
  - **LINE** command
  - **POLYLINE** command
  - **ERASE** command
  - **COPY** command
  - **LAYER PROPERTIES** command

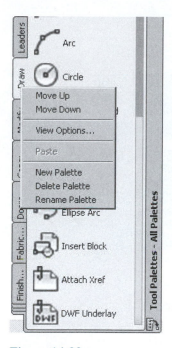

Figure 14-23

Create new palette

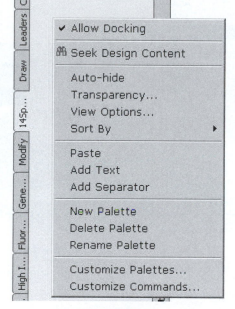

Figure 14-24

Customize tool palette menu

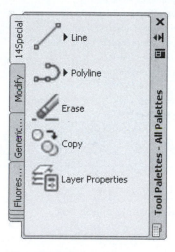

Figure 14-25

Completed new tool palette

- Close the **Customize User Interface** dialog box to stop adding commands to the palette (see Figure 14-26).

- On the new **14Special** palette, right-click on the **LINE** command and pick **Copy** (see Figure 14-27).

- Right-click in an open area on the **14Special** palette and **Paste** the **LINE** command on the current palette twice (see Figure 14-28).

- Right-click on the second copy of the **LINE** command and choose **Properties** (see Figure 14-29).

- Edit the **Name** of the command to be **Red Line** and modify the color to **Red** (see Figure 14-30).

- Right-click on the third copy of the **LINE** command and choose **Properties**.

- Edit the **Name** of the command to be **Yellow Line** and modify the color to **Yellow**, similar to what is shown in Figure 14-30.

- Click on each **LINE** command in the palette (see Figure 14-31) and draw a few line segments in the drawing. Although only color was changed in this tutorial, more properties could have been changed. Tailoring your commands in this way can result in more productive drawing sessions.

- Save the drawing in your **Workskills** folder as **T14-2**.

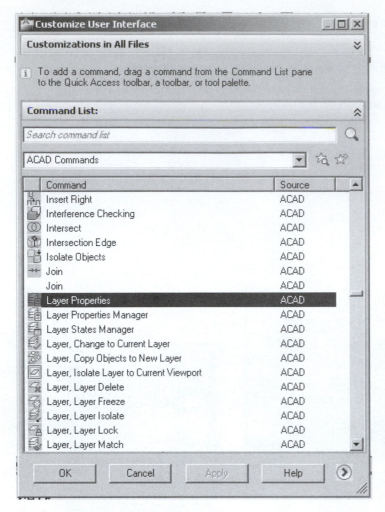

Figure 14-26

Customize palette dialog box

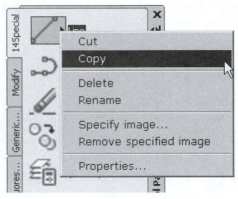

Figure 14-27

Right-click on palette item

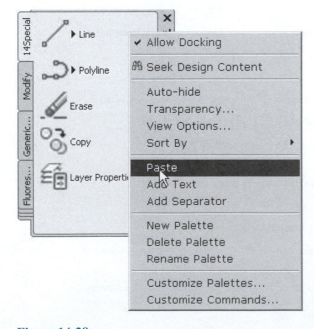

Figure 14-28

Palette right-click menu

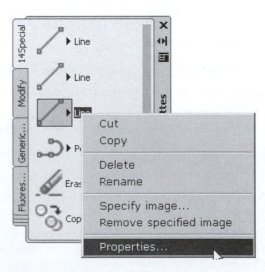

Figure 14-29

Modify Properties right-click menu

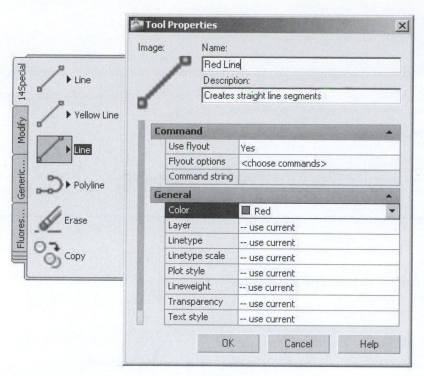

Figure 14-30

Tool palette command properties for the **Red Line**

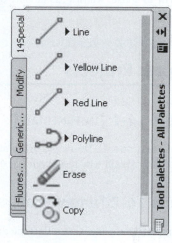

Figure 14-31

Completed new palette for Tutorial 14-2

Chapter Test Questions

Multiple Choice

Circle the correct answer.

1. Which of the following is **not** an alias?

   a. H

   b. DL

   c. Undo

   d. E

2. Templates have a(n) _____ extension in their name.

   a. .dwg

   b. .dwt

   c. .dws

   d. .xtp

3. Tool palettes cannot contain

   a. Commands

   b. Blocks

   c. Hatches

   d. Templates

4. The **Tool Properties** palette can place the object

   a. At a scale

   b. On a specified layer

   c. With a plot style

   d. All the above

5. Initial settings for an AutoCAD drawing come from the

   a. Toolbars

   b. Template

   c. Aliases

   d. Standards

Matching

Write the number of the correct answer on the line.

a. .dwg _____

b. .xtp _____

c. Transparency _____

d. .dwt _____

e. Icon _____

1. AutoCAD template

2. Used to access a command

3. Exported tool palette

4. AutoCAD drawing file

5. The setting to see through the object to the drawing underneath

True or False

Circle the correct answer.

1. **True or False:** Using the menu is always faster than using an icon.

2. **True or False:** Templates are essentially empty drawings.

3. **True or False:** Aliases can be only one character long.

4. **True or False:** Toolbars must be docked to be usable.

5. **True or False:** Templates are stored in the same place as AutoCAD drawings.

Chapter Projects

Project 14-1 [INTERMEDIATE]

Examine Appendix C. Develop a list of at least five changes to the aliases that you would recommend to your supervisor and explain why these changes should be made.

Project 14-2 [INTERMEDIATE]

Develop three templates that reflect the disciplines of architecture, civil engineering, and mechanical engineering. Explain what is common to all three and what the differences are.

Project 14-3 [INTERMEDIATE]

Discuss within your team and with other professional users of AutoCAD which commands are better as menu items, aliases, in toolbars, or on palettes. Is there a pattern based on discipline (architectural, civil, mechanical, etc.) or on the level of drawing detail? What else may determine the best placement of commands and blocks?

Project 14-4 [ADVANCED]

Check with area companies on the use of customized toolbars and palettes. Make a presentation to the class on the findings.

Chapter Practice Exercises

ⓖ Practice Exercise 14-1: *Creating Toolbars* [BASIC]

Create a toolbar with at least six of the commands that you use most often. Name this toolbar with your name or initials. Save the drawing in your **Workskills** folder as **EX14-1**.

ⓖ Practice Exercise 14-2: *Creating Palettes* [INTERMEDIATE]

Create a palette with at least six of the commands that you use most often. Modify properties on some of the commands based on the use of the commands. Also add four of the blocks you created or used in the Chapter 10 Tutorials to this palette by accessing those saved drawings with **DesignCenter** (<Ctrl> + <2> or the alias **DC**). Being able to combine commands and blocks with customized properties offers you great productivity in creating drawings. Use the commands in the palette to draw a few items, and place a few blocks from the palette in the drawing. Save the drawing in your **Workskills** folder as **EX14-2**.

A AutoCAD Commands

3D
3DALIGN
3DARRAY
3DCLIP
3DCONFIG
3DCORBIT
3DDISTANCE
3DDWF
3DEDITBAR
3DFACE
3DFLY
3DFORBIT
3DMESH
3DMOVE
3DORBIT
3DORBITCTR
3DOSNAP
3DPAN
3DPOLY
3DPRINT
3DROTATE
3DSCALE
3DSIN
3DSWIVEL
3DWALK
3DZOOM

ABOUT
ACISIN
ACISOUT
ACTBASEPOINT
ACTMANAGER
ACTRECORD
ACTSTOP
ACTUSERINPUT
ACTUSERMESSAGE
ADCCLOSE
ADCENTER
ADCNAVIGATE
ADDSELECTED
ADJUST
ALIGN
AMECONVERT

ANALYSISCURVATURE
ANALYSISDRAFT
ANALYSISOPTIONS
ANALYSISZEBRA
ANIPATH
ANNORESET
ANNOUPDATE
APERTURE
APPLOAD
ARC
ARCHIVE
AREA
ARRAY
ARX
ATTACH
ATTACHURL
ATTDEF
ATTDISP
ATTEDIT
ATTEXT
ATTIPEDIT
ATTREDEF
ATTSYNC
AUDIT
AUTOCONSTRAIN
AUTOPUBLISH

BACTION
BACTIONBAR
BACTIONSET
BACTIONTOOL
BASE
BASSOCIATE
BATTMAN
BATTORDER
BAUTHORPALETTE
BAUTHORPALETTECLOSE
BCLOSE
BCONSTRUCTION
BCPARAMETER
BCYCLEORDER
BEDIT
BESETTINGS

BGRIPSET
BHATCH
BLIPMODE
BLOCK
BLOCKICON
BLOOKUPTABLE
BMPOUT
BOUNDARY
BOX
BPARAMETER
BREAK
BREP
BROWSER
BSAVE
BSAVEAS
BSETTINGS
BTABLE
BTESTBLOCK
BVHIDE
BVSHOW
BVSTATE

CAL
CAMERA
CHAMFER
CHAMFEREDGE
CHANGE
CHECKSTANDARDS
CHPROP
CHSPACE
CIRCLE
CLASSICIMAGE
CLASSICLAYER
CLASSICXREF
CLEANSCREENOFF
CLEANSCREENON
CLIP
CLOSE
CLOSEALL
COLOR
COMMANDLINE
COMMANDLINEHIDE
COMPILE

CONE
CONSTRAINTBAR
CONSTRAINTSETTING
CONVERT
CONVERTCTB
CONVERTOLDLIGHTS
CONVERTOLDMATERIALS
CONVERTPSTYLES
CONVTOMESH
CONVTONURBS
CONVTOSOLID
CONVTOSURFACE
COPY
COPYBASE
COPYCLIP
COPYHIST
COPYLINK
COPYTOLAYER
CUI
CUIEXPORT
CUIIMPORT
CUILOAD
CUIUNLOAD
CUSTOMIZE
CUTCLIP
CVADD
CVHIDE
CVREBUILD
CVREMOVE
CVSHOW
CYLINDER

DATAEXTRACTION
DATALINK
DATALINKUPDATE
DBCONNECT
DBLIST
DCALIGNED
DCANGULAR
DCCONVERT
DCDIAMETER
DCDISPLAY
DCFORM
DCHORIZONTAL
DCLINEAR
DCRADIUS
DCVERTICAL
DDEDIT
DDPTYPE
DDVPOINT
DELAY

DELCONSTRAINT
DETACHURL
DGNADJUST
DGNATTACH
DGNCLIP
DGNEXPORT
DGNIMPORT
DGNLAYERS
DGNMAPPING
DIM
DIM1
DIMALIGNED
DIMANGULAR
DIMARC
DIMBASELINE
DIMBREAK
DIMCENTER
DIMCONSTRAIN
DIMCONTINUE
DIMDIAMETER
DIMDISASSOCIATE
DIMEDIT
DIMINSPECT
DIMJOGGED
DIMJOGLINE
DIMLINEAR
DIMORDINATE
DIMOVERRIDE
DIMRADIUS
DIMREASSOCIATE
DIMREGEN
DIMSPACE
DIMSTYLE
DIMTEDIT
DIST
DISTANTLIGHT
DIVIDE
DONUT
DRAGMODE
DRAWINGRECOVERY
DRAWINGRECOVERY-HIDE
DRAWORDER
DSETTINGS
DSVIEWER
DVIEW
DWFADJUST
DWFATTACH
DWFCLIP
DWFFORMAT
DWFLAYERS
DWGPROPS

DXBIN

EATTEDIT
EATTEXT
EDGE
EDGESURF
EDITSHOT
ELEV
ELLIPSE
ERASE
ETRANSMIT
EXPLODE
EXPORT
EXPORTDWF
EXPORTDWFX
EXPORTLAYOUT
EXPORTPDF
EXPORTSETTINGS
EXPORTTOAUTOCAD
EXTEND
EXTERNALREFERENCES
EXTERNALREFERENCESCLOSE
EXTRUDE

FBXEXPORT
FBXIMPORT
FIELD
FILL
FILLET
FILLETEDGE
FILTER
FIND
FLATSHOT
FOG
FREESPOT
FREEWEB

GCCOINCIDENT
GCCOLLINEAR
GCCONCENTRIC
GCEQUAL
GCFIX
GCHORIZONTAL
GCPARALLEL
GCSMOOTH
GCSYMMETRIC
GCTANGENT
GCVERTICAL
GEOGRAPHICLOCATION
GEOMCONSTRAINT
GOTOURL

GRADIENT	LAYMCH	MESHEXTRUDE
GRAPHICSCONFIG	LAYMCUR	MESHMERGE
GRAPHSCR	LAYMGR	MESHOPTIONS
GRID	LAYOFF	MESHPRIMITIVEOPTIONS
GROUP	LAYON	MESHREFINE
	LAYOUT	MESHSMOOTH
HATCH	LAYOUTWIZARD	MESHSMOOTHLESS
HATCHEDIT	LAYTHW	MESHSMOOTHMORE
HATCHGENERATEBOUNDARY	LAYTRANS	MESHSPIN
HATCHSETBOUNDARY	LAYULK	MESHSPLIT
HATCHSETORIGIN	LAYUNISO	MESHUNCREASE
HATCHTOBACK	LAYVPI	MIGRATEMATERIALS
HELIX	LAYWALK	MINSERT
HELP	LEADER	MIRROR
HIDE	LENGTHEN	MIRROR3D
HIDEOBJECTS	LIGHT	MLEADER
HIDEPALETTES	LIGHTLIST	MLEADERALIGN
HLSETTINGS	LIGHTLISTCLOSE	MLEADERCOLLECT
HYPERLINK	LIMITS	MLEADEREDIT
HYPERLINKOPTIONS	LINE	MLEADERSTYLE
	LINETYPE	MLEDIT
ID	LIST	MLINE
IMAGE	LIVESECTION	MLSTYLE
IMAGEADJUST	LOAD	MODEL
IMAGEATTACH	LOFT	MOVE
IMAGECLIP	LOGFILEOFF	MREDO
IMAGEQUALITY	LOGFILEON	MSLIDE
IMPORT	LTSCALE	MSPACE
IMPRINT	LWEIGHT	MTEDIT
INSERT		MTEXT
INSERTOBJ	MARKUP	MULTIPLE
INTERFERE	MARKUPCLOSE	MVIEW
INTERSECT	MASSPROP	MVSETUP
ISOLATEOBJECT	MATBROWSERCLOSE	
ISOPLANE	MATBROWSEROPEN	NAVBAR
	MATCHCELL	NAVSMOTION
JOIN	MATCHPROP	NAVSMOTIONCLOSE
JPGOUT	MATEDITORCLOSE	NAVSWHEEL
JUSTIFYTEXT	MATEDITOROPEN	NAVVCUBE
	MATERIALASSIGN	NETLOAD
LAYCUR	MATERIALATTACH	NEW
LAYDEL	MATERIALMAP	NEWSHEETSET
LAYER	MATERIALS	NEWSHOT
LAYERCLOSE	MATERIALSCLOSE	NEWVIEW
LAYERP	MEASURE	
LAYERPALETTE	MEASUREGEOM	OBJECTSCALE
LAYERPMODE	MENU	OFFSET
LAYERSTATE	MESH	OLELINKS
LAYFRZ	MESHCAP	OLESCALE
LAYISO	MESHCOLLAPSE	OOPS
LAYLCK	MESHCREATE	OPEN

OPENDWFMARKUP

OPENSHEETSET

OPTIONS

ORTHO

OSNAP

PAGESETUP

PAN

PARAMETERS

PARAMETERSCLOSE

PARTIALOAD

PARTIALOPEN

PASTEASHYPERLINK

PASTEBLOCK

PASTECLIP

PASTEORIG

PASTESPEC

PCINWIZARD

PDFADJUST

PDFATTACH

PDFCLIP

PDFLAYERS

PEDIT

PFACE

PLAN

PLANESURF

PLINE

PLOT

PLOTSTAMP

PLOTSTYLE

PLOTTERMANAGER

PNGOUT

POINT

POINTCLOUD

POINTCLOUDATTACH

POINTCLOUDINDEX

POINTLIGHT

POLYGON

POLYSOLID

PRESSPULL

PREVIEW

PROJECTGEOMETRY

PROPERTIES

PROPERTIESCLOSE

PSETUPIN

PSFACE

PUBLISH

PUBLISHTOWEB

PURGE

PYRAMID

QCCLOSE

QDIM

QLEADER

QNEW

QSAVE

QSELECT

QTEXT

QUICKCALC

QUICKCUI

QUIT

QVDRAWING

QVDRAWINGCLOSE

QVLAYOUT

QVLAYOUTCLOSE

RAY

RECOVER

RECOVERALL

RECTANG

REDEFINE

REDO

REDRAW

REDRAWALL

REFCLOSE

REFEDIT

REFSET

REGEN

REGENALL

REGENAUTO

REGION

REINIT

RENAME

RENDER

RENDERCROP

RENDERENVIRONMENT

RENDEREXPOSURE

RENDERPRESETS

RENDERWIN

RESETBLOCK

RESUME

REVCLOUD

REVERSE

REVOLVE

REVSURF

RIBBON

RIBBONCLOSE

ROTATE

ROTATE3D

RPREF

RPREFCLOSE

RSCRIPT

RULESURF

SAVE

SAVEAS

SAVEIMG

SCALE

SCALELISTEDIT

SCALETEXT

SCRIPT

SECTION

SECTIONPLANE

SECTIONPLANEJOG

SECTIONPLANESETTINGS

SECTIONPLANETOBLOCK

SECURITYOPTIONS

SEEK

SELECT

SELECTSIMILAR

SETBYLAYER

SETIDROPHANDLER

SETVAR

SHADEMODE

SHAPE

SHAREWITHSEEK

SHEETSET

SHEETSETHIDE

SHELL

SHOWPALETTES

SIGVALIDATE

SKETCH

SLICE

SNAP

SOLDRAW

SOLID

SOLIDEDIT

SOLPROF

SOLVIEW

SPACETRANS

SPELL

SPHERE

SPLINE

SPLINEDIT

SPOTLIGHT

STANDARDS

STATUS

STLOUT

STRETCH

STYLE

STYLESMANAGER

SUBTRACT

SUNPROPERTIES

SUNPROPERTIES CLOSE

SURFBLEND

SURFEXTEND

SURFFILLET

SURFNETWORK

SURFOFFSET

SURFPATCH
SURFSCULPT
SURFUNTRIM
SWEEP
SYSWINDOWS

TABLE
TABLEDIT
TABLEEXPORT
TABLESTYLE
TABLET
TABSURF
TARGETPOINT
TASKBAR
TEXT
TEXTEDIT
TEXTSCR
TEXTTOFRONT
THICKEN
TIFOUT
TIME
TINSERT
TOLERANCE
TOOLBAR
TOOLPALETTES
TOOLPALETTESCLOSE
TORUS
TPNAVIGATE
TRACE
TRANSPARENCY
TRAYSETTINGS
TREESTAT

TRIM

U
UCS
UCSICON
UCSMAN
ULAYERS
UNDEFINE
UNDO
UNION
UNISOLATEOBJECTS
UNITS
UPDATEFIELD
UPDATETHUMBSNOW

VBAIDE
VBALOAD
VBAMAN
VBARUN
VBASTMT
VBAUNLOAD
VIEW
VIEWGO
VIEWPLAY
VIEWPLOTDETAILS
VIEWRES
VISUALSTYLES
VISUALSTYLESCLOSE
VLISP
VPCLIP
VPLAYER
VPMAX

VPMIN
VPOINT
VPORTS
VSCURRENT
VSLIDE
VSSAVE
VTOPTIONS

WALKFLYSETTINGS
WBLOCK
WEBLIGHT
WEDGE
WHOHAS
WIPEOUT
WMFIN
WMFOPTS
WMFOUT
WORKSPACE
WSSAVE
WSSETTINGS

XATTACH
XBIND
XCLIP
XEDGES
XLINE
XOPEN
XPLODE
XREF

ZOOM

B Menus, Toolbars, Ribbons, and Palettes

Menus

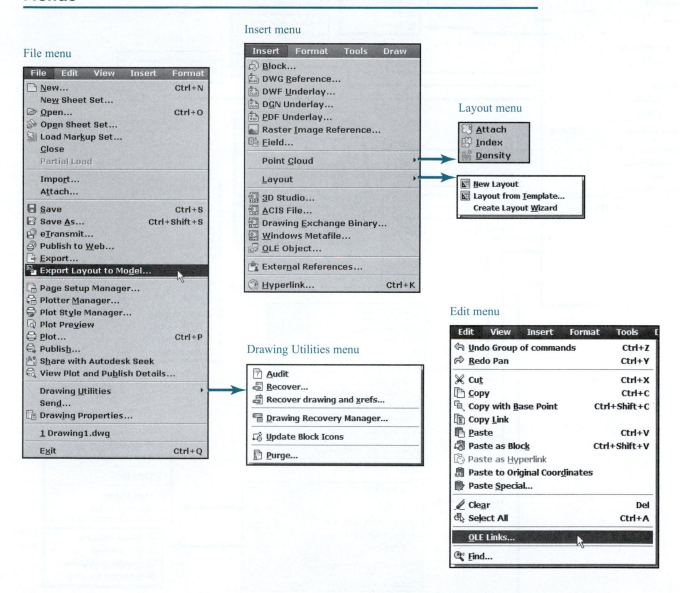

File menu

Insert menu

Layout menu

Drawing Utilities menu

Edit menu

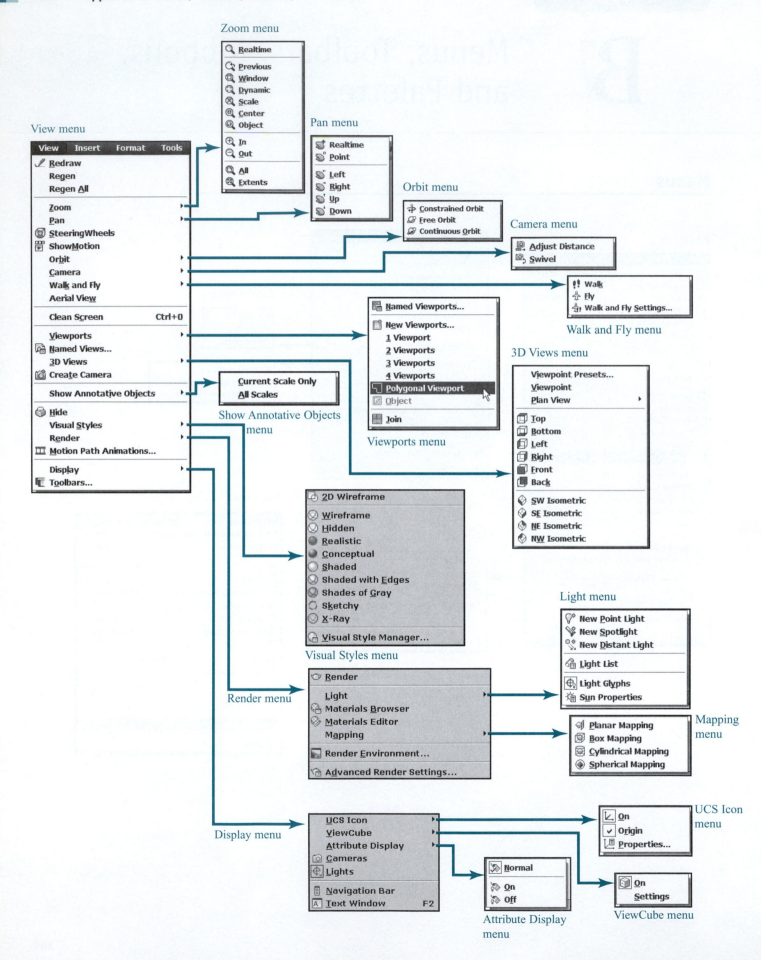

Zoom menu

Pan menu

View menu

Orbit menu

Camera menu

Walk and Fly menu

3D Views menu

Show Annotative Objects menu

Viewports menu

Visual Styles menu

Light menu

Render menu

Mapping menu

Display menu

UCS Icon menu

Attribute Display menu

ViewCube menu

Format menu

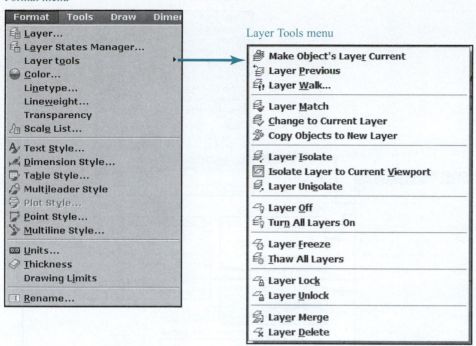

Layer Tools menu

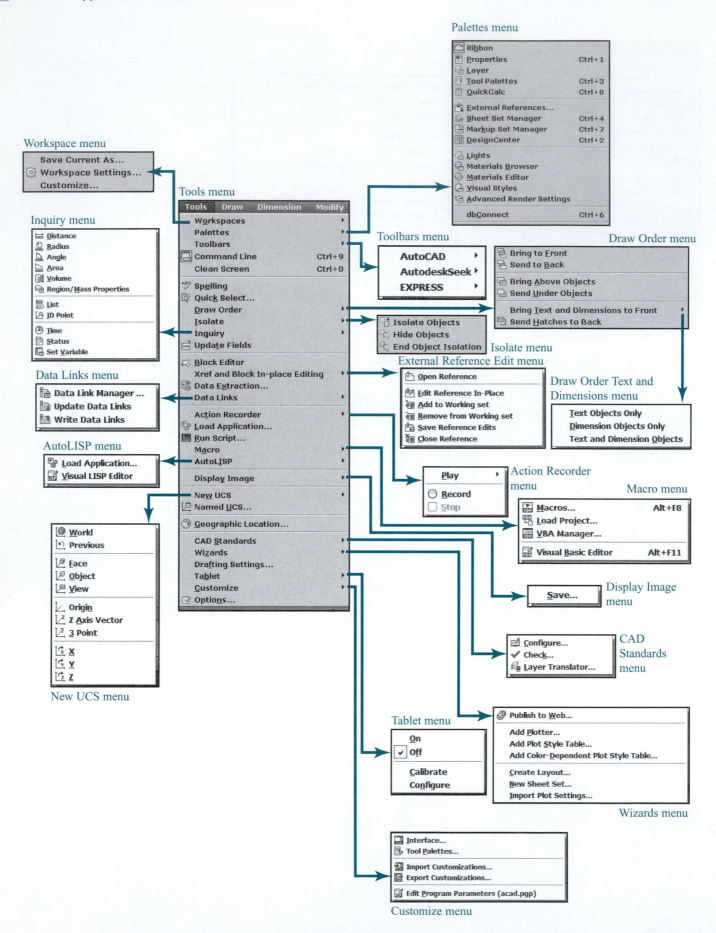

Palettes menu

Ribbon		
Properties	Ctrl+1	
Layer		
Tool Palettes	Ctrl+3	
QuickCalc	Ctrl+8	
External References...		
Sheet Set Manager	Ctrl+4	
Markup Set Manager	Ctrl+7	
DesignCenter	Ctrl+2	
Lights		
Materials Browser		
Materials Editor		
Visual Styles		
Advanced Render Settings		
dbConnect	Ctrl+6	

Workspace menu

Save Current As...
Workspace Settings...
Customize...

Tools menu

Tools **Draw** **Dimension** **Modify**

Workspaces	▶
Palettes	▶
Toolbars	▶
Command Line	Ctrl+9
Clean Screen	Ctrl+0
Spelling	
Quick Select...	
Draw Order	▶
Isolate	▶
Inquiry	▶
Update Fields	
Block Editor	
Xref and Block In-place Editing	▶
Data Extraction...	
Data Links	▶
Action Recorder	▶
Load Application...	
Run Script...	
Macro	▶
AutoLISP	▶
Display Image	▶
New UCS	▶
Named UCS...	
Geographic Location...	
CAD Standards	▶
Wizards	▶
Drafting Settings...	
Tablet	▶
Customize	▶
Options...	

Inquiry menu

Distance
Radius
Angle
Area
Volume
Region/Mass Properties
List
ID Point
Time
Status
Set Variable

Toolbars menu

AutoCAD	▶
AutodeskSeek	▶
EXPRESS	▶

Draw Order menu

Bring to Front	
Send to Back	
Bring Above Objects	
Send Under Objects	
Bring Text and Dimensions to Front	▶
Send Hatches to Back	

Isolate menu

Isolate Objects
Hide Objects
End Object Isolation

External Reference Edit menu

Open Reference
Edit Reference In-Place
Add to Working set
Remove from Working set
Save Reference Edits
Close Reference

Draw Order Text and Dimensions menu

Text Objects Only
Dimension Objects Only
Text and Dimension Objects

Data Links menu

Data Link Manager ...
Update Data Links
Write Data Links

AutoLISP menu

Load Application...
Visual LISP Editor

Action Recorder menu

Play	▶
Record	
Stop	

Macro menu

Macros...	Alt+F8
Load Project...	
VBA Manager...	
Visual Basic Editor	Alt+F11

Display Image menu

Save...

New UCS menu

World
Previous
Face
Object
View
Origin
Z Axis Vector
3 Point
X
Y
Z

CAD Standards menu

Configure...
Check...
Layer Translator...

Tablet menu

On
Off
Calibrate
Configure

Wizards menu

Publish to Web...
Add Plotter...
Add Plot Style Table...
Add Color-Dependent Plot Style Table...
Create Layout...
New Sheet Set...
Import Plot Settings...

Customize menu

Interface...
Tool Palettes...
Import Customizations...
Export Customizations...
Edit Program Parameters (acad.pgp)

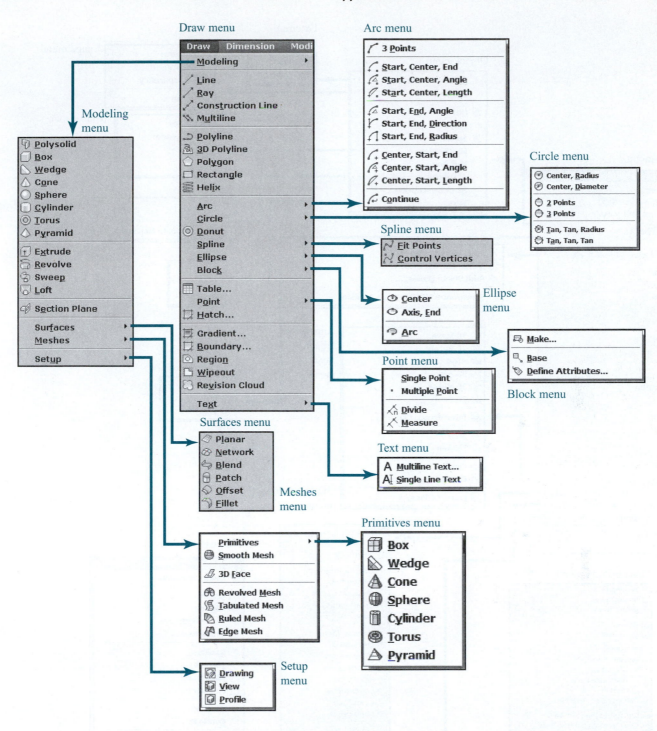

Draw menu

Arc menu

Modeling menu

Circle menu

Spline menu

Ellipse menu

Point menu

Block menu

Surfaces menu

Text menu

Meshes menu

Primitives menu

Setup menu

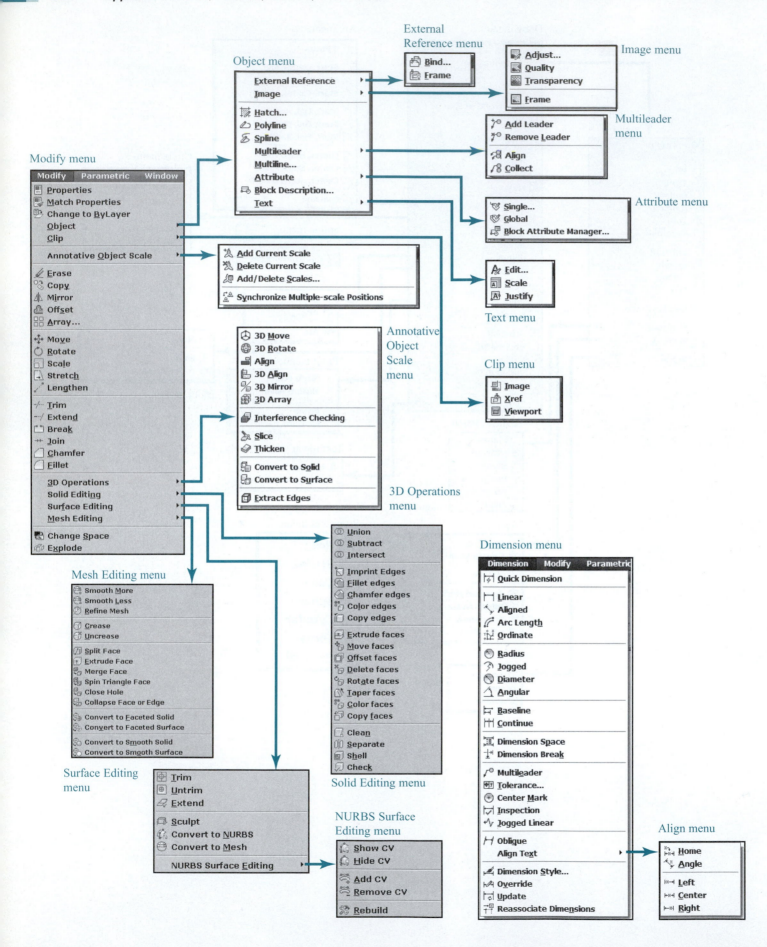

External
Reference menu

Image menu

Object menu

Modify menu

Multileader
menu

Attribute menu

Text menu

Annotative
Object
Scale
menu

Clip menu

3D Operations
menu

Dimension menu

Mesh Editing menu

Solid Editing menu

Surface Editing
menu

NURBS Surface
Editing menu

Align menu

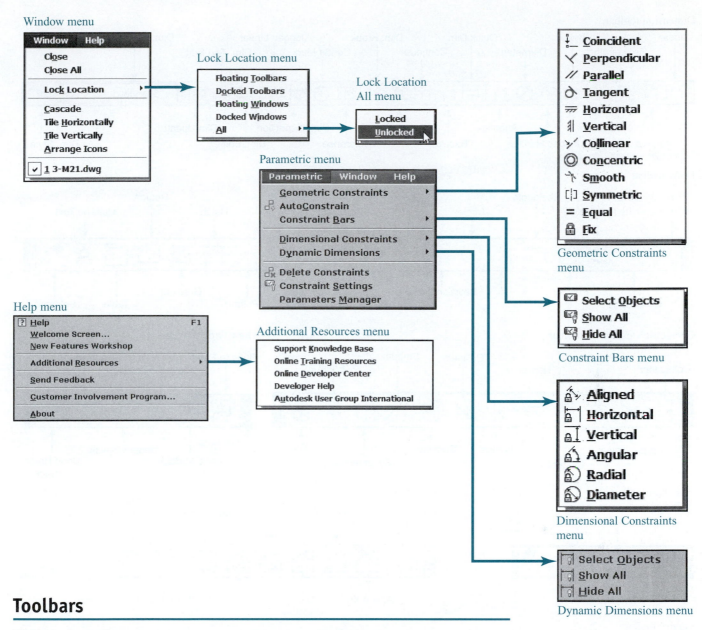

Window menu

Lock Location menu

Lock Location
All menu

Parametric menu

Geometric Constraints
menu

Constraint Bars menu

Dimensional Constraints
menu

Dynamic Dimensions menu

Help menu

Additional Resources menu

Toolbars

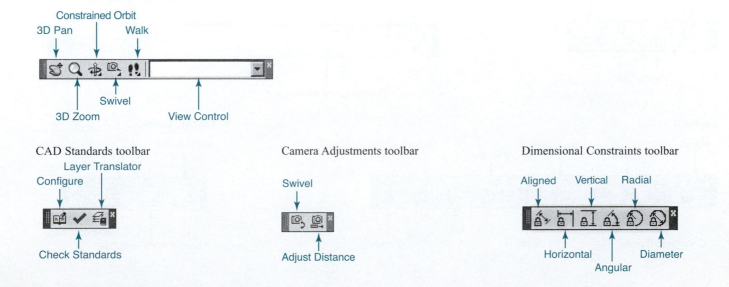

3D Navigation toolbar

CAD Standards toolbar

Camera Adjustments toolbar

Dimensional Constraints toolbar

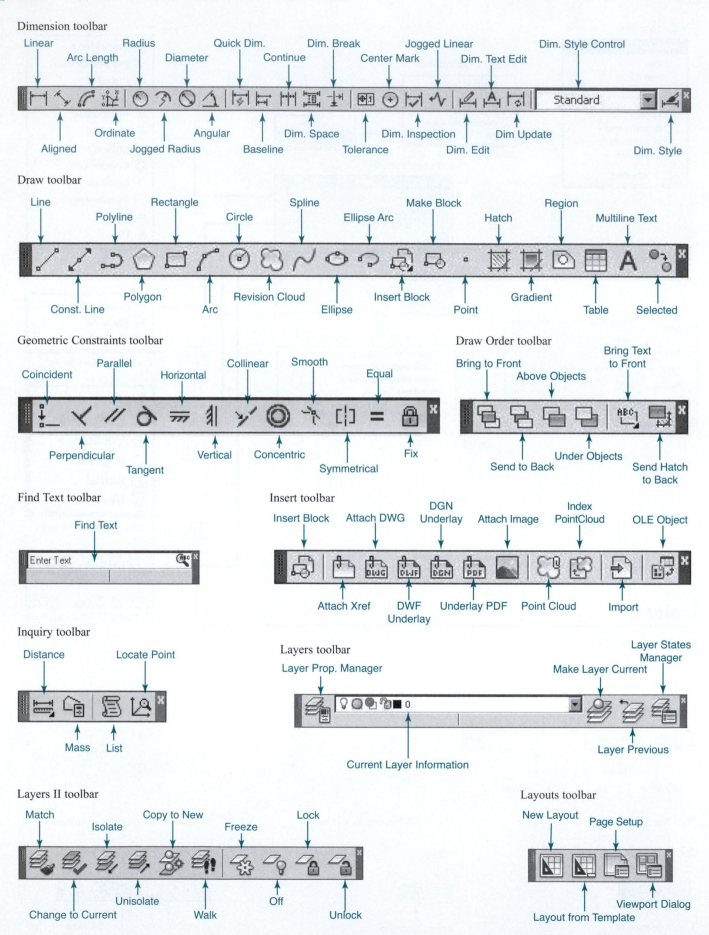

Dimension toolbar

Linear
Arc Length
Radius
Diameter
Quick Dim.
Continue
Dim. Break
Center Mark
Jogged Linear
Dim. Text Edit
Dim. Style Control

Aligned
Ordinate
Jogged Radius
Angular
Baseline
Dim. Space
Tolerance
Dim. Inspection
Dim. Edit
Dim Update
Dim. Style

Draw toolbar

Line
Polyline
Rectangle
Circle
Spline
Ellipse Arc
Make Block
Hatch
Region
Multiline Text

Const. Line
Polygon
Arc
Revision Cloud
Ellipse
Insert Block
Point
Gradient
Table
Selected

Geometric Constraints toolbar

Coincident
Parallel
Horizontal
Collinear
Smooth
Equal

Perpendicular
Tangent
Vertical
Concentric
Symmetrical
Fix

Draw Order toolbar

Bring to Front
Above Objects
Bring Text to Front

Send to Back
Under Objects
Send Hatch to Back

Find Text toolbar

Find Text

Enter Text

Insert toolbar

Insert Block
Attach DWG
DGN Underlay
Attach Image
Index PointCloud
OLE Object

Attach Xref
DWF Underlay
Underlay PDF
Point Cloud
Import

Inquiry toolbar

Distance
Locate Point

Mass
List

Layers toolbar

Layer Prop. Manager
Layer States Manager
Make Layer Current

Current Layer Information
Layer Previous

Layers II toolbar

Match
Isolate
Copy to New
Freeze
Lock

Change to Current
Unisolate
Walk
Off
Unlock

Layouts toolbar

New Layout
Page Setup

Layout from Template
Viewport Dialog

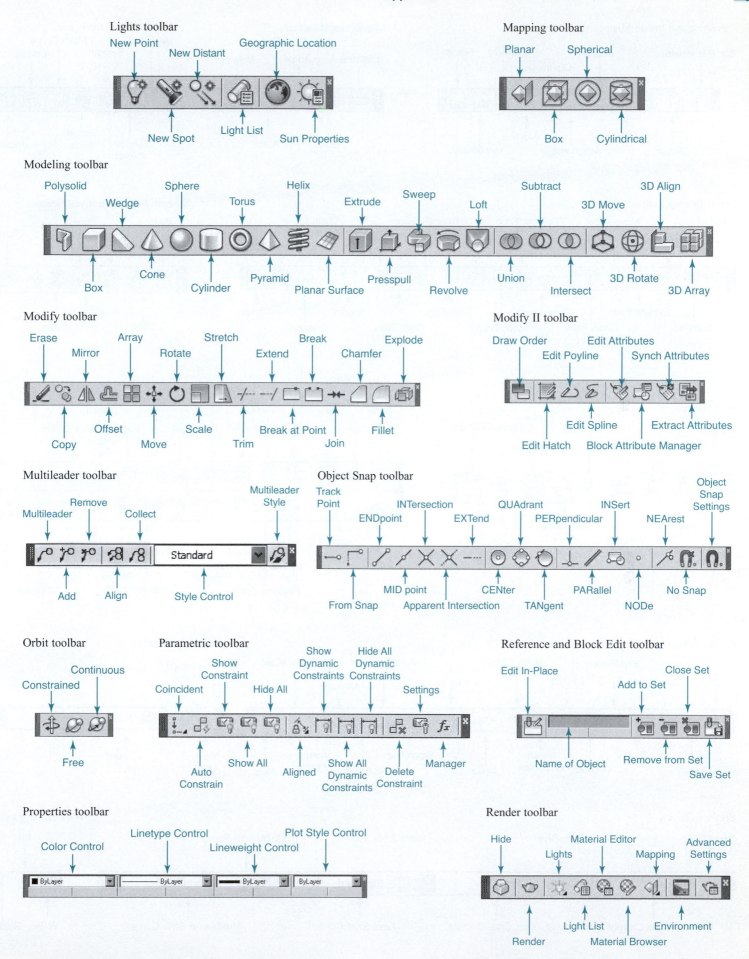

Lights toolbar
New Point
New Distant
Geographic Location
New Spot
Light List
Sun Properties

Mapping toolbar
Planar
Spherical
Box
Cylindrical

Modeling toolbar
Polysolid
Wedge
Sphere
Torus
Helix
Extrude
Sweep
Loft
Subtract
3D Move
3D Align
Cone
Cylinder
Pyramid
Planar Surface
Presspull
Revolve
Union
Intersect
3D Rotate
3D Array
Box

Modify toolbar
Erase
Mirror
Array
Rotate
Stretch
Extend
Break
Chamfer
Explode
Offset
Scale
Break at Point
Fillet
Copy
Move
Trim
Join

Modify II toolbar
Draw Order
Edit Attributes
Edit Poyline
Synch Attributes
Edit Spline
Extract Attributes
Edit Hatch
Block Attribute Manager

Multileader toolbar
Multileader
Remove
Collect
Multileader Style
Standard
Add
Align
Style Control

Object Snap toolbar
Track Point
INTersection
QUAdrant
INSert
Object Snap Settings
ENDpoint
EXTend
PERpendicular
NEArest
MID point
CENter
PARallel
No Snap
From Snap
Apparent Intersection
TANgent
NODe

Orbit toolbar
Continuous
Constrained
Free

Parametric toolbar
Show Dynamic Constraints
Hide All Dynamic Constraints
Show Constraint
Hide All
Coincident
Settings
Auto Constrain
Show All
Aligned
Show All Dynamic Constraints
Delete Constraint
Manager

Reference and Block Edit toolbar
Edit In-Place
Close Set
Add to Set
Name of Object
Remove from Set
Save Set

Properties toolbar
Color Control
Linetype Control
Plot Style Control
Lineweight Control
ByLayer
ByLayer
ByLayer
ByLayer

Render toolbar
Hide
Material Editor
Lights
Mapping
Advanced Settings
Render
Light List
Material Browser
Environment

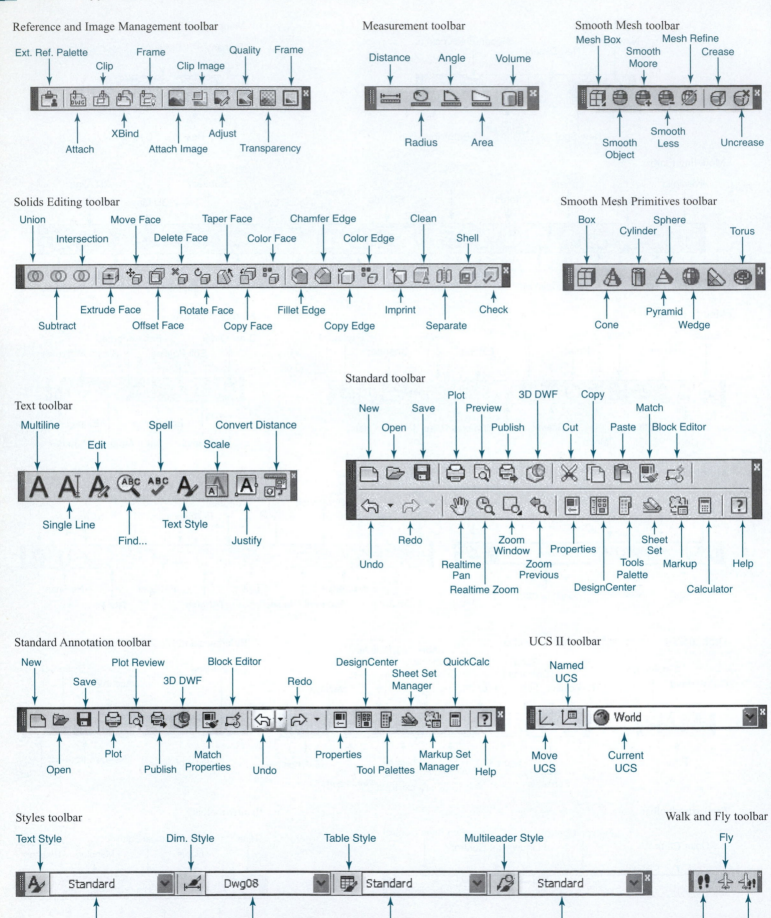

UCS toolbar

UCS
UCS Previous
Object
Origin
3 Point
Y Axis
Apply
World
Face UCS
View
Z Axis Vector
X Axis
Z Axis

Viewports toolbar

Viewport Dialog
Polygon
Clip
Viewport Scale
Single
Convert Object

1/4" = 1'-0"

View toolbar

Named
Top
Bottom
Left
Right
Front
Rear
SW
SE
NE
NW
Camera
Previous
Current View

Detail 1

Visual Styles toolbar

2D Wireframe
3D Hidden
3D Wireframe
Realistic
Conceptual
Manage

Surface Creation toolbar

Extrude
Surface Network
Planar Surface
Surface Blend
Surface Patch
Surface Offset
Surface Fillet

Surface Creation II toolbar

Extrude
Sweep
Loft
Revolve

Surface Editing toolbar

Untrim
Sculpt
Convert to Mesh
Hide CV
Remove CV
Trim
Extend
Converts to NURBS
Show CV
Add CV
Rebuilt CV

Web toolbar

Forward
Browse
Back
Stop

Workspaces toolbar

2D Drafting & Annotation

Workspace Setting
Current Workspace
My Workspace

Zoom toolbar

Dynamic
Center
In
All
Window
Scale
Object
Out
Extents

Ribbons

Home Ribbon

Insert Ribbon

Annotate Ribbon

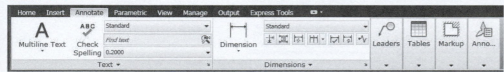

Parametric Ribbon

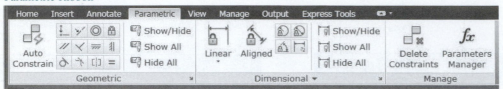

View Ribbon

Manage Ribbon

Output Ribbon

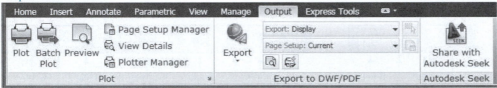

3D Home ribbon

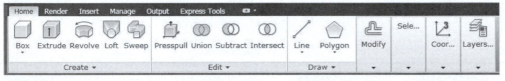

3D Insert ribbon

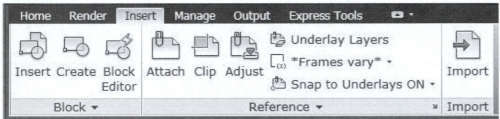

3D Render ribbon

3D Manage ribbon

3D Output ribbon

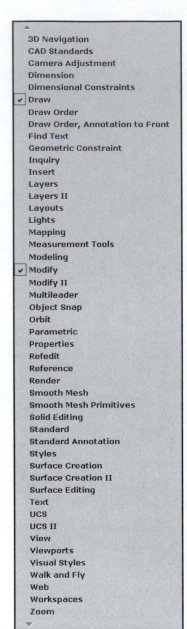

3D Navigation
CAD Standards
Camera Adjustment
Dimension
Dimensional Constraints
✓ Draw
Draw Order
Draw Order, Annotation to Front
Find Text
Geometric Constraint
Inquiry
Insert
Layers
Layers II
Layouts
Lights
Mapping
Measurement Tools
Modeling
✓ Modify
Modify II
Multileader
Object Snap
Orbit
Parametric
Properties
Refedit
Reference
Render
Smooth Mesh
Smooth Mesh Primitives
Solid Editing
Standard
Standard Annotation
Styles
Surface Creation
Surface Creation II
Surface Editing
Text
UCS
UCS II
View
Viewports
Visual Styles
Walk and Fly
Web
Workspaces
Zoom

3D Modeling Home ribbon

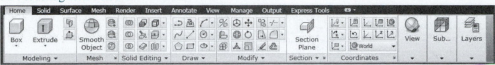

3D Modeling Solid ribbon

3D Modeling Surface ribbon

3D Modeling Mesh ribbon

3D Modeling Render ribbon

3D Modeling Insert ribbon

3D Modeling Annotate ribbon

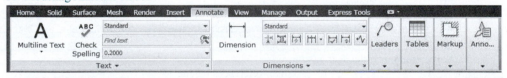

3D Modeling View ribbon

3D Modeling Manage ribbon

3D Modeling Output ribbon

Hatch Creation ribbon

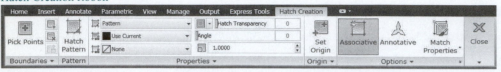

Hatch Editor ribbon

Text Editor ribbon

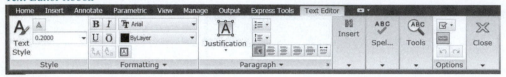

Table Cell ribbon

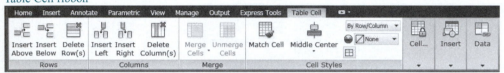

Palettes

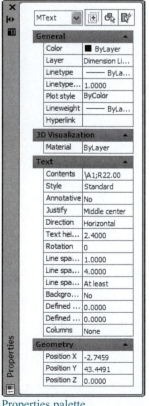

Properties palette

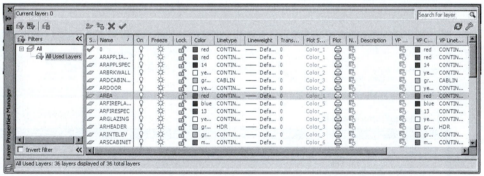

Layer Properties Manager palette

Calculator palette   External References palette

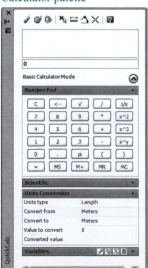

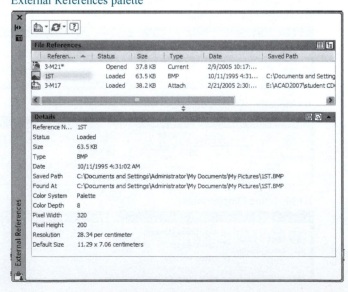

Markup Set Manager palette

DesignCenter palette

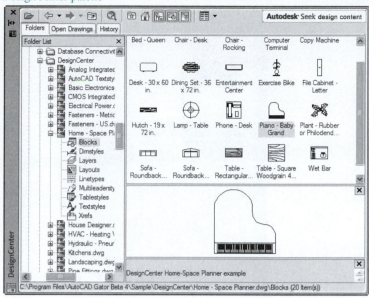

Tool palettes

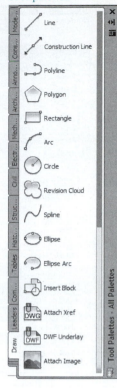

Lights palette

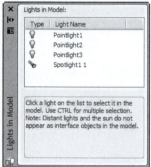

Sheet Set Manager palette

Materials palette

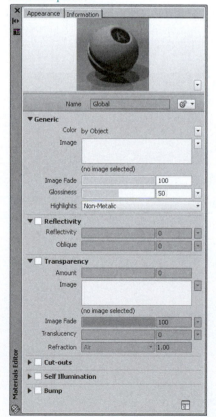

Visual Styles Manager palette

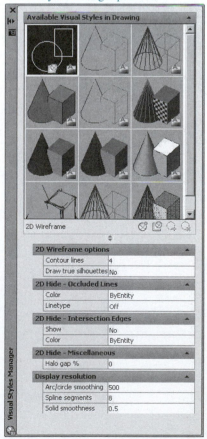

Advanced Render Settings palette

Materials Browser palette

dbConnect Manager palette

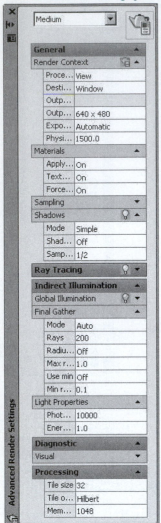

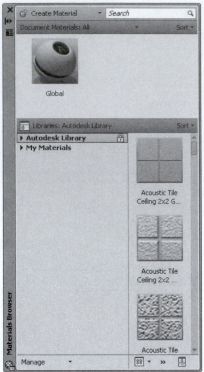

C Command Alias List

Alias	Command (Standard)	Alternate Alias	Command Line Version Only
Single Stroke (Most Used)			
A	ARC		
B	BLOCK	-B	-BLOCK
C	CIRCLE		
D	DIMSTYLE		
E	ERASE		
F	FILLET		
G	GROUP	-G	-GROUP
H	HATCH	-H	-HATCH
I	INSERT	-I	-INSERT
J	JOIN		
L	LINE		
M	MOVE		
O	OFFSET		
P	PAN	-P	-PAN
R	REDRAW		
S	STRETCH		
T	MTEXT	-T	-MTEXT
U	UNDO		
V	VIEW	-V	-VIEW
W	WBLOCK	-W	-WBLOCK
X	EXPLODE		
Z	ZOOM		
Block and Xref Commands			
AC	BACTION		
ATT	ATTDEF	-ATT	-ATTDEF
ATE	ATTEDIT	-ATE	-ATTEDIT
ATI	ATTIPEDIT		
ATTE	-ATTEDIT		
B	BLOCK	-B	-BLOCK
BC	BCLOSE		
BE	BEDIT		
BS	BSAVE		
BVS	BVSTATE		
CPARAM	BCPARAMETER		
ED	DDEDIT		
ER	EXTERNALREFERENCES		
I	INSERT	-I	-INSERT
PA	PASTESPEC		
PARAM	BPARAMETER		
W	WBLOCK	-W	-WBLOCK
XA	XATTACH		
XB	XBIND	-XB	-XBIND
XC	XCLIP		
XR	XREF	-XR	-XREF
Draw Commands			
3F	3DFACE		
3P	3DPOLY		

Alias	Command (Standard)	Alternate Alias	Command Line Version Only
A	ARC		
BH	BHATCH		
BO	BOUNDARY	-BO	-BOUNDARY
C	CIRCLE		
CREATESOLID	SURFSCULPT		
CYL	CYLINDER		
DO	DONUT		
DT	TEXT		
EL	ELLIPSE		
EXT	EXTRUDE		
GD	GRADIENT		
H	HATCH	-H	-HATCH
L	LINE		
ML	MLINE		
MT	MTEXT		
PL	PLINE		
PO	POINT		
POL	POLYGON		
PSOLID	POLYSOLID		
PYR	PYRAMID		
REC	RECTANG		
REG	REGION		
SO	SOLID		
SPL	SPLINE		
T	MTEXT	-T	-MTEXT
TB	TABLE		
TOR	TORUS		
WE	WEDGE		
XL	XLINE		

Dimension Commands

Alias	Command (Standard)
D	DIMSTYLE
DAL	DIMALIGNED
DAN	DIMANGULAR
DAR	DIMARC
DBA	DIMBASELINE
DCE	DIMCENTER
DCO	DIMCONTINUE
DCON	DIMCONSTRAINT
DDA	DIMDISASSOCIATE
DDI	DIMDIAMETER
DED	DIMEDIT
DJL	DIMJOGLINE
DJO	DIMJOGGED
DLI	DIMLINEAR
DOR	DIMORDINATE
DOV	DIMOVERRIDE
DRA	DIMRADIUS
DRE	DIMREASSOCIATE
DST	DIMSTYLE
JOG	DIMJOGGED
LE	QLEADER
MEA	MEASUREGEOM
MLA	MLEADERALIGN
MLC	MLEADERCOLLECT
MLD	MLEADER
MLE	MLEADEREDIT
MLS	MLEADERSTYLE
TOL	TOLERANCE

Alias	Command (Standard)	Alternate Alias	Command Line Version Only
File Commands			
3DP	3DPRINT		
3DPLOT	3DPRINT		
AECTOACAD	EXPORTTOAUTOCAD		
DRM	DRAWINGRECOVERY		
EXIT	QUIT		
EXP	EXPORT		
IMP	IMPORT		
IO	INSERTOBJ		
LO	-LAYOUT		
PARTIALOPEN	-PARTIALOPEN		
PRE	PREVIEW		
PRINT	PLOT		
PTW	PUBLISHTOWEB		
RAPIDPROTOTYPE	3DPRINT		
SSM	SHEETSET		
Format Commands			
COL	COLOR	COLOUR	COLOR
CT	CTABLESTYLE		
D	DIMSTYLE		
DST	DIMSTYLE		
LA	LAYER	-LA	-LAYER
LAS	LAYERSTATE		
LMAN	LAYERSTATE		
LT	LINETYPE	-LT	-LINETYPE
LTS	LTSCALE		
LTYPE	LINETYPE	-LTYPE	-LINETYPE
LW	LWEIGHT	LINEWEIGHT	LWEIGHT
ST	STYLE		
TH	THICKNESS		
TS	TABLESTYLE		
UN	UNITS	-UN	-UNITS
Image Commands			
IAD	IMAGEADJUST		
IAT	IMAGEATTACH		
ICL	IMAGECLIP		
IM	IMAGE	-IM	-IMAGE
Modify Commands			
3A	3DARRAY		
3AL	3DALIGN		
3DMIRROR	MIRROR3D		
3DS	3DSCALE		
3M	3DMOVE		
3R	3DROTATE		
AL	ALIGN		
AR	ARRAY	-AR	-ARRAY
BLENDSRF	SURFBLEND		
BR	BREAK		
CBAR	CONSTRAINTBAR		
CONVTOMESH	MESHSMOOTH		
CH	PROPERTIES	-CH	CHANGE
CHA	CHAMFER		
CO	COPY		
CP	COPY		
CREASE	MESHCREASE		
CSETTINGS	CONSTRAINTSETTINGS		
CURVATUREANALYSIS	ANALYSISCURVATURE		

Alias	Command (Standard)	Alternate Alias	Command Line Version Only
DELCON	DELCONSTRAINT		
DIV	DIVIDE		
E	ERASE		
ED	DDEDIT		
EX	EXTEND		
EXTENDSURF	SURFEXTEND		
F	FILLET		
FILLETSURF	SURFFILLET		
G	GROUP	-G	-GROUP
GCON	GEOMCONSTRAINT		
GD	GRADIENT		
GENERATESECTION	SECTIONPLANETOBLOCK		
HE	HATCHEDIT		
HB	HATCHTOBACK		
IN	INTERSECT		
INF	INTERFERE		
J	JOIN		
JOGSECTION	SECTIONPLANEJOG		
LEN	LENGTHEN		
LESS	MESHSMOOTHLESS		
M	MOVE		
MA	MATCHPROP		
ME	MEASURE		
MI	MIRROR		
MO	PROPERTIES		
MORE	MESHSMOOTHMORE		
NETWORKSRF	SURFNETWORK		
O	OFFSET		
OFFSETSRF	SURFOFFSET		
PAR	PARAMETERS		
-PAR	-PARAMETERS		
PATCH	SURFPATCH		
PE	PEDIT		
PR	PROPERTIES		
PRCLOSE	PROPERTIESCLOSE		
PROPS	PROPERTIES		
PU	PURGE	-PU	-PURGE
REFINE	MESHREFINE		
REN	RENAME	-REN	-RENAME
REV	REVOLVE		
RO	ROTATE		
S	STRETCH		
SC	SCALE		
SEC	SECTION		
SL	SLICE		
SMOOTH	MESHSMOOTH		
SP	SPELL		
SPE	SPLINEDIT		
SPLANE	SECTIONPLANE		
SPLIT	MESHSPLIT		
SU	SUBTRACT		
TEDIT	TEXTEDIT		
TR	TRIM		
UNCREASE	MESHUNCREASE		
UNI	UNION		
X	EXPLODE		

Tool Commands

AA	AREA
ADC	ADCENTER

Alias	Command (Standard)	Alternate Alias	Command Line Version Only
AL	ALIGN		
AP	APPLOAD		
ARM	ACTUSERMESSAGE	-ARM	-ACTUSERMESSAGE
ARR	ACTRECORDER		
ARS	ACTSTOP	-ARS	-ACTSTOP
ARU	ACTUSERINPUT		
CHK	CHECKSTANDARDS		
CLI	COMMANDLINE		
DBC	DBCONNECT		
DC	ADCENTER	DCENTER	ADCENTER
DI	DIST		
DL	DATALINK		
DLU	DATALINKUPDATE		
DR	DRAWORDER		
DRAFTANGLEANALYSIS	ANALYSISDRAFTANGLE		
DS	DSETTINGS		
DX	DATAEXTRACTION		
FI	FILTER		
GEO	GEOGRAPHICLOCATION		
GR	DDGRIPS		
LI	LIST		
LS	LIST		
MSM	MARKUP		
NORTH	GEOGRAPHICLOCATION		
NORTHDIR	GEOGRAPHICLOCATION		
OP	OPTIONS		
OS	OSNAP	-OS	-OSNAP
PC	POINTCLOUD		
PCATTACH	POINTCLOUDATTACH		
PCINDEX	POINTCLOUDINDEX		
POFF	HIDEPALLETES		
PON	SHOWPALLETES		
QC	QUICKCALC		
QCUI	QUICKCUI		
SCR	SCRIPT		
SE	DSETTINGS		
SET	SETVAR		
SN	SNAP		
STA	STANDARDS		
TA	TABLET		
TO	TOOLBAR		
TP	TOOLPALETTES		
ZEBRA	ANALYSISZEBRA		

View Commands

Alias	Command
3DNAVIGATE	3DWALK
3DO	3DORBIT
3DW	3DWALK
AAPLAY	ALLPLAY
CAM	CAMERA
CUBE	NAVCUBE
DV	DVIEW
ESHOT	EDITSHOT
FREEPOINT	POINTLIGHT
FSHOT	FLATSHOT
HI	HIDE
INSERTCONTROLPOINT	CVADD
ISOLATE	ISOLATEOBJECTS
LO	-LAYOUT
MAT	MATBROWSEROPEN

Alias	Command (Standard)	Alternate Alias	Command Line Version Only
MOTION	NAVSMOTION		
MOTIONCLS	NAVSMOTIONCLOSE		
MS	MSPACE		
MV	MVIEW		
NSHOT	NEWSHOT		
NVIEW	NEWVIEW		
ORBIT	3DORBIT		
P	PAN	-P	-PAN
POINTON	CVSHOW		
POINTOFF	CVHIDE		
PS	PSPACE		
QVD	QVDRAWING		
QVDC	QVDRAWINGCLOSE		
QVL	QVLAYOUT		
QVLC	QVLAYOUTCLOSE		
R	REDRAW		
RA	REDRAWALL		
RC	RENDERCROP		
RE	REGEN		
REA	REGENALL		
REBUILD	CVREBUILD		
REMOVECONTROLPOINT	CVREMOVE		
RP	RENDERPRESETS		
RPR	RPREF		
RR	RENDER		
RW	RENDERWIN		
SHA	SHADEMODE		
SPLAY	SEQUENCEPLAY		
TI	TILEMODE		
UC	UCSMAN		
UNHIDE	UNISOLATEOBJECTS		
UNISOLATE	UNISOLATEOBJECTS		
V	VIEW	-V	-VIEW
VGO	VIEWGO		
VP	DDVPOINT	-VP	VPOINT
VPLAY	VIEWPLAY		
VS	VSCURRENT		
VSM	VISUALSTYLES	-VSM	-VISUALSTYLES
WHEEL	NAVSWHEEL		
XC	XCLIP		
Z	ZOOM		

APPENDIX

D AutoCAD Setting Variables (with Typical Initial or Default Values)

Variable Name	Value	
3DCONVERSIONMODE	1	
3DDWFPREC	2	
3DOSMODE		
3DSELECTIONMODE	1	
ACADLSPACDOC	0	
ACADPREFIX	"C:\Documents and Settings\ username\Application\data\ Autodesk\Aut…"	(read only)
ACADVER	"18.1 (LMS Tech)"	(read only)
ACISOUTVER	70	
ACTPATH		
ACTRECORDERSTATE	0	(read only)
ACTRECPATH	"C:\documentation\administration\ application\data\autodesk\…"	
ACTUI	6	
AECEIPINPROGRESS	OFF	
AFLAGS	16	
ANGBASE	0	
ANGDIR	0	
ANNOALLVISIBLE	1	
ANNOAUTOSCALE	−4	
ANNOTATIVEDWG	0	
APBOX	0	
APERTURE	10	
APPFRAMERESOURCE	" "	
APPLYGLOBALOPACITIES	0	
AREA	0.0000	(read only)
ATTDIA	0	
ATTIPE	0	
ATTMODE	1	
ATTMULTI	1	
ATTREQ	1	
AUDITCTL	0	
AUNITS	0	
AUPREC	0	
AUTODWFPUBLISH	0	
AUTOMATICPUB	0	
AUTOSNAP	55	
BACKGROUNDPLOT	2	
BACKZ	0.0000	(read only)
BACTIONBARMODE	1	
BACTIONCOLOR	"7"	
BCONSTATUSMODE	0	
BDEPENDENCYHIGHLIGHT	1	
BGRIPOBJCOLOR	"141"	
BGRIPOBJSIZE	8	

Variable Name	Value	
BINDTYPE	0	
BLIPMODE	0	
BLOCKEDITLOCK	0	
BLOCKEDITOR	0	(read only)
BLOCKTESTWINDOW	0	
BPARAMETERCOLOR	"7"	
BPARAMETERFONT	"Simplex.shx"	
BPARAMETERSIZE	12	
BPTEXTHORIZONTAL	1	
BTMARKDISPLAY	1	
BVMODE	0	
CALCINPUT	1	
CAMERADISPLAY	0	
CAMERAHEIGHT	0.0000	
CANNOSCALE	"1:1"	
CANNOSCALEVALUE	1.000000000	(read only)
CAPTURETHUMBNAILS	1	
CBARTRANSPARENCY	50	
CCONSTRAINTFORM	0	
CDATE	20050915.01344651	(read only)
CDYNDISPLAYMODE	0	
CECOLOR	"BYLAYER"	
CELTSCALE	1.0000	
CELTYPE	"BYLAYER"	
CELWEIGHT	−1	
CENTERMT	0	
CETRANSPARENCY	BYLAYER	
CHAMFERA	0.0000	
CHAMFERB	0.0000	
CHAMFERC	0.0000	
CHAMFERD	0	
CHAMMODE	0	
CIPMODE	1	(read only)
CIRCLERAD	0.0000	
CLASSICKEYS	0	
CLAYER	"0"	
CLEANSCREENSTATE	0	(read only)
CMATERIAL	"ByLayer"	
CMDACTIVE	1	(read only)
CMDDIA	1	
CMDECHO	1	
CMDINPUTHISTORYMAX	20	
CMDNAMES	"SETVAR"	(read only)
CMLEADERSTYLE	"standard"	
CMLJUST	0	
CMLSCALE	1.0000	
CMLSTYLE	"STANDARD"	
COMPASS	0	
CONSTRAINTBARDISPLAY	3	
CONSTRAINTCURSORDISPLAY	1	
CONSTRAINTINFER	0	
CONSTRAINTBARMODE	4095	
CONSTRAINTNAMEFORMAT	2	
CONSTRAINTRELAX	0	
CONSTRAINTSOLVEMODE	3	

Variable Name	Value	
COORDS	1	
COPYMODE	0	
CPLOTSTYLE	"ByColor"	
CPROFILE	"standard"	(read only)
CROSSINGAREACOLOR	100	
CSHADOW	Cast And Receive Shadows	
CTAB	"Model"	
CTABLESTYLE	"Standard"	
CULLINGOBJ	1	
CULLINGOBJSELECTION	0	
CURSORSIZE	15	
CVPORT	2	
DATALINKNOTIFY	2	
DATE	2455233.06584183	(read only)
DBLCLKEDIT	ON	
DBMOD	5	(read only)
DCTCUST	"C:\Documents and Settings\ username\Application\Data\ Autodesk\Aut..."	
DCTMAIN	"enu"	
DEFAULTGIZMO	0	
DEFAULTINDEX	0	
DEFAULTLIGHTING	1	
DEFAULTLIGHTINGTYPE	1	
DEFLPLSTYLE	"ByColor"	(read only)
DEFPLSTYLE	"ByColor"	(read only)
DELOBJ	3	
DEMANDLOAD	3	
DGNFRAME	0	
DGNIMPORTMAX	10000000	
DGNMAPPINGPATH	"C:\documentation\administration\ local settings\application..."	
DGNOSNAP	1	
DIASTAT	1	(read only)
DIGITIZER	0	
DIMADEC	0	
DIMALT	OFF	
DIMALTD	2	
DIMALTF	25.4000	
DIMALTRND	0.0000	
DIMALTTD	2	
DIMALTTZ	0	
DIMALTU	2	
DIMALTZ	0	
DIMANNO	0	(read only)
DIMAPOST	""	
DIMARCSYM	0	
DIMASO	ON	
DIMASSOC	2	
DIMASZ	0.1800	
DIMATFIT	3	
DIMAUNIT	0	
DIMAZIN	0	
DIMBLK	""	
DIMBLK1	""	

Variable Name	Value	
DIMBLK2	""	
DIMCEN	0.0900	
DIMCLRD	0	
DIMCLRE	0	
DIMCLRT	0	
DIMCONSTRAINTICON	3	
DIMDEC	4	
DIMDLE	0.0000	
DIMDLI	0.3800	
DIMDSEP	"."	
DIMEXE	0.1800	
DIMEXO	0.0625	
DIMFIT	3	
DIMFRAC	0	
DIMFXL	1.0000	
DIMFXLON	OFF	
DIMGAP	0.0900	
DIMJOGANG	45	
DIMJUST	0	
DIMLDRBLK	""	
DIMLFAC	1.0000	
DIMLIM	OFF	
DIMLTEX1	""	
DIMLTEX2	""	
DIMLTYPE	""	
DIMLUNIT	2	
DIMLWD	−2	
DIMLWE	−2	
DIMPOST	""	
DIMRND	0.0000	
DIMSAH	OFF	
DIMSCALE	1.0000	
DIMSD1	OFF	
DIMSD2	OFF	
DIMSE1	OFF	
DIMSE2	OFF	
DIMSHO	ON	
DIMSOXD	OFF	
DIMSTYLE	"Standard"	(read only)
DIMTAD	0	
DIMTDEC	4	
DIMTFAC	1.0000	
DIMTFILL	0	
DIMTFILLCLR	0	
DIMTIH	ON	
DIMTIX	OFF	
DIMTM	0.0000	
DIMTMOVE	0	
DIMTOFL	OFF	
DIMTOH	ON	
DIMTOL	OFF	
DIMTOLJ	1	
DIMTP	0.0000	
DIMTSZ	0.0000	
DIMTVP	0.0000	

Variable Name	Value	
DIMTXSTY	"Standard"	
DIMTXT	0.1800	
DIMTXTDIRECTION	OFF	
DIMTZIN	0	
DIMUNIT	2	
DIMUPT	OFF	
DIMZIN	0	
DISPSILH	0	
DISTANCE	0.0000	(read only)
DIVMESHBOXHEIGHT	3	
DIVMESHBOXLENGTH	3	
DIVMESHBOXWIDTH	3	
DIVMESHCONEAXIS	8	
DIVMESHCONEBASE	3	
DIVMESHCONEHEIGHT	3	
DIVMESHCYLAXIS	5	
DIVMESHCYLBASE	3	
DIVMESHCYLHEIGHT	3	
DIVMESHPYRBASE	3	
DIVMESHPYRHEIGHT	3	
DIVMESHPYRLENGTH	3	
DIVMESHMESHSPHEREAXIS	12	
DIVMESHSPHEREHEIGHT	6	
DIVMESHTORUSPATH	8	
DIVMESHTORUSSECTION	8	
DIVMESHWEDGEBASE	3	
DIVMESHWEDGEHEIGHT	3	
DIVMESHWEDGELENGTH	4	
DIVMESHWEDGESLOPE	3	
DIVMESHWEDGEWIDTH	3	
DONUTID	0.5000	
DONUTOD	1.0000	
DRAGMODE	2	
DRAGP1	10	
DRAGP2	25	
DRAGVS	""	
DRAWORDERCTL	3	
DTEXTED	2	
DWFFRAME	2	
DWFOSNAP	1	
DWGCHECK	1	
DWGCODEPAGE	"ANSI_1252"	(read only)
DWGNAME	"Drawing1.dwg"	(read only)
DWGPREFIX	"C:\Documents and Settings\ username\My Documents\"	(read only)
DWGTITLED	0	(read only)
DXEVAL	12	
DYNCONSTRAINTMODE	1	
DYNDIGRIP	31	
DYNDIVIS	1	
DYNMODE	−3	
DYNPICOORDS	0	
DYNPIFORMAT	0	
DYNPIVIS	1	
DYNPROMPT	1	

Variable Name	Value	
DYNTOOLTIPS	1	
EDGEMODE	0	
ELEVATION	0.0000	
ENTERPRISEMENU	"."	(read only)
ERHIGHLIGHT	1	
EXPERT	0	
EXPLMODE	1	
EXPORTEPLOTFORMAT	2	
EXPORTMODELSPACE	0	
EXPORTPAGESETUP	0	
EXPORTPAPERSPACE	0	
EXTMAX	$-1.0000E+20,-1.0000E+20,$	
	$-1.0000E+20$	(read only)
EXTMIN	$1.0000E+20,1.0000E+20,$	
	$1.0000E+20$	(read only)
EXTNAMES	1	
FACETERDEVNORML	40	
FACETERDEVSURFACE	0.0010	
FACETERGRIDRATIO	0.00	
FACETERMAXEDGELENGTH	0.0	
FACETERMAXGRID	4096	
FACETERMESHTYPE	0	
FACETERMINUGRID	0	
FACETERMINVGRID	0	
FACETERPRIMITIVEMODE	1	
FACETERSMOOTHLEV	1	
FACETRATIO	0	
FACETRES	0.5000	
FBXIMPORTLOG	1	
FIELDDISPLAY	1	
FIELDEVAL	31	
FILEDIA	1	
FILLETRAD	0.0000	
FILLETRAD3D	1.0000	
FILLMODE	1	
FONTALT	"simplex.shx"	
FONTMAP	"C:\Documents and Settings\	
	username\Application\Data\	
	Autodesk\Aut..."	
FRONTZ	0.0000	(read only)
FULLOPEN	1	(read only)
FULLPLOTPATH	1	
GEOLATLONGFORMAT	0	
GEOMARKERVISIBILITY	1	
GFANG	0	
GFCLR1	"5"	
GFCLR2	"2"	
GFCLRLUM	1.000000000	
GFCLRSTATE	0	
GFNAME	1	
GFSHIFT	0	
GLOBALOPACITY	0	
GRIDDISPLAY	2	
GRIDMAJOR	5	
GRIDMODE	0	

Variable Name	Value	
GRIDSTYLE	0	
GRIDUNIT	0.5000,0.5000	
GRIPBLOCK	0	
GRIPCOLOR	150	
GRIPCONTOUR	251	
GRIPDYNCOLOR	140	
GRIPHOT	12	
GRIPHOVER	11	
GRIPMULTIFUNCTION	3	
GRIPOBJLIMIT	100	
GRIPS	5	
GRIPSIZE		
GRIPSUBOBJMODE	1	
GRIPTIPS	1	
GTAUTO	1	
GTDEFAULT	0	
GTLOCATION	0	
HALOGAP	0	
HANDLES	1	(read only)
HATCHBOUNDSET	0	
HATCHCREATION	0	
HATCHTYPE	0	
HELPPREFIX	" "	
HIDEPRECISION	0	
HIDETEXT	ON	
HIDEXREFSCALES	1	
HIGHLIGHT	1	
HPANG	0	
HPANNOTATIVE	0	
HPASSOC	1	
HPBACKGROUNDCOLOR	"NONE"	
HPBOUND	1	
HPBOUNDRETAIN	0	
HPCOLOR	"use current"	
HPDLMODE	2	
HPDOUBLE	0	
HPDRAWORDER	3	
HPGAPTOL	0.0000	
HPINHERIT	0	
HPISLANDDETECTION	1	
HPISLANDDETECTIONMODE	1	
HPLASTPATTERN	"ANSI31"	
HPLAYER	"use current"	
HPMAXLINES	1000000	
HPNAME	"ANSI31"	
HPOBJWARNING	10000	
HPORIGIN	0.0000,0.0000	
HPORIGINMODE	0	
HPORIGINSTOREASDEFAULT	0	
HPQUICKPREVIEW	ON	
HPRELATIVEPS	OFF	
HPSCALE	1.0000	
HPSEPARATE	0	
HPSPACE	1.0000	
HPTRANSPARENCY	"use current"	

Variable Name	Value	
HYPERLINKBASE	""	
IMAGEFRAME	1	
IMAGEHLT	0	
IMPLIEDFACE	1	
INDEXCTL	0	
INETLOCATION	"http://www.autodesk.com"	
INPUTHISTORYMODE	15	
INSBASE	0.0000,0.0000,0.0000	
INSNAME	""	
INSUNITS	1	
INSUNITSDEFSOURCE	1	
INSUNITSDEFTARGET	1	
INTELLIGENTUPDATE	20	
INTERFERECOLOR	"1"	
INTERFEREOBJVS	"Realistic"	
INTERFEREVPVS	"Wireframe"	
INTERSECTIONCOLOR	257	
INTERSECTIONDISPLAY	OFF	
ISAVEBAK	1	
ISAVEPERCENT	50	
ISOLINES	4	
LARGEOBJECTSUPPORT	0	
LASTANGLE	0	(read only)
LASTPOINT	0.0000,0.0000,0.0000	
LASTPROMPT	"LASTANGLE 0"	(read only)
LATITUDE	37.7950	
LAYERDLGMODE	1	
LAYEREVAL	1	
LAYEREVALCTL	1	
LAYERFILTERALERT	2	
LAYERNOTIFY	0	
LAYLOCKFADECTL	50	
LAYOUTREGENCTL	2	
LEGACYCTRPICK	2	
LENSLENGTH	50.0000	(read only)
LIGHTGLYPHDISPLAY	1	
LIGHTINGUNITS	2	
LIGHTSINBLOCKS	1	
LIMCHECK	0	
LIMMAX	12.0000,9.0000	
LIMMIN	0.0000,0.0000	
LINEARBRIGHTNESS	0	
LINEARCONTRAST	0	
LOCALE	"ENU"	(read only)
LOCALROOTPREFIX	"C:\Documents and Settings\ username\Local Settings\ application\Da…"	(read only)
LOCKUI	0	
LOFTANG1	90	
LOFTANG2	90	
LOFTMAG1	0.0000	
LOFTMAG2	0.0000	
LOFTNORMALS	1	
LOFTPARAM	7	
LOGEXPBRIGHTNESS	65.0	

Variable Name	Value	
LOGEXPCONTRAST	50.0	
LOGEXPDAYLIGHT	2	
LOGEXPMIDTONES	1.00	
LOGEXPPHYSICALSCALE	1500.000	
LOGFILEMODE	0	
LOGFILENAME	"C:\documents and settings\ username\local settings\ application\da..."	(read only)
LOGFILEPATH	"C:\documents and settings\ username\local settings\ application\da..."	
LOGINNAME	"UserName"	(read only)
LONGITUDE	−122.3940	
LTSCALE	1.0000	
LUNITS	2	
LUPREC	4	
LWDEFAULT	25	
LWDISPLAY	OFF	
LWUNITS	1	
MATERIALSPATH	" "	
MAXACTVP	64	
MAXSORT	1000	
MAXTOUCHES	0	
MBUTTONPAN	1	
MEASUREINIT	0	
MEASUREMENT	0	
MENUBAR	1	
MENUCTL	1	
MENUECHO	0	
MENUNAME	"C:\Documents and Settings\ username\Application\Data Autodesk\Aut..."	(read only)
MESHTYPE	1	
MIRRHATCH	0	
MIRRTEXT	0	
MLEADERSCALE	10000	
MODEMACRO	""	
MSLTSCALE	1	
MSOLESCALE	1.0000	
MTEXTCOLUMN	2	
MTEXTED	"Internal"	
MTEXTFIXED	2	
MTEXTTOOLBAR	2	
MTJIGSTRING	"abc"	
MYDOCUMENTSPREFIX	"C:\Documents and Settings\ username\My Documents"	(read only)
NAVBARDISPLAY	1	
NAVSWHEELMODE	2	
NAVSWHEELOPACITYBIG	50	
NAVSWHEELOPACITYMINI	50	
NAVSWHEELSIZEBIG	1	
NAVSWHEELSIZEMINI	1	
NAVVCUBEDISPLAY	3	
NAVVCUBELOCATION	0	
NAVVCUBEOPACITY	50	

Variable Name	Value	
NAVVCUBEORIENT	1	
NAVVCUBESIZE	4	
NOMUTT	0	
NORTHDIRECTION	0	
OBJECTISOLATIONMODE	0	
OBSCUREDCOLOR	257	
OBSCUREDLTYPE	0	
OFFSETDIST	−1.0000	
OFFSETGAPTYPE	0	
OLEFRAME	2	
OLEHIDE	0	
OLEQUALITY	3	
OLESTARTUP	0	
OPENPARTIAL	1	
ORTHOMODE	0	
OSMODE	20517	
OSNAPCOORD	2	
OSNAPHATCH	0	
OSNAPZ	0	
OSOPTIONS	3	
PALETTEOPAQUE	0	
PAPERUPDATE	0	
PARAMETERCOPYMODE	1	
PDFOSNAP	1	
PDFRAME	1	
PDMODE	0	
PDSIZE	0.0000	
PEDITACCEPT	0	
PELLIPSE	0	
PERIMETER	0.0000	(read only)
PERSPECTIVE	0	
PERSPECTIVECLIP	5.0000	
PFACEVMAX	4	(read only)
PICKADD	2	
PICKAUTO	1	
PICKBOX	5	
PICKDRAG	0	
PICKFIRST	1	
PICKSTYLE	1	
PLATFORM	"Microsoft Windows …"	(read only)
PLINECONVERTMODE	0	
PLINEGEN	0	
PLINETYPE	2	
PLINEWID	0.0000	
PLOTOFFSET	0	
PLOTROTMODE	2	
PLOTTRANSPARENCYOVERRIDE	1	
PLQUIET	0	
POINTCLOUDAUTOUPDATE	1	
POINTCLOUDDENSITY	15	
POINTCLOUDLOCK	0	
POINTCLOUDRTDENSITY	5	
POLARADDANG	"0"	
POLARANG	90	
POLARDIST	0.0000	

Variable Name	Value	
POLARMODE	0	
POLYSIDES	4	
POPUPS	1	(read only)
PREVIEWEFFECT	2	
PREVIEWFACEEFFECT	1	
PREVIEWFILTER	7	
PREVIEWTYPE	0	
PROJECTNAME	""	
PROJMODE	1	
PROXYGRAPHICS	1	
PROXYNOTICE	1	
PROXYSHOW	1	
PROXYWEBSEARCH	0	
PSLTSCALE	1	
PSOLHEIGHT	4.0000	
PSOLWIDTH	0.2500	
PSPROLOG	""	
PSQUALITY	75	
PSTYLEMODE	1	(read only)
PSTYLEPOLICY	1	
PSVPSCALE	0.00000000	
PUBLISHALLSHEETS	1	
PUBLISHCOLLATE	1	
PUBLISHHATCH	1	
PUCSBASE	""	
QPLOCATION	0	
QPMODE	−1	
QTEXTMODE	0	
QVDRAWINGPIN	0	
QVLAYOUTPN	0	
RASTERDPI	300	
RASTERPERCENT	20	
RASTERPREVIEW	1	
RASTERTHRESHOLD	20	
REBUILD2DCV	6	
REBUILD2DDEGREE	3	
REBUILD2DOPTION	1	
REBUILDDEGREEU	3	
REBUILDDEGREEV	3	
REBUILDOPTIONS	1	
REBUILDU	6	
REBUILDV	6	
RECOVERAUTO	0	
RECOVERYMODE	2	
REFEDITNAME	""	(read only)
REGENMODE	1	
REMEMBERFOLDERS	1	
RENDERQUALITY	1	
RENDERUSERLIGHTS	1	
REPORTERROR	1	
RIBBONCONTEXTSELECT	0	
RIBBONCONTEXTSELLIM	2500	
RIBBONDOCKHEIGHT	100	
RIBBONSELECTMODE	1	
RIBBONSTATE	1	

Variable Name	Value	
ROAMABLEROOTPREFIX	"C:\Documents and Settings\ username\Application\Data\ Autodesk\Aut…"	(read only)
ROLLOVEROPACITY	0	
ROLLOVERTIPS	1	
RTDISPLAY	1	
SAVEFIDELITY	1	
SAVEFILE	""	(read only)
SAVEFILEPATH	"C:\Documents and Settings\ username\Local Settings\Temp\"	
SAVENAME	""	(read only)
SAVETIME	10	
SCREENBOXES	0	(read only)
SCREENMENU	0	
SCREENMODE	3	(read only)
SCREENSIZE	937.0000,485.0000	(read only)
SELECTIONANNODISPLAY	1	
SELECTIONAREA	1	
SELECTIONAREAOPACITY	25	
SELECTIONCYCLING	0	
SELECTIONPREVIEW	3	
SELECTSIMILARMODE	130	
SETBYLAYERMODE	255	
SHADEDGE	3	
SHADEDIF	70	
SHADOWPLANELOCATION	0.0000	
SHORTCUTMENU	11	
SHOWHIST	1	
SHOWLAYERUSAGE	0	
SHOWMOTIONPIN	1	
SHPNAME	""	
SIGWARN	1	
SKETCHING	0.1000	
SKPOLY	0	
SKTOLERANCE	.5000	
SKYSTATUS	0	
SMOOTHMESHCONVERT	0	
SMOOTHMESHGRID	3	
SMOOTHMESHMAXFACE	312803	
SMOOTHMESHMAXLEV	4	
SMSTATE	0	
SNAPANG	0	
SNAPBASE	0.0000,0.0000	
SNAPISOPAIR	0	
SNAPMODE	0	
SNAPSTYL	0	
SNAPTYPE	0	
SNAPUNIT	0.5000,0.5000	
SOLIDCHECK	1	
SOLIDHIST	1	
SORTENTS	127	
SPLDEGREE	3	
SPLFRAME	0	
SPLINESEGS	8	
SPLINETYPE	6	

Variable Name	Value	
SPLKNOTS	0	
SPLMETHOD	0	
SSFOUND	""	(read only)
SSLOCATE	1	
SSMAUTOOPEN	1	
SSMPOLLTIME	60	
SSMSHEETSTATUS	2	
STANDARDSVIOLATION	2	
STARTUP	1	
STATUSBAR	1	
STEPSIZE	6.0000	
STEPSPERSEC	2.0000	
SUBOBJSELECTIONMODE	0	
SUNSTATUS	0	
SURFACEASSOCIATIVITY	1	
SURFACEASSOCIATIVITYDRAG	1	
SURFACEAUTOTRIM	0	
SURFACEMODELINGMODE	0	
SURFACEOFFSETCONNECT	0	
SURFACETRIMAUTOEXTEND	1	
SURFACETRIMPROJECTION	0	
SURFTAB1	6	
SURFTAB2	6	
SURFTYPE	6	
SURFU	6	
SURFV	6	
SYSCODEPAGE	"ANSI_1252"	(read only)
TABLEINDICATOR	1	
TABLETOOLBAR	1	
TABMODE	0	
TARGET	0.0000,0.0000,0.0000	(read only)
TDCREATE	2453629.06304220	(read only)
TDINDWG	0.00123557	(read only)
TDUCREATE	2453629.22970887	(read only)
TDUPDATE	2453629.06304220	(read only)
TDUSRTIMER	0.00123128	(read only)
TDUUPDATE	2453629.22970887	(read only)
TEMPOVERRIDES	1	
TEMPPREFIX	"C:\Documents and Settings\ username\Local Settings\Temp\"	(read only)
TEXTED	2	
TEXTEDITOR	0	
TEXTEVAL	0	
TEXTFILL	1	
TEXTOUTPUTFILEFORMAT	0	
TEXTQLTY	50	
TEXTSIZE	0.2000	
TEXTSTYLE	"Standard"	
THICKNESS	0.0000	
THUMBSIZE	1	
TILEMODE	1	
TIMEZONE	−8000	
TOOLTIPMERGE	0	
TOOLTIPS	1	
TRACEWID	0.0500	

Variable Name	Value	
TRACKPATH	0	
TRANSPARENCYDISPLAY	0	
TRAYICONS	1	
TRAYNOTIFY	1	
TRAYTIMEOUT	0	
TREEDEPTH	3020	
TREEMAX	10000000	
TRIMMODE	1	
TSPACEFAC	1.0000	
TSPACETYPE	1	
TSTACKALIGN	1	
TSTACKSIZE	70	
UCSAXISANG	90	
UCSBASE	""	
UCSDETECT	0	
UCSFOLLOW	0	
UCSICON	3	
UCSNAME	""	(read only)
UCSORG	0.0000,0.0000,0.0000	(read only)
UCSORTHO	1	
UCSVIEW	1	
UCSVP	1	
UCSXDIR	1.0000,0.0000,0.0000	(read only)
UCSYDIR	0.0000,1.0000,0.0000	(read only)
UNDOCTL	61	(read only)
UNDOMARKS	0	(read only)
UNITMODE	0	
UOSNAP	1	
UPDATETHUMBNAIL	15	
VIEWCTR	8.7025,4.5000,0.0000	(read only)
VIEWDIR	0.0000,0.0000,1.0000	(read only)
VIEWMODE	0	(read only)
VIEWSIZE	9.0000	(read only)
VIEWTWIST	0	(read only)
VISRETAIN	1	
VPLAYEROVERRIDES	0	(read only)
VPLAYEROVERRIDESMODE	1	
VPMAXIMIZEDSTATE	0	(read only)
VPROTATEASSOC	1	
VSACURVATUREHIGH	1.0000	
VSACURVATURELOW	−1.0000	
VSACURVATURETYPE	0	
VSADRAFTANGLEHIGH	3.0000	
VSADRAFTANGLELOW	−3.0000	
VSAZEBRACOLOR1	"RGB:255,255,255"	
VSAZEBRACOLOR2	"RGB:0,0,0"	
VSAZEBRADIRECTION	90	
VSAZEBRASIZE	45	
VSAZEBRATYPE	1	
VSBACKGROUNDS	1	
VSEDGE	−6	
VSEDGECOLOR	"ByEntity"	
VSEDGEJITTER	−2	
VSEDGEOVERHANG	−6	
VSEDGES	1	

Variable Name	Value	
VSEDGESSMOOTH	1	
VSFACECOLORMODE	0	
VSFACEHIGHLIGHT	−30	
VSFACEOPACITY	−60	
VSFACESTYLE	0	
VSHALOGAP	0	
VSHIDEPRECISION	0	
VSICONTOP	0	
VSINTERSECTIONCOLOR	"7(white)"	
VSINTERSECTIONEDGES	0	
VSINTERSECTIONLTYPE	1	
VSISOONTOP	0	
VSLIGHTINGQUALITY	1	
VSMATERIALMODE	0	
VSMAX	52.2149,27.0000,0.0000	(read only)
VSMIN	−34.8099,−18.0000,0.0000	(read only)
VSMONOCOLOR	"RCB:255,255,255"	
VSOBSCUREDCOLOR	"ByEntity"	
VSOBSCUREDEDGES	1	
VSOBSCUREDLTYPE	1	
VSOCCLUDEDCOLOR	"by entity"	
VSOCCLUDEDDLTYPE	1	
VSOCCLUDEDEDGES	1	
VSSHADOWS	0	
VSSILHEDGES	0	
VSSILHWIDTH	5	
VTDURATION	750	
VTENABLE	3	
VTFPS	7	
WBDEFAULTBROWSER	0	
WBHELPONLINE	1	
WBHELPTYPE	1	
WHIPARC	0	
WINDOWAREACOLOR	150	
WMFBKGND	OFF	
WMFFOREGND	OFF	
WORLDUCS	1	(read only)
WORLDVIEW	1	
WRITESTAT	1	(read only)
WSCURRENT	""	
XCLIPFRAME	2	
XDWGFADECTL	70	
XEDIT	1	
XFADECTL	50	
XLOADCTL	2	
XLOADPATH	"C:\Documents and Settings\ username\Local Settings\Temp\"	
XREFCTL	0	
XREFNOTIFY	2	
XREFTYPE	0	
ZOOMFACTOR	60	
ZOOMWHEEL	0	

Glossary

absolute coordinate entry: The process of specifying a point by typing in a coordinate. The coordinate is measured from the origin or 0,0 point in the drawing.

absolute coordinate system: Coordinate values measured from a coordinate system's origin point. *See also* origin, relative coordinate system, user coordinate system **(UCS)**, world coordinates, and world coordinate system **(WCS)**.

acquired point: Object tracking feature used to locate a point as an intermediate location in order to locate temporary alignment paths. Acquired points show up as a small cross in the drawing. Some points are acquired by simply placing your cursor over key object definition points while other acquired points require selecting a point with your mouse.

acquisition marker: During tracking or object snap tracking, the temporary plus sign displayed at the location of an acquired point.

action: Defines how the geometry of a dynamic block reference will move or change when the custom properties of a block reference are manipulated in a drawing. A dynamic block definition usually contains at least one action that is associated with a parameter. **(BACTION)**

activate: Part of the Autodesk software registration process. It allows you to run a product in compliance with the product's end-user license agreement.

adaptive sampling: A method to accelerate the anti-aliasing process within the bounds of the sample matrix size. *See also* anti-aliasing.

adjacent cell selection: A selection of table cells that share at least one boundary with another cell in the same selection.

affine calibration: A tablet calibration method that provides an arbitrary linear transformation in two-dimensional space. Affine calibration requires three calibration points to allow a tablet transformation that combines translation, independent X and Y scaling, rotation, and some skewing. Use affine calibration if a drawing has been stretched differently in the horizontal or vertical direction. **(TABLET)**

alias: A shortcut for a command. For example, CP is an alias for **COPY**, and Z is an alias for **ZOOM**. You define aliases in the acad.pgp and aclt.pgp files.

aliasing: The jagged or stepped appearance of discrete picture elements, or pixels, aligned as a straight or curved edge on a fixed grid. *See also* anti-aliasing.

aligned dimension: A dimension that measures the distance between two points at any angle. The dimension line is parallel to the line connecting the dimension's definition points. **(DIMALIGNED)**

aligned system: A dimension style in which all the text entities are written in line with or parallel to the dimension line and are read from the bottom and/or right-hand side of the paper.

alpha channel: Alpha is a type of data, found in 32-bit bitmap files, that assigns transparency to the pixels in the image. A 24-bit truecolor file contains three channels of color information: red, green, and blue, or RGB. Each channel of a truecolor bitmap file is defined by 8 bits, providing 256 levels of intensity. The intensity of each channel determines the color of the pixel in the image. Thus, an RGB file is 24-bit with 256 levels each of red, green, and blue. By adding a fourth, alpha channel, the file can specify the transparency, or opacity, of each of the pixels. An alpha value of 0 is transparent, an alpha value of 255 is opaque, and values in between are semitransparent. An RGBA file (red, green, blue, alpha) is 32-bit, with the extra 8 bits of alpha providing 256 levels of transparency. To output a rendered image with alpha, save in an alpha-compatible format such as PNG, TIFF, or Targa.

ambient color: The color of an object where it is in shadow; the color is what the object reflects when illuminated by ambient light rather than direct light.

ambient light: Light that illuminates all surfaces of a model with equal intensity. Ambient light has no single source or direction and does not diminish in intensity over distance.

angular dimension: A dimension that measures acute or obtuse angles or arc segments and consists of text, extension lines, and leaders.

angular unit: The unit of measurement for an angle. Angular units can be measured in decimal degrees, degrees/minutes/seconds, grads, and radians.

annotate: To add text, notes, and dimensions to a drawing to communicate a complete design by indicating materials, locations, distances, and other key information.

annotation scale: A setting that is saved with model space, layout viewports, and model views. When annotative objects are created, they are scaled based on the current annotation scale setting and automatically displayed at the correct size.

annotations: Text, dimensions, tolerances, symbols, notes, and other types of explanatory symbols or objects that are used to add information to a model.

anonymous block: An unnamed block created by a number of features, including associative and nonassociative dimensions.

ANSI: For American National Standards Institute. Coordinator of voluntary standards development for both private and public sectors in the United States. Standards pertain to programming languages, Electronic Data Interchange (EDI), telecommunications, and the physical properties of diskettes, cartridges, and magnetic tapes.

anti-aliasing: A method that reduces aliasing by shading the pixels adjacent to the main pixels that define a line or boundary. *See also* aliasing.

approximation points: Point locations that a B-spline must pass near, within a fit tolerance. *See also* fit points and interpolation points.

arc: A portion of a circle that forms a curve.

array: 1. Multiple copies of selected objects in a rectangular or polar (radial) pattern. **(ARRAY)** 2. A collection of data items, each identified by a subscript or key, arranged so a computer can examine the collection and retrieve data with the key.

arrowhead: A terminator, such as an arrowhead, slash, or dot, at the end of a dimension line showing where a dimension begins and ends.

ASCII: For American Standard Code for Information Interchange. A common numeric code used in computer data communications. The code assigns meaning to 128 numbers, using seven bits per character with the eighth bit used for parity checking. Nonstandard versions of ASCII assign meaning to 255 numbers.

aspect ratio: Ratio of display width to height.

associative dimension: A dimension that automatically adapts as the associated geometry is modified. Controlled by the **DIMASSOC** system variable. *See also* nonassociative dimension and exploded dimension.

associative hatch: Hatching that conforms to its bounding objects such that modifying the bounding objects automatically adjusts the hatch. **(BHATCH)**

associative property: The ability to connect entities together so that when changes are made the changes will be reflected in the new edited dimension.

attenuation: The diminishing of light intensity over distance.

Attribute A data: Oriented object that can be connected to a block.

attribute definition: An object that is included in a block definition to store alphanumeric data. Attribute values can be predefined or specified when the block is inserted. Attribute data can be extracted from a drawing and inserted into external files. **(ATTDEF)**

attribute extraction file: A text file to which extracted attribute data are written. The contents and format are determined by the attribute extraction template file. *See also* attribute extraction template file.

attribute extraction template file: An ASCII text file that determines which attributes are extracted and how they are formatted when written to an ASCII attribute extraction file. *See also* attribute extraction file.

attribute prompt: The text string displayed when you insert a block with an attribute whose value is undefined. *See also* attribute definition, attribute tag, and attribute value.

attribute tag: A text string associated with an attribute that identifies a particular attribute during extraction from the drawing database. *See also* attribute definition, attribute prompt, and attribute value.

attribute value: The alphanumeric information associated with an attribute tag. *See also* attribute definition, attribute prompt, and attribute tag.

AutoCAD Library search path: The search order for a support file: current directory, drawing directory, directory specified in the support path, and directory containing the executable file, acad.exe.

AutoCAD window: The drawing area, its surrounding menus, and the command line.

autosave: The practice of AutoCAD automatically saving your drawing at regular intervals. The default save interval is 10 minutes. Autosave files have a .5V$ file extension by default and are automatically deleted when the drawing is closed normally.

AutoTracking: AutoCAD feature that helps you to draw objects at specific angles or in specific relationships to other objects. When you turn on AutoTracking, temporary alignment paths help you create objects at precise positions and angles. Both orthogonal and polar tracking are available.

axis tripod: Icon with X, Y, and Z coordinates that is used to visualize the viewpoint (view direction) of a drawing without displaying the drawing. **(VPOINT)**

B-spline curve: A blended piecewise polynomial curve passing near a given set of control points. *See also* Bezier curve. **(SPLINE)**

back face: The opposite side of an object's normal face. Back faces are not visible in a rendered image. *See also* normal.

BAK: A standard file name extension used by many programs to be the last saved version of a document, drawing, or spreadsheet before the most recently saved version.

base point: A control point within several applications. 1. In the context of editing grips, the grip that changes to a solid color when selected to specify the focus of the subsequent editing operation. 2. A point for relative distance and angle when copying, moving, rotating, scaling, and making other modifications to objects. 3. The insertion base point of the current drawing. **(BASE)** 4. The insertion base point for a block definition. **(BLOCK)**

baseline: An imaginary line on which text characters appear to rest. Individual characters can have descenders that drop below the baseline. *See also* baseline dimension.

baseline dimension: Multiple dimensions measured from the same datum location on an object. Also called *parallel dimensions*. *See also* baseline.

Bezier curve: A polynomial curve defined by a set of control points, representing an equation of an order one less than the number of points being considered. A Bezier curve is a special case of a B-spline curve. *See also* B-spline curve.

bitmap: The digital representation of an image having bits referenced to pixels. In color graphics, a different value represents each red, green, and blue component of a pixel.

blips: Temporary screen markers displayed in the drawing area when you specify a point or select objects. **(BLIPMODE)**

block: A generic term for one or more objects that are combined to create a single object. Commonly used for either block definition or block reference. *See also* block definition and block reference. **(BLOCK)**

block attribute: A dynamic text-like object that can be included in a block definition to store alphanumeric data. Attribute values can be preset, specified when the block is inserted, or updated anytime during the life of a drawing. Attribute data can be automatically extracted from a drawing and output to an AutoCAD table or an external file.

Block Authoring palettes: Tool palettes used in the **Block Editor** to add actions and parameters to dynamic block definitions.

Block Authoring tools: Actions, parameters, and parameter sets on the tabs of the **Block Authoring** palettes window. Used in the **Block Editor** to create dynamic blocks.

block definition: A user-defined collection of drawing objects assigned a base point and a name that is stored centrally in a drawing. A block can be inserted in a drawing multiple times as a block reference. When a block definition is updated, all block references with the same name are automatically updated. *See also* block and block reference.

block definition table: The nongraphical data area of a drawing file that stores block definitions. *See also* named object.

block instance: *See* block reference.

block reference: An instance of a block definition inserted in a drawing that references the central block definition drawing data. All that is stored with the block reference is an insertion point, scale, and rotation angle. All other data is derived from the block definition. Also called *instance*. *See also* block and block definition. **(INSERT)**

bump map: A map in which brightness values are translated into apparent changes in the height of the surface of an object.

button menu: The menu for a pointing device with multiple buttons. Each button on the pointing device (except the pick button) can be defined in the customization file (acad.cui).

BYBLOCK: A special object property used to specify that the object inherits the color or linetype of any block containing it. **(BYLAYER)**.

BYLAYER: A special object property used to specify that the object inherits the color or linetype associated with its layer. **(BYBLOCK)**.

callout block: A block used as symbol to reference another sheet. Callout blocks have many industry-specific terms, such as reference tags, detail keys, and detail markers. *See also* label block.

camera: Defines the current eye-level position in a 3D model. A camera has a location XYZ coordinate, a target XYZ coordinate, and a field of view or lens length, which determines the magnification or zoom factor.

camera target: Defines the point being viewed by specifying the coordinate at the center of the view.

candela: The SI unit of luminous intensity (perceived power emitted by a light source in a particular direction) (symbol: cd); lm × sr

Cartesian coordinate system: A three-dimensional coordinate system in which the **X-axis** or direction is typically horizontal and increasing to the right, the **Y-axis** or direction is vertical and increasing upward, and the **Z-axis** or direction follows the right-hand rule. The origin of the system is the intersection of the three axes and is called 0,0,0.

category: *See* view category.

cell: The box at the intersection of a table row and column that contains the table data or a formula. A cell is typically referenced using its column letter and row number separated with a colon. For example, the cell in column A and row 1 is referenced as A:1.

cell boundary: The four gridlines surrounding a table cell. An adjacent cell selection can be surrounded with a cell boundary.

cell style: A style that contains specific formatting for table cells.

chain actions: In a dynamic block definition, a property of point, linear, polar, XY, and rotation parameters. When set to Yes, a change in an action that contains the parameter in the action's selection set triggers any actions associated with that parameter, just as if the parameter in the block reference had been edited through a grip or custom property.

chamfer: To cut off a corner with a slight angle or bevel.

circle: An unbroken line that has no angles and is drawn around a center point where every point is the same distance from the center point.

circular external reference: An externally referenced drawing (Xref) that references itself directly or indirectly. The Xref that creates the circular condition is ignored.

circumscribe: An option for constructing an entity on the outside of a circle.

clipping planes: The boundaries that define or clip the field of view. **(DVIEW)**

CMYK: For cyan, magenta, yellow, and key color. A system of defining colors by specifying the percentages of cyan, magenta, yellow, and the key color, which is typically black.

coincident: Two points that have the same X, Y, and Z coordinates.

color bleed scale: A measure of the degree of saturation of the reflected color from the material.

color map: A table defining the intensity of red, green, and blue (RGB) for each displayed color.

column: A vertically adjacent table cell selection spanning the height of the table. A single column is one cell in width.

command alias: An abbreviated definition of a command name that enables you to enter commands more quickly at the keyboard by entering the first one or two letters of the command name. Appendix C contains a complete list of the default AutoCAD command aliases.

command line: A text area reserved for keyboard input, prompts, and messages.

composite solid: A solid created from two or more individual solids. **(INTERSECT, SUBTRACT, UNION)**

computer-aided drafting (CAD): The process of producing engineering drawings and documentation through a computer system.

constraints: A series of controls that govern the position, slope, tangency, and/or the dimensions of the drawing elements.

construction plane: A plane on which planar geometry is constructed. The XY plane of the current UCS represents the construction plane. *See also* elevation and user coordinate system **(UCS)**.

continued dimension: A type of linear dimension that uses the second extension line origin of a selected dimension as its first extension line origin, breaking one long dimension into shorter segments that add up to the total measurement. Also called *chain dimension*. **(DIMCONTINUE)**

control frame: A series of point locations used as a mechanism to control the shape of a B-spline. These points are connected by a series of line segments for visual clarity and to distinguish the control frame from fit points. The **SPLFRAME** system variable must be turned on to display control frames.

control point: *See* control frame.

Coons patch: In 3D surface meshes, the bicubic surface (one curved in the M direction and another in the N direction) interpolated between four edges.

coordinate entry: The process of specifying point locations.

coordinate filters: Functions that extract individual X, Y, and Z coordinate values from different points to create a new, composite point. Also called *X, Y, Z point filters*.

cross sections: Generally, curves or lines that define the profile (shape) of a lofted solid or surface. Cross sections can be open or closed. A lofted solid or surface is drawn in the space between the cross sections. **(LOFT)**

crosshairs: A type of cursor consisting of two lines that intersect.

crossing window: A rectangular area drawn to select objects fully or partly within its borders.

CTB file: A color-dependent plot style table.

current layer: The layer that is active to receive all newly created entities.

cursor: *See* pointer and crosshairs.

cursor menu: *See* shortcut menu.

custom grips: Found in a dynamic block reference, used to manipulate the geometry and custom properties.

custom object: A type of object that is created by an ObjectARX application and that typically has more specialized capabilities than standard objects. Custom objects include parametric solids (Autodesk Mechanical Desktop), intelligently interactive door symbols (Autodesk Architectural Desktop), polygon objects (Autodesk Map®), and associative dimension objects (AutoCAD and AutoCAD LT®). *See also* proxy object and object enabler.

customization (CUI) file: An XML-based file that stores customization data. A customization file is modified through the **Customize User Interface** dialog box. CUI files replace MNU, MNS, and MNC files that were used to define menus in releases prior to AutoCAD 2006.

data link: A connection between a table and an external source of data.

default: A predefined value for a program input or parameter. Default values and options for commands are denoted by angle brackets (< >).

default drawing: *See* initial environment.

default lighting: The lighting in a shaded viewport when the sun and user lights are turned off. Faces are lighted by two distant light sources that follow the viewpoint as it is moved around the model.

definition points: Points for creating a dimension. The program refers to the points to modify the appearance and value of a nonassociative dimension when the dimensioned object is modified. Also called *defpoints* and stored on the special layer **DEFPOINTS**.

definition table: The nongraphical data area of a drawing file that stores block definitions.

delta distance: The horizontal or vertical measured distance between two points.

dependency highlighting: In a dynamic block definition, how associated objects are displayed when a parameter, grip, or action is selected.

dependent named objects: (in xrefs) Named objects brought into a drawing by an external reference.

dependent symbols: *See* dependent named objects (in Xrefs).

DesignCenter: A tool palette that allows you to drag and drop definition-based entities from other AutoCAD files into the resident file.

desktop: The initial screen of a Windows operating system.

DGN underlay: *See* underlay.

dialog box: A window that appears on top of the drawing screen allowing for random input of command data and options.

DIESEL: For Direct Interpretively Evaluated String Expression Language. A macro language for altering the status line with the **MODEMACRO** system variable and for customizing menu items.

diffuse color: An object's predominant color.

dimension line arc: An arc (usually with arrows at each end) spanning the angle formed by the extension lines of an angle being measured. The dimension text near this arc sometimes divides it into two arcs. *See also* angular dimension.

dimension style: A named group of dimension settings that determines the appearance of the dimension and simplifies the setting of dimension system variables. **(DIMSTYLE)**

dimension text: The measurement value of dimensioned objects.

dimension variables: A set of numeric values, text strings, and settings that control dimensioning features. **(DIMSTYLE)**

dimensional constraints: Controls that apply a value related to the size or location of an entity, for example, the length of a line, the diameter of a circle, or the location of a circle off an edge.

direct distance entry: The process of specifying a point by dragging the AutoCAD cursor to specify direction and typing in a distance.

directory: A location on a disk or a drive for saving existing files, sometimes referred to as a *folder*.

dithering: Combining color dots to give the impression of displaying more colors than are actually available.

dockable window: A user interface element that can be either docked or floating in the drawing area. Dockable windows include the command window, tool palettes, **Properties** palette, and so on.

drawing aids: A series of on/off toggles such as **SNAP, GRID, ORTHO,** and **POLAR** that assist with input.

drawing area: The area in which drawings are displayed and modified. The size of the drawing area varies depending on the size of the AutoCAD window and on how many toolbars and other elements are displayed. *See also* AutoCAD window.

drawing extents: The smallest rectangle that contains all objects in a drawing, positioned on the screen to display the largest possible view of all objects. **(ZOOM)**

drawing limits: A defined area within model space used to control drawing area size. *See* grid limits.

drawing scale: A mathematical ratio between the design's full size or real size and the size needed to fit on the piece of paper.

drawing set: A collection of drawings assembled using the **Publish** dialog box.

drawing template: A drawing used as a starting point when creating a new drawing. Drawing templates can include title blocks, dimension styles, layer definitions, or any information found in a regular drawing. Drawing templates have a file extension of .DWT. *See also* initial environment.

drop-down list: A selection method for a list of options within a dialog box.

DSD: For drawing set descriptions. A file format for saving a description of a drawing set that has been assembled using the **Publish** dialog box.

DST: For sheet set data. The XML file format used to store the associations and information that define a sheet set.

DWF™: For Design Web Format. A highly compressed file format that is created from a DWG file, DWF files are easy to publish and view on the Web. *See also* DWG and DXF.

DWF underlay: *See* underlay.

DWG: Standard file format for saving vector graphics in AutoCAD. *See also* DWF and DXF.

DWT: The file format for an AutoCAD drawing template. Templates contain predefined objects and properties from which you start a drawing session.

DXF™: For drawing interchange format. An ASCII or binary file format of a drawing file for exporting drawings to other applications or for importing drawings from other applications. *See also* DWF and DWG.

edge: The boundary of a face.

edge modifiers: Effects such as overhang and jitter that control how edges are displayed in a shaded model.

edge primitives: A solid modeling version of **FILLET** or **CHAMFER** that will place a curve or beveled edge on an already created solid object.

electronic drawing set: The digital equivalent of a set of plotted drawings. An electronic drawing set is created by publishing drawings to a PLT file.

elevation: The default Z value above or below the XY plane of the current user coordinate system, used for entering coordinates and digitizing locations. **(ELEV)**

ellipse: A closed curve shaped like an egg for which the sum of the squares of the projected distances equals a constant.

embed: To use object linking and embedding (OLE) information from a source document in a destination document. An embedded object is a copy of the information from a source document that is placed in the destination document and has no link to the source document. *See also* link.

enterprise customization file: A CUI file that is typically controlled by a CAD manager. It is often accessed by many users and is stored in a shared network location. The file is read-only to users to prevent the data in the file from being changed. A CAD manager creates an enterprise CUI file by modifying a main CUI file and then saving the file to the support location defined in the **Options** dialog box, **Files** tab.

environment map: A bitmap used to simulate reflections in materials that have reflective properties. The map is "wrapped" around the scene and any reflective object will show the appropriate portion of the map in the reflective parts of its material.

environment variable: A setting stored in the operating system that controls the operation of a program.

explode: To disassemble a complex object, such as a block, dimension, solid, or polyline, into simpler objects. In the case of a block, the block definition is unchanged. The block reference is replaced by the components of the block. *See also* block, block definition, and block reference. **(EXPLODE)**

exploded dimension: Independent objects that have the appearance of a dimension but are not associated with the dimensioned object or each other. Controlled by the **DIMASSOC** system variable. *See also* associative dimension, nonassociative dimension, and explode. **(EXPLODE)**

extents: *See* drawing extents.

external reference (Xref): An alternative to inserting a block that creates and maintains a link between the two drawing files. A drawing file referenced by another drawing. **(XREF)**

extrude: A way of creating a 3D solid by sweeping an object that encloses an area along a linear path.

face: A triangular or quadrilateral portion of a surface object. Also, a subobject of mesh shape that is made up of vertices and edges.

face color mode: A setting in the visual style that controls how color is displayed on a face.

face style: A setting in the visual style that defines the shading on a face.

facet: A subobject of a face used to define the smoothness of the mesh object.

falloff angle: Specifies the angle that defines the full cone of light, which is also known as the *field angle*.

feature control frame: The tolerance that applies to specific features or patterns of features. Feature control frames always contain at least a geometric characteristic symbol to indicate the type of control and a tolerance value to indicate the amount of acceptable variation.

fence: A multisegmented line specified to select objects it passes through.

field: A specialized text object set up to display data that may change during the life cycle of the drawing. When the field is updated, the latest value of the field is displayed. **(FIELD)**

file management: The process of saving, copying, moving, and deleting the files produced by a computer system.

fill: A solid color covering an area bounded by lines or curves. **(FILL)**

fillet: To round off an inside or outside corner at a specific radius.

filters: *See* coordinate filters.

final gathering: An optional, additional step to calculating global illumination. Using a photon map to calculate global illumination can cause rendering artifacts such as dark corners and low-frequency variations in the lighting. These artifacts can be reduced or eliminated by turning on final gathering, which increases the number of rays used to calculate global illumination. Final gathering can greatly increase rendering time. It is most useful for scenes with overall diffuse lighting, less useful for scenes with bright spots of indirect illumination. Final gathering is turned on in the **Advanced Render Settings** palette. *See also* global illumination.

fit points: Locations that a B-spline must pass through exactly or within a fit tolerance. *See also* interpolation points and approximation points.

fit tolerance: The setting for the maximum distance by which a B-spline can pass for each of the fit points that define it.

floating viewports: Paper space viewport created in a drawing layout tab that can have almost any size and shape—including circles and polygons. Paper space viewports are referred to as "floating" because they can be modified using standard AutoCAD editing commands so that they can be moved, resized, and erased. Unlike model space, tiled viewports, and paper space, floating viewports can overlap and have space in between them. *See* layout viewports.

font: A character set comprising letters, numbers, punctuation marks, and symbols of a distinctive proportion and design.

foot-candle: The U.S. unit of illuminance (symbol: fc); lm/ft^2

frame: An individual, static image in an animated sequence. *See also* motion path.

freeze: A setting that suppresses the display of objects on selected layers. Objects on frozen layers are not displayed, regenerated, or plotted. Freezing layers shortens regenerating time. *See also* thaw. **(LAYER)**

front faces: Faces with their normals pointed outward.

full size/full scale: Creating a drawing in which $1''=1''$, $1'=1'$, 1 m = 1 m, 1 km = 1 km, etc., making the drawing the true size of the object.

function keys: The 10 or 12 programmable keys typically located across the top of the keyboard.

geometric constraints: Controls that place one or more objects into a fixed relationship such as making a line horizontal or two lines parallel.

geometry: All graphical objects such as lines, circles, arcs, polylines, and dimensions. Nongraphical objects such as linetypes, lineweights, text styles, and layers are not considered geometry. *See also* named object.

gizmo: A boxlike apparatus that some modifiers display in viewports that initially surrounds the selected object. A gizmo acts somewhat like a container that transfers the modification to the object to which it is attached.

global illumination: An indirect illumination technique that allows for effects such as color bleeding. As light hits a colored object in the model, photons bounce to adjacent objects and tint them with the color of the original object.

Gooch shading: A type of shading that uses a transition from cool to warm colors rather than from dark to light.

graphics area: *See* drawing area.

graphics screen: *See* drawing area.

graphics window: *See* AutoCAD window and drawing area.

grid: An area covered with regularly spaced dots or lines to aid drawing. The spacing between grid dots is adjustable. Grid dots are not plotted. *See also* grid limits. **(GRID)**

grid limits: The user-defined rectangular boundary of the drawing area covered by dots when the grid is turned on. Also called *drawing limits*. **(LIMITS)**

grip box: Graphic symbol used to show grip control points.

grip control points: Predefined locations on an entity used to modify the selected object.

grip modes: The editing capabilities activated when grips are displayed on an object: stretching, moving, rotating, scaling, and mirroring.

grip tool: An icon that is used in a 3D view to easily constrain the movement or rotation of a selection set of objects to an axis or a plane. **(3DMOVE, 3DROTATE)**

grips: Editing points that appear at key locations on drawing objects. Once grips are activated, you can directly modify drawing objects by selecting their grips.

ground plane: The XY plane of the user coordinate system when perspective projection is turned on. The ground plane displays with a color gradient between the ground horizon (nearest to the horizon) and the ground origin (opposite the horizon). *See also* sky and underground.

groups: A command used to manipulate a group of objects as if it were one. **(GROUP)**

guide curves: Lines or curves that intersect each cross section of a lofted solid or surface and that define the form by adding additional wireframe information to the object. **(LOFT)**

handle: A unique alphanumeric tag for an object in the program's database.

hatch: A pattern of lines or symbols used to fill a closed boundary of a shape to identify parts of a drawing.

hatch boundary: The edges of a hatched area. These edges can be closed objects (such as a circle or closed polyline) or a combination of objects that define a closed area.

hatch islands: Closed areas within a hatch boundary. You have the option of telling AutoCAD how to deal with island areas when creating hatch objects.

hatch patterns: The pattern used to fill a hatch boundary. Hatch patterns are defined in .pat files and also include solid and gradient fill patterns.

HDI: For Heidi® Device Interface. An interface for developing device drivers that are required for peripherals to work with the program and other Autodesk products.

helix: An open 2D or 3D spiral. **(HELIX)**

HLS: For hue, luminance, and saturation. A system of defining color by specifying the amount of these three variables.

home page: The main navigating screen for a website.

horizontal landing: An optional line segment connecting the tail of a leader line with the leader content.

hot spot angle: Specifies the angle that defines the brightest cone of light, which is known to lighting designers as the *beam angle*.

hover grip: The status of a grip control point when there are multiple choices in a grip location.

icon: A small picture or symbol used as a shortcut to launch a command.

i-drop®: A method by which a drawing file, object, or entity can be dragged from a Web page and inserted into a drawing.

IGES: For Initial Graphics Exchange Specification. An ANSI-standard format for digital representation and exchange of information between CAD/CAM systems. *See also* ANSI.

illuminance: In photometry, the total luminous flux incident on a surface per unit area.

implied windowing: Feature that allows you to create a window or a crossing selection automatically by picking an empty space in a drawing to define the first corner point. The opposite corner point defines a window selection if it is picked to the right of the first corner point and a crossing selection if it is picked to the left.

indirect bump scale: A measure of the effect of the base material's bump mapping in areas lit by indirect light.

indirect illumination: Illumination techniques such as global illumination and final gathering that enhance the realism of a scene by simulating radiosity, or the interreflection of light between objects in a scene.

initial environment: The variables and settings for new drawings as defined by the default drawing template, such as acad.dwg, aclt.dwg or acadiso.dwg, acltiso.dwg. *See also* template drawing.

input property: In a dynamic block definition, a parameter property other than that of a lookup, alignment, or base point parameter that can be added as a column to a lookup table. When the parameter values in a dynamic block reference match a row of input property values, the corresponding lookup property values in that table row are assigned to the block reference. **(BLOOKUPTABLE)**

inquiry: The process of retrieving information from a drawing file.

inscribe: An option for constructing an entity inside a circle.

insert The process of merging an object (drawing, block, image, etc.) into the resident drawing file.

interface element: A user interface object that can be customized: a toolbar, pull-down menu, shortcut key, or dockable window.

interpolation points: Defining points through which a B-spline passes. *See also* approximation points and fit points.

island: An enclosed area within another enclosed area. Islands may be detected as part of the process of creating hatches, polylines, and regions. **(BHATCH, BOUNDARY)**

ISO: For International Standards Organization. The organization headquartered in Geneva, Switzerland, that sets international standards in all fields except electrical and electronics.

isometric snap style: A drafting option that aligns the cursor with two of three isometric axes and displays grid points or lines, making isometric drawings easier to create.

justify: A method used to place text.

key point: In a dynamic block definition, the point on a parameter that drives its associated action when edited in the block reference.

label block: A block used to label views and details. Labels contain data, such as a title, view number, and scale, that are associated with the referenced view. *See also* callout block.

landing: The portion of a leader object that acts as a pointer to the object being called out. A landing can be either a straight line or a spline curve.

landing gap: An optional space between a leader tail and the leader content.

layer: A logical grouping of data that are like transparent acetate overlays on a drawing. Layers can be viewed individually or in combination. **(LAYER)**

layer index: A list showing the objects on each layer. A layer index is used to locate what portion of the drawing is read when a drawing is partially opened. Saving a layer index with a drawing also enhances performance when a person works with external references. The **INDEXCTL** system variable controls whether layer and spatial indexes are saved with a drawing.

layer translation mappings: Assignments of a set of layers to another set of layers that define standards. These standards include layer names and layer properties. Also called *layer mappings*.

layering scheme: A plan to create and manage a series of layers within a complex design.

layout: The tabbed environment in which paper space layout viewports are created and designed to be plotted. Multiple layouts can be created for each drawing.

layout space: One of two spaces in which entities can be created. Layout space is used for creating finished views of a design with annotations. It is used for printing or plotting, as opposed to doing design work.

layout viewport: The user-defined window created in a paper space layout that allows you to view drawing information that resides in model space. Layout viewports are sometimes referred to as "floating" viewports because they can be moved, copied, and resized, unlike the "tiled" viewports created in model space that are static and must abut each other. *See also* paper space. **(VPORTS)**

leader: A text-based entity used to add clarification to a detail through a dimensioning function.

leader tail: The portion of a leader line that is connected to the annotation.

lens length: A measure of the magnification properties of a camera's lens. The greater the lens length, the narrower the field of view.

light glyph: The graphic representation of a point light or a spotlight.

limits: *See* drawing limits.

line font: *See* linetype.

linear dimension: A projected straight-line distance between two points in space parallel to the *X*-, *Y*-, or *Z*-axis.

linetype: The display of a line or curve. For example, a continuous line has a different linetype than a dashed line. Also called *line font*. **(LINETYPE)**

lineweight: A width value that can be assigned to all graphical objects except TrueType® fonts and raster images.

link: To use object linking and embedding (OLE) to reference data in another file. When data are linked, any changes in the source document are automatically updated in any destination document. *See also* embed.

lofted solid/surface: A solid or surface that is drawn through a set of two or more cross-sectional curves. The cross sections define the profile (shape) of the resulting solid or surface. Cross sections (generally, curves or lines) can be open or closed. **(LOFT)**

lookup property: In a dynamic block definition, a lookup parameter that is added to a lookup table. The lookup parameter label is used as the property name. When the parameter values in a dynamic block reference match a row of input property values, the corresponding lookup property values in that table row are assigned to the block reference. **(BLOOKUPTABLE)**

lookup table: Defines properties for and assigns property values to a dynamic block. Assigns property values to the dynamic block reference based on how the block is manipulated in a drawing. **(BLOOKUPTABLE)**

lumen: The SI unit of luminous flux (symbol: lm); cd/sr

luminaire: The aggregation of a lamp or lamps and their fixtures. The fixture may be a simple can or a complex armature with constrained joints.

luminance: The value of light reflected off a surface. A measure of how bright or dark the surface is perceived.

luminous flux: The perceived power per unit of solid angle. The total luminous flux for a lamp is the perceived power emitted in all directions.

lux: The SI unit of illuminance (symbol: lx); lm/m^2

main customization file: A writable CUI file that defines most of the user interface elements (including the standard menus, toolbars, keyboard accelerators, and so on). The acad.cui file (the default main CUI file) is automatically loaded when AutoCAD is started.

markup: A single comment or a redline geometry correction inserted into a DWF file using Autodesk® DWF™ Composer.

markup set: A group of markups contained within a single DWF file.

merge: In tables, an adjacent cell selection that has been combined into a single cell.

mirror: To create a new version of an existing object by reflecting it symmetrically with respect to a prescribed line or plane. **(MIRROR)**

mode: A software setting or operating state.

model: A two- or three-dimensional representation of an object.

model space: One of the two primary spaces in which objects reside. Typically, a geometric model is placed in this three-dimensional coordinate space. A final layout of specific views and annotations of this model is placed in layout space. *See also* paper space or layout space. (MSPACE)

model viewports: A type of display that splits the drawing area into two or more adjacent rectangular viewing areas. *See also* layout viewports, **TILEMODE**, and viewport. **(VPORTS)**

motion path: The path or target of a camera. A path can be a line, arc, elliptical arc, circle, polyline, 3D polyline, or spline.

multileader: A leader object that creates annotations with multiple leader lines.

multisheet DWF: A DWF file that contains multiple sheets.

named object: The various types of nongraphical information, such as styles and definitions, stored with a drawing. Named objects include linetypes, layers, dimension styles, text styles, block definitions, layouts, views, and viewport configurations. Named objects are stored in definition (symbol) tables.

named path: A saved motion path object that is linked to a camera or target.

named range: In Microsoft Excel, a cell or cell range that is given an alphanumeric name.

named view: A view saved for later restoration. **(VIEW)**

node: An object snap specification for locating points, dimension definition points, and dimension text origins.

nonassociative dimension: A dimension that does not automatically change as the associated geometry is modified. Controlled by the **DIMASSOC** system variable. *See also* associative dimension and exploded dimension.

normal: A vector that is perpendicular to a face.

noun-verb selection: The procedure of selecting an object first and then performing an operation on it rather than entering a command first and then selecting the object.

NURBS: For nonuniform rational B-spline curve. A B-spline curve or surface defined by a series of weighted control points and one or more knot vectors. *See also* B-spline curve.

object: One or more graphical elements, such as text, dimensions, lines, circles, or polylines, treated as a single element for creation, manipulation, and modification. Formerly called *entity*.

object enabler: A tool that provides specific viewing and standard editing access to a custom object when the **ObjectARX** application that created the custom object is not present. *See also* custom object and proxy object.

Object Snap: Method for selecting predefined positions on an object while a drawing is being created or edited. *See also* running object snap and object snap override.

object snap override: To turn off or change a running **Object Snap** mode to input a single point. *See also* Object Snap and running object snap.

object snaps/osnaps: Geometric points on objects such as the endpoints or midpoint of a line or the center of an arc of a circle. Object snaps can be construction points on objects or calculated points such as a point of tangency, a perpendicular point, or the projected intersection of two drawing objects

ObjectARX® (AutoCAD Runtime Extension): A compiled-language programming environment for developing AutoCAD applications.

offset: To create a parallel copy of an object.

OLE: For object linking and embedding. An information-sharing method in which data from a source document can be linked to or embedded in a destination document. Selecting the data in the destination document opens the source application so that the data can be edited. *See also* embed and link.

opacity map: Projecting opaque and transparent areas onto an object. A solid surface that appears to have holes or gaps.

operating system: The code that runs all commands for the computer system.

orbit: The ability to dynamically rotate an object through mouse movement around any point in space to establish a new viewpoint.

ordinate dimensioning: A method of dimensioning that describes the X and Y locations of a feature based on a fixed origin.

origin: The point where coordinate axes intersect. For example, the origin of a Cartesian coordinate system is where the *X, Y,* and *Z* axes meet at 0,0,0.

ORTHO: A drawing aid for creating objects at right angles.

Ortho mode: A setting that limits pointing device input to horizontal or vertical (relative to the current snap angle and the user coordinate system). *See also* snap angle and user coordinate system (UCS).

orthogonal: Having perpendicular slopes or tangents at the point of intersection.

orthographic: 90° increments. When the ORTHO mode is turned on, AutoCAD locks the cursor movement to 0°, 90°, 180°, and 270° angles.

orthographic projection: The two-dimensional graphic representation of an object formed by the perpendicular intersections of lines drawn from points on the object to a plane of projection. Orthographic projection is a drafting technique commonly used to create multiple view drawings by creating one view, then projecting perpendicular lines from the complete view to create the other views. This approach limits the number of times you need to measure in your drawing, thus reducing errors and increasing productivity.

page setup: A collection of plot device and other settings that affect the appearance and format of the final output. These settings can be modified and applied to other layouts.

palette: A special window that can access drawings, blocks, and commands in the AutoCAD environment.

pan: To shift the view of a drawing without changing magnification. **(PAN)**

paper space: One of two primary spaces in which objects reside. Paper or layout space is used for creating a finished layout for printing or plotting, as opposed to doing drafting or design work. Paper space viewports are designed using a **Layout** tab. Model space is used for creating the drawing. A model is designed using the **Model** tab. *See also* model space and viewpoint. **(PSPACE)**

parameter: In a dynamic block definition, defines custom properties for the dynamic block by specifying positions, distances, and angles for geometry in the block.

parameter set: A tool on the **Parameter Sets** tab of the **Block Authoring** palettes window that adds one or more parameters and one or more associated actions to the dynamic block definition.

parametric: Automated creation of a drawing based on a given set of dimensions referred to as *parameters*. These input parameters are applied against algorithms that create points, distances, and angles for the creation of drawing geometry. A simple example of creating a drawing parametrically is entering a width (*X*) and a height (*Y*) to create a rectangle.

parametric constraints: Drawing controls that allow the designer to apply relationships between objects in a drawing file.

partial customization file: Any CUI file that is not defined as the main CUI file. Partial CUI files can be loaded and unloaded as needed during a drawing session.

path curve: Defines the direction and length that a profile curve is lofted, swept, or extruded to create a solid or surface. **(LOFT, SWEEP, EXTRUDE)**

PC2 file: Complete plotter configuration file. PC2 files contain all plot settings and device-specific settings that were saved in previous versions. *See also* PCP file and PC3 file.

PC3 file: Plotter configuration file used to store and manage printer/plotter settings. PC3 files control plot device settings such as port connections and output settings, media, graphics, physical pen configuration, custom properties, initialization strings, calibration, and user-defined paper sizes. *See also* PMP file, STB file, and CTB file.

PCP file: Partial plotter configuration file. PCP files contain basic plot specifications and pen parameters that were saved in previous versions. Plot settings that are stored in a PCP file include pen assignments, plotting units, paper size, plot rotation, plot origin, scale factor, and pen optimization level. *See also* PC2 file and PC3 file.

personalization: Customization of the executable files acad.exe and aclt.exe during installation with user name, company, and other information.

perspective view: Objects in 3D seen by an observer positioned at the viewpoint looking at the view center. Objects appear smaller when the distance from the observer (at the viewpoint) to the view center increases. Although a perspective view appears realistic, it does not preserve the shapes of objects. Parallel lines seemingly converge in the view, so measurements cannot be made to scale from perspective views. The program has perspective view settings for VPORTS table entries as well as viewport objects. The UCS icon for a viewport observed with a perspective view has a different appearance.

photometric lights: Physically correct lights. Physically correct lights attenuate as the square of the distance. Photometry is the science of measurement of visible light in terms of its perceived brightness.

photon map: The product of a technique for generating the indirect illumination effects of global illumination used by the renderer by tracing photons emitted from a light. The photon is traced through the model, being reflected or transmitted by objects, until it strikes a diffuse surface. When it strikes a surface, the photon is stored in the photon map.

photorealistic rendering: Rendering that resembles a photograph.

pick button: The button on a pointing device that is used to select objects or specify points on the screen. For example, the left button on a two-button mouse.

pickbox: Square box that replaces the cursor crosshairs whenever AutoCAD prompts you to *Select objects:*. It is used to pick objects in a drawing to create a selection set.

plan view: A view orientation from a point on the positive Z-axis toward the origin (0,0,0). **(PLAN)**

planar face: A flat face that can be located anywhere in 3D space.

planar projection: Mapping of objects or images onto a plane.

planar surface: A flat surface that can be located anywhere in 3D space. **(PLANESURF)**

PLINE: *See* polyline.

plot: The process of printing through a CAD system.

plot style: A collection of property settings defined in a plot style table that is applied when the drawing is plotted to control the appearance of the drawing objects on the printed drawing. Plot styles can be used to control line thickness, grayscale, screening, and other plot features.

plot style table: A set of plot styles. Plot styles defined in plot style tables apply to objects only when the plot style table is attached to a layout or viewport.

plotting: The process of printing a drawing in AutoCAD. Plotting includes outputting your drawing to printers and plotters as well as various electronic file formats.

plug-ins: Libraries of reusable content that extend the functionality of AutoCAD. Plug-ins are created by third-party developers and can be accessed from the **Featured Technologies and Content** channel of the **Communications Center**.

PMP file: Plot Model Parameter. File containing custom plotter calibration and custom paper size information associated with a plotter configuration file.

point: 1. A location in three-dimensional space specified by X, Y, and Z coordinate values. 2. An object consisting of a single coordinate location. **(POINT)**

point filters: *See* coordinate filters.

pointer: A cursor on a video display screen that can be moved around to place textual or graphical information. *See also* crosshairs.

polar array: A pattern of objects copied around a specified center point a specified number of times. **(ARRAY)**

polar coordinate system: Input method based on an angle and a distance.

polar snap: A precision drawing tool used to snap to incremental distances along the polar tracking alignment path. *See also* polar tracking.

polar tracking: A process where AutoCAD will lock the cursor movement to predefined angles. When the cursor gets close to one of these predefined angles, AutoCAD will lock onto that angle and display the angle measurement at the cursor. *See also* polar snap.

polygon window selection: A multisided area specified to select objects. *See also* crossing window and window selection.

polyline: An object composed of one or more connected line segments or circular arcs treated as a single object. Also called *pline*. **(PLINE, PEDIT)**

polysolid: A swept solid that is drawn in the same way as a polyline or that is based on an existing line. By default, a polysolid always has a rectangular profile. The height and width of the profile can be specified. **(POLYSOLID)**

primary table fragment: The part of a broken table that contains the beginning set of rows up to the first table break.

printable area: The actual physical area that can be printed for the currently specified plotting device and paper size. Most printers cannot print to the very edge of the paper because of mechanical limitations.

procedural materials: Materials that generate a 3D pattern in two or more colors and apply it to an object. These include marble, granite, and wood. Also called *template materials*.

profile curve: An object that is swept, extruded, or revolved and defines the shape of the resulting solid or surface. **(SWEEP, EXTRUDE, REVOLVE)**

prompt: A message on the command line that asks for information or requests an action such as specifying a point.

properties: The settings that control how and where a drawing object is shown in the drawing. Some properties are common to all objects (layer, color, linetype, and lineweight) or specific to a particular type of drawing object (the radius of a circle or the endpoint of a line).

proxy object: A substitute for a custom object when the ObjectARX application that created the custom object is not available. *See also* custom object and object enabler.

PWT: A template file format used to publish drawings to the Web.

ray-traced shadows: A way of generating shadows. Ray tracing follows the path of rays sampled from a light source. Shadows appear where rays have been blocked by objects. Ray-traced shadows have sharp edges. Ray-traced shadows are active when **Shadow Map** is turned off on the **Advanced Render Settings** palette.

ray tracing: Following the path of rays sampled from a light source. Reflections and refractions generated this way are physically accurate. Ray tracing is turned on in the **Advanced Render Settings** palette.

radial dimension: A dimension style that describes the center point and radius/diameter of a circle or an arc.

radio button: A button used as an input method to select a single option in a dialog box.

raster: A data file generally composed of a rectangular grid of picture elements or color points.

rectangle: A four-sided geometric shape with equal-length opposite sides and right angles in each corner.

rectangular break: To break a table into multiple parts that are evenly spaced and set at a user-specified height using the table breaking grips.

REDRAW: To quickly refresh or clean up blip marks in the current viewport without updating the drawing's database. *See also* regenerate. **(REDRAW)**

reference: A definition, known as an *external reference* or *block reference,* that is used and stored in the drawing. *See also* block **(BLOCK)** and external reference. **(XREF)**

reflectance scale: A measure of the amount of energy reflected by a material.

reflection color: The color of a highlight on shiny material. Also called *specular color.*

reflection line: In a dynamic block reference, the axis about which a flip action's selection set flips when the associated parameter is edited through a grip or the **Properties** palette.

reflection mapping: The creation of the effect of a scene reflected on the surface of a shiny object.

refraction: The distortion of light through an object.

regenerate: To update a drawing's screen display by recomputing the screen objects and coordinates from the database. *See also* **REDRAW**. **(REGEN)**

regular polygon: A multisided closed figure in which all sides and interior angles are equal.

relative coordinate system: Coordinates specified in relation to previous coordinates or an object.

relative polar coordinate system: Coordinates specified in relation to previous coordinates based on an angle and a distance.

resource drawing: A data resource for the sheet set. A saved model space view can be placed from a resource drawing onto a sheet.

return button: The button on a pointing device used to accept an entry. For example, the right button on a two-button mouse.

reverse lookup: Adds a lookup grip to a dynamic block reference. When this grip is clicked, a drop-down list of the lookup values for that lookup property (column in the lookup table) is displayed. When a value is selected from the list, the corresponding input property values are assigned to the block reference. Depending on how the block was defined, this usually results in a change in the block reference's geometry. **(BLOOKUPTABLE)**

RGB: For red, green, and blue. A system of defining colors by specifying percentages of red, green, and blue.

ribbon: A special palette that provides a single, compact placement for the tools and commands needed for a particular workspace. The ribbon is made of tabs and panels that are totally customizable.

roughness: Value that simulates how light hitting a face is reflected back to the user. A high roughness value simulates a nonshiny or rough object (sandpaper/carpet). A low roughness value simulates a very shiny object (metals, some plastics.)

row: A horizontally adjacent table cell selection spanning the width of the table. A single row is one cell in height.

RSS feed: For Rich Site Summary (or Really Simple Syndication). Information published by a subscription website. Usually allows users to receive notifications when new content (articles) is posted.

rubber band: A live preview of a drawing object as it is being drawn. The rubber-band preview allows you to see objects as they are being created.

rubber-band line: A line that stretches dynamically on the screen with the movement of the cursor. One endpoint of the line is attached to a point in a drawing, and the other is attached to the moving cursor or crosshairs.

running object snap: An **Object Snap** mode set to continue for subsequent selections. *See also* Object Snap and object snap override. **(OSNAP)**

sampling: An antialiasing technique that provides a "best guess" color for each rendered pixel. The renderer first samples the scene color at locations within the pixel or along the pixel's edge then uses a filter to combine the samples into a single pixel color.

save back: To update the objects in the original reference (external or block reference) with changes made to objects in a working set during in-place reference editing.

scale factor: Multiplier that determines the size of annotation features such as text height, dimension features, and linetype appearance when a drawing is plotted or printed. The scale factor is typically the reciprocal of the plot scale or view scale.

scale representation: The display of an annotative object based on the annotation scales that the object supports. For example, if an annotative object supports two annotation scales, it has two scale representations.

script file: A set of commands executed sequentially with a single SCRIPT command. Script files are created outside the program using a text editor, saved in text format, and stored in an external file with the file extension .scr.

secondary table fragment: Any part of a broken table that does not contain the beginning set of rows.

section object: An AutoCAD entity that allows you to temporarily slice 3D objects and create 2D and 3D sections from them. Section objects are created with the **SECTIONPLANE** command.

section plane: A 2D plane locating the position along which a solid object is to be cut.

selected grip: The status of a grip control point involved in an editing function.

selection set: One or more selected objects on which a command can act at the same time. In a dynamic block definition, the geometry associated with an action.

shadow casting: Controls whether light casts shadows. To be displayed, shadows must be turned on in the visual style applied to the current viewport.

shadow map: A bitmap that the renderer generates during a prerendering pass of the scene. Shadow maps do not show the color cast by transparent or translucent objects, but they can have soft-edged shadows, which ray-traced shadows cannot. Shadow-mapped shadows provide softer edges and can require less calculation time than ray-traced shadows but are less accurate. On the **Advanced Render Settings** palette, shadow-mapped shadows are active when **Shadow Map** is turned on.

ShapeManager: The technology used to produce 3D solids.

sheet: A layout selected from a drawing file and assigned to a sheet set. *See also* sheet set.

sheet list table: A table listing all sheets in a sheet set. A sheet list table can be generated automatically with the **Sheet Set Manager**.

sheet selection: A named selection of sheets in a sheet set that can be conveniently recalled for archiving, transmitting, and publishing operations.

sheet set: An organized and named collection of sheets from several drawing files. *See also* sheet. **(SHEETSET)**

shortcut keys: Keys and key combinations that start commands; for example, **<Ctrl>** + **<S>** saves a file. The function keys (**<F1>**, **<F2>**, and so on) are also shortcut keys. Also known as *accelerator keys*.

shortcut menu: The menu displayed at the cursor location when the pointing device is right-clicked. The shortcut menu and the options it provides depend on the pointer location and other conditions, such as whether an object is selected or a command is in progress.

sky: The background color of the drawing area when perspective projection is turned on. The sky displays with a color gradient between the sky horizon (nearest to the horizon) and the sky zenith (opposite the horizon). *See also* ground plane.

slide file: A file that contains a raster image or snapshot of the objects displayed in the drawing area. Slide files have the file extension .sld. **(MSLIDE, VSLIDE)**

slide library: A collection of slide files organized for convenient retrieval and display. Slide library names have the extension .slb and are created with the slidelib.exe utility.

smooth shading: Smoothing of the edges between polygon faces.

snap: The ability to choose exactly a known location.

snap angle: The angle at which the snap grid is rotated.

snap grid: The invisible grid that locks the pointer into alignment with the grid points according to the spacing set by **SNAP.** Snap grid does not necessarily correspond to the visible grid, which is controlled separately by **GRID. (SNAP)**

Snap mode: A mode for locking a pointing device into alignment with an invisible rectangular grid. When **Snap** mode is on, the screen crosshairs and all input coordinates are snapped to the nearest point on the grid. The snap resolution defines the spacing of this grid. *See also* Object Snap.

snap resolution: The spacing between points of the snap grid.

software: Programs that control the operations of a computer and its peripherals.

solid history: A property of a solid that allows the original forms of the solid to be seen and modified.

solid object: An object that represents the entire volume of an object, for example a box.

solid primitive: A basic solid form. Solid primitives include box, wedge, cone, cylinder, sphere, torus, and pyramid.

spatial index: A list that organizes objects based on their location in space. A spatial index is used to locate what portion of the drawing is read when a drawing is partially opened. Saving a spatial index with a drawing also enhances performance when working with external references. The **INDEXCTL** system variable controls whether layer and spatial indexes are saved with a drawing.

specular reflection: The light in a narrow cone where the angle of the incoming beam equals the angle of the reflected beam.

spline: A smooth curve based on a mathematical formula that passes through a series of control points.

status bar: A series of readouts and on/off buttons, for drawing aids, located on the bottom of the screen.

STB file: Plot style table file. Contains plot styles and their characteristics.

stretch frame: In a dynamic block definition that contains a stretch action or a polar stretch action, determines how the objects within or crossed by the frame are edited in the block reference.

Subscription Center: A resource available from the **Help** menu for subscription members to access the latest releases of Autodesk software, incremental product enhancements, personalized Web support, and self-paced e-learning.

subobject: Any part of a solid: a face, an edge, or a vertex. Also, an original individual form that is part of a composite solid.

subset: A named collection of sheets in a sheet set that is often organized by discipline or workflow stage. *See also* view category.

surface normal: Positive direction perpendicular to the surface of an object.

sweep: A 3D operation that takes a 2D shape and makes it follow a predefined path. The result will be a 3D object.

swept primitive: An object created by extruding, revolving, sweeping, or lofting a 2D shape along an axis or path.

swept solid/surface: A solid or surface created in the shape of the specified profile (the swept object) swept along the specified path. **(SWEEP)**

symbol: A representation of an item commonly used in drawings. Symbols are inserted in drawings as blocks.

symbol library: A collection of block definitions stored in a single drawing file.

system variable: A named setting maintained by AutoCAD that controls an aspect of a drawing or the drawing environment. Most system variables can be changed by entering the variable name at the command line, although some variables are read-only and cannot be changed.

table: A rectangular array of cells that contain annotation, primarily text but also blocks. In the AEC industry, tables are often referred to as *schedules* and contain information about the materials needed for the construction of the building being designed. In the manufacturing industry, they are often referred to as *BOM* (bills of materials). **(TABLE)**

table break: The point at the bottom of a table row where the table will be split into a supplementary table fragment.

table style: A style that contains a specific table format and structure. A table style contains at least three cell styles.

tangent: A location on a circle where a line and a circle touch at one point and only one point.

template: Predefined collection of specific properties and property settings that gives a material a specific appearance. *See also* initial environment.

temporary files: Data files created during a program session. The files are deleted by the time the session is ended. If the session ends abnormally, such as during a power outage, temporary files might be left on the disk.

tessellation lines: Lines that help in visualizing a curved surface.

text screen (text window): One of two screens within AutoCAD. This screen houses the history of the current drawing session.

text style: A named, saved collection of settings that determines the appearance of text characters—for example, stretched, compressed, oblique, mirrored, or set in a vertical column.

texture map: The projection of an image (such as a tile pattern) onto an object (such as a chair).

thaw: A setting that displays previously frozen layers. *See also* freeze.

thickness: The distance certain objects are extruded to give them a 3D appearance. **(PROPERTIES, CHPROP, ELEV, THICKNESS)**

tiled viewports: *See* model viewports.

TILEMODE: A system variable that controls whether viewports can be created as movable, resizable objects (layout viewports), or as nonoverlapping display elements that appear side by side (model viewports). *See also* viewport.

Tool Palettes: Customizable AutoCAD window that allows the user to organize tools and many other settings by palettes. You can add a tool by dragging objects into a palette. You can create a tool palette by right-clicking on the **Tool Palettes** title bar and selecting **New Palette**.

toolbar: A collection of icons representing commands or operations.

tracking: A way to locate a point relative to other points on the drawing.

translucency: The scattering of light through an object.

transmittance scale: A measure of the amount of energy a transparent material transmits out to the scene.

transparency: A quantity defining how much light is let through an object.

transparent command: A command that can be used without interrupting the currently active command. Most display commands can be used transparently so that you can pan and zoom in a drawing while simultaneously using the drawing and editing commands. Transparent commands are run by entering an apostrophe (') before the command name.

two-sided material: The positive and negative normals of a material during the rendering process.

UCS: *See* user coordinate system **(UCS)**.

UCS icon: An icon that indicates the orientation of the **UCS** axes. **(UCSICON)**

underground: The XY plane of the user coordinate system when perspective projection is turned on and when viewed from below ground. The underground plane displays with a color gradient between the earth horizon (nearest to the horizon) and the earth azimuth (opposite the horizon). ground plane and sky.

underlay: A DWF or DGN file used to provide visual context in a drawing file. Underlays cannot be edited and do not provide the full range of notification. Underlays cannot be bound to a drawing. *See also* external reference (Xref).

unidirectional system: A dimensional system in which all text entities are placed parallel to the **X-axis** and read from the bottom of the document.

unselected grip: The status of a grip control point identifying an object.

user coordinate system (UCS): A user-defined coordinate system that defines the orientation of the **X, Y,** and **Z** axes in 3D space. The UCS determines the default placement of geometry in a drawing. *See also* world coordinate system (WCS).

UVW: The material's coordinate space. Used instead of XYZ because that is usually reserved for the world coordinate system (WCS). Most material maps are a 2D plane assigned to a 3D surface. The U, V, and W coordinates parallel the relative directions of X, Y, and Z coordinates. On a 2D map image, U is the equivalent of X and represents the horizontal direction of the map. V is the equivalent of Y and represents the vertical direction of the map. W is the equivalent of Z and represents a direction perpendicular to the UV plane of the map.

value set: In a dynamic block definition, a range or list of values specified for a linear, polar, XY, or rotation parameter.

vector: A mathematical object with precise direction and length but without specific location.

vertex: A location where edges or polyline segments meet.

view: A graphical representation of a model from a specific location (viewpoint) in space. *See also* viewpoint and viewport. **(VPOINT, DVIEW, VIEW)**

view category: A named collection of views in a sheet set that is often organized by function. *See also* subset.

viewpoint: The location in 3D model space from which a model is viewed. *See also* view and viewport. **(DVIEW, VPOINT)**

viewport: A bounded area that displays some portion of the model space of a drawing. The **TILEMODE** system variable determines the type of viewport created. When **TILEMODE** is off (0), viewports are objects that can be moved and resized on a layout. **(MVIEW)** When **TILEMODE** is on (1), the entire drawing area is divided into nonoverlapping model viewports. *See also* **TILEMODE**, view, and viewpoint. **(VPORTS)**

viewport configuration: A named collection of model viewports that can be saved and restored. **(VPORTS)**

virtual screen display: The area in which the program can pan and zoom without regenerating the drawing.

visibility mode: Controls whether geometry that is invisible for a visibility state is displayed or not (in a dimmed state). **(BVMODE)**

visibility state: In a dynamic block, a custom property that allows only specified geometry to be displayed in the block reference. **(BVSTATE)**

visual style: A collection of settings that control the display of edges and shading in a viewport.

volumetric shadow: A photorealistically rendered volume of space cast by the shadow of an object.

WCS: *See* world coordinate system **(WCS)**.

window selection: A rectangular area specified in the drawing area for selecting multiple objects simultaneously. *See also* crossing selection, polygon window selection.

wipeout object: A polygonal area that masks underlying objects with the current background color. This area is bounded by the wipeout frame, which can be turned on for editing and turned off for plotting.

wireframe model: The representation of an object using lines and curves to represent its boundaries.

wizard: A tool that uses a step-by-step routine to establish a series of drawing settings.

working drawing: A drawing for manufacturing or building purposes.

working set: A group of objects selected for in-place reference editing.

workplane: Another name for the XY plane of the user coordinate system. *See also* elevation and user coordinate system **(UCS)**.

workspace: A set of menus, toolbars, and dockable windows (such as the **Properties** palette, **DesignCenter**, and the **Tool Palettes**) that are grouped and organized so that work can be performed in a custom, task-oriented drawing environment.

world coordinate system (WCS): A coordinate system used as the basis for defining all objects and other coordinate systems. *See also* user coordinate system **(UCS)**.

world coordinates: Coordinates expressed in relation to the world coordinate system **(WCS)**.

WYSIWYG: For What You See Is What You Get.

X,Y,Z point filters: *See* coordinate filters.

Xref: *See* external reference.

zoom: To reduce or increase the apparent magnification of the drawing area. **(ZOOM)**

Index